Securing Privacy in the Internet Age

Securing Privacy in the Internet Age

Edited by Anupam Chander, Lauren Gelman,

and Margaret Jane Radin

STANFORD LAW BOOKS
An imprint of Stanford University Press
Stanford, California

Stanford University Press
Stanford, California

©2008 by the Board of Trustees of the Leland Stanford Junior University.

This book has been published with the assistance of The Center for Internet and Society.

Printed in the United States of America on acid-free, archival-quality paper

Library of Congress Cataloging-in-Publication Data
Securing privacy in the Internet age / edited by Anupam Chander, Lauren Gelman, and Margaret Jane Radin.
    p. cm.
 Includes bibliographical references and index.
 ISBN 978-0-8047-5918-2 (pbk. : alk. paper)
 1. Data protection--Law and legislation. 2. Privacy, Right of. 3. Internet--Law and legislation. I. Chander, Anupam. II. Gelman, Lauren. III. Radin, Margaret Jane.
 K3264.C65S43 2008
 342.08'58--dc22   2008012382

Typeset by Bruce Lundquist in 10/14 Minion

CONTENTS

Securing Privacy in the Internet Age

INTRODUCTION

Securing Privacy in the Internet Age

Anupam Chander

Anupam Chander is professor of law, University of California, Davis and visiting professor, Yale Law School. The author is grateful to Maren Ahnberg, Joseph Boufadel, Christopher Camp, Audrey Goodwater, Kathryn Lee, and Ryan Walters for excellent research assistance, and to coeditors Lauren Gelman and Margaret Jane Radin for the vision that made this book possible. The author also thanks Deans Rex Perschbacher and Kevin Johnson for their support.

A child born in 2008 will have many of the major and minor events of her life recorded in digital form. Her performance as a rabbit in a primary school play will be filmed on digital video cameras. Her school papers will be submitted and the grades recorded on digital media. The forms she fills out during her life will often be stored electronically. Doctors will dictate or type notes from her visits on computers. Radiologists in distant offices will interpret many of the tests ordered by her doctors. Computers might even sequence her genome and test it for disease susceptibility. Her running shoes might record her daily local running regimen, while her mobile phone provider records her travels across town and the identities of her friends. Security cameras will record her activities in public and private spaces. She will share the photos from her vacations online. Her parody of a favorite professor in a law school skit may find its way onto YouTube. Her emails and instant messages to friends may linger on computer servers. She will do much of her banking and buying online. This twenty-first-century child will face a lifetime's worth of personal events that will be catalogued, compiled, and digested by remote computers. In a networked, digitized world, as Lawrence Lessig presciently warned, "Your life becomes an ever-increasing record."[1]

The goal of this volume is to reduce the risks that this information about this child of the Internet Age will be misused. Law can help limit such risks—by incentivizing more limited collection of information, more robust security for stored information, and the purging of information over time.

Privacy becomes difficult to sustain in a world characterized by the ready flow of information. The threat to privacy cannot be trivialized as an irrational fear of unwanted electronic solicitations. Rather it takes more sinister form in identity theft, fraud, stalking, increased expenditures for security, hesitations about otherwise desirable marketplace transactions, spying on people, intrusions into intimacy, difficulty in obtaining employment or insurance, and increased conformity to social norms. To put a monetary figure on just one of these harms, consider a report for the Federal Trade Commission, which estimates that consumers lost $5 billion in 2003 due to identity theft.[2] Making our systems for securing private information more robust becomes an economic imperative.

As recent debacles involving financial information collectors such as Choice-Point and MasterCard reveal, protecting privacy turns centrally on something as mundane as securing computer databases and setting the terms for access. Yet privacy and security typically are considered in isolation, with academic attention focused on granting individuals rights against corporations that seek to exploit information about them, and corporate attention focused on protecting corporate information in the face of determined hackers. Advocates of privacy have sought to protect individuals from snooping corporations, while advocates of security have sought to protect corporations from snooping individuals. *Securing Privacy in the Internet Age*, growing out of a major symposium at the Stanford Law School, brings the two goals together. It gathers many of the world's leading academics, litigators, and public policy advocates, putting their heads together in a common endeavor to enhance privacy security. The traditional bugbear of privacy has been the government, which can take on the role of the Orwellian Big Brother, monitoring any deviations from publicly approved behavior—but the principal focus of the authors in this collection is the fraternity of Little Brothers—the corporations and individuals who seek to profit from gathering personal information about others.

In the main, the experts we have drawn together agree that the privacy of individuals is unduly compromised by the burgeoning digital databases pooling personally identifiable information. Although this problem has been anticipated since the dawn of the computer age, the Internet Age heightens the risks because of a number of factors:

1. Databases can be shared readily over electronic networks
2. The volume and quality of activities engaged in online increase the types of activity susceptible to easy cataloging
3. The Internet increases the vulnerability of databases to remote hackers

Most of the authors find the legal infrastructure inadequate to secure privacy: in Daniel Solove's indictment, "The problem is caused in significant part by the law, which has allowed the construction and use of digital dossiers without adequately regulating the practices by which companies keep them secure."[3]

In 2007—after seemingly weekly disclosures of large-scale breaches of privacy security covering a wide array of data collection services, from consumer service agencies such as ChoicePoint, Lexis-Nexis, MasterCard, the Veteran's Administration, and even the local doctor's office, the existence of a problem seems hard to deny.

CURRENT LAW ON SECURING PRIVACY

The law securing privacy in the United States is cobbled together from a disparate array of federal statutes, a few state laws, and common law. There is no overarching framework, but rather episodic privacy protections for limited domains and in certain circumstances. For the most part, existing federal statutes applicable to privacy predate the Internet Age. Statutes such as the Right to Financial Privacy Act of 1978 and the Electronic Communications Privacy Act of 1986 were designed principally to combat governmental intrusions into privacy. Attempts to deploy these statutes against the collection of personal information have generally tripped over the fact that they permit either party in a communication to divulge that communication to others, thus permitting a Website to authorize others to collect information given to that Website by Web surfers.

Congress has enacted *sui generis* rules for certain special cases. The Gramm-Leach-Bliley Act (GLB), for example, imposes special protections for information gathered by financial institutions. Similarly, the Health Insurance Portability and Accountability Act (HIPAA) requires healthcare service providers to take various steps to safeguard privacy, including the ubiquitous privacy notices whose receipt you are asked to certify with every medical appointment. Although HIPAA's privacy requirements have been visibly in place for years, HIPAA's security requirements became effective only in 2005. HIPAA may have a broader reach than may at first be apparent. Its security rule covers not just healthcare providers but also their "business associates," including potentially everything from transcription services to law firms. The principal World Wide Web-era innovation is the Children's Online Privacy Protection Act (COPPA), which requires Websites to obtain parental permission before gathering personal information online from children under thirteen.

Given the lacunae in federal law, which has preferred narrowly applicable privacy rules, California recently stepped into the breach with its own Online Privacy Protection Act (Cal OPPA). That statute, which requires companies to post privacy notices, applies not just to California companies but to any company, presumably worldwide, that gathers personal information online from Californians. Another California statute, California Civil Code § 1798.82, requires companies to disclose breaches of security with respect to personal information of any resident of California if this personal information includes the person's name and any of the following (1) social security number, (2) driver's license number, or (3) financial account access information. Unlike many of their federal counterparts, both California statutes grant private rights of action, § 1798.82 explicitly and Cal OPPA via California's unfair competition law. Given the breadth of the California legislation and the importance of the California market to the national economy, California privacy law may become the de facto national standard. Indeed, in the recent ChoicePoint debacle, ChoicePoint initially planned to reveal the breach of its database only to California residents, who were covered by § 1798.82. After complaints from residents across the country, the company rapidly decided that it could not treat Californians as a privileged class, and extended its disclosure to encompass all Americans.

But to understand American law securing privacy, it is not sufficient to look at federal or state law. Brussels has proved itself an important source of norms securing privacy, imposing broad obligations on American data collectors with facilities in Europe or American entities processing European data. Asian, Latin American, and African states may not be far behind in imposing demands on foreign collectors of information regarding their citizens.

SECURITY AND PRIVACY VALUES

Despite their close link in practice, security and privacy are differing values, with separate motivation. Security seems the less contested value. Few people argue for less security, though many question how much of society's resources should be devoted to it and how best security is to be attained. But security holds pitfalls as well. Robust encryption can defeat government surveillance of criminal as well as legitimate activity. Excessive focus on security can dampen risk-taking endeavors, threatening innovation and increasing costs.

Privacy is a complicated value. Privacy helps restrain the world from prying intrusions into personal affairs, but at the same time immunizes private realms from the demands of justice. Feminists in particular have sought to bring the light of law into the private realm, exposing the oppression in domestic spheres—while at the same time seeking to preserve a realm of privacy with respect to a woman's right to choose to have a child. Gay rights proponents, confronted with a sometimes hostile majority population, often prefer fewer infringements on privacy. Libertarians might also prefer fewer infringements on privacy, yet are generally not inclined to protect that privacy through the expansion of the law. Not only do they distrust the state, they worry that one person's ability to protect privacy might intrude on another's right to speak about that person. Perhaps the strongest lobby against increased privacy protection is business, which prefers as much information about potential customers as possible—that is, knowledge about who wants what where. Databases of consumer information are increasingly a principal corporate asset; privacy protections would limit the creation and deployment of such databases, and thereby erode their value.

Privacy and security are not the only values in designing an information regime. There are many other values, including innovation; efficient production and distribution; access to cheaper goods and services, especially for the poor; simplicity; functionality; and free speech. Society accordingly must approach privacy security with care—protecting against the intrusions of a database society with ever-more powerful search algorithms and ever-more sophisticated thieves, while ensuring robust commerce, innovation, and wide distribution of society's goods.

Privacy and security are linked, but they are not identical. An institution that gathers information can breach an individual's privacy even without a security lapse simply by giving that information away voluntarily. That is, privacy breaches do not arise solely from security lapses. Data collectors transfer private information not only unintentionally to hackers but also intentionally to affiliated companies.

SECURING PRIVACY BREACHES AND CONSENT

There are four types of actions that might constitute a breach of privacy security:

1. *Data Gathering*: The collection and maintenance of personal information contrary to the wishes of the data subjects

2. *Data Misuse*: The use of personal information in ways contrary to the wishes of the data subjects

3. *Data Sharing*: The voluntary disclosure of personal information by data collectors to third parties in ways contrary to the wishes of the data subjects

4. *Security Breach*: The unauthorized accessing of personal information held by data collectors

The absence of consent plays a central role in all of these breaches, but consent here is a fraught concept. Does the availability of the right to opt out of information gathering establish consent for data gathering when the right is not exercised? Lilian Edwards observes, "Consent, a seemingly simple idea, is much less clear when faced in terms of opt-in and opt-out, pre-ticked tick boxes, half-buried links to privacy policies, and incomprehensible legal language."[4] The Children's Online Privacy Protection Act requires "verifiable parental consent," thus requiring affirmative actions on the part of a parent more akin to opt-in to data collection. Similarly, the European Data Protection Directive requires consent to be "unambiguous." The "safe harbor" under this directive for United States companies, however, permits consent to be expressed through "opt-out" (except for very sensitive information, such as that about race, sex, and religion). Most businesses strongly prefer opt-out systems, recognizing that few consumers will take the trouble to flip the privacy setting to deny data collection. Raymond Nimmer believes that this suggests consumer indifference to the exploitation of personal information. But it is possible that, for many, the failure to opt out of data collection reflects not indifference to that collection but rather a lack of awareness. It is also possible that consumers often find the process of opting out too cumbersome to be worthwhile. Overall, it seems hard to conclude that opt-out systems reflect consumer choice adequately, let alone "unambiguously," as required by the European Data Protection Directive.

Notice and consent seem inadequate to establish privacy security. The privacy notices given with every hospital visit pursuant to HIPAA are destined, after the most cursory of glances, for the trashcan. That is not to say that notice is unhelpful. California's simple requirement that breaches of privacy security must be notified to California residents led to the disclosure of the large-scale ChoicePoint intrusion, an intrusion that would have likely passed without notice in the absence of the California law.

ESTABLISHING PRIVACY SECURITY

Security is a process, not a product.[5] Security consists of an ongoing process of identifying threats and vulnerabilities and taking appropriate responses. A firewall, a password, and a lock on the door to the computer server room are not a one-size-fits-all solution. The process of establishing privacy security must be multidimensional, recognizing that privacy security will thrive only through careful attention to an array of components, including the following:

1. What information can be collected from the individual
2. How information can be used by the data collector
3. With whom that information may be shared by the data collector
4. How securely the information, once collected, is maintained
5. The process of authenticating identity

Because no single corporation controls all of these components, privacy security is best viewed from the societal level. This is simply another facet of the economics of information. There are too many externalities in the choices required in information regimes—for example, what kind of authentication to use, what kind of data to gather, and for what purposes information may be used—to expect the price system to ensure an optimal level of privacy security. The marketplace is also unequipped to address the methods by which privacy security is undermined. The harms that arise are often difficult to trace to the source of the breach.

WHAT IS TO BE DONE

Although the experts agree that a problem exists, they do not agree on what must be done. The difference of opinion is to be expected—the writers include, for example, on one side, a lawyer pressing full-time for increased federal regulation of privacy and security (Chris Hoofnagle) and, on the other side, a legal academic who has a more skeptical view of regulation (Raymond Nimmer).

Three broad approaches are offered:

1. *Laissez-faire/Market*: Some experts favor a laissez-faire approach, with the market dictating a solution
2. *Common law*: Others seek to regulate via the common law, offering more vigorous or novel uses of existing law to discipline privacy security abuses
3. *Statutory*: Many contributors would like to see additional regulation of entities that gather and process data

Many authors have faith that the common law can improve privacy and security. Daniel Solove recommends the imposition of fiduciary duties on data collectors. Jennifer Chandler offers the possibility of a product-liability-type of claim against the makers of "unreasonably insecure software." Marcy Peek proposes the use of claims for restitution to make data collectors pay for their unjust enrichment from personal information. But there are many impediments to such suits. Privacy infractions often represent the kind of losses that traditional legal claims proved inadequate to handle. They often involve small harms to individuals, worthwhile to pursue in judicial setting only through the aggregation of multiple claims. Class actions would thus seem like the ideal vehicle for vindicating wrongs and disciplining those who are careless about protecting others' privacy. But Jonathan Sobel, Karen Petrulakis, and Denelle Dixon-Thayer, reporting from the front lines, tell us that class action lawyers typically need something more: a statutory setting of damages and attorneys' fees to avoid individualized determination of harm, which proves difficult both at the class certification stage and at the remedy stage. Ian Ballon notes that certification of class actions may be impossible when users enter into click-through agreements that send disputes to arbitration, a forum that is inhospitable to class relief. Sobel and his coauthors conclude that private litigation has thus far "failed" in the absence of federal statutes authorizing specified damages and attorneys' fees.

The price of privacy security should not be a loss of innovation or inordinate constraints on business. As Susan Brenner argues, too heavy a regulatory hand might stifle business. If grocers, clothing stores, and the like could not share information with third parties without consent, such companies might find it difficult to conduct routine back office transactions such as customer and inventory management and credit processing, processes that are often outsourced. The concern about hampering technology through excessive regulation is perhaps most clear with radio frequency identification tags

(RFIDs), which allow products to identify themselves wirelessly to nearby readers. In Japan, schools are planting RFIDs in children's backpacks for additional safety, though some worry about the misuse of surveillance data. Want to know more about what you eat? RFID technology permits Japanese steak consumers to determine, for example, that a source cow was born on January 5, 2001; supervised by Toshiyuki Arimura of Miyazaki prefecture; and shipped to Marusho Foods on February 13, 2003, where it was processed on the next day.[6]

But perhaps RFIDs may be safer for cattle than for people. For example, *Wired* magazine advised its American readers to bring a hammer down on the RFID chip implanted in the latest passports.[7]

OUTLINE OF THE BOOK

Securing Privacy in the Internet Age begins with a review of the existing landscape of security and privacy law.

Reviewing Existing Security and Privacy Law

Thomas J. Smedinghoff offers an overview of the obligations of businesses to provide information security. He suggests that a panoply of laws, both statutory and common law, result in a cognizable legal standard for information security. He finds a consistency between the various rules that have developed—from those protecting the privacy of children to those protecting health or financial information. He argues that security measures must be calibrated to the particular context of risk and threat. He delineates the questions that a corporation's executives, lawyers, and compliance officers should ask in designing security systems. Smedinghoff mentions the special concerns that arise when a company outsources certain of its business processes. Outsourcing, of course, has become almost as politically controversial as it is endemic to modern business practice. He observes that "you can outsource the work, but not the responsibility."

Ian C. Ballon reviews three of the major statutes that impose security obligations on companies:

1. The Gramm-Leach-Bliley Act, which covers customer information held by financial institutions
2. The Health Insurance Portability and Accountability Act, which covers individual health information held by health plans, healthcare clearinghouses, and most healthcare providers

3. California's security reporting statute, California Civil Code § 1798.82, which requires any company doing business in California to disclose breaches of databases holding personal information

Neither GLB nor HIPAA provides a private cause of action, and thus enforcement of these obligations is limited to the federal government. The principal federal agency enforcing security obligations is the Federal Trade Commission, which has settled charges of insecure practices with respect to consumer information against such prominent corporations as Eli Lilly & Co., Guess, and even Microsoft.

Jonathan K. Sobel, Karen J. Petrulakis, and Denelle M. Dixon-Thayer review the existing landscape and conclude that privacy security law in large part consists of the contracts created between data collectors and data subjects, often through privacy policies posted on Websites. If Sobel and his co-authors are correct, then the question is whether consumers will value their privacy sufficiently to ensure it via contract or whether they will cede it readily for small favors or conveniences. This is ultimately a question of market alienability—should personal information be readily available for sale if the individual is willing to sell it? Complicating the discussion is that market inalienability operates at two levels at least—alienation from the data subject to the data collector, and alienation from the data collector to third persons, such as credit services.

So what do these privacy contracts say? Andrea M. Matwyshyn studies the evolution of contracts offered by the Websites of seventy-five publicly traded companies. She compares the terms of use and privacy policies at two points in time—the late 1990s and March 2004. Although terms of use and privacy policies were not common in the late 1990s, she finds that they have become increasingly common with time. She finds that companies have increased the detail in their privacy policies, while seeking to transfer risk to users through terms-of-use policies. She sees the results as distressing, and suggests that consumers seek technological tools to protect their privacy.

If we want to learn privacy security law, we must look not just at Washington, D.C., or Sacramento (or even the "code" produced in Redmond, Washington, or Silicon Valley), but also Brussels. The European Union, Timothy Wu tells us, has enacted the world's most stringent and broad data privacy law. Will this law become de facto our own? Will the world's strictest law govern, as multinational enterprises bring their operations in line with it, or will the world's weakest law govern, as corporations relocate to offer their services from unregulated jurisdictions? Wu suggests that the answer will differ, depending on the type of regulatory problem at issue.

Promoting Privacy and Security Through the Common Law

Daniel J. Solove observes that the abuse of personal information arises out of leaks of information, which themselves arise out of insecure computer systems. He argues that the law has concentrated its energies on the abuses that actually emerge, where it might better concentrate on the underlying insecurity that leads indirectly to the abuses. He suggests two legal theories that might motivate better security: (1) a fiduciary duty imposed on data collectors to keep information private and (2) tort claims for data insecurity leading to either emotional distress or increased risk of future harm. Solove recognizes that the damages in such anticipatory cases are likely to be small, and suggests that aggregation of multiple small claims might still lead to an effective private attorney general. Solove also promotes an invigorated role for the Federal Trade Commission, which has on occasion sought to improve privacy and security practices in, for example, Microsoft's Passport system and Guess.com Inc.'s customer information database.

Marcy E. Peek focuses on what she calls "shadow offenders"—companies that traffic in personal data without any direct commercial or contractual relationship with the data subject. She turns to the common law remedy of restitution as a method to discipline such third-party actors, who are not by definition reached by contractual claims. She argues that restitution can provide a remedy when a plaintiff's damages are hard to measure but a defendant's profits are clear. The broad reach of the restitution claim will prove attractive to privacy advocates but alarming to corporations, which are accustomed to benefiting from information gathered from disparate sources without necessarily compensating all data subjects.

Jennifer A. Chandler analogizes what she calls "unreasonably insecure software" to a defective product, subject therefore to a strict liability claim in tort. She argues that the market in software does not represent an ideal security-cost trade-off because of market failure—due to heavy concentration in production; information failures, especially on the part of the ordinary software purchaser; and negative externalities of insecurity. She rejects the possibility of direct regulation of software standards to guarantee security because regulation (1) is slow, (2) is subject to industry capture, and (3) may impose a one-size-fits-all approach rather than a more tailored security standard.

Chandler explores the possibility of bringing a claim for negligence against the developers of unreasonably insecure software. She recognizes doctrinal hurdles that a purchaser of software would face in such a novel products liability case. She suggests that a particular type of plaintiff might have better success in bringing such a suit. This is the victim of a distributed denial of service (DDOS) attack, whose computer is temporarily disabled by other computers ("zombies," in the inventive language of computer scientists) that barrage a victim's computer with requests that exhaust that computer's resources.[8] To wage such an attack, the attacker takes advantage of security lapses in the zombies' computer systems. Unlike many consumers of insecure software, victims of DDOS attacks cannot be readily dismissed for having contracted with a software provider to purchase the faulty software. Although Chandler's paradigmatic case is not software insecurity leading to the breach of privacy but rather insecurity leading to business interruption, she illuminates the doctrinal difficulties of a products liability claim for harm arising from unreasonably insecure software.

Shubha Ghosh and Vikram Mangalmurti propose more generally that information security systems be subject to strict liability for insecure systems. Holding software companies to this high standard would create strong incentives to improve security. Ghosh and Mangalmurti consider a number of difficult doctrinal issues raised by their approach. Is software a product (subject to a strict liability standard) or a service (subject to a negligence standard)? Should open source software systems be subject to strict liability? Ghosh and Mangalmurti offer some thoughtful initial suggestions on these and other questions.

Promoting Privacy and Security Through Statutory Reforms

Chris Jay Hoofnagle, of the leading privacy advocacy group Electronic Privacy Information Center, offers the example of Clifford J. Dawg, a canine cardholder of a Chase Manhattan Platinum Visa Card since 2004. Mr. Dawg does not need his master to buy him doggie treats because an overeager bank has supplied him with credit. This carefree attitude also infects credit reporting agencies, who are all too willing to share information with their clients because that is how they make money. By "freezing" credit information, Hoofnagle would require prior approval—either on a blanket basis or on a one-off basis—from the individual before the credit agency could release information about him or her. Potential identity thieves would find it more difficult to obtain information about a possible victim. And this change would reduce the number of unsolicited credit card offers to man's best friend.

Edward J. Janger and Paul M. Schwartz offer the only argument for regulation that many economists understand: market failure. They argue that there are externalities to security breaches of financial information held by financial institutions and payment intermediaries. They suggest that information about security breaches is a "public good" and thus likely to be undersupplied if the market is left to itself. The externality arises in part because sensitive data, once released to the public domain, do not carry their own provenance. Because of this, consumers and others with an interest in preventing such leaks may not be able to discipline the institution releasing (intentionally or accidentally) the data. This argument might suggest a strong disclosure mandate, requiring financial institutions to report publicly releases of data that should be held private. But Janger and Schwartz challenge intuitions by suggesting that less disclosure of privacy breaches in financial data might improve privacy protections. They suggest the creation of an anonymous disclosure intermediary to which a financial institution could turn in the event of a leak. Because of anonymity, the financial institution would not suffer any reputational harm from the disclosure of the leak, a disclosure that it might be reluctant to make otherwise. The intermediary could then inform both other financial institutions and the individuals whose data were leaked about the problem, permitting them to adopt mitigating measures.

The technological cutting edge of this book is most evident in Jonathan Weinberg's appraisal of the privacy implications of RFIDs, described by Senator Leahy as "barcodes on steroids." Weinberg's early study of this emerging technology helps us recognize that the technological architecture is crucial to protecting privacy. Consider the possibility of limiting the unwanted release of information (or "blabbing," as Weinberg colorfully puts it) by requiring that the RFID tag emit not a single unique identifier but a series of random pseudonyms, understandable only by authorized readers. Even the most technical issue has hidden consequences for privacy; for example, if the tag's meaning is subject to open standards, it can be deciphered by anyone; if the meaning is restricted to proprietary databases, only those with access to those databases can interpret the tag. Weinberg identifies three specific privacy threats. First, RFIDs might be used to profile a person, with tag readers recognizing the tagged items carried by that person. Second, RFIDs enable surveillance because the tags, once tied to a particular person, can be used to identify that person's physical location. Finally, information gained from an RFID can be used to take an action in response. Weinberg considers a number of ways to alleviate the privacy risk, from the voluntary adoption by the RFID industry of more privacy protecting technological standards to legislation mandating protections, such as the ability to easily identify and remove an RFID.

Susan W. Brenner proposes perhaps the most potent and, for data collectors, terrifying regulatory reform: a new criminal statute creating a misuse of personal data offense. Treating personal information as a kind of property, she concludes that certain kinds of data collection are theft. She recognizes that this poses a problem for most privacy invasions because, for any individual, the harm may be difficult to establish. She thus suggests that the "data crime" would not turn on harms to individual victims but rather on the systemic harm to society. Implementing this crime as a "public welfare" offense, she seems to favor doing away with *mens rea* in favor of strict liability.

The idea of a national ID card may send shudders down the spines of privacy advocates, but A. Michael Froomkin offers a thoughtful case for it nonetheless. Froomkin seeks to lessen the alarm by arguing that we already have a national ID card system in place de facto. The de facto system arises from the coincidence of the following events: (1) large legislatively authorized databases for specialized purposes, (2) the use of credit cards and other identifying cards that enable companies to amass enormous databases of personal information, (3) the increasing use of surveillance cameras by both public and private actors, and (4) the advances in computing technologies that have enabled companies to amass such enormous databases. A *de jure* system would have the virtue that it could build in privacy protections. One clear benefit of such a system is that, with appropriate biometric or other security measures, it would provide the possibility of better authentication, thereby reducing the possibility of identity theft. What remains unclear to the editors is whether the creation of a regulated *de jure* system would mean the elimination or control of an unregulated de facto system.

Promoting Privacy and Security Through the Market

Offering a dissenting view, Raymond T. Nimmer argues that advocates of increased privacy regulation seek data control, specifically, the reordering of the relationship between individuals and businesses with respect to information. He observes that United States law generally permits either side of a transaction to exploit information gained through that transaction in the absence of a confidentiality agreement between the parties. For Nimmer, privacy regulations such as the European Union's Data Privacy Directive impose costs on ordinary transactions not justified by consumers' increased control over information. Nimmer accordingly prefers the status quo for the great bulk of consumer transactions, requiring individuals to act affirmatively to control information.

Jay P. Kesan, Ruperto P. Majuca, and William J. Yurcik argue for private insurance as the most efficient method for spurring optimal investment in information security. As long as premiums are tied to the level of self-protection measures undertaken by the firm, cyberinsurance is consistent with such measures. They offer an economic model of a firm's security behavior to make their case that a firm will likely benefit from insuring against the losses that might arise from an information security breach. If they are right, smart corporations should be purchasing such insurance, and indeed, they suggest that this is increasingly the case.

NOTES

1. Lawrence Lessig, *Code and the Laws of Cyberspace* 152 (2000).

2. Federal Trade Commission, *Identity Theft Survey Report* 4 (Sept. 2003).

3. *See* Daniel J. Solove, The New Vulnerability: Data Security and Personal Information, Chapter 6 in this volume.

4. Lilian Edwards, The Problem with Privacy: A Modest Proposal, 18 *Int'l Rev. L., Comp. & Tech.* 309, 323 (Nov. 2004).

5. *See* Thomas J. Smedinghoff, Defining the Legal Standard for Information Security, Chapter 1 in this volume.

6. *RFID in Japan*, June 1, 2004, available at http://ubiks.net/local/blog/jmt/archives3/cat_applications.html.

7. Jenna Wortham, Disable Your Passport's RFID Chip, *Wired* 46 (Jan. 2007).

8. *See generally* Margaret Jane Radin, Distributed Denial of Service Attacks: Who Pays? (Part I), 6 *Cyberspace Lawyer* 2 (Dec. 2001); Distributed Denial of Service Attacks: Who Pays? (Part II), 6 *Cyberspace Lawyer* 2 (Jan. 2002).

REVIEWING EXISTING SECURITY AND PRIVACY LAW

Part 1

1 DEFINING THE LEGAL STANDARD FOR INFORMATION SECURITY

What Does "Reasonable" Security Really Mean?

Thomas J. Smedinghoff

Thomas J. Smedinghoff is a partner in the Privacy, Data Security, and Information Law Practice at the law firm of Wildman Harrold in Chicago. He currently serves as a member of the U.S. Delegation to the United Nations Commission on International Trade Law (UNCITRAL), where he participates in the Working Group on Electronic Commerce that recently completed negotiation of the "United Nations Convention on the Use of Electronic Communications in International Contracts." He served as an advisor to the National Conference of Commissioners on Uniform State Laws (NCCUSL) and participated in drafting the Uniform Electronic Transactions Act (UETA). He chaired the Illinois Commission on Electronic Commerce and Crime and authored the Illinois Electronic Commerce Security Act. He can be reached at smedinghoff@wildman.com.

Protecting the security of corporate information and computer systems was once just a technical issue to be addressed by a company's IT department. Today, however, what we call "information security" has become a legal obligation, and responsibility for compliance has been put directly on the shoulders of senior management. Yet the nature of that obligation is often poorly understood by management, as well as by the technical experts who must implement it and the lawyers who must ensure legal compliance.

The fundamental question is quite simple. What is the scope of a company's legal obligations to implement information security measures? In other words, just what exactly is it required to do? In the past, answering that question has proved to be quite difficult.

Recently enacted security statutes and regulations, as well as a series of government enforcement actions,[1] suggest that we are now witnessing the development of a fairly well-defined answer to that question. In particular, they indicate the emergence of a new "legal" standard for information security that will help to clarify the scope and extent of a company's obligation to implement information security.

This chapter seeks to define that developing legal standard for corporate information security obligations. To do that, it begins with an overview of the legal obligation itself. Then, by reviewing the requirements of the major statutes, regulations, and government enforcement actions relating to information security, it identifies the parameters of the legal standard for security compliance.

I. THE LEGAL OBLIGATION TO PROVIDE INFORMATION SECURITY

The legal issues surrounding information security are rooted in the fact that, in today's business environment, virtually all of a company's daily transactions, and all of its key records, are created, used, communicated, and stored in electronic form using networked computer technology. Electronic communications have become the preferred way of doing business, and electronic records have become the primary means for storing information. As a consequence, most business entities are now "fully dependent upon information technology and the information infrastructure."[2]

This widespread implementation of networked information systems has provided companies with tremendous economic benefits, including significantly reduced costs and increased productivity. But the resulting dependence on a networked computer infrastructure also creates significant potential vulnerabilities that can result in major harm to the business and its stakeholders.[3] Thus concerns regarding corporate governance, ensuring individual privacy, protecting sensitive business data, accountability for financial information, and the authenticity and integrity of transaction data are driving the enactment of laws and regulations, both in the United States and globally, that are imposing obligations on businesses to implement information security measures to protect their own data.

As a result, almost all businesses now have some legal obligation to provide security for their own information. And satisfying that obligation is critical, especially in today's highly charged environment, in which a failure to do so is likely to bring on significant public relations problems as well as legal risk.

A. Sources of the Duty

Corporate legal obligations to implement security measures are set forth in an ever-expanding patchwork of federal and state laws, regulations, and government enforcement actions, as well as common law fiduciary duties and other implied obligations to provide "reasonable" security. (A list of some of the key security laws and regulations is set out in the Appendix that accompanies this chapter.) Many of the requirements are industry-specific (for example, focused on the financial industry or the healthcare industry) or data-specific (for example, focused on personal information or financial data). Others focus only on public companies. But viewing the recent laws, regulations, and enforcement actions as a group shows a clear trend of extending those obligations to all companies and all corporate data.

Some of the key sources of the corporate duty to provide information security include the following:[4]

- Corporate governance legislation and case law designed to protect public companies and their shareholders, investors, and business partners— The Sarbanes-Oxley Act and the related regulations, for example, require public companies to ensure that they have implemented appropriate information security controls with respect to their financial information.[5] Similarly, SEC regulations impose requirements for internal controls over information systems.[6]

- Privacy laws and regulations designed to protect the personal interests of individual employees, customers, or prospects—These laws require companies to implement information security measures to protect certain personal data they maintain about individuals. At the federal level, such laws and regulations include Gramm-Leach-Bliley in the financial sector, HIPAA in the healthcare sector, and COPPA, which governs information about children.[7] Several states have also enacted laws imposing a general obligation to ensure the security of personal information.[8]

- FTC Act Section 5 and similar state laws—Through a series of enforcement actions and consent decrees, both the FTC and several state attorneys general have, in effect, extended security obligations to nonregulated industries by virtue of Section 5 of the FTC Act and similar state laws.[9] Initially, cases were based on the alleged failure of companies to provide adequate information security contrary to representations they made to customers. In other words, these were claims of deceptive trade practices. But beginning in June 2005, the FTC significantly broadened the scope of its enforcement actions by asserting that a failure to provide appropriate information security was, itself, an unfair trade practice—even in the absence of any false representations by the defendant as to the state of its security.[10]

- E-transaction laws designed to ensure the enforceability and compliance of electronic documents generally—Both the federal and state electronic transaction statutes (E-SIGN and UETA) require all companies to provide security for storage of electronic records relating to online transactions.[11]

- Sector-specific regulations—Many federal and state regulations address security. For example, IRS regulations require companies to implement information security to protect electronic tax records.[12] Similarly, as a condition to engaging in certain electronic transactions, SEC regulations address security in a variety of contexts,[13] and FDA regulations require security for certain records.[14]

- Fiduciary obligations—Evolving case law suggests that, by virtue of their fiduciary obligations to the company, corporate directors will find that their duty of care includes responsibility for the security of the company's information systems.[15]

- Evidentiary rules—Recent case law suggests that information security is a requirement for the admissibility of electronic records.[16]

- Common law—Recent case law also recognizes that there may be a common law duty to provide security, the breach of which constitutes a tort.[17]

The bottom line is that a company's duty to provide security may come from several different sources—each perhaps asserting jurisdiction over a different aspect of corporate information—but the net result (and certainly the trend) is a general obligation to provide security for all corporate data and information systems.

B. Scope and Objectives of the Duty

When laws addressing security are viewed in the aggregate, it is clear that the obligation is expansive in scope. All types of corporate information need to be protected, including financial information, personal information, tax-related records, employee information, transaction information, and trade secret and other confidential information. Moreover, protecting electronic information alone is not sufficient. It is also important to address the means by which such information is created, stored, and communicated. Thus statutes and regulations governing information security typically focus on the protection of both *information systems*—computer systems, networks, and software—and the *data*, *messages*, and *information* that those systems record, process, communicate, store, share, transmit, or receive.

The objectives of information security often are stated in two ways. In some cases, statutes and regulations define the primary objectives in terms of positive results to be achieved, such as ensuring the availability of systems and information; controlling access to systems and information; and ensuring the confidentiality, integrity, and authenticity of information.[18] In other cases, they define the goals or objectives of security in terms of the harms to be avoided, such as mandating that companies protect systems and information against unauthorized access, use, disclosure, transfer, modification, alteration or processing, and accidental loss or destruction.[19]

Regardless of approach, achieving these objectives involves implementing security measures designed to protect systems and information from the various threats they face. What those threats are, where they come from, what is at risk, and how serious the consequences are will vary greatly from case to case. But responding to the threats a company faces with appropriate physical, technical, and organizational security measures is the focus of the duty to provide security.

Often unanswered, however, is a key question: Just what exactly is a business obligated to do? In other words, what is the legal standard against which the obligation to implement information security is to be measured?

II. THE LEGAL STANDARD FOR INFORMATION SECURITY

Laws and regulations rarely specify the security measures a business should implement to satisfy its legal obligations. Most simply obligate companies to establish and maintain "reasonable" or "appropriate" security procedures, controls, safeguards, or measures,[20] but give no further direction or guidance. There are, of course, many standards that seek to define the scope of information security requirements from a "technical" perspective.[21] But a careful review of newer statutes, regulations, and cases reveals an amazingly consistent approach that also defines the parameters of a "legal" standard.

The legal standard involves a relatively sophisticated approach to compliance, and recognizes what security consultants have been saying for some time: "Security is a process, not a product."[22] Thus the standard does not literally dictate what security measures are required to achieve "reasonable security." Instead, it focuses on a process to identify and implement measures that are reasonable under the circumstances to achieve the desired security objectives.[23] This means companies must engage in an ongoing and repetitive process that assesses risks, identifies and implements responsive security measures, verifies that they are effectively implemented, and ensures that they are continually updated in response to new developments. In other words, merely implementing seemingly strong security measures is not sufficient. Those measures must be responsive to existing threats facing the company, and must constantly evolve in light of changes in threats, technology, the company's business, and other factors.

This "process oriented" legal standard for corporate information security was first set forth in a series of financial industry security regulations required under the Gramm-Leach-Bliley Act (GLB) titled *Guidelines Establishing Standards for Safeguarding Consumer Information*. They were issued by the Federal Reserve, the OCC, the FDIC, and the Office of Thrift Supervision on February 1, 2001,[24] and later adopted by the FTC in its GLB Act *Safeguards Rule* on May 23, 2002.[25] The same approach was also incorporated in the Federal Information Security Management Act of 2002 (FISMA),[26] and in the HIPAA *Security Standards* issued by the Department of Health and Human Services on February 20, 2003.[27]

The FTC has since adopted the view that the "process oriented" approach to information security outlined in these regulations sets forth a general "best practice" for legal compliance that should apply to all businesses in all industries.[28] Thus it has, in effect, implemented this "process oriented" approach in all of its decisions and consent decrees relating to alleged failures to provide appropriate information security.[29] The National Association of Insurance Commissioners has also recommended the same approach,[30] and to date, several state insurance regulators have adopted it.Several state attorneys general have also adopted this approach in their actions against perceived offenders.[31] And now we are starting to see some cases take the same approach.[32]

III. WHAT IS REQUIRED FOR THE COMPREHENSIVE SECURITY PROGRAM?

The essence of the process-oriented approach to security compliance is implementation of a comprehensive written security program[33] addressing seven topics: identification of assets, risk assessment, implementation of security controls, third-party service providers, education, monitoring and testing, and review and adjustment. That legally-mandated process can be summarized as follows.

A. Identification of Assets

When addressing information security, the first step is to define the scope of the effort. What information, communications, and processes are to be protected? What information systems are involved? Where are they located? What laws potentially apply to them? As is often the case, little known but sensitive data files are found in a variety of places within the company.

B. Periodic Risk Assessment

Once the information assets are identified, implementing a comprehensive security program to protect them requires a thorough assessment of the potential risks to the organization's information systems and data. This involves identifying all reasonably foreseeable internal and external threats to the information assets to be protected. For each identified threat, the organization should then evaluate the risk posed by the threat by doing the following:

- Assessing the likelihood that the threat will materialize
- Evaluating the potential damage that will result if it materializes
- Assessing the sufficiency of the policies, procedures, and safeguards in place to guard against the threat[34]

This process will be the baseline against which security measures can be selected, implemented, measured, and validated.[35] The goal is to understand the risks the business faces, determine what level of risk is acceptable, and identify appropriate and cost-effective safeguards to combat any unacceptable risks.

C. Security Controls to Manage and Control Risk

The next step is to design and implement appropriate security measures to manage and control the risks identified during the risk assessment. Such security measures are generally grouped into three categories,[36] which are typically referred to as follows:

- *Physical security measures.* These are tangible means of preventing unauthorized physical access to the computer systems and networks that process and store the data, including servers, terminals used to access the system, storage devices, and the like.[37] Examples include fences, walls, and other barriers; locks, safes, and vaults; dogs and armed guards; sensors and alarm bells.

- *Technical security measures.*[38] This involves the use of safeguards incorporated into computer hardware, software, and related devices. They are designed to ensure system availability, provide access control, authenticate persons seeking access, protect the integrity of information communicated via and stored on the system, and ensure confidentiality where appropriate. Examples include firewalls, access control software, antivirus software, passwords, PIN numbers, smart cards, biometric tokens, encryption, dial-up access control, and callback systems.

- *Administrative security measures*[39] (sometimes referred to as organizational or procedural security measures[40]). These consist of management procedures and constraints, operational procedures, accountability procedures, and supplemental administrative controls to prevent unauthorized access and to provide an acceptable level of protection for computing resources and data.[41] Administrative security procedures frequently include personnel management, training, and discipline.

It is not enough merely to implement impressive-sounding security measures in each of these categories. The measures selected must be responsive to the particular threats a business faces and must address its specific vulnerabilities, taking account of factors such as the company's size and capabilities, the nature and scope of its business activities, the nature and sensitivity of the information to be protected, the state of the art of the technology and security, and the costs of the security measures.

In all cases, selecting and implementing security measures that are responsive to the identified threats is critical. Posting armed guards around a building, for example, sounds impressive, but if the primary threat the company faces is unauthorized remote access to its data via the Internet, that particular security measure is of little value. Likewise, firewalls and intrusion detection software can be effective to stop hackers and protect sensitive databases from outside attack, but if a company's major vulnerability is careless (or malicious) employees who inadvertently (or intentionally) disclose passwords or protected information, then even those sophisticated technical security measures, while important, will not adequately address the problem.

Implementing this process—that is, doing a risk assessment and then deploying security measures that address the identified threats—may well help to insulate the company from liability in the event a breach occurs. According to the recent federal court decision in *Guin* v. *Brazos Higher Education Service*, when a proper risk assessment has been done and responsive security measures implemented, the inability to foresee and deter a specific security breach does not constitute a failure to satisfy the duty to provide reasonable security.[42]

The key question, however, remains: "What specific security measures should a company implement?" Generally, developing law in the United States does not require companies to implement specific security measures or use a particular technology. As expressly stated in the HIPAA security regulations, for example, companies "may use any security measures" reasonably designed to achieve the objectives specified in the regulations.[43] This focus on flexibility means that, like the obligation to use "reasonable care" under tort law, determining compliance may ultimately become more difficult, as there are unlikely to be any safe harbors for security.

Nonetheless, developing law seems to consistently require that companies consider certain *categories* of security measures, even if the way in which each category is addressed is not specified. Thus, many security regulations that require covered organizations to implement physical, technical, and administrative security measures[44] also specify some subcategories of each of those measures that companies should consider. Although by no means an exclusive list, the legal standard for security generally requires that companies consider the need for, and adopt as necessary, appropriate security measures in the following categories:[45]

- Physical facility protection—measures to protect against destruction or loss of, or damage to, equipment or information due to potential environmental hazards, such as fire and water damage or technological failures; procedures that govern the receipt and removal of hardware and electronic media into and out of a facility; and procedures that govern the use and security of physical workstations.

- Physical access controls—restrictions at buildings, computer facilities, and records storage facilities to permit access only to authorized individuals.

- Technical access controls—policies and procedures to ensure that authorized persons who need access to the system have it, and that those who should not have access don't, including procedures for determining access authorization, granting and controlling access, authenticating persons or entities seeking access, and terminating access.

- Intrusion detection procedures—procedures to monitor log-in attempts and report discrepancies; procedures to detect actual and attempted attacks on or intrusions into company information systems; and procedures for preventing, detecting, and reporting malicious software such as viruses and Trojan horses.

- Employee procedures—procedures to ensure employee honesty and proper job performance, and controls to prevent employees from compromising system security.
- System modification procedures—procedures designed to ensure that all changes made to the company's system are consistent with the company's security program.
- Data integrity, confidentiality, and storage—procedures to protect information from unauthorized access, alteration, disclosure, or destruction during storage or transmission.
- Data destruction and hardware and media disposal—procedures regarding final disposition of information or hardware on which it resides, and procedures for removal from media before the media is reused.
- Audit controls—maintenance of records to document repairs and modifications to the physical components of the facility related to security (such as walls, doors, locks, and so on); and hardware, software, or procedural audit control mechanisms that record and examine activity in the systems.
- Contingency plan—procedures designed to ensure the ability to continue operations in the event of an emergency, such as a data backup plan, disaster recovery plan, and emergency mode operation plan.
- Incident response plan—a plan for taking responsive actions in the event the company suspects or detects that a security breach has occurred, including ensuring that appropriate persons within the organization are quickly notified and that prompt action is taken, both in terms of responding to the breach (for example, to stop further information compromise and to work with law enforcement), and notifying those who may have been injured by the breach.

Again, the law does not typically require implementation of any particular security control. The key is to implement security controls responsive to the identified threats. Thus, for example, although encryption is one approach to providing data confidentiality, one court recently held that the law does not specifically require encryption as the only acceptable solution.[46]

D. Oversight of Third-Party Service Provider Arrangements

Corporate obligations to provide security extend not only to the data in a company's possession but also to a company's data in the possession of a third-party service provider. Thus third-party relationships should be subject to the same risk management, security, privacy, and other protection policies that would be expected if a business were conducting the activities directly.[47]

The developing legal standard for security imposes three basic requirements on businesses that outsource: they must exercise due diligence in selecting service providers; they must contractually require outsource providers to implement appropriate security measures; and they must monitor the performance of the outsource providers.[48]

E. Awareness, Training, and Education

Training and education for employees is a critical component of any security program. Even the very best physical, technical, and administrative security measures are of little value if employees do not understand their roles and responsibilities. For example, installing heavy-duty doors with state-of-the art locks (whether of the physical or virtual variety) will not provide the intended protection if the employees authorized to have access leave the doors open and unlocked for others to pass through.

Security education begins with communication to employees of applicable security policies, procedures, standards, and guidelines. It also includes implementing a security awareness program, periodic security reminders, and developing and maintaining relevant employee training materials, such as user education concerning virus protection, password management, and discrepancy reporting.[49] Applying appropriate sanctions against employees who fail to comply with security policies and procedures also is important.

F. Monitoring and Testing

Once security measures are implemented, companies must ensure that they have been properly put in place and are effective. This includes assessing whether the chosen security measures are sufficient to control the identified risks and conducting regular testing or monitoring of the effectiveness of those measures. Existing precedent also suggests that companies must monitor compliance with their security programs. To that end, a regular review of records of system activity, such as audit logs, access reports, and security incident tracking reports, is important.[50]

G. Review and Adjustment

Perhaps most significantly, the legal standard for information security recognizes that security is a moving target. Businesses must constantly keep up with ever-changing threats, risks, and vulnerabilities, as well as the security measures available to respond to them. It is an ongoing process. As a consequence, businesses must conduct periodic internal reviews to evaluate and adjust their information security program[51] in light of the following:

- The results of the testing and monitoring
- Any material changes to the business
- Changes in technology
- Changes in internal or external threats
- Environmental or operational changes
- Any other circumstances that may have a material impact

In addition to periodic internal reviews, businesses should obtain a periodic review and assessment (audit) by qualified independent third-party professionals using procedures and standards generally accepted in the profession to certify that the security program meets or exceeds applicable requirements and is operating with sufficient effectiveness to provide reasonable assurances that the security, confidentiality, and integrity of information is protected. Of course, the findings and recommendations that come from such a review should prompt a company to appropriately adjust its security program.

IV. RESPONSIBILITY FOR THE SECURITY PROGRAM

Finally, it is important to recognize that as information security has evolved into a legal obligation, responsibility for compliance has been put directly on the shoulders of senior management, and in many cases the board of directors. It is, in many respects, a corporate governance issue.

For public companies, the Sarbanes-Oxley Act places responsibility with the CEO and the CFO.[52] In the financial industry, the Gramm-Leach-Bliley security regulations place responsibility for security with the board of directors.[53] In the healthcare industry, the HIPAA security regulations require an identified security official to be responsible for compliance.[54] Several FTC consent decrees involving companies in a variety of nonregulated industries do likewise.[55]

Evolving case law suggests that, by virtue of their fiduciary obligations to the company, corporate directors will find that their duty of care may "extend from safeguarding corporate financial data accuracy to safeguarding the integrity of all stored data."[56] In the *Caremark International Inc. Derivative Litigation*, for example, the Delaware court noted that "it is important that the board exercise a good faith judgment that the corporation's information and reporting system is in concept and design adequate to assure the board that appropriate information will come to its attention in a timely manner as a matter of ordinary operations, so that it may satisfy its responsibility."[57]

Companies also are beginning to recognize that the responsibility for security lies with upper management and the board of directors. The Business Roundtable, for example, has noted both that "[i]nformation security requires CEO attention" and that "[b]oards of directors should consider information security as an essential element of corporate governance and a top priority for board review."[58] The Corporate Governance Task Force Report has taken a similar position.[59]

The scope of that responsibility can be significant. The Gramm-Leach-Bliley security regulations, for example, require the board of directors to approve the written security program; to oversee the development, implementation, and maintenance of the program; and to require regular reports (at least annually) regarding the overall status of the security program, the company's compliance with regulations, and material matters relating to the security program.[60]

V. CONCLUSION

All of the major statutes, regulations, and government enforcement actions of the past few years directed toward corporate obligations to implement information security measures show an amazing consistency in approach. When viewed as a group, they set forth a rather clearly defined standard for legal compliance, which is reflected in the process-oriented approach to a comprehensive security program outlined in the preceding text.

Of course, not all information activities of all companies are regulated by existing security statutes or regulations. But in those cases in which the law requires companies to provide information security, the foregoing process-oriented approach is likely to be the standard against which legal compliance is measured, even if not explicitly addressed in the applicable law. Moreover, as the law expands corporate obligations to implement reasonable information security measures, we can expect this standard to be the one applied, either directly or by analogy.

APPENDIX: KEY INFORMATION SECURITY LAW REFERENCES

A. Federal Statutes

1. COPPA: Children's Online Privacy Protection Act of 1998, 15 U.S.C. § 6501 *et seq.*
2. E-SIGN: Electronic Signatures in Global and National Commerce Act, 15 U.S.C. § 7001(d).
3. FISMA: Federal Information Security Management Act of 2002, 44 U.S.C. §§ 3541-49.
4. FTC Act Section 5: Federal Trade Commission Act, 15 U.S.C § 45(a)(1).
5. GLB Act: Gramm-Leach-Bliley Act, Public L. 106-102, §§ 501 and 505(b), 15 U.S.C. §§ 6801, 6805.
6. HIPAA: Health Insurance Portability and Accountability Act, 42 U.S.C. §§ 1320d-2, 1320d-4.
7. Homeland Security Act of 2002: 44 U.S.C. § 3532(b)(1).
8. Sarbanes-Oxley Act: Pub. L. 107-204, §§ 302, 404, 15 U.S.C. §§ 7241, 7262.
9. Federal Rules of Evidence 901(a): see *American Express* v. *Vinhnee*, 2005 Bankr. LEXIS 2602 (9th Cir. Bk. App. Panel, 2005) and *Lorraine* v. *Markel*, 2007 U.S. Dist. LEXIS 33020 (D. Md. May 4, 2007).

B. State Statutes

1. UETA: Uniform Electronic Transaction Act, Section 12 (now enacted in forty-six states).
2. Law imposing obligations to provide security for personal information:

Arkansas	Ark. Code Ann. § 4-110-104(b)
California	Cal. Civ. Code § 1798.81.5(b)
Connecticut	Pub. Act No. 08–167
Maryland	Md. Code, § 14-3503
Massachusetts	Mass. Gen. Laws. Ch. 93H, § 2(a)
Nevada	52 Nev. Rev. Stat. § 23(1)
Oregon	2007 S.B. 583, Section 12
Rhode Island	R.I. Stat. 11-49.2-2(2)-(3)
Texas	Tex. Bus. & Com. Code Ann. § 48.102(a)
Utah	Utah Code Ann. § 13-42-201

3. Data destruction laws:

Arkansas	Ark. Code Ann. § 4-110-104(a)
California	Cal. Civil Code § 1798.81

Connecticut	Pub. Act No. 08–167
Georgia	Ga. Stat. § 10-15-2
Hawaii	Haw. Stat. Section § 487R-2
Illinois	815 Ill. Comp. Stat. 530 / 30
	(state agencies only)
Indiana	Ind. Code § 24-4-14
Kentucky	Ken. Rev. Stat. Ch. 365.720
Maryland	Md. Code, § 14-3502; Md. HB 208 & SB 194
Massachusetts	Mass. Gen. laws. Ch. 93I
Michigan	MCL § 445.72a
Montana	Mont. Stat. § 30-14-1703
Nevada	Nev. Rev. Stat. 603A.200
New Jersey	N.J. Stat. 56:8-162
North Carolina	N.C. Gen. Stat. § 75-65
Oregon	2007 S.B. 583, Section 12
Texas	Tex. Bus. & Com. Code Ann. § 48.102(b)
Utah	Utah Code Ann. § 13-42-201
Vermont	Vt. Stat. Tit. 9 § 2445 *et seq.*
Washington	RCWA 19.215.020

4. Security breach notification laws

Alaska	Ala. Stat. §§ 45.48.010-45.48.090
Arizona	Ariz. Rev. Stat. § 44-7501
Arkansas	Ark. Code Ann. § 4-110-101 *et seq.*
California	Cal. Civ. Code § 1798.82
Colorado	Col. Rev. Stat. § 6-1-716
Connecticut	Conn. Gen. Stat. 36A-701(b)
Delaware	De. Code Ann. tit. 6, §§ 12B-101 *et seq.*
District of Columbia	DC Official Code § 28-3851 *et seq.*
Florida	Fla. Stat. Ann. § 817.5681
Georgia	Ga. Code Ann. § 10-1-910 *et seq.*[61]
Hawaii	Hawaii Rev. Stat. § 487N-2
Idaho	Id. Code §§ 28-51-104 through 28-51-107
Illinois	815 Ill. Comp. Stat. 530 / 1 *et seq.*
Indiana	Ind. Code § 24-4.9
Iowa	2008 Iowa S.F. 2308
Kansas	Kansas Stat. 50-7a01, 50-7a02
Louisiana	La. Rev. Stat. Ann. § 51:3071 *et seq.*
Maine	Me. Rev. Stat. Ann. tit. 10, §§ 1347 *et seq.*

Maryland	Md. Code, §§ 14-3501 thru 14-3508
Massachusetts	Mass. Gen. Laws. Ch. 93H
Michigan	MCL 445.63, §§ 12, 12a, and 12b
Minnesota	Minn. Stat. § 325E.61 and § 609.891
Montana	Mont. Code Ann. § 30-14-1701 *et seq.*
Nebraska	Neb. Rev. Stat. 87-801 *et seq.*
Nevada	Nev. Rev. Stat. 603A.010 *et seq.*
New Hampshire	N.H. RSA 359-C:19 *et seq.*
New Jersey	N.J. Stat. 56:8-163
New York	N.Y. Bus. Law § 899-aa
North Carolina	N.C. Gen. Stat. § 75-65
North Dakota	N.D. Cent. Code § 51-30-01 *et seq.*
Ohio	Ohio Rev. Code § 1349.19
Oklahoma	Okla. Stat. title 24 § 161 *et seq.*
Oregon	Ore. Rev. Stat. § 646A
Pennsylvania	73 Pa. Cons. Stat. § 2303
Rhode Island	R.I. Gen. Laws § 11-49.2-1 *et seq.*
South Carolina	S.C. Code § 39-1-90
Tennessee	Tenn. Code Ann. § 47-18-2107
Texas	Tex. Bus. & Com. Code Ann. § 48.001 *et seq.*
Utah	Utah Code Ann. § 13-42-101 *et seq.*
Vermont	Vt. Stat. Tit. 9 § 2430 *et seq.*
Virginia	Va. Code 18.2-186.6
Washington	Wash. Rev. Code § 19.255.010
West Virginia	W. Va Code §§ 46A-2A-101--46A-2A-105
Wisconsin	Wis. Stat. § 895.507
Wyoming	Wyo. Stat. §§ 40-12-501-40-12-502

C. Federal Regulations

1. COPPA Regulations: 16 C.F.R. 312.8.

2. FDA Regulations: 21 C.F.R. pt. 11.

3. GLB Security Breach Notification Rule: Interagency Guidance on Response Programs for Unauthorized Access to Customer Information and Customer Notice, 12 C.F.R. Part 30 (OCC), 12 C.F.R. Part 208 (Federal Reserve System), 12 C.F.R. Part 364 (FDIC), and 12 C.F.R. Part 568 (Office of Thrift Supervision).

4. GLB Security Regulations: Interagency Guidelines Establishing Standards for Safeguarding Consumer Information (to implement §§ 501 and 505(b)

of the Gramm-Leach-Bliley Act), 12 C.F.R. Part 30, Appendix B (OCC), 12 C.F.R. Part 208, Appendix D (Federal Reserve System), 12 C.F.R. Part 364, Appendix B (FDIC), and 12 C.F.R. Part 568 (Office of Thrift Supervision).

5. GLB Security Regulations (FTC): FTC Safeguards Rule (to implement §§ 501 and 505(b) of the Gramm-Leach-Bliley Act), 16 C.F.R. Part 314 (FTC).

6. HIPAA Security Regulations: Final HIPAA Security Regulations, 45 C.F.R. Part 164.

7. IRS Regulations: Rev. Proc. 97-22, 1997-1 C.B. 652, 1997-13 I.R.B. 9, and Rev. Proc. 98-25.

8. IRS Regulations: IRS Announcement 98-27, 1998-15 I.R.B. 30, and Tax Regs. 26 C.F.R. § 1.1441-1(e)(4)(iv).

9. OFHEO Regulations: Safety and Soundness Regulation, 12 C.F.R. Part 1720, Appendix C.

10. SEC Regulations: 17 C.F.R. 240.17a-4, and 17 C.F.R. 257.1(e)(3).

D. State Regulations

1. NAIC Model Regulations: National Association of Insurance Commissioners, Standards for Safeguarding Consumer Information, Model Regulation.

2. Attorneys-New Jersey Advisory Committee on Professional Ethics, Opinion 701 (2006).

E. Court Decisions

1. *Wolfe* v. *MBNA America Bank*, 485 F. Supp. 2d 874, 882 (W.D. Tenn. 2007).

2. *Lorraine* v. *Markel*, 2007 U.S. Dist. LEXIS 33020 (D. Md. May 4, 2007).

3. *Guin* v. *Brazos Higher Education Service*, 2006 U.S. Dist. LEXIS 4846 (D. Minn. Feb. 7, 2006).

4. *American Express* v. *Vinhnee*, 336 B.R. 437; 2005 Bankr. LEXIS 2602 (9th Cir. December 16, 2005).

5. *Bell* v. *Michigan Council 25*, No. 246684, 2005 Mich. App. LEXIS 353 (Mich. App. Feb. 15, 2005) (Unpublished opinion).

F. FTC Decisions and Consent Decrees

1. *In re* The TJX Companies, Inc., FTC File No. 072-3055 (Agreement Containing Consent Order, March 27, 2008), available at www.ftc.gov/os/caselist/0723055.

2. *In re* Reed Elsevier, Inc. and Seisint, Inc., FTC File No. 052-3094 (Agreement Containing Consent Order, March 27, 2008), available at www.ftc.gov/os/caselist/0523094.

3. U.S. v. ValueClick, Inc., Case No. CV08-01711 MMM (RZx), FTC File Nos. 072-3111 and 072-3158 (Stipulated Final Judgment, C.D. Cal. March 17, 2008), available at www.ftc.gov/os/caselist/0723111.

4. *In re* Goal Financial, LLC (Agreement Containing Consent Order, FTC File No. 072-3013, March 4, 2008), available at www.ftc.gov/os/caselist/0723013.

5. *In re* Life is good, Inc. (Agreement containing Consent Order, FTC File No. 072 3046, January 17, 2008), available at www.ftc.gov/os/caselist/0723046/index.shtm.

6. *In re* Guidance Software (Agreement containing Consent Order, FTC File No. 062 3057, November 16, 2006), available at www.ftc.gov/opa/2006/11/guidance.htm.

7. *In re* CardSystems Solutions, Inc. (Agreement containing Consent Order, FTC File No. 052 3148, Feb. 23, 2006), available at www.ftc.gov/opa/2006/02/cardsystems_r.htm.

8. *United States* v. *ChoicePoint, Inc.* (Stipulated Final Judgment, FTC File No. 052 3069, N.D. Ga. Jan. 26, 2006), available at www.ftc.gov/os/caselist/choicepoint/choicepoint.htm.

9. *In re* DSW Inc. (Agreement containing Consent Order, FTC File No. 052 3096, Dec. 1, 2005), available at www.ftc.gov/opa/2005/12/dsw.htm.

10. *In re* BJ's Wholesale Club, Inc. (Agreement containing Consent Order, FTC File No. 042 3160, June 16, 2005), available at www.ftc.gov/opa/2005/06/bjswholesale.htm.

11. *In re* Sunbelt Lending Services, Inc. (Agreement containing Consent Order, FTC File No. 042 3153, Nov. 16, 2004), available at www.ftc.gov/os/caselist/0423153/04231513.htm.

12. *In re* Petco Animal Supplies, Inc. (Agreement containing Consent Order, FTC File No. 042 3153, Nov. 7, 2004), available at www.ftc.gov/os/caselist/0323221/0323221.htm.

13. *In re* MTS, Inc., d/b/a Tower records/Books/Video (Agreement containing Consent Order, FTC File No. 032-3209, Apr. 21, 2004), available at www.ftc.gov/os/caselist/0323209/040421agree0323209.pdf.

14. *In re* Guess?, Inc. (Agreement containing Consent Order, FTC File No. 022 3260, June 18, 2003), available at www.ftc.gov/os/2003/06/guessagree.htm.

15. *FTC* v. *Microsoft* (Consent Decree, Aug. 7, 2002), available at www.ftc.gov/os/2002/08/microsoftagree.pdf.

16. *In re* Eli Lilly & Co. (Decision and Order, FTC Docket No. C-4047, May 8, 2002), available at www.ftc.gov/os/2002/05/elilillydo.htm.

G. State Attorneys General Consent Decrees

1. *In re* Providence Health System-Oregon (Attorney General of Oregon, Assurance of Discontinuance, September 26, 2006), available at www.doj .state.or.us/media/pdf/finfraud_providence_avc.pdf.

2. *In re* Barnes & Noble.com, LLC (Attorney General of New York, Assurance of Discontinuance, Apr. 20, 2004), available at www.bakerinfo.com/ ecommerce/barnes-noble.pdf.

3. *In re* Ziff-Davis Media Inc. (Attorneys General of California, New York, and Vermont), Assurance of Discontinuance, Aug. 28, 2002), available at www.oag.state.ny.us/press/2002/aug/aug28a_02_attach.pdf.

H. European Union

1. EU Data Protection Directive: European Union Directive 95/46/EC of February 20, 1995, on the protection of individuals with regard to the processing of personal data and on the free movement of such data (Data Protection Directive), art. 17, available at http://europa.eu.int/comm/ internal_market/privacy/docs/95-46-ce/dir1995-46_part1_en.pdf.

2. EU Data Protection Directive: European Union Directive 2006/24/EC of March 15, 2006, on the retention of data generated or processed in connection with the provision of publicly available electronic communications services or of public communications networks and amending Directive 2002/58/EC, available at http://eurocrim.jura.uni-tuebingen.de/cms/en/ doc/745.pdf.

NOTES

1. A list of some of the key statutes, regulations, and enforcement actions addressing corporate obligations to implement information security measures is set out in the Appendix at the end of this chapter.

2. *National Strategy to Secure Cyberspace* 6 (Feb. 14, 2003), available at www.whitehouse .gov/pcipb.

3. "As a result of increasing interconnectivity, information systems and networks are now exposed to a growing number and a wider variety of threats and vulnerabilities. This raises new issues for security." *OECD Guidelines for the Security of Information Systems and Networks* 7 (July 25, 2002), available at www.oecd.org/dataoecd/16/22/15582260.pdf.

4. Citations to these sources are in the Appendix at the end of this chapter.

5. *See generally* Bruce H. Nearon, Jon Stanley, Steven W. Teppler, & Joseph Burton, Life

After Sarbanes-Oxley: The Merger of Information Security and Accountability 45 *Jurimetrics J.* 379-412 (2005).

6. *See, e.g.*, 17 C.F.R. 240.17a-4 & 17 C.F.R. 257.1(e)(3).

7. *See, e.g.*, Gramm-Leach-Bliley (GLB) Act §§ 501, 505(b), 15 U.S.C. §§ 6801, 6805, GLB Security Regulations at 12 C.F.R. pt. 30, app. B (OCC), 12 C.F.R. pt. 208, app. D (Federal Reserve System), 12 C.F.R. pt. 364, app. B (FDIC), 12 C.F.R. pt. 568 (Office of Thrift Supervision),16 C.F.R. pt. 314 (FTC); Health Insurance Portability and Accountability Act (HIPAA), 42 U.S.C. §§ 1320d-2, 1320d-4, HIPAA Security Regulations at 45 C.F.R. pt. 164; Children's Online Privacy Protection Act of 1998 (COPPA), 15 U.S.C. § 6501 *et seq.*, COPPA regulations at 16 C.F.R. pt. 312.8. *See also* EU Data Protection Directive, art. 17.

8. *See* list in the Appendix at the end of this chapter.

9. *See* list in the Appendix at the end of this chapter.

10. *See* the FTC enforcement actions involving *CardSystems Solutions, Inc., ChoicePoint, Inc., DSW, Inc.*, and *BJ's Wholesale Club, Inc.* listed in the Appendix.

11. *See* Electronic Signatures in Global and National Commerce Act (E-SIGN), 15 U.S.C. § 7001(d); Uniform Electronic Transaction Act (UETA), § 12.

12. *See, e.g.*, IRS Rev. Proc. 97-22, 1997-1 C.B. 652, 1997-13 I.R.B. 9; Rev. Proc. 98-25; IRS Announcement 98-27; 1998-15 I.R.B. 30; Tax Regs. 26 C.F.R. § 1.1441-1(e)(4)(iv).

13. *See, e.g.*, 17 C.F.R. 240.17a-4; 17 C.F.R. 257.1(e)(3).

14. *See, e.g.*, 21 C.F.R. pt. 11.

15. *See, e.g.*, Caremark International Inc. Derivative Litigation, 698 A. 2d 959, 970 (Del. Ch. 1996).

16. *See, e.g., American Express v. Vinhnee*, 2005 Bankr. LEXIS 2602 (9th Cir. Bk. App. Panel, 2005); *Lorraine v. Markel*, 2007 U.S. Dist. LEXIS 33020 (D. Md. May 4, 2007).

17. *See, e.g., Wolfe v. MBNA America Bank*, 485 F. Supp. 2d 874, 882 (W.D. Tenn. 2007); *Guin v. Brazos Higher Education Service*, Civ. No. 05-668, 2006 U.S. Dist. Lexis 4846 (D. Minn. Feb. 7, 2006); *Bell v. Michigan Council*, 2005 Mich. App. LEXIS 353 (Mich. App. Feb. 15, 2005) (all affirming a negligence cause of action).

18. *See, e.g.*, Homeland Security Act of 2002 (Federal Information Security Management Act of 2002), 44 U.S.C. § 3542(b)(1); GLB Security Regulations (OCC), 12 C.F.R. pt. 30 app. B, pt. II.B; HIPAA Security Regulations, 45 C.F.R. § 164.306(a)(1); Microsoft Consent Decree at II, p. 4.

19. *See, e.g.*, FISMA, 44 U.S.C. § 3542(b)(1). Most of the foreign privacy laws also focus their security requirements from this perspective. This includes, for example, the EU Data Protection Directive, and the privacy laws in Canada, Finland, Italy, and the UK.

20. *See, e.g.*, FDA regulations at 21 C.F.R. pt. 11 (procedures and controls); SEC regulations, 17 C.F.R. 257.1(e)(3) (procedures); SEC regulations at 17 C.F.R. 240.17a-4 (controls); GLB regulations (FTC) 16 C.F.R. Part 314 (safeguards); Canada, Personal Information Protection and Electronic Documents Act, Schedule I, § 4.7 (safeguards); EU Data Privacy Directive, art. 17(1) (measures).

21. These include ISO, NIST, COBIT, and other standards. *See* Jody Westby (ed.), *International Strategy for Cyberspace Security*, ch. 4 (2004).

22. Bruce Schneier, *Secrets & Lies: Digital Security in a Networked World*, p. xii (2000).

23. *See, e.g., Guin v. Brazos Higher Education Service*, Civ. No. 05-668, 2006 U.S. Dist. Lexis 4846 (D. Minn. Feb. 7, 2006) (rejecting an argument that a specific security measure (encryption) was legally mandated, and focusing instead on the fact that the defendant had followed the

proper "process," *i.e.*, had put in place written security policies, had done current risk assessments, and had implemented proper safeguards as required by the GLB Act).

24. 66 Fed. Reg. 8616, Feb. 1, 2001; 12 C.F.R. pt. 30, app. B (OCC), 12 C.F.R. pt. 208, app. D (Federal Reserve System), 12 C.F.R. pt. 364, app. B (FDIC), 12 C.F.R. pt. 568 (Office of Thrift Supervision).

25. 67 Fed. Reg. 36484, May 23, 2002; 16 C.F.R. pt. 314.

26. 44 U.S.C. § 3544(b).

27. 45 C.F.R. pt. 164.

28. *See* Final Report of the FTC Advisory Committee on Online Access and Security 26 (May 15, 2000), available at www.ftc.gov/acoas/papers/finalreport.htm (noting that "security is more a process than a state"); Prepared Statement of the Federal Trade Commission before the Subcommittee on Technology, Information Policy, Intergovernmental Relations, and the Census, Committee on Government Reform, U.S. House of Representatives on "Protecting Our Nation's Cyberspace" 5 (Apr. 21, 2004) (noting that "security is an ongoing process of using reasonable and appropriate measures in light of the circumstances"), available at www.ftc.gov/os/2004/04/042104cybersecuritytestimony.pdf.

29. *See, e.g.*, FTC Decisions and Consent Decrees listed in the Appendix at the end of this chapter.

30. *See, e.g.*, National Association of Insurance Commissioners, *Standards for Safeguarding Customer Information Model Regulation* IV-673-1, available at www.naic.org.

31. *See, e.g.*, State Attorneys General Consent Decrees listed in the Appendix at the end of this chapter.

32. *See supra* n. 17.

33. *See, e.g.*, FISMA, 44 U.S.C. § 3544(b) ("Develop, document, and implement an agency-wide information security program"); GLB Regulations (Federal Reserve), 12 C.F.R. 208, app. D-2.II(A) ("Implement a comprehensive written information security program"); GLB Regulations (FTC), 16 C.F.R. 314.3(a) ("Develop, implement, and maintain a comprehensive information security program that is written in one or more readily accessible parts"); Microsoft Consent Decree ("Establish and maintain a comprehensive information security program in writing").

34. *See, e.g.*, FISMA, 44 U.S.C. §§ 3544(a)(2)(A) ,3544(b)(1); GLB Security Regulations, 12 C.F.R. pt. 30, app. B, pt. III.B(2).

35. *See, e.g.*, *Guin v. Brazos Higher Education Service*, Civ. No. 05-668, 2006 U.S. Dist. Lexis 4846 (D. Minn. Feb. 7, 2006).

36. Laws and regulations regarding security typically require regulated entities to implement security measures designed to address each of these three categories. *See, e.g.*, GLB, 15 U.S.C. § 6801 (addressing "administrative, technical, and physical safeguards"); HIPAA, 42 U.S.C. § 1320d-2(d)(2) (requiring covered entities to "maintain reasonable and appropriate administrative, technical, and physical safeguards . . .").

37. Internet RFC 2828, available at www.faqs.org/rfcs/rfc2828.html.

38. *See, e.g.*, HIPAA Security Regulations, 45 C.F.R. § 164.312.

39. *See, e.g.*, HIPAA Security Regulations, 45 C.F.R. § 164.308.

40. *See, e.g.*, GLB Security Regulations, 12 C.F.R. pt. 30 app. B, pt. II.A.

41. RFC 2828, available at www.faqs.org/rfcs/rfc2828.html. *See also* HIPAA regulations, 45 C.F.R. 164.304.

42. *See Guin, supra* note 23 at 12.

43. HIPAA Security Regulations, 45 CFR § 164.306(b)(1).

44. *See, e.g.,* HIPAA regulations 45 C.F.R. §§ 164.308, 164.310, 164.312; GLB Regulations 12 C.F.R. 208, app. D-2.II(A), 12 C.F.R. pt. 30, app. B, pt. II; Microsoft Consent Decree, at p. 4.

45. These are the security controls identified in the statutes and regulations listed in the Appendix at the end of this chapter.

46. *See Guin, supra* n. 23 at 11.

47. *See, e.g.,* Office of the Comptroller of the Currency, Administrator of National Banks, OCC Bulletin 2001-47 on Third Party Relationships (Nov. 21, 2001), available at www.OCC.treas.gov/ftp/bulletin/2001-47.doc.

48. *See, e.g.,* GLB Security Regulations, 12 C.F.R. pt. 30 app. B, pt. II.D(2); HIPAA Security Regulations, 45 C.F.R. §§ 164.308(b)(1), 164.314(a)(2).

49. *See, e.g.,* FISMA, 44 U.S.C. § 3544(b)(4); HIPAA Security Regulations, 45 C.F.R. §§ 164.308(a)(1)(ii)(C), 164.308(a)(5)(i); Ziff Davis Assurance of Discontinuance, paras. 24(d), p. 5 and 27(c), p. 7.

50. *See, e.g.,* FISMA, 44 U.S.C. § 3544(b)(5); GLB Security Regulations, 12 C.F.R. pt. 30, app. B, pt. III(c)(3); HIPAA Security Regulations, 45 C.F.R. § 164.308(a)(1)(ii)(D); Eli Lilly Decision at II.C; Microsoft Consent Decree at II, p. 4; Ziff Davis Assurance of Discontinuance, para. 27(e) and (f), p. 7.

51. *See, e.g.,* GLB Security Regulations, 12 C.F.R. pt. 30, app. B, pt. III.E; HIPAA Security Regulations, 45 C.F.R. § 164.306(e), 164.308(a)(8); Microsoft Consent Decree at II, p. 4, and III, p. 5; Ziff Davis Assurance of Discontinuance, para. 27(e), (f), and (h), p. 7; Eli Lilly Decision at II.D.

52. Sarbanes-Oxley Act, § 302, 15 U.S.C. § 7241.

53. *See, e.g.,* GLB Security Regulations (Federal Reserve) 12 C.F.R. 208, app. D-2.III(A).

54. HIPAA Security Regulations, 45 C.F.R. § 164.308(a)(2).

55. *See* FTC Decisions and Consent Decrees listed in the Appendix at the end of this chapter.

56. E. Michael Power & Roland L. Trope, *Sailing in Dangerous Waters: A Director's Guide to Data Governance* 13 (2005); Roland L. Trope, Directors' Digital Fiduciary Duties, *IEEE Security & Privacy* 78 (Jan.-Feb. 2005).

57. 698 A. 2d 959, 970 (Del. Ch. 1996).

58. Securing Cyberspace: Business Roundtable's Framework for the Future, Business Roundtable 1, 2 (May 19, 2004), available at www.businessroundtable.org/pdf//20040518000CyberSecurityPrinciples.pdf.

59. *Information Security Governance: A Call to Action,* Corporate Governance Task Force Report, National Cyber Security Partnership 12-13 (Apr. 2004), available at www.cyberpartnership.org/InfoSecGov4_04.pdf. The National Cyber Security Partnership (NCSP) is a public-private partnership established to develop shared strategies and programs to better secure and enhance America's critical information infrastructure.

60. GLB Security Regulations (OCC), 12 C.F.R. pt. 30, app. B, pt. III.A, pt. III.F.

61. Applies to information brokers only.

62. Applies to state agencies only.

2 THE COMING WAVE OF INTERNET-RELATED SECURITY LITIGATION

Ian C. Ballon

Ian C. Ballon is a shareholder in the Silicon Valley and Santa Monica offices of Greenberg Traurig, LLP, the author of the four-volume legal treatise E-Commerce and Internet Law: A Legal Treatise with Forms *(West LegalWorks, 2001 and Cum. Supp.), and executive director of Stanford University Law School's Center for E-Commerce. This article is adapted in part from materials in Mr. Ballon's treatise. In addition, Jubin Meraj and Demondre Edwards provided research and other valuable assistance. Mr. Ballon may be reached at (650) 289-7881, (310) 586-6575, or Ballon@GTlaw.com.*

The field of Internet security law today resembles privacy law in 1995,[1] when there was an incomplete patchwork of remedies available under state law; there were a few specific, narrow federal statutes (most of which addressed hacking or related computer crimes); and the FTC had just begun to study online privacy issues pursuant to its broad jurisdiction over unfair or deceptive consumer practices. Today, federal law imposes security obligations on businesses in a limited number of specific fields (such as financial services and healthcare); state legislators are just beginning to consider online security as an important issue (following California's adoption of a security reporting statute, which took effect in 2003); and the FTC is focusing increasing attention on security as an important aspect of privacy protection. As with privacy in 1995, engineering and technological solutions, more than legal standards, define the security practices of most businesses today. There is no uniform "safe harbor" protection nor "best practices" standards to shield businesses from liability in this emerging area of law.

Although various proposals have been advanced, there is no single U.S. or international standard that, if complied with, could insulate a company from state, federal, or regulatory liability in all instances. Moreover, there is disagreement over whether legal standards should be detailed enough to provide certainty to businesses seeking to avoid liability through compliance, or flexible enough to adapt to changing technological standards.[2] Ultimately, as with privacy law, technological innovations will continue to change the definition of "reasonable conduct" and effectively will impose new obligations on companies to protect the security of digital information.

Just as there is presently a rich body of law relating to Internet privacy, the coming years will see an increase in security-related legislation and litigation, including class action litigation. Businesses should anticipate these trends and adjust their internal practices accordingly.

I. THE CURRENT PATCHWORK OF LAWS GOVERNING INTERNET SECURITY

A. Overview

Internet security is relevant to multiple areas of both civil and criminal law. With respect to digital data or other electronic information, the term *security law* typically refers to the internal and external security obligations imposed on businesses and the civil or regulatory liability that may result from unauthorized access or other security breaches (including the related question of whether a company has taken adequate precautions to ensure security). From a legal perspective, "Internet security" usually refers to three separate potential security concerns: (1) Website or gateway security (or the security at the point at which customer data or a company's internal computer network are potentially accessible to third parties); (2) Internet security (with respect to which federal law generally prohibits the unauthorized interception of communications); and (3) internal security (or the security of systems and information accessible to employees or other authorized personnel that are not otherwise generally available outside a company).[3]

Although security lawyers must be knowledgeable about technological issues that may raise legal questions—such as the use of digital signatures or certificates or other means of encrypting communications and authenticating the identity of individuals or entities online—the legal framework for evaluating security concerns and potential solutions has not yet fully developed.

There is no uniform federal regulatory scheme governing a business's obligation to ensure the security of electronic information. The federal Gramm-

Leach-Bliley Act and Health Insurance Portability and Accountability Act (HIPAA) and their implementing regulations impose extensive, specific legal obligations on companies to maintain the security of electronic data in, respectively, the financial services and healthcare industries. These statutes and their implementing regulations, which created the most detailed rules governing U.S. data security in existence today, subject companies to regulatory oversight but do not afford private causes of action.

Most states do not expressly regulate the security of electronic data. State laws generally impose civil or criminal penalties on hackers who break into systems or networks or otherwise access information without authorization. In addition, in most states, existing tort, consumer protection, and unfair trade laws may implicitly regulate Internet security—albeit without providing much concrete guidance to companies—by creating a financial disincentive for businesses to use anything other than "industry standard" security technologies and practices. By contrast, California has adopted a security reporting statute that creates an even more tangible disincentive for companies to deviate from industry standard practices by expressly requiring that notification of security breaches be provided to consumers in certain circumstances.

As with privacy law in the 1990s, the FTC, more than courts or legislatures, increasingly is imposing de facto security law standards (through enforcement actions) on businesses (such as those outside the financial services and healthcare fields) that are not otherwise subject to specific federal regulation. FTC enforcement actions, in turn, may lead to class action litigation since many plaintiffs' lawyers closely monitor the activities of the FTC and state attorneys general.

Internet-related privacy class actions have proven difficult to maintain when brought under federal anti-hacking statutes or other laws that, arguably, impose civil or criminal penalties on those who breach Internet security.[4] State unfair competition statutes may provide a better vehicle for class action lawyers to successfully pursue remedies in litigation, although Internet privacy claims to date often have involved *de minimis* damages. By contrast, certain types of security breaches potentially could result in large damage awards.

Absent the enactment of appropriate safe harbors and federal preemption of state laws, the coming wave of security-related litigation may eclipse anything seen in the field of Internet privacy law and could represent a significant cost of doing business for Internet companies.

B. Gramm-Leach-Bliley Act of 1999

The Gramm-Leach-Bliley Act of 1999 imposes security obligations on financial institutions.[5] Under Subtitle A of the Act, which deals with the disclosure of nonpublic information, every financial institution has an affirmative and continuing obligation to respect the privacy and protect the confidentiality of nonpublic personal customer information. Specific regulatory agencies, including the FTC, were assigned the task of establishing standards for financial institution safeguards that (1) ensure the security and confidentiality of customer records and information and (2) protect against hazards or unauthorized access to such information.

For a financial institution to disclose the nonpublic information of its customers to a nonaffiliated third party, it must comply with the statute's consumer notification provisions, which require, among other things, that financial institutions provide (1) a clear and conspicuous disclosure that its customers' information may be disseminated to third parties and (2) the opportunity for consumers to prevent such disclosures. The statute also prohibits a financial institution from disclosing a consumer's access number or code to a nonaffiliated third party for use in telemarketing, direct mail marketing, or other marketing through electronic mail to the consumer. The enforcement of Subtitle A of the statute rests with certain designated federal agencies, state insurance authorities, and the FTC.[6]

Pursuant to the Safeguards Rule, financial institutions subject to the FTC's jurisdiction are required to develop and implement appropriate safeguards to protect consumer information, including a written information security plan. Among other things, such financial institutions must designate one or more employees to coordinate the safeguards; identify and access the risks to consumer information in relevant areas of operations; design, implement, and regularly monitor a safeguards program; hire appropriate service providers and contract with them to implement the safeguards; and evaluate and adjust the program in light of relevant circumstances.[7]

Subtitle B of the Act, which addresses fraudulent access to financial information, establishes guidelines that prohibit anyone from obtaining, disclosing, or providing documents under false pretenses that pertain to a financial institution's customer information. Violations of these prohibitions are subject to FTC enforcement actions, as well as civil and criminal penalties.

This general prohibition, however, does not apply to (1) law enforcement agencies; (2) financial institutions and insurance institutions that are engaged in certain specified activities; (3) customer information of a financial institution that is available as a public record under federal securities laws; and (4) state-licensed private investigators acting pursuant to judicial authorization to collect child support from a person adjudged to be delinquent.

Pursuant to the statute, federal banking and securities regulatory agencies are required to update security guidelines applicable to financial institutions to deter and detect the activities proscribed by this Act. In addition, the comptroller general is required to report to Congress on (1) the efficacy and adequacy of the remedies provided in the Act and (2) recommendations for additional actions to address threats to financial information privacy. The FTC and the attorney general are also required to report annually to Congress on enforcement actions taken pursuant to this Act. The statute, however, does not afford a private cause of action.

C. The Health Insurance Portability and Accountability Act (HIPAA)

Under the U.S. Department of Health and Human Services' final security rule (the "Security Rule") issued in February 2003 pursuant to the Health Insurance Portability and Accountability Act of 1996 (HIPAA), health plans, healthcare clearinghouses, and most healthcare providers (referred to as "covered entities") are required to employ certain administrative, physical, and technical safeguards to ensure the confidentiality and integrity of protected health information maintained or transmitted by electronic media.[8] Among other things, the Security Rule requires that business associate agreements incorporate specified language regarding electronic data security. It also requires covered entities to appoint a single security official to oversee compliance.

HIPAA allows companies some flexibility to respond to changing technological standards. The Security Rule is organized around general "standards," many of which are divided into more detailed "implementation specifications." Although there are certain implementation specifications that covered entities are required to meet, other "addressable specifications" allow covered entities the flexibility to (1) assess whether the specification is reasonable and appropriate given the environment in which the entity operates; (2) implement the specification if it is deemed to be reasonable and appropriate; or (3) implement an equivalent, alternative security measure that is reasonable and appropriate (and document the reasons for concluding that the alternative measure is reasonable and appropriate). Addressable specifications relate to, among other things, encryption, employee access authorization procedures, security reminders, virus protection, log-in monitoring, password management policies, and testing and revision of contingency plans.

Although the Security Rule includes some required specifications, it is intended to be "scalable" to allow covered entities to develop reasonable, individually tailored approaches to security. In fact, the preamble to the Security Rule emphasizes that risk analysis and risk management form "the foundation on which all of the other standards depend." According to the rule, the reasonableness of a particular security measure will be judged by (1) the size, complexity, and capabilities of the covered entity; (2) the covered entity's technical infrastructure, hardware, and software capabilities; (3) the cost of alternative security measures; and (4) the probability and severity of potential risks.

To ensure compatibility with the Privacy Rule, the Security Rule adopts the same definition of "protected health information" as the Privacy Rule. However, unlike the Privacy Rule, the Security Rule applies only to "electronic protected health information," which is protected health information maintained in or transmitted by "electronic media."[9]

Although covered entities did not need to comply with the Security Rule until April 21, 2005, the Privacy Rule, which took effect on April 14, 2003, imposed some overlapping obligations, including a general requirement that covered entities adopt "administrative, physical and technical safeguards" to maintain the privacy of protected health information. For this reason, covered entities as a practical matter could follow the Security Rule even before its effective date in order to comply with the Privacy Rule, such as when negotiating business associate contracts.

As with the Gramm-Leach-Bliley Act, HIPAA does not afford a private cause of action against companies that violate its provisions.

D. California's Security Reporting Statute

California's security reporting statute,[10] which took effect on July 1, 2003, does not impose specific compliance requirements or offer any safe harbors. Rather, it focuses on the end result—security—and establishes a notification procedure to deter security breaches and encourage careful preplanning.

The statute requires a state agency or a person or entity that conducts business in California and owns or licenses computerized data that include personal information to disclose in specified ways any security breach[11] to a resident of California whose unencrypted personal information was, or is reasonably believed to have been, acquired by an unauthorized person. The statute, which preempts any local regulations, also requires an agency, person, or business that maintains computerized data that include personal information owned by another to notify the owner or licensee of the information of any security breach.

Under the statute, "personal information" means an individual's first name, or first initial, and last name, in combination with any one or more of the following data elements, when either the name or the data elements are not encrypted: (1) social security number; (2) driver's license number or California identification card number; (3) account, credit, or debit card number, in combination with any required security code, access code, or password that would permit access to an individual's financial account.

Notice, under the statue, may be provided by (1) written notice; (2) electronic notice, if consistent with the provisions governing electronic records and signatures set forth in the federal E-SIGN law;[12] or (3) substitute notice, if the person, business, or agency demonstrates that the cost of providing actual notice would exceed $250,000, or that the affected class of subject persons to be notified exceeds 500,000, or that the person, business, or agency does not have sufficient contact information to provide actual notice. Substitute notice must include (1) email notice, if the person, business, or agency has an email address for a person; (2) a conspicuous Website posting; or (3) notification through "major" statewide media. Notification may be delayed, however, if a law enforcement agency determines that it would impede a criminal investigation.

Although the threat of compelled notification undoubtedly encourages businesses that might not otherwise do so to provide adequate security for customer information, even the best system may be breached by a hacker or as a result of human error. However well intended, the effect of the law could be harsh for California businesses. Notifications under California's security reporting statute could lead to litigation under California's notoriously broad Unfair Competition Statute,[13] including potentially class action litigation. Regardless of when or how they arrive, notifications, in addition to alerting consumers, may generate adverse publicity and attract the attention of plaintiff's lawyers.

E. FTC Enforcement Actions

For businesses outside the financial services and healthcare industries, FTC guidelines for Internet security are implemented through enforcement actions brought against companies that are alleged to have acted unfairly or deceptively by making express or implicit promises about protecting sensitive information from consumers that allegedly have not been kept due to inadequate security measures. Prominent security-related enforcement actions have involved Eli Lilly & Co.,[14] Microsoft,[15] Guess, Inc.,[16] Tower Records,[17] and Petco.[18]

According to a November 19, 2003, release,[19] FTC enforcement actions are intended to illustrate the following principles:

- Security measures should be "reasonable and appropriate under the circumstances," which may vary depending on factors such as a company's size and complexity, the nature of its business, and the sensitivity of the information it collects.

- Not all security breaches constitute FTC violations; the FTC recognizes that "security breaches sometimes can happen when a company has taken every reasonable precaution."

- Because appropriate information security practices are necessary to protect consumers' privacy, businesses cannot simply wait for a breach to occur and be detected before taking action, particularly when they have made explicit promises to consumers.

- Good security requires an ongoing process of assessing and responding to risks and vulnerabilities, which change over time.

FTC enforcement actions, although limited to cases in which a company fails to follow stated or implied practices and procedures relating to security, effectively promote the development of *de facto* security standards.

F. The Threat of Class Action Litigation

Breaches of Internet security may lead to litigation under state tort, unfair competition, or consumer protection laws. Privacy-related class action suits to date, though expensive to defend, generally have not yielded large settlements or judgments. Federal privacy statutes contain minimum damage requirements and other technical requirements that may be difficult to meet in litigation arising out of online consumer transactions, and generally are targeted at deterring hacking or other computer crimes rather than consumer protection.[20] Low potential recoveries also may serve as a deterrent to litigation. In addition, certification of a privacy- or security-related class action may be difficult to obtain when users enter into a binding click-through or other agreements that provide for binding arbitration of disputes.[21]

Although privacy violations generally have not yielded significant damage awards or settlements, security violations could prove to be a more fertile area of growth for plaintiffs' class action lawyers because of the potentially greater damages that may accrue in certain kinds of security breach cases.

Businesses may seek to limit the risk of exposure to class action litigation in some cases by entering into contracts with consumers that contain binding arbitration clauses. However, judges may closely scrutinize unilateral contracts with consumers. Among other things, courts to date have not uniformly enforced online arbitration agreements, either because they find that a binding online contract has not been formed[22] or that the agreement itself was procedurally or substantively unconscionable.[23] California has also limited the enforceability of arbitration provisions in potential class action suits.[24]

Marketing considerations also may limit a company's ability to disclaim responsibility for Internet security. As with privacy, there is a tension between the commercial need to promise adequate protection and the risk-management imperative of disclaiming express and implied warranties. Because online contracts serve a marketing function in addition to ordering legal relationships,[25] there are sometimes practical business limitations on the extent to which a company may disclaim any pretense of affording reasonable security. It also remains to be seen whether, or on what terms, extremely broad disclaimers could even withstand scrutiny by the FTC or state attorneys given general consumer expectations that companies that collect their data will at least undertake some effort to protect against their disclosure.

Although reasonable disclaimers and contractual limitations may be generally enforced, they may be of only limited value in litigation brought under state unfair competition laws or for intentional torts, given that statutory violations and intentional torts generally may not be disclaimed. Reputable businesses may take measures to prevent intentional security violations. By contrast, unfair competition claims potentially could be based on unintended breaches allegedly occasioned by the failure to follow adequate security precautions and may not be limited by contractual provisions.

FTC enforcement actions have encouraged the development of security-related practices and procedures, including the adoption of information security programs. California's security notification statute has created an even stronger disincentive for businesses operating in California to ignore security concerns. Indeed, the requirement that companies disclose security breaches to consumers creates a tangible risk to companies—especially because California's broad unfair competition statute allows a private cause of action to be brought for violations of statutes that do not expressly create independent causes of action.[26] Moreover, courts evaluating state tort law claims are not bound by the principle recognized by the FTC that "security breaches sometimes can happen when a company has taken every reasonable precaution."[27]

In the absence of specific guidelines—such as those applied to financial institutions and covered healthcare entities under federal law—what constitutes *adequate* or *reasonable* conduct ultimately may present a fact question in litigation. The absence of any safe harbor for businesses outside of the healthcare and financial services industries (whose failure to comply with federal regulations may not support a private cause of action) means that even businesses that implement the latest security technologies and industry "best practices" may be forced to defend themselves in litigation if a security breach occurs.

II. CONCLUSION

As with the more developed field of privacy law, the FTC is actively shaping industry best practices through enforcement actions and settlements involving businesses that fail to adhere to express or implied representations about their security practices. Laws such as California's security reporting statute underscore the need for all Internet businesses to implement the latest technologies and adhere to industry standard practices and procedures, but do not offer a safe harbor for doing so.

Despite a company's best efforts, it is impossible to anticipate all actions potentially undertaken by hackers or effectively guarantee absolute security. Although insurance coverage may help businesses limit their risk of exposure, the absence of a uniform federal standard defining what constitutes adequate security or providing safe harbors for reasonable compliance efforts, coupled with potential exposure for state law tort and unfair competition claims for failing to ensure the security of digital data and information, ultimately leaves Internet companies potentially at risk for a coming wave of litigation that may be difficult to fully anticipate or avoid.

NOTES

1. For a discussion of the development of U.S. data privacy law, *see* Ian C. Ballon, *E-Commerce and Internet Law* §§ 32.01, 32.03, 32.05 (West LegalWorks 2001 & 2003 Supp.), available at www.ballononecommerce.com.

2. *See* Thomas J. Smedinghoff, "Defining the Legal Standard for Information Security," paper submitted at the "Securing Privacy in the Internet Age" conference, Stanford University Law School, March 13-14, 2004.

3. *See* Ballon, *supra* note 1, at § 4.07. .

4. Such statutes include the Electronic Communications Privacy Act, 18 U.S.C. § 2510 *et seq.* and the Computer Fraud and Abuse Act, 18 U.S.C. § 1030.

5. *See* 15 U.S.C. §§ 6801-09, 6821-27 (2004).

6. The statute also amended the Fair Credit Reporting Act enforcement guidelines to require certain federal banking agencies to jointly prescribe regulations governing dissemination by holding companies, and their affiliates, of the nonpublic personal information of its customers.

7. *See* http://www.ftc.gov/opa/2003/11/cybersecurity.htm.

8. *See* 45 C.F.R. § 164.312 (2004).

9. The definition of *electronic media* includes telephone voice response and faxback systems, but excludes fax-to-fax and regular telephone transmissions.

10. Cal. Civ. Code §§ 1798.29, 1798.82. Since 2003, a majority of the other states have enacted similar statutes modeled on the California law. *See* Ballon, *supra* note 1, at § 4.07.

11. *Breach of the security system* means an unauthorized acquisition of computerized data that compromises the security, confidentiality, or integrity of any personal information maintained by the agency.

12. *See* 15 U.S.C. § 7001.

13. *See* Cal. Bus. & Prof. Code § 17200 *et seq.*

14. In January 2002, Eli Lilly settled charges with the FTC after it sent an email to Prozac users (reminding them to refill their prescriptions) in which the recipients were identified in the "TO," rather than the "BCC" line of the email message. Although the disclosure was unintentional, Eli Lilly agreed to take appropriate steps to ensure the security of the identity of the recipients in the future. *See Eli Lilly and Company*, 2002 F.T.C. LEXIS 22 (2002); *see also* http://www.ftc.gov/opa/2002/01/elililly.htm.

15. In August 2002, Microsoft settled with the FTC in response to an allegation that Microsoft made false security and privacy promises regarding its "Passport" Web services. Microsoft's Passport Web services stored and collected personal and financial information, allowing users to conduct online transactions without separately inputting this data on each Website. Among other charges, the FTC alleged that Microsoft's privacy policy falsely represented that Microsoft employed reasonable and appropriate security measures to protect the confidentiality of collected information. As part of the settlement, Microsoft agreed to implement a comprehensive information security program, certified by an independent third party, that would meet or exceed the security standards set forth in the consent order. *See Microsoft, Inc.*, 2002 F.T.C. LEXIS 43 (2002); *see also* http://www.ftc.gov/opa/2002/08/microsoft.htm.

16. In June 2003, Guess settled charges that security flaws had exposed consumers' credit card information to hackers. The FTC alleged that Guess did not use reasonable and appropriate security measures to protect the confidentiality of the collected information. As part of the settlement, Guess agreed to implement a comprehensive information security program. *See Guess, Inc.*, 2003 F.T.C. LEXIS 85 (2003); *see also* http://www.ftc.gov/opa/2003/06/guess.htm.

17. In June 2004, Tower Records settled charges that its Website had exposed customers' personal information to other users. *See In the Matter of MTS, Inc.*, File No. 032 3209 (F.T.C. Consent Order entered June 2004).

18. In *The Matter of Petco Animal Supplies, Inc.*, File No. 032 3221 (F.T.C. Consent Order entered Nov. 8, 2004), Petco settled charges that it had failed to implement reasonable and appropriate security measures to protect sensitive consumer information on its Website.

19. *See* http://www.ftc.gov/opa/2003/11/cybersecurity.htm.

20. For example, in *Chance v. Avenue A, Inc.*, 165 F. Supp. 2d 1153 (W.D. Wash. 2001), the court granted defendants' motion for summary judgment and denied as moot plaintiffs' motion for class certification in a case arising out of defendants' alleged placement of cookies on user computers, permitting user communications to be monitored allegedly without their knowledge. The court granted summary judgment on plaintiffs' Computer Fraud and Abuse Act claim because the minimum $5,000 damage requirement had not been met. The court further granted summary judgment on plaintiffs' claim under the Stored Communications Act, 18 U.S.C. § 2701 *et seq.*, because, given the technological and commercial relationship between users and the defendant's Website, it was implausible to suggest that "access" was not intended or authorized. Summary judgment likewise was granted on plaintiffs' claim under the Wiretap Act, 18 U.S.C. § 2510 *et seq.*, based on the finding that it was implicit in the code instructing users' computers to contact the Website that consent had been obtained to the interception of communication between users and defendants.

Similarly, in *In re Doubleclick Inc. Privacy Litig.*, 154 F. Supp. 2d 497 (S.D.N.Y. 2001), the court granted defendant's motion to dismiss plaintiffs' federal claims, declined to exercise supplemental jurisdiction over plaintiffs' state law claims, and dismissed with prejudice plaintiffs' amended complaint based on various claims arising out of Doubleclick's proposed plan to allow participating Websites to exchange cookie files obtained by users to better target banner advertisements. Plaintiffs, Web users, had alleged that defendant's cookies collected information about them, such as names, email addresses, home and business addresses, telephone numbers, searches performed on the Internet, and Web pages or sites, which plaintiffs considered personal in nature and that users would not ordinarily expect advertisers to be able to collect. Among other things, the court ruled that because defendant's affiliated Websites were the relevant "users" of Internet access under the Electronic Communications Privacy Act (ECPA), and submissions containing personal data made by users to defendant's affiliated Websites were intended for those Websites, the sites' authorization was sufficient to grant defendant's access under 18 U.S.C. § 2701(c)(2).

The court similarly granted defendant's motion to dismiss most federal claims, and declined to exercise supplemental jurisdiction over state law claims in *In re Intuit Privacy Litig.*, 138 F. Supp. 2d 1272 (C.D. Cal. 2001). In that case, which arose out of the collection of data in cookie files, defendant's motion to dismiss claims under 18 U.S.C. § 2511 and 18 U.S.C. § 1030 was granted without prejudice because plaintiffs had failed to sufficiently allege a tortious or criminal purpose, or that they had suffered damage or loss. The motion was denied, however, with respect to plaintiffs' claim under 18 U.S.C. § 2701 for intentionally accessing electronically stored data. *See also, e.g., In re Pharmatrak Privacy Litig.*, 329 F. 3d 9 (1st Cir. 2003) (reversing and remanding for further consideration the entry of summary judgment on plaintiffs' claim under the Electronic Communications Privacy Act (ECPA) that their privacy rights had been violated when the defendants' practice of collecting personal information on Websites was not disclosed to users). But *see In re Toys R Us, Inc. Privacy Litig.*, MDL No. M-00-1381, 2001 U.S. Dist. LEXIS

16947 (N.D. Cal. Oct. 9, 2001) (denying a motion to dismiss in a case based on the defendant's alleged use of cookies to collect user data based on the finding that plaintiffs had stated a claim under the Computer Fraud and Abuse Act and granting leave to amend the complaint to assert a Wiretap Act claim).

21. *See In re RealNetworks, Inc. Privacy Litig.*, Civil No. 00 C 1366, 2000 U.S. Dist. LEXIS 6584 (N.D. Ill. May 8, 2000) (denying an intervenor's motion for class certification where the court found that RealNetworks had entered into a contract with putative class members that provided for binding arbitration).

22. *See, e.g., Specht v. Netscape Communications, Inc.*, 306 F. 3d 17 (2d Cir. 2002) (holding posted terms accessible via a link to not be binding on users because assent was not obtained).

23. *See, e.g., Comb v. PayPal, Inc.*, 218 F. Supp. 2d 1165 (N.D. Cal. 2002) (holding a click-through contract that contained an arbitration provision to be substantively and procedurally unconscionable under California law).

24. *See Discover Brank v. Superior Court*, 36 Cal. 4th 148 (2005).

25. Ballon, *supra* note 1, at § 57.01 *et seq.*

26. *See, e.g., Kasky v. Nike*, Inc., 27 Cal. 4th 939, 950 (2002); *StopYouth Addiction, Inc. v. Lucky Stores, Inc.*, 17 Cal. 4th 553, 561-67 (1998).

27. *See* http://www.ftc.gov/opa/2003/11/cybersecurity.htm.

3 THE EVOLUTION OF DATA PROTECTION AS A PRIVACY CONCERN, AND THE CONTRACT LAW DYNAMICS UNDERLYING IT

Jonathan K. Sobel, Karen J. Petrulakis, and Denelle M. Dixon-Thayer

Jonathan K. Sobelis currently group president, media, at Sourceforge. Previously he was senior vice president, general counsel, and secretary of the board of directors for Yahoo! Inc. He was also a partner at Folger Levin & Kahn LLP. Karen J. Petrulakis is a partner at Folger Levin & Kahn LLP. Denelle M. Dixon-Thayer is senior legal director at Yahoo! Inc. Previously she was a partner at Folger Levin & Kahn LLP.

A deceptively simple term, *privacy* has a multitude of meanings and dimensions, all depending on the context. As Professor Raymond Nimmer thoughtfully discusses, not only is the term *privacy* now widely used to cover those zones and activities that are inherently private and that connote freedom from intrusion by the state or by others, but it has come also to encompass the important concept of data protection.[1] As only one example of its breadth, some commentators also include in the concept of privacy the ability to prevent unwanted communications, such as "spam" and telemarketing. As a result, when considering privacy we are ultimately thinking about a whole range of activities that are not solitary or limited to designated private places such as the home, but more often involve relationships (both known and unknown) between people and commercial entities.

The obvious reason why data protection has moved to the forefront of privacy issues: the Internet. Offline practices concerning data mining, usage, collection, and sharing are not transparent or instantaneous. A person may receive, via regular mail, an offer for certain baby products just after having a baby and may consider it a coincidence or not notice. However, these same practices on the Internet are more instantaneous and visible.[2] Less visible, equally pervasive, and perhaps even more significant, is the widespread, relatively recent adoption of databases, interconnected networks, and other digital tools for collecting and disseminating data.

The digital collection of data has increased the debate concerning the protection of personal data.[3] The debate was fueled by the desire of many users to remain anonymous while on the Internet and to not have their behavioral data logged and disseminated. Obvious concerns arose stemming from the digital collection of data and the development of new technology (such as Web beacons) that offered increased and more precise mechanisms for the consolidation, transfer, and use of personal data. The debate has centered on the appropriate mechanisms (such as legislation, industry self-regulation, and litigation) to protect personal data, without undermining the benefits of the Internet. The growing recognition of complex relationship matrices involving data (including third parties who assist commercial entities, "offshoring" of data management and access, data matching practices, and the online-offline mixing) also precipitated the development of data protection issues.[4]

Recognizing the role of relationships in data protection perhaps does not dictate anything at all about the ultimate balance of rights or the correct rules to govern the collection, use, and security of data. Property concepts, tort concepts, and contract concepts may be useful. However, in describing the current reality, it is important to acknowledge the primacy of contract. For the constituencies most often involved in developing data protection policies—the public, the government, the plaintiffs' bar, various interest groups, and companies that must identify and apply relevant rules—the entire policy debate is conducted over an unacknowledged tectonic plate of contract principles.

The underlying reality that contract law may be the mechanism best suited to address the privacy concerns only makes the debate more complicated. Some believe that market principles through contract can and do effectively protect individual rights, and point to individuals' actual practices as confirmation of this. On the other side of the debate, there is an implicit, often unspoken, belief that if left up to individuals (through contract law), individuals may not adequately protect the privacy of their personal data.[5]

After almost a decade of public debate, litigation, and initial attempts at regulation, the data protection issues raised in the digital era remain challenging. Some of this (particularly the early rounds of privacy litigation) is the result of a fundamental misunderstanding of the Internet medium and technology. But much of it reflects the complexity of the issues and the failure of current legal regimes to neatly fit the issues.

This chapter will first discuss the legislative standards of data protection in the United States and show that these statutes attempt to regulate the structure of contracts concerning "personal data." It will then consider private class action litigation and its failures due to its lack of focus on contract principles. The chapter will also analyze the activity of the Federal Trade Commission (FTC) and the state attorneys general—institutions that have focused on contract principles and have become significant leaders in the data protection discussion. The chapter will conclude that much of the confusion and frustration involved in considering privacy issues arises from unexpressed tensions around the application of contract principles to the issues. Finally, the chapter will offer advice to corporations about how to develop useful practices regarding both privacy and security and to navigate the current legal regime in the United States.

I. LEGISLATORS HAVE ENACTED STANDARDS OF DATA PROTECTION UNDER THE GUISE OF PRIVACY PROTECTION

Lawmakers, responding to concerns about the protection of personal data and information, have shifted from traditional notions of privacy rights as protecting an individual's property and body.[6] As privacy became an area of increasing interest, and as information flowed ever faster, it became readily apparent that an all-encompassing statutory regime was not practical.[7] Therefore legislators initially turned their attention to specific areas of perceived abuse and vulnerability. As a result, some subject areas, such as health and financial data, have become heavily regulated, while others have remained largely devoid of specific legislative protections. Some argue that this piecemeal approach has left holes in privacy protection.[8]

The regulations passed thus far follow a predictable pattern. Repeatedly, Congress has turned to concepts of notice, opt-out, and information access to protect privacy rights. Without clear recognition (or more precisely, without clear admission), the subject matter statutes are obvious examples of attempts to regulate the structure of contracts concerning "personal data."

A. Fair Credit Reporting Act

The Fair Credit Reporting Act (FCRA)[9] was the first federal law to regulate the use of personal information by private businesses. Enacted in 1970, it focused on the growing credit reporting industry and was intended to promote accuracy, fairness, and the privacy of personal information assembled by that industry.[10] The Act sets forth the cardinal elements of modern privacy legislation. It requires that credit reporting agencies follow "reasonable procedures" to protect the confidentiality, accuracy, relevancy, and proper utilization of credit information.[11] To ensure procedures are followed, the Act also provides consumers with important rights, specifically, rights to notice, consent, and accountability.[12] The FCRA also provides procedures permitting consumers to correct misinformation in their files.[13] This simplistic approach in the FCRA, notice and consent and access to information, has become the mantra to protect individual privacy rights nearly three decades after its passage. The Act also established a pseudo-contractual approach to privacy protection, permitting consumers essentially to change the "terms" of their relationships with credit reporting agencies by placing restrictions on their confidential information.

B. Gramm-Leach-Bliley

The Financial Modernization Act of 1999,[14] commonly known as the Gramm-Leach-Bliley Act (GLB), also follows the pattern established by the FCRA. GLB includes three principal sections regulating the disclosure of personal financial information by covered financial institutions. First, the Financial Privacy Rule provides consumers with rights of notice and opt-out with respect to certain types of disclosures.[15] Second, GLB's pretexting provisions protect consumers from companies that obtain financial information under false pretenses.[16] Finally, the Act requires the Federal Trade Commission to promulgate a Safeguards Rule, requiring all financial institutions to take steps to keep consumer information secure.[17] Thus the GLB relies heavily on notice and opt-out to protect consumers, another attempt to regulate the structure of contracts concerning personal information.

C. Health Insurance Portability and Accountability Act

Likewise, the Health Insurance Portability and Accountability Act (HIPAA)[18] and related regulations[19] create a comprehensive system for regulating the privacy of health information. HIPAA requires medical providers, insurers, and other entities with access to health information to institute procedures for notice, opt-out of disclosures, and access to private information.[20] It also requires that consumers have opportunities to amend incorrect information.[21] HIPAA also provides the authorization for regulations implementing comprehensive security standards for the transmission of health data.[22] HIPAA thus follows the same pattern as the FCRA and GLB, relying on contractual principles to protect consumers.

D. Children's Online Privacy Protection Act

Conversely, the Children's Online Privacy Protection Act (COPPA)[23] is designed to protect a specific segment of the population that is considered particularly vulnerable, rather than a particular type of information. The Act regulates the collection of information from children under the age of thirteen.[24] It imposes various requirements on commercial Website operators and online service providers that either target children or have actual knowledge that children use their service or site.[25] With limited exceptions, businesses that are subject to COPPA must comply with stringent notice requirements and obtain verifiable parental consent before making any disclosures of a child's personal information.[26] Similar to other privacy statutes, COPPA provides access and modification rights, permitting parents to view and modify or delete their child's personal information from a covered entity's information system.[27] The parent thus takes responsibility for guarding a child's privacy through the use of the same contractual principles as provided under other laws.

Each of the identified statutes is an attempt by Congress to respond to the demand for protection of personal data. These statutes set the base-level rules of engagement between companies and their individual users, and explicitly structure the contractual relationships. This movement toward investing individual consumers with quasi-contractual rights to protect their personal data represents an important shift away from classic notions of privacy as an expression of societal norms.

II. HOW HAVE THE PRIVATE LITIGATION AND GOVERNMENT ENFORCEMENT ACTIONS SHAPED THE DATA PROTECTION DISCUSSION?

Private litigation and regulatory activity, although attempting to address the same harm, have had different results. Because the private litigation was driven by the plaintiffs' bar, it did not focus on traditional contract principles, and it presumptively failed when an applicable federal statute allowing for specified damages and attorneys fees could not be identified. In contrast, the regulatory activity, at both the federal and state levels, has influenced the data protection discussion by requiring that industry provide notice, choice, and access concerning the collection, use, maintenance, and distribution of personal data. Regulators, focusing on the contracts that were struck between companies and users, have become significant leaders in creating what is now the industry standard.

A. Private Litigation Failed Because It Did Not Focus on Contract Law as a Tool for Data Protection

For a relatively brief period between 1999 and 2001, a wave of privacy class action litigation arose that seized upon the ubiquitous data-gathering practices utilized by Website businesses and advertisers on the Internet as a potential source of economic benefit for the plaintiff's bar. Class action plaintiffs achieved some early successes such as winning certification of a nationwide class in May 2000 in a case against Amazon.com and Alexa Internet.[28] Nevertheless, "privacy litigation" (as it was termed) was ultimately unsuccessful because it did not focus on the contract rights underlying the relationships, and instead focused on inapplicable federal statutes offering statutory damages and attorney fees provisions. Since that time nearly all (if not all) of the privacy litigation that was filed either has been resolved on dispositive motions or has settled.[29]

1. Privacy Litigation Necessarily Focused on Federal Statutes That Provided a Potential for Substantial Monetary Recovery   The fundamental economics of class action litigation require that there be a profit incentive for plaintiffs' lawyers. Class actions are filed only when there exists a potential for a substantial monetary recovery for the class and recovery of attorneys' fees. Without such a potential, plaintiffs' law firms have no incentive to shoulder the financial burden-in both attorney time and out-of-pocket costs-of complex class action litigation. This economic reality caused plaintiffs' firms bringing privacy lawsuits to focus their pleadings on federal statutes that offered a potential for recovery of significant statutory penalties and statutory attorneys' fees. State common law theories such as invasion of privacy, standing alone, could not support a class action because of the need to, and inherent difficulty of, proving individual damages.[30] As one plaintiffs' lawyer acknowledged, "the costs of continuing expensive class action lawsuits are burdensome and not insignificant if the answer is that the damages are non-existent, nominal, or minimal."[31]

These economics are equally important from the other side of the class action equation. From a defense perspective, class actions get the attention of corporate decision makers and serve as a catalyst for a change in practices only when they pose a threat of a large monetary judgment. Thus for class action litigation to succeed as a mechanism for enhancing consumers' privacy protection, it was essential that the litigation focus on federal statutory claims that raised the specter of substantial damages or penalties.

The federal statutes typically relied upon in the privacy class action cases included Titles I and II of the Electronic Communications Privacy Act (ECPA) (18 U.S.C. § 2701 and 18 U.S.C. § 2510, respectively). Title I of the ECPA (commonly known as the Federal Wiretap Act) prohibits unauthorized interception of communications while the communications are in transit.[32] Title II of the ECPA prohibits the intentional and unauthorized access of electronic communications while in electronic storage.[33]

These statutes offered the potential for recovery of substantial monetary penalties and attorneys' fees.[34] Under Title II of the ECPA, for example, "in no case shall a person entitled to recover [for a violation of the Act] receive less than the sum of $1,000."[35] Similarly, for each violation the Wiretap Act provides civil litigants with possible statutory damages of between $50 and $500 for a first offense and between $100 and $1,000 if the defendant had previously been held liable under the Act.[36] Both statutes provide for recovery of reasonable attorneys' fees and costs.[37]

2. The Federal Statutes Failed to Reach the Relevant Contract Rights, and Reliance on the Statutes Was Rejected by the Courts   Basing privacy claims on these federal statutes, which were passed to address entirely different issues before the ascendance of Internet commerce, was akin to fitting a square peg into a round hole. For example, use of Title II of the ECPA, an anti-hacker statute, as a vehicle for class plaintiffs was impeded by the reality that the defendants did not obtain the personal data through hacking. Indeed, in most cases, the personal data was received through relationships with affiliated Websites or from the class plaintiffs themselves.[38] These statutes were not designed to cover what were inherently breach-of-contract disputes (for example, claims alleging a company's failure to abide by the agreed upon and disclosed use of personal data, or failure to disclose the company's use of personal data). The result was that federal courts began dismissing privacy claims brought under these federal statutes.

The *DoubleClick* action in the United States District Court for the Southern District of New York exemplifies the failure of the privacy litigation.[39] In *DoubleClick,* the plaintiffs' claims under Titles I and II of the ECPA and the

CFAA (as well as state law privacy claims) concerned DoubleClick's data-gathering practices through the use of cookies. DoubleClick's business focused on collecting, compiling, and analyzing information about Internet users and using that information to target online advertising.[40] The claims were fueled by DoubleClick's purchase of a catalog marketer and announcement of plans to merge consumers' offline and online data. Although DoubleClick defused the public furor by publicly retracting these plans,[41] the litigation proceeded.

The court dismissed the federal claims and declined to exercise supplemental jurisdiction over the state law claims, thus dismissing the entire lawsuit.[42] First, with respect to Title II of the ECPA (the anti-hacker statute), the plaintiffs had alleged that DoubleClick's placement of cookies on class members' hard drives and collection of information from those cookies without their knowledge or consent constituted "unauthorized access" to stored electronic communications.[43] The plaintiffs' complaint thus focused on the relationship between the individual computer users and DoubleClick. In dismissing the claim, however, the federal court focused on the relationship between the DoubleClick-affiliated Websites and DoubleClick. The court held that DoubleClick's conduct fell within the statutory exception for "conduct authorized . . . by a user," reasoning that the "user" in this context was the DoubleClick-affiliated Website and that DoubleClick's conduct was authorized by its commercial arrangements with those Websites.[44] The plaintiff's argument that "[t]he most natural reading of 'user' is the person who has signed up for Internet access" was unavailing under the court's reading of the statute.[45]

Similarly, the *DoubleClick* court rejected the plaintiffs' Wiretap Act claim that focused on the consent of the individual to intercept or use his or her personal information. The court found that DoubleClick's conduct fell within a statutory exception applicable "where one of the parties to the communication has given prior consent to such interception."[46] As with regard to Title II, the court easily found that the DoubleClick-affiliated Websites were "parties to the communication[s]" with the plaintiffs and had given consent to DoubleClick to intercept those communications.[47] As to both statutes, the court was constrained by the statutory language that was not intended to address the harms at the heart of the litigation.[48]

After the *DoubleClick* decision, other courts followed its reasoning and dismissed similar privacy claims under these statutes. For instance, the United States District Court for the Western District of Washington nearly duplicated the reasoning in *DoubleClick* when it granted summary judgment to Avenue A (another Internet advertiser) on claims brought under the same federal statutes in a privacy class action.[49]

3. After the Federal Claims Were Effectively Removed from the Plaintiffs' Arsenal, the Settlements That Followed Reverted to Contract Principles to Enforce the Protection of Personal Data   Once the federal claims were effectively eliminated as a basis for the privacy class actions, many of the cases settled. The resulting settlements required enhanced notice by the defendant companies concerning the collection and use of personal data—essentially, focusing on the contract between the parties.

For instance, the *DoubleClick* litigation settled (presumably to eliminate the threat of an appeal) when DoubleClick agreed to (among other things) provide a privacy policy that clearly described its practices concerning personal data. DoubleClick also agreed to purge certain data files containing personal data it had collected, and to obtain permission ("opt-ins") before it linked any personal data with Web surfing history.[50] The plaintiffs' lawyers were quoted as saying the settlement was "reasonable" under the circumstances because the plaintiffs were given "limited tools under the law to prosecute the case."[51]

The settlements reached in the litigations demonstrate the constant interplay between contract law and privacy issues. The privacy policy is the underlying agreement between the user and the company, and governs the rules of the relationship.[52] The requirement that DoubleClick include a privacy policy that clearly describes its practices concerning personal data is a demand for more specificity in the contract so both sides are aware of the rules of the relationship. This also helps to ensure that if the rules are broken, plaintiffs can clearly identify which rights have been violated. The focus on requiring clearer and more precise contracts (privacy policies) has not helped the plaintiff's bar salvage the class actions, but it has helped to create an industry standard concerning data protection issues.

B. The Regulatory Activity (Both Federal and State) Has Focused on the Protection of Personal Data By Enforcing Contract Obligations

The FTC and the state attorneys general have proved to be influential in developing the data protection rules and practices. Unlike the private litigation, which attempted to redefine statutory schemes that were not intended to apply to privacy issues, the FTC approaches privacy concerns by relying on its broad authority to regulate businesses' practices (which more directly implicates the contracts between the individuals and the companies).[53] The regulators have brokered settlements with several large companies, and those settlements have in turn created a standard of acceptable industry practice concerning data protection. In essence, the regulators have legislated standards, using the powers they believe are available to them.

The FTC relies on its authority to regulate "unfair or deceptive acts or practices in or affecting commerce,"[54] under Section 5 of the Federal Trade Commission Act (FTC Act), in targeting several businesses for allegedly failing to provide promised protections to personal information. Because the FTC views the FTC Act as a means to enforce the terms of a company's privacy policy, these actions are heavily rooted in contract principles. This section "deliberately incorporates a flexible standard, so that the Commission may react to changes in the marketplace."[55] With this flexible standard in place, the FTC views its actions as not "an overly expansive view of the unfairness doctrine, but instead represent[ing] a reasoned and tailored response to the circumstances presented."[56] Unlike the federal statutes relied upon in the class action litigation, which could be (and were) challenged as substantively inapplicable, the FTC inquiries and actions are based on such broad and amorphous power, that few companies challenge the scope and appropriateness of the FTC action.[57]

FTC actions often prompt cooperation from target companies, which often leads to settlements. Many companies, after receiving notice of action by the FTC, in an effort to avoid burdensome government investigations and additional hassle, quickly enter into the settlements. The corporate response to potential government litigation differs from the mostly uncooperative reaction to potential private litigation, making the government agencies more influential in changing corporate practices. In the privacy arena, the settlements reached by the FTC have included prohibitions on future misrepresentations regarding the security or use of personal data, clearer privacy statements, and the requirement that companies take proactive measures to create information security systems and maintain and test these systems.[58]

The FTC's first foray involving Internet privacy was its action against Geocities for allegedly misrepresenting how it was using the personal data collected from the users of its Website. A settlement was reached soon after the inquiry was initiated.[59] Under the settlement, Geocities agreed to post a clear privacy statement on its Website notifying consumers what information was being collected, the purpose for the collection, to whom it would be disclosed, and how consumers could access and remove the information.[60] In addition, Geocities was required to obtain parental consent to collect information regarding children users.[61] The FTC highly publicized its settlement with Geocities, and used it as an example of its leadership in shaping standards for data protection.[62]

Since the Geocities settlement, the FTC has initiated a number of actions under the guise of ensuring that a company's posted privacy statements were an actual reflection of company procedures.[63] For example, in March 2005, the FTC announced a settlement of its action against an Internet service provider of "shopping cart" software, which allegedly collected and rented the information of nearly one million consumers in violation of the privacy policies of the merchants using the "shopping cart" services.[64] The settlement bars disclosure of previously collected personal data and requires either a change in practices to be consistent with merchants' privacy policies or clear and conspicuous disclosure to consumers that personal information would be disclosed to third parties.[65]

A notable FTC action was brought against Microsoft related to the misrepresentations concerning the security of its Passport services. The complaint alleged that Microsoft represented to users a higher degree of security than was actually available, and had failed to describe the full extent of the personal information collected by Microsoft.[66] The consent order reached prohibits any further misrepresentations by Microsoft and requires it to implement and maintain a comprehensive information security program, including monitoring and regular testing, for Passport and similar services.[67]

In several actions, the FTC has focused on data security, pursuing companies with privacy policies that promise security of personal information but also include disclaimers of liability for privacy breaches.[68] In consent decrees resolving these actions, the FTC has established parameters (with increasing specificity) of what it believes should be involved in corporate information security programs. For example, the FTC attacked Tower Record's privacy policy, which represented that Tower was using "state of the art technology" to protect the personal information of consumers on its Website. In reality, Tower's Website contained security flaws and allowed access to personal information provided by consumers on the Website.[69] The settlement reached required Tower to design and implement reasonable safeguards to control the identified risks to information security and to ensure their capabilities through regular testing.[70] Similar programs were designated in the settlements reached in the FTC's actions against Guess.com and Petco Animal

Supplies, Inc., which targeted Guess.com's claims that it was taking "reasonable and appropriate measures" to protect the personal data that it collected and Petco's assertion that its Website was "completely safe."[71]

The offices of the state attorneys general have mirrored the actions of the FTC and pursued companies by relying on state unfair business practices laws modeled after the FTC Act. Most of these cases have resulted in settlements that impose stricter requirements on the company's policies and procedures to ensure protection of the consumers' private information. In addition to requirements to establish and maintain privacy and security protocols, the settlements by the AGs often result in the payment of monetary damages. As is the case with the FTC, the AGs' use of broad unfair business practice laws and the corporate response to government action results in the AGs being influential regulators.

New York has been particularly active in relying on its "mini-FTC" statute to pursue companies for allegedly misleading consumers about the confidentiality of their personal information. The New York State AG has relied on the New York General Business Law 22-A as a mechanism for regulating "unfair or deceptive" business practices. From Victoria's Secret to Yahoo!, the New York AG has initiated investigations purportedly seeking to ensure that companies are abiding by the terms of their contracts with their users.[72] In well-publicized actions in March 2006, the New York AG settled with Datran Media, a leading email marketer, and filed suit against Gratis Internet in connection with the allegedly improper disclosure of personal information of more than six million consumers.[73] Calling Gratis's sale of seven million files of data to Datran the "largest deliberate breach of a privacy policy discovered by U.S. law enforcement to date," New York AG Eliot Spitzer emphasized the binding nature of the privacy policy contract: "Companies must adhere to known privacy policies and promises."[74]

III. PRACTICAL OBSERVATIONS ABOUT THE APPLICATION OF CONTRACT LAW AND SUGGESTIONS FOR THE IMPERFECT STATE OF AFFAIRS

The frustration and confusion associated with data protection issues is in large part due to the implicit notion that contract law forms the basis of the rights to be addressed. It is further complicated by the reality that because of how the rights are created, a single overarching statute or regulatory regime may be impractical. However, the fact that most people do not read most contracts most of the time[75] makes contract law an imperfect tool. In addition, that many contracts (including privacy policies) can be alleged to be unclear (for example, What does it mean not to "rent" or "sell" really?) also may make reliance on contract law problematic.

Faced with the imperfect state of affairs, a company must strive for "transparency" in data collection, use, and distribution practices. Most violations by reputable companies are unintended. Privacy statements often become treaties focused on rectifying the internal tensions in companies between marketing, legal, and operational staffs. Because it is very difficult to know how data is collected and used inside a company, companies must rigorously audit data collection and use, train all involved employees, and use the privacy policy as much for internal purposes as for external purposes.

The average individual has a very large number of relationships to manage. Because of the dissonance between answers in the abstract to questions concerning privacy of personal data, and an individual's actual behavior, it is unclear how concerned the individual is about data protection issues. The simple truth is that most individuals do not go to a lot of trouble to manage the use of their data. The result may be that public policy concerns and media attention have distorted the significance of the data protection issue.

Nevertheless, the privacy policy is an important contract. It must be accurate, comprehensive, clear, and available in order to offer protection to companies facing claims concerning the release, dissemination, or collection of personal data. Given the nature of the claims and rights involved, a company's best defense is that in its contract it said what it did, and in its actions, it did what it said.

NOTES

1. Raymond T. Nimmer, 1 *Information Law* Ch. 8 (2003).

2. In fact, this was the subject of the FTC's action against Gateway Learning Corporation, which allegedly changed its privacy policy to permit it to share personal information previously collected from consumers on its "Hooked on Phonics" Website—"including their names, addresses, phone numbers, and age ranges and gender of their children"—to third parties for marketing purposes. *See* FTC Press Release, July 7, 2004, available at http://www.ftc.gov/opa/2004/07/gateway.htm.

3. Daniel Solove, The Origins and Growth of Information Privacy Law, 748 *PLI/Pat* 29 (2003).

4. Not surprisingly, immediately following September 11, 2001, privacy briefly disappeared from the public policy agenda, suggesting an implicit double standard between commercial notions of privacy and law enforcement or national security standards. It is unlikely that without the horrific acts that transpired on September 11, 2001, and the resulting public fear, the passage

of the PATRIOT Act, which implicates significant data protection issues, could have occurred. *See* USA PATRIOT Act of 2001, Pub. L. No. 107-56, 115 Stat. 272 (2001). Although outside the scope of this chapter, the repercussions of this double standard are a key area in the development of privacy law. *See, e.g.,* Electronic Frontier Foundation's suit accusing AT&T of collaborating with the National Security Agency's massive program to wiretap and data-mine American's communications, which a federal court allowed to proceed on July 20, 2006, available at http://www.eff.org/legal/cases/att.

5. *See* Google's Email "Violates Privacy Laws," available at http://news.zdnet.co.uk/internet/ecommerce/0,39020372,39150936,00.htm, Apr. 30, 2004; Bob Sullivan, Letter Calls on Firm to Suspend E-mail Scanning Test, available at http://msnbc.msn.com/id/4679359/, Apr. 6, 2004.

6. U.S. Const. Amend. 4. *See* Matthew C. Keck, Cookies, the Constitution, and the Common Law: A Framework for the Right of Privacy on the Internet, 13 *Alb. L. J. Sci. & Tech.* 83, 97 (2002) for a discussion of the significance of the Fourth Amendment.

7. Henry Valetk, Mastering the Dark Arts of Cyberspace: A Quest for Sound Internet Safety Policies, 2004 *Stan. Tech. L. Rev.* 2 (2004).

8. *Id.*

9. 15 U.S.C. § 1681 *et seq. See also* http://www.epic.org/privacy/fcra for a history of the Act.

10. *Id.*

11. *Id.* at § 1681(b).

12. *Id.* at § 1681(b), 1681(e).

13. *Id.* at § 1681(i).

14. 15 U.S.C. § 6801 *et seq.*

15. *Id.* at § 6802.

16. *Id.* at § 6821.

17. 16 C.F.R. pt. 314.

18. 42 U.S.C. § 1301 *et seq.*

19. 45 C.F.R. pts. 160 and 164.

20. *Id.* at §§ 164.520, 164.530.

21. *Id.* at § 164.526.

22. *Id.* at pts. 160, 162, and 164.

23. 15 U.S.C. § 6501 *et seq.*

24. *Id.* at § 6502.

25. *Id.*

26. *Id.*

27. *Id.;* 16 C.F.R. § 312.

28. *Supnick v. Amazon.com, Inc., et al.,* U.S. District Court, Western District of Washington, Case No. COO-0221-P (May 18, 2000). The plaintiffs in *Supnick* claimed that the Alexa software allowed Alexa (and Amazon, its parent company) to "intercept and access user's personal information, including user names, passwords, and other private information that is embedded in the URL of secure sites that are password protected, and transmits that information back to [Alexa] on a frequent basis through an open [I]nternet connection."

29. *See, e.g., Supnick* (settled Apr. 16, 2001, settlement approved July 27, 2001); *In re Doubleclick Inc. Privacy Litigation,* (dismissed Mar. 28, 2001, settled Mar. 29, 2002, settlement approved

May 21, 2002); *In re broadcast.com Privacy Litigation* (summary judgment granted Dec. 11, 2001); *In re Intuit Privacy Litigation*, 138 F. Supp. 2d 1272 (CDCal 2001) (dismissed in part Apr. 10, 2001); *Avenue A*, 2001 U.S. Dist. LEXIS 17503 (WD Wash. 2001) (dismissed Sept. 14, 2001).

30. The need to prove damages is destructive to any class action because it complicates the class certification motion (as the claims are more individualized), it requires more time and effort on behalf of the class plaintiffs (and their lawyers), and it makes a quick settlement more unlikely (because unlike statutory damages, which are easily quantifiable, individualized damages are difficult to assess).

31. Seth Richard Lesser, *Internet Privacy Litigation and the Current Normative Rules of Internet Privacy Protection*, published on the Website of the Center for Democracy and Technology (http://cdt.org/).

32. 18 U.S.C. § 2510. Although the ECPA's primary purpose was to address government interception of electronic communications, it also enacted privacy rights concerning inspection of electronic communications by private parties. *See* R. Ken Pippen, Consumer Privacy on the Internet: It's Surfer Beware, 47 *A.F. L. Rev.* 125, 147-48 (1999).

33. 18 U.S.C. § 2701.

34. Privacy class action complaints from this era also typically plead a claim under the Computer Fraud and Abuse Act (CFAA) (18 U.S.C. § 1030). The CFAA is the "anti-hacking law" that protects against the unauthorized access of information stored on protected computers. This statute, however, did not offer statutory penalties but instead required proof that economic damages exceeded $5,000, a requirement that proved problematic for the plaintiffs in these cases. *See, e.g., In re DoubleClick Inc. Privacy Litigation*, 154 F. Supp. 2d 497 (S.D.N.Y., Mar. 28, 2001); *In re Broadcast.com, Inc. Privacy Litigation*, United States District Court, Eastern District of Texas, Case No. 2:00CV18-TJW (Dec. 11, 2001, Order granting summary judgment to Broadcast.com.).

35. 18 U.S.C. § 2707(c).

36. 18 U.S.C. § 2520(c)(1)(A), and § 2520(c)(1)(B).

37. 18 U.S.C. § 2707(c), 2707(b)(3), and § 2520(b)(3).

38. *See, e.g., Crowley v. Cybersource Corp. and Amazon.com Inc.*, 2001 U.S. Dist. LEXIS 17020 (N.D. Cal. 2001) (concluding that the ECPA claims against Amazon.com failed because Amazon had received the information from the plaintiff voluntarily when he purchased items from Amazon.com).

39. *In re DoubleClick Inc. Privacy Litigation*, 154 F. Supp. 2d 497 (S.D.N.Y., Mar. 28, 2001).

40. *Id.* at 500.

41. *Id.* at 505.

42. *Id.* at 526.

43. *Id.* at 507.

44. *Id.* at 507-11 (quoting 18 U.S.C. § 2707(c)).

45. *Id.* at 509.

46. *Id.* at 514.

47. *Id.*

48. Other litigation was resolved on dispositive motions, with the courts finding that the federal statutes were not broad enough to cover the named defendants. *See, e.g., In re broadcast.*

com Privacy Litigation, Memorandum and Order Dec. 12, 2001, U.S. Dist. Eastern Dist. of Tex. (Marshall Div.) (finding that the ECPA is not applicable because broadcast.com does not provide "electronic communication service to the public" as required by the statute); *Crowley v. Cybersource Corp. and Amazon.com Inc.,* 2001 U.S. Dist. LEXIS 17020 (N.D. Cal. 2001) (concluding that Amazon was an online retailer, not a provider of electronic communication services as required by the ECPA).

49. *Chance v. Avenue A, Inc.,* 165 F. Supp. 2d 1153, 1161 (Sept. 14, 2001).

50. As an add-on DoubleClick also agreed to conduct a public information campaign consisting of three hundred million banner advertisements educating consumers on Internet privacy.

51. CNET News.com, May 21, 2002, "DoubleClick Able to Settle Privacy Suits."

52. As with the *DoubleClick* settlement, the settlement in *Supnick* obligated Alexa to more clearly define and provide notice about Alexa's contractual rights concerning personal data. For instance, Alexa agreed to add a list of FAQs about its privacy policy and to provide additional links explaining Alexa's practices concerning personal data.

53. http://www.pwcglobal.com/Extweb/manissue.nsf/docid/EC7961F9AB6C93FC85256 B8F006E0E95.

54. 15 U.S.C. § 45(a)(1).

55. FTC Press Release January 6, 2000, http://www.ftc.gov/opa/2000/01/reverse4.htm.

56. *Id.*

57. http://www.pcworld.com/news/article/),aid,103868,00.asp.

58. http://www.ftc.gov/privacy/privacyinitiatives/promises_enf.html.

59. Agreement Containing Consent Order, http://www.ftc.gov/os/1998/08/geo-ord.htm.

60. *Id.*

61. *Id.*

62. *See* Internet Site Agrees to Settle FTC Charges of Deceptively Collecting Personal Information in Agency's First Internet Privacy Case (Aug. 13, 1998), available at http://www.ftc.gov/opa/1998/08/geocitie.htm; Debra Valentine, General Counsel FTC, About Privacy: Protecting the Consumer on the Global Information Infrastructure (Dec. 8, 1998), available at http://www.ftc.gov/speeches/other/dvaboutprivacy.htm.

63. *See* http://www.ftc.gov/privacy/privacyinitiatives/promises_enf.html.

64. *See* FTC Press Release, Mar. 10, 2005, available at http://www.ftc.gov/opa/2005/03/cartmanager.htm (Vision I Properties, LLC, doing business as CartManager International).

65. *Id.*

66. Complaint, http://www.ftc.gov/os/2002/12/microsoftcomplaint.pdf.

67. Agreement Including Consent Order, http://www.ftc.gov/os/2002/08/microsoftagree.pdf.

68. The United States Law Week, FTC, Business Lawyers Recommend Careful Drafting of Online Privacy Policies to Avoid Incongruent Terms, Vol. 72, No. 39 p. 2623. Recently the FTC has focused on data security breaches outside the Internet context, such as in credit card authorization systems. *See, e.g.,* FTC Press Release, Feb. 23, 2006, http://www.ftc.gov/opa/2006/02/cardsystems_r.htm (CardSystems Solutions); FTC Press Release, Mar. 14, 2006, http://www.ftc.gov/opa/2006/03/fyi0616.htm (DSW Inc.).

69. FTC Press Release, April 21, 2004, http://www.ftc.gov/opa/2004/04/towerrecords.htm

70. *See* Agreement Including Consent Order, http://www.ftc.gov/os/caselist/0323209/040 421agree0323209.pdf.

71. *See* Agreement Containing Consent Order, http://www.ftc.gov/os/2003/06/guessagree. pdf; FTC Press Release, Nov. 17, 2004, http://www.ftc.gov/opa/2004/11/petco.htm.

72. The New York AG often acts in concert with other state AGs. An investigation against Ziff-Davis involved three attorneys general: those from New York, California, and Vermont. The controversy centered on the unencrypted storing of the personal data of those who bought magazines online, which allowed the information to be accessible from an online file. The investigations resulted in a settlement requiring Ziff-Davis to maintain practices on par with industry standards and make accurate representations to its users about its privacy and security practices. Assurance of Discontinuance, http://www.oag.state.ny.us/press/2002/aug/aug28a_02_attach.pdf.

73. Press Release, Mar. 13, 2006, http://www.oag.state.ny.us/press/2006/mar/mar13a_06. html (Datran settlement); Press Release, Mar. 23, 2006, http://www.oag.state.ny.us/press/2006/mar/mar23a_06.html (Gratis filing).

74. Press Release, Datran settlement, *supra* note 73.

75. Todd D. Rakoff, Contracts of Adhesion: An Essay in Reconstruction, 96 *Harv. L. Rev.* 1173, 1178 (1983) (finding that virtually every scholar and empirical study has concluded that consumers do not read contracts prior to signing them); Lee Goldman, Contractually Expanded Review of Arbitration Awards, 8 *Harv. Negot. L. Rev.* 171, 191-92 (2003) (noting that if it is a complete fiction to believe consumers read form contracts, it is "ludicrous" to believe consumers actually read or consent to online "clickwrap" and "browsewrap" contracts).

4 MUTUALLY ASSURED PROTECTION

Toward Development of Relational Internet
Data Security and Privacy Contracting Norms

Andrea M. Matwyshyn

Andrea M. Matwyshyn is an assistant professor of legal studies and business ethics at the Wharton School at University of Pennsylvania; and affiliate, Centre for Economics & Policy, University of Cambridge. The author invites comments at amatwysh@wharton.upenn.eduand wishes to thank Sharon M. Gordon, Cem Paya, Martin H. Redish, and Anupam Chander for their insightful commentary and critiques.

The Internet is a complex adaptive system[1] with emergent structures.[2] It is a system in which multiple actors dynamically interact on the basis of local rules, resulting in visible aggregate behaviors and norms.[3] As such, problems of Internet regulation should be viewed, first and foremost, as problems of complexity,[4] and a more stable and trusted Internet marketplace will require legal structures that facilitate the coexistence and evolution of these different actors and local rules. An element of this complexity is regulation that arises from the dynamic strategic interactions of a system, a type of "organizational code." Legal constructions such as contract norms are an integral part of and arise out of this organizational code; as such, they can function in either a harmonizing or disruptive manner.

The initial legal structures of the Internet were those of private ordering through contract,[5] a bottom-up method of ordering.[6] Consequently, this chapter adopts the bottom-up analytical lens of complexity theory to empirically identify emerging legal structures in the context of Internet data security contracting practices. It then normatively analyzes the social and commercial desirability of emergent Internet data security contracting constructions from an interdisciplinary perspective.

This chapter presents an empirical study across time of seventy-five Websites of publicly traded companies, tracking legal emergence of data security contracting practices. The two primary constructions of data security contracting—terms of use and privacy policies—were content analyzed. Terms of use in the sample were found to have become more restrictive across time, shifting more liability onto users, and to be generally unenforceable under current Internet contracting doctrine. Meanwhile, privacy policies were found to have become more developed in their privacy promises to users across time. These constructions were determined to be nonadaptive, pitting users and content providers against each other as adversaries instead of business partners in Internet commerce.

Consequently, this chapter argues that a new legal construction for data security contracting is needed to replace the current regime of terms of use and privacy policies. A new legal construction should be inherently relational; it should create confluence of interests in data security between content providers and users and better reflect the commercial value of user data. It must also strike a better balance among content entrepreneurship and consumer protection, standardization and customization,[7] and development of both content providers and users. Finally, and perhaps most important, adoption of a relational data security contracting paradigm calls for cooperation among technologists and lawyers and facilitating the education of Internet users.

I. INTERNET DATA SECURITY CONTRACTS IN A COMPLEX SYSTEM

Part of the difficulty in crafting legal scaffolding to support trusted systems of Internet commerce arises as a consequence of the organizational structure of the Internet, a complex adaptive system. Complex systems are characterized by a large number of similar but independent actors who persistently move, respond, and evolve in relation to each other in an increasingly sophisticated manner.[8] The result of this evolution is a form of self-organization in which order in the system forms spontaneously. The Internet has demonstrated itself to be such a complex system; it is composed of numerous independent actors, acting in clustered groups at least in the context of the Web,[9] frequently following local rules[10] and demonstrating increasingly complicated visible patterns of natural organization of behaviors and norms.[11] The behavior of complex adaptive systems frequently cannot be accurately predicted and can naturally evolve to a state of self-organization on the border between order and disorder.[12] Therefore, the incursion of commercial legal safeguards into the Internet marketplace must be sensitive to the contours of this organizational code; Internet commerce regulation should be approached as an organized complexity problem.[13] If thoughtfully incorporated and monitored, legal tools can assist in socially engineering this complex system toward order rather than disorder in its emergence.

Data security has been a heated topic of legal discussion since the mid-1990s, and Internet data security contracting presents an area ripe for an examination of emergent organizational code. A successful Internet data security contracting approach can be crafted only within the context of the broader architectural dynamics of the Internet marketplace. Specifically, we should consider not only the effects of hierarchical Internet architectures of control[14]—law[15] and computer code[16]—on Internet data security contracting, but also the influence of nonhierarchical organizational code on Internet data security contracting—the behavioral strategic norms of Internet actors, including end users in the aggregate, entities doing business, and the technology transactions bar—in shaping and reshaping the comparative power and legal strategies of Internet actors in the data security contracting context. The next section undertakes an empirical study of current Internet data security contracting practices of public companies to track legal emergence across time and normatively examines the fit of current data security legal constructs within broader Internet contracting doctrine.

II. EMERGENT LEGAL DATA SECURITY CONSTRUCTIONS

Section II undertakes an empirical exploration of current Internet data security contracting norms, specifically assessing, first, the extent of legal emergence in the organizational code of Internet data security transactions, and, second, whether these emerging legal constructions are optimal and adaptive. In other words, Section II conducts an empirical analysis of the issues raised in Section I—whether current data security contracting practices facilitate trusted Internet commerce in the long run. To this end, Section II surveys the Websites of seventy-five publicly traded entities and analyzes the evolution of data security contracting practices of each one. The content of each Website's privacy policy and terms of use was analyzed at two points in time—the time of the first available fully archived version of each Website from the 1990s[17] and the Website as available in March 2004.

A. Hypotheses and Sample (n = 75)

Prior to conducting this section's inquiry into data security contracting legal emergence, the following two results were hypothesized:

1. The two legal data security constructions that have emerged across time—privacy policies and terms of use—will reflect that entities have more clearly articulated their privacy practices in privacy policies across time, but have shifted more risk and liability associated with Websites onto users through increasingly draconian terms of use.

2. Entities' terms and conditions of use will frequently be unenforceable under current Internet contract best practices and doctrine.

The empirical inquiry was conducted on a sample of Websites of seventy-five NYSE- and NASDAQ-listed companies.[18] Each Website in the sample had been fully archived in 1999 or earlier in the Internet Archive.[19] The pre-2000 archived version of each Website was compared with the current live version of the Website to ascertain change over time. The reason publicly traded companies were selected for the sample stems from the additional risk and liability concerns faced by these companies in connection with the content of their Websites. Frequently, publicly traded companies use their Websites as a locus of communications with their shareholders. Possible sources of liability include running afoul of securities law speech restrictions[20] on graphical user interfaces or providing piped-in stock quote information upon which a user might rely to his or her detriment.[21] Terms of use are also an additional place where safe-harbor language is included by entities with regard to forward-looking statements and projections.[22] For these reasons, publicly traded companies face a particularly strong incentive to attempt to limit liability on their Websites through contract while making the Website as user-friendly and legally compliant as possible. The sample also included variation in industry sectors. Twenty-one of the Websites were Websites of entities in the technology sector; twenty were those of (nontechnology) manufacturing entities; twelve were Websites of entities in the finance sector; eleven were Websites of retail sector entities; five were from the energy sector; four were in services; one was in real estate; and one Website belonged to a traditional media entity.

B. Methodology

To test Hypothesis 1, each Website's data security contracting constructions, privacy policies, and terms of use were analyzed at two points in time—the time of the earliest archived version of the Website in the Internet Archive from 1999 or earlier, Time 1, and the live version of the Website as of March 2004, Time 2. Two scales were developed to enable coding of the content of these two legal constructions. Content analysis of the privacy policies of each Website assessed the extent of privacy disclosures using a scale of 1–10, with each privacy disclosure scoring one point.[23] Similarly, content analysis of terms of use of each Website assessed extent of risk and liability-shifting onto users using a scale of 1–26, with each liability-shifting provision scoring one point.[24] The differences of these scores were then compared for change across time using a one-tailed t-test to determine the significance of the difference of the means of these two correlated samples.[25]

To test Hypothesis 2, the probable enforceability of the current terms of use of each Website in the sample was assessed in terms of Internet contracting "best practices" derived from Internet contracting case law. Currently, Internet contracting best practices can be deduced from holdings and dicta of four lead cases—*ProCD, Inc. v. Zeidenberg*,[26] *Register.com, Inc. v. Verio, Inc.*,[27] *Specht v. Netscape Communications Corp.*,[28] and the most recent iteration of *Ticketmaster Corp. v. Tickets.com, Inc.*[29] In *ProCD, Inc. v. Zeidenberg*, an individual purchased software that displayed license terms in a "clickwrap" format[30] on the computer screen every time the user executed the software program. In other words, the user affirmatively demonstrated assent to the terms of use by selecting "yes" or "OK" on the screen. The 7th Circuit deemed the user to have had sufficient opportunity and notice in order to review the terms and to return the software if he did not wish to assent. Consequently, in the eyes of the court the purchaser was contractually bound because of click-through assent to the terms that were conspicuously displayed on his screen.[31] *Register.com, Inc. v. Verio, Inc.* presented a slightly more nuanced Internet contracting inquiry. A domain name registrar sued a service provider who repeatedly electronically requested data for marketing purposes from the Website of the domain name registrar in violation of the registrar's terms of use. After each such query, the service provider was presented with a notice that the act of querying constituted consent to the registrar's terms of use. Because of the very large number of times the service provider was met with the explicit, conspicuous notice of being bound by the registrar's terms of use, and because of the service provider's acknowledgment that it was aware of the existence of the terms of use, the court ruled in favor of the plaintiff registrar.[32] Thus repeated exposure to a conspicuous notice of terms of use presented in a sentence was deemed to constitute affirmative consent to the terms.

However, *Specht* v. *Netscape Communications Corp.* explained that if a Website does not explicitly and clearly communicate that by clicking a download button or taking another action, a consumer is assenting to terms of use, such terms of use will not be upheld. In *Specht*, the defendants moved to compel arbitration under the terms of a linked license agreement that was presented through a small link at the bottom of the home page.[33] The defendants in *Specht* argued that the plaintiffs should be held to a standard of "reasonable prudence" and that they should have known to scroll to the bottom of the Webpage to look for license terms. The court rejected this argument, noting that license terms on a screen not readily visible are not enforceable when the defendant does not provide conspicuous notice of their existence to users.[34] Finally, the second iteration of *Ticketmaster Corp.* v. *Tickets.com, Inc.*[35] introduced a new generation of home page terms of use.[36] In this case, Ticketmaster argued that Tickets.com, among other things, violated the Ticketmaster terms of use by copying ticket and show information off the Ticketmaster Website through the use of spiders and bots[37] on a continuous basis. Ticketmaster asserted that Tickets.com was bound by the terms of use because it had received reasonable notice of being bound by them: a notice sentence across the top of the Ticketmaster home page stated that using the Website constituted consent to the Ticketmaster terms of use, which were presented through a browsewrap,[38] a link to the full text of the terms. Tickets.com sought summary judgment on all counts, and the court deciding the matter dismissed all counts by Ticketmaster against Tickets.com except for this allegation in contract. The court deemed the contract issue worthy of surviving summary judgment; the obvious placement of the link to the terms of use at the top of the Ticketmaster home page and the link's being embedded in an explicit notice sentence of contract formation "could not be missed,"[39] said the court.

When taken together, these four cases can be said to create a sliding scale of terms-of-use enforceability. On the one hand, clickwrap agreements[40] that prevent the user from accessing content without an explicit affirmative demonstration of consent will tend to be enforced by courts.[41] On the other hand, courts tend to decline to enforce a browsewrap agreement[42] with an ambiguous link[43] located below the fold[44] with no requirement of affirmative demonstration of consent by the user.[45] In between these two extremes are browsewrap agreements that might be called "notice-sentence browsewraps."[46] These notice-sentence browsewraps intend to provide notice to a user of terms of use through their placement and presentation of a link to the terms, usually in a sentence above the fold on the home page. In other words, the user is conspicuously advised that taking a certain action constitutes consent to the terms of the linked agreement, modeling the terms-of-use presentation discussed by the *Ticketmaster* court.[47] Although an enforceable notice-sentence browsewrap does not prevent the user from accessing the content of the Website, it must clearly inform a reasonable user of the consequences of such access-agreement to the terms of the linked agreement. Each of the Websites in the sample was analyzed for presence of a clickwrap, a notice browsewrap, or a standard browsewrap. A clickwrap terms-of-use agreement was deemed enforceable, a notice-sentence browsewrap agreement was deemed probably enforceable, and a standard browsewrap agreement was deemed unenforceable.

C. Results and Analysis

An examination of the graphical user interfaces of the Websites in the sample across time showed that terms of use and privacy policies significantly increased as data security contracting constructions online. At Time 1, 16 percent of the Websites in the sample had some sort of terms of use in place, whereas at Time 2, 91 percent had terms of use in place. Similarly, at Time 1, 7 percent of the Websites in the sample had a privacy policy, but at Time 2, 49 percent had privacy policies in place. Turning to the content of these terms of use and privacy policies, a one-tailed t-test for correlated samples revealed a statistically significant change in both terms of use and privacy policy content. Terms of use at Time 2 tended to score significantly higher on the terms-of-use scale than at Time 1 and therefore reflected significantly greater shifting of risk and liability onto users. Privacy policies at Time 2 tended to score significantly higher on the privacy policy scale and to be more developed in their privacy promises (Table 4.1).

Table 4.1. Change in scale scores of terms of use and privacy policies across time

($n = 75$)	Terms of Use	Privacy Policies
Mean Time 1	1.8133	.3333
Mean Time 2	6.96	3.2667
Mean 1-Mean 2	−5.1467	−2.9333
T	−6.85	−3.2667
Df	74	74
p (one-tailed)	<.0001	<.0001

Therefore, Hypothesis 1, which postulated that terms of use were increasingly shifting risk onto users and that privacy policies had become increasingly developed in their privacy promises was supported by the data. From Time 1 to Time 2, terms of use significantly increased in the extent of business risk "assumed" by users as a consequence of using the Website. Meanwhile, the privacy policies of the Websites in the sample increasingly articulated with detail the extent of their privacy practices, frequently assuming greater voluntary duties of care associated with collected user data.[48] In the case of both results, there was a 99.99 percent likelihood that the results did not occur by chance. The results of this analysis demonstrate a statistically significant aggregate increase in both the extent of development of privacy promises in privacy policies and the extent of risk and liability shifting by the content providers onto users through terms of use.

With regard to Hypothesis 2, an examination of the probable enforceability of terms of use on the Websites in the sample at Time 2 found that none of the Websites used clickwrap or notice-sentence browsewrap terms of use. All of the Websites in the sample either had terms of use that consisted solely of a copyright notice or used a traditional browsewrap agreement format. As such, the terms of use of the forty-nine Websites in the sample whose terms of use consisted of more than a simple copyright notice[49] would most likely be deemed unenforceable under current Internet contracting case law.[50] Consequently, Hypothesis 2, that most of the Websites in the sample will have unenforceable terms of use, was also supported. 65 percent of the Websites in the sample had terms of use at Time 2 that consisted of a linked agreement without a notice sentence. All of these terms of use were presented in a traditional browsewrap format that does not provide the requisite notice to users mandated by the standard set forth in *ProCD, Verio, Specht,* and *Ticketmaster.* As such, these browsewrap terms of use would likely be set aside by courts.

These results indicate two trends. First, a fundamental tension exists in contracting paradigms adopted by entities in their Website privacy policies as opposed to their terms of use. Privacy policies became more elaborate over time, disclosing more information to users and adopting a relational paradigm with the user. This paradigm demonstrates the expectation of a long-term, iterated interaction with the user. Conversely, however, terms of use also became more developed over time, shifting more risk onto users, demonstrating an adversarial paradigm more in line with a one-shot exchange between parties with unequal bargaining power than a paradigm of relational commercial trust.

Second, current browsewrap constructions of terms of use in the sample appear to benefit neither users nor content providers—they are both unlikely to be found by users and unlikely to be enforced by courts. This finding is consistent with the previous finding that content providers and users are treating each other as adversaries in the context of terms of use: if the relationship were a cooperative one between trusted business partners in an iterated exchange, incentives would be in place to ensure that both sides have an accurate understanding of terms and knowledge that an agreement was being formed. Those incentives appear to be absent. Currently, content providers in the sample tend not to be concerned with users' interaction with their terms of use, preferring to engage in contractual obscurity rather than contractual transparency, even if it means their terms of use are consequently unenforceable. Case law is clear on the point that without clear and conspicuous placement, content providers can have no assurance that users saw the terms of use and understood, or should have understood, the legal implications of their use of the Website.

D. Conclusions from the Empirical Inquiry

The results of the empirical study lead to the conclusion that current Internet data security constructions are not facilitating development of commercial trust online. They do not successfully reconcile the needs of the actors involved in the complex system in a way that is likely to lead to commercial growth. The sample did not reflect a picture in the aggregate of a balance being struck between predictable mitigation of liability for content providers and assumption of obligations to securely treat user data. Instead, the content of the terms of use and privacy policies analyzed reflected an inherently irreconcilable tension in legal strategy adopted in the two constructions: the terms of use tended to reflect a nonrelational approach best suited to a one-shot game of adversaries, while the privacy policies tended to reflect a more relational approach with a continuing obligation to maintain data in accordance with security promises, reflecting an iterated game of commercial partners.[51] Similarly, Internet contracting doctrine appears either consciously ignored or not understood by content providers, exacerbating the conflict of interest between content providers and users.

To build a trusted system of Internet commerce, the better paradigm is that of trusted commercial partners engaged in an iterated exchange in which all parties understand their contractual obligations. As such, the conflict in contracting paradigms between terms of use and privacy policies makes current legal emergence in data security contracting "nonadaptive";[52] current paradigms do not effectively reconcile the divergent interests of Internet actors in a sustainable manner. Consequently, the current data security contracting constructions need to be replaced with new, "adaptive" legal data security contracting constructions. As demonstrated by the conflicting commercial paradigms adopted by privacy policies and terms of use, the current nonadaptive emergence is moving the system toward chaos and away from order. Adaptivity will eventually lead to stable architectures that are well-suited to the environment and the goals of the actors operating within it and that can evolve along with the complex adaptive system. These stable architectures might be termed "architectures of growth."

III. FUTURE INTERNET DATA SECURITY CONTRACTING PARADIGMS— FACILITATING ARCHITECTURES OF GROWTH

Section II recognized that the current organizational code of the data security transactional Internet space demonstrates nonadaptive legal emergence and an absence of an architecture of growth. Section III attempts to articulate the elements of an adaptive data security contracting legal regime and growth architecture: a data security contracting growth architecture will be inherently relational and will reconcile three fundamental tensions—tension between content innovation and consumer protection, tension between legal customization and legal standardization,[53] and tension between development and economic self-realization of the content provider and the user.

Architectures of growth[54] are adaptive[55] emergent legal constructions whose creation occurs in tandem with, and arises out of, the natural emergence processes of organizational code[56] in a manner that facilitates the further development of the system. Legal social engineering[57] can occur either through architectures of growth or, as has been previously noted by scholars, through "architectures of control."[58] In other words, Internet architectures can act as either an agent of social development or an agent of social containment. Architectures of growth guide bottom-up development of technology behaviors and commerce. Architectures of control, conversely, refer to hierarchical impositions of social values that occur through legal code on the one hand and computer code on the other.[59] Architectures of growth and architectures of control must work in tandem for trusted Internet commerce to flourish. Thus a successful Internet data security contracting regime will be governed by both architectures. It will exist within architectures of control, but strive toward maintaining its architectures of growth.[60]

The nonadaptive nature of current data security contracting constructions arises primarily from two deficits that prevent them from developing into architectures of growth. First, current Internet data security contract constructions do not adequately recognize that user data has emerged as a key corporate intangible asset.[61] Thus the user data transfer is not conceptualized as a bargained-for exchange in any meaningful sense and discounts the commercial value of user data. A new adaptive data security contracting paradigm that recognizes and leverages the commercial value of user data in a relational transactional context of continuing obligations is more likely to result in a growth architecture and build mutual trust.

Second, the current nonadaptive data security contract regime suffers from a legal complexity problem that arises from the lack of cooperation among attorneys, businesspeople, and technologists within entities. The lawyers drafting terms of use may be inadequately sensitive to the natural structures of the Internet and business concerns about the way people use the Internet.[62] Meanwhile, privacy policies are sometimes written by marketing departments or technologists who may be unaware of the legal implications of particular contract presentation on the user interface. When these pieces are placed together, they do not form a structure that accomplishes the business goals the pieces were intended to further-liability limitation and user disclosure.[63]

Facilitating emergence of data security growth architectures will necessitate reconciliation of three fundamental tensions in data security contracting: (1) tension between content entrepreneurship and consumer protection, (2) tension between legal content customization and legal standardization, and (3) tension in simultaneously aiding development of both content providers and users, despite an information power imbalance in favor of the content provider. Multiple iterations of policy trial and error may await as lawmakers, businesses, and consumers strive for finding a successful balance among these factors. At the end of this trial and error, however, a trusted Internet marketplace may await us.

IV. CONCLUSION

This chapter has empirically and normatively analyzed current Internet data security legal constructions, terms of use, and privacy policies, and found them to be nonadaptive constructions that will not yield a legal architecture of growth in the long term. It has called for emergence of a new adaptive relational legal construction for data security contracting. Finally, this chapter has identified elements that should be considered in crafting this new data security contracting regime. These elements include eliminating contractual enforceability problems while balancing content innovation with consumer protection, balancing customization and standardization, and balancing development of content providers and users. Ultimately, the future of data security contracting will be determined in part by our ability to educate and empower Internet users to guide their own development toward a technologically adept commercial identity.

NOTES

1. Complexity, in general, is the science examining the interrelationship, interaction, and interconnectivity of various elements within a system and between a system and the environment in which it exists. The hallmarks of complex adaptive systems are distributed control, connectivity, coevolution, sensitive dependence on initial conditions, emergent order, a state not in equilibrium, and a paradoxical condition of both order and chaos. *See, e.g.,* Mitchell Resnick, *Turtles, Termites and Traffic Jams* (1997); John H. Holland, *Hidden Order: How Adaptation Builds Complexity* (1995). Law and legal norms are part of this web of mutual causation within a system, which I call "organizational code."

2. Emergence is order that arises from the interactions of individual actors within a complex system, demonstrating a global pattern that could not have been forecast simply from understanding the behavior of one particular actor. *See, e.g.,* Steven Johnson, *Emergence: The Connected Lives of Ants, Brains, Cities and Software* (2001).

3. *Id.*

4. For further discussion of complexity theory, *see, e.g.,* Y. Bar-Yam, *Dynamics of Complex Systems: Studies in Nonlinearity* (1997); Alberto Laszlo Barabasi, *Linked* (2002).

5. *See, e.g.,* Henry H. Perritt Jr., Towards a Hybrid Regulatory Scheme for the Internet, *U. Chi. Legal F.* 215, 215 (2001) (arguing for private ordering as the primary governing construct of Internet activity within broad public law frameworks as a hybrid system of regulation).

6. At least one noted legal scholar has highlighted the importance of considering bottom-up norms and legal emergence. *See* Margaret Jane Radin, Online Standardization and the Integration of Text and Machine, 70 *Fordham L. Rev.* 1125, 1135-37 (2002). However, most Internet regulation scholarly work to date has focused on top-down governance.

7. *See* Radin, *supra* note 6.

8. For various applications of complex systems theory to other legal contexts, *see, e.g.,* David G. Post & David R. Johnson, Chaos Prevailing on Every Continent: Toward a New Theory of Decentralized Decision-making in Complex Systems, 73 *Chi-Kent L. Rev.* 1055 (1998) (arguing that legal theory would be enriched by paying attention to algorithms derived from the study of complex systems in contexts such as competitive federalism and the "patching" algorithm).

9. Barabasi, *supra* note 4.

10. For example, outside of terms of use, online communities often have additional community rules of conduct. *See, e.g.,* AOL Community Rules, available at http://www.aol.com/community/rules.html (last visited May 3, 2004).

11. For example, the Milgram "six degrees of separation" study was replicated using email to demonstrate the hubbed nature of the Web. *See* Email Updates Six Degrees, available at http://www.technologyreview.com/articles/rnb_081803.asp (last visited May 3, 2004).

12. Garnett P. Williams, *Chaos Theory Tamed* 234 (1997).

13. Barabasi, *supra* note 4.

14. Lawrence Lessig, *Code and Other Laws of Cyberspace* (1999). In *Code*, Lessig argues that computer code, which he terms "West Coast Code," is an architecture of control and a powerful source of social regulation, as is law, or "East Coast Code." *See also* Gordon Pask, "The Architectural Relevance of Cybernetics," *Architectural Design* 9/69 (1969) ("[R]apid advances will be made in . . . a proper and systematic formulation of the sense in which architecture acts as a social control.").

15. Lessig, *supra* note 14, at 53.

16. *Id.*

17. The archived versions of Websites were provided by the Internet Archive, http://www.archive.org. (last visited May 3, 2004).

18. 02Micro International Limited; 1-800-Flowers.com; ABElectrolux; ADC Telecommunications, Inc.; AirNet Communications Corporation; ALCATEL; American Woodmark Corporation; BCSB Bancorp, Inc.; BlackRock, Inc.; BSQUARE Corporation; Buckle, Inc. (The); C-Cor.net Corporation; Centillium Communications, Inc.; Cleveland-Cliffs, Inc.; Cooper Companies, Inc. (The); Cortech, Inc.; D&E Communications, Inc.; De Rigo Spa; Dean Foods, Inc.; Dell, Inc.; E-Loan, Inc.; Erie Indemnity Company; Famous Dave's; First Financial Holdings, Inc.; First Industrial Realty Trust, Inc.; Futuremedia Public Limited Company; Gabelli Asset Management, Inc.; Gray Television, Inc.; H&R Block, Inc.; Habersham Bancorp; Heritage Propane Partners, L.P.; Hughes Electronics Corporation; Innovative Solutions and Support, Inc.; J.Jill Group, Inc.; Kerr-McGee Corporation; K-V Pharmaceutical Company; Landacorp, Inc.; Lehman Brothers Holdings, Inc.; Lithia Motors, Inc.; Magma Design Automation, Inc.; Magnetek, Inc.; MDU Resources Group, Inc.; Merisel, Inc.; Mitek Systems, Inc.; Monsanto Company; M-Systems Flash Disk Pioneers, Ltd.; Murphy Oil Corporation; Neose Technologies, Inc.; Nicor, Inc.; NSD Bancorp, Inc.; Nymagic, Inc.; Pac-West Telecomm, Inc.; Par Technology Corporation; Payless Shoesource, Inc.; Persistence Software, Inc.; Post Properties, Inc.; Publicis Groupe S.A.; Reliv International, Inc.; Rockwell Automation, Inc.; Saks Incorporated; Sangamo BioSciences, Inc.; Silver Standard Resources, Inc.; Spartech Corporation; Stage Stores, Inc.; Stryker Corporation; Tennant Company; TradeStation Group, Inc.; Triton PCS Holdings, Inc.; Unity Bancorp, Inc.; Varco International, Inc.; W Holding Company Incorporated; Walgreens; XOMA, Ltd.; Zale Corporation; Zimmer Holdings, Inc.

19. *See supra* note 17.

20. *See, e.g.,* American Law Institute, Brian E. Pastuszenski, Jordan D. Hershman, & Inez H. Friedman-Boyce, Communicating with Analysts and Investors in the Wake of New SEC Regulation FD: A Practical Guide for Issuers and Advisors, SG091 *ALI-ABA* 875 (2002).

21. *Id.* It is possible that a small percentage of Websites in the sample required a click-through of the terms of use if the user completed a transaction. However, most of the corporate Websites in the sample did not include transactions.

22. *Id.*

23. Privacy Policies Scale (1-10)—The privacy policy scale consisted of the total number of the following elements that were present in a particular privacy policy: (1) a statement of corporate policy that the entity values data privacy and cares about its users; (2) a description of what types of data are collected on the Website; (3) a description of under what circumstances data is collected on the Website; (4) a description of how the data is collected on the Website, in particular what technologies are used to collect data; (5) a description of how the collected data is used by the Website and the owner of the Website currently and in the future; (6) a statement setting forth whether and with whom the data collected on the Website will be shared; (7) a description of data security processes of the Website and how data will be protected; (8) a statement of whether a user can update or delete data and the process of doing so; (9) a listing of contact information for questions about the data practices of the Website; and (10) a statement regarding treatment and special consideration of children's data in line with the Children's Online Privacy Protection Act.

24. Terms-of-Use Scale (1-26)—The terms-of-use scale consisted of the total number of the following elements that were present in particular terms of use: (1) an explicit statement that the user assents to be bound by the terms simply by using the Website; (2) a statement incorporating other agreements outside the terms of use, such as product-specific agreements; (3) a statement retaining all intellectual property rights to the owner of the content unless explicit rights are otherwise granted to the user in the intellectual property on the Website; (4) a statement granting a limited license to the user to view and use the intellectual property on the Website; (5) an explicit assignment by the user of all right, title, and interest in and to the user's communications with the Website to the content provider; (6) a disclaimer of any representations and warranties in connection with the Website and its content that is provided on an "as is, where is" basis and the user accepts at the user's own risk; (7) a disclaimer of any responsibility by the Website for third-party content on or connected with the Website; (8) a statement limiting or disclaiming the content provider's liability for any harm that occurs to a user as a consequence of use of the Website; (9) an agreement by the user to indemnify the content provider for any harm the content provider suffers as a consequence of the user's use of the Website; (10) a statement prohibiting linking by other Websites to the Website without express consent of the content provider; (11) a code of conduct for users of the Website; (12) a securities disclaimer disclaiming accuracy of forward-looking statements; (13) a securities disclaimer stating that nothing on the Website should be construed as an offer of securities; (14) a securities disclaimer disclaiming responsibility for updating of content of the Website; (15) an acknowledgment by the user of the insecurity of Internet communications and the possibility of interception of data transmissions; (16) an agreement of the user to exercise care in safeguarding passwords and other data associated with use of the Website; (17) an agreement of the user to provide notice of change in any information provided through the Website; (18) a statement reserving the right to the content provider to terminate the user's ability to use the Website; (19) an agreement by the user to be governed under particular state law articulated by the content provider; (20) an

agreement of the user to resolve disputes with the content provider in a particular forum and the user's consent to the jurisdiction of that forum; (21) a statement that should any provision be deemed unenforceable in the agreement, it shall not influence the enforceability of the other provisions in the agreement; (22) a reservation of the right of the content provider to unilaterally amend the terms without notice; (23) a statement that obligations of users survive the termination of the terms of use and the user's use of the Website; (24) a statement articulating that the terms constitute the entire understanding of the user and content provider on the subject matter of the terms of use; (25) a statement reserving the right of the content provider to selectively enforce the terms of use and that a failure to enforce them shall not constitute a waiver of the right to enforce them subsequently; and (26) a prohibition on the user's assignment of any rights or obligations under the terms of use.

25. For a description of t-test methodology, *see, e.g.,* Lee A. Becker, http://web.uccs.edu/lbecker/spss80/ttest.htm (last visited May 3, 2004).

26. 86 F. Supp. 2d 1165 (7th Cir. 1996).

27. 126 F. 2d 238 (S.D.N.Y. 2000), *aff'd as modified,* 356 F. 3d 393 (2d Cir. 2004).

28. 150 F. Supp. 2d 585 (S.D.N.Y. 2001), *aff'd,* 306 F. 3d 17 (2d Cir. 2002).

29. 2003 WL 21406289, 2003 Copr.L.Dec. P 28,607 (C.D. Cal., Mar. 7, 2003).

30. *Clickwrap* is the term used to describe an agreement presentation that appears in a window which opens to reveal the text of the agreement and is accompanied by a dialogue box with the button label "I agree," which the user must click prior to gaining access to the Website content. For a discussion of clickwrap and browsewrap agreements, *see, e.g.,* Ryan J. Casamiquela, Contractual Assent and Enforceability in Cyberspace, 17 *Berkeley Tech. L. J.* 475 (2002).

31. 86 F. Supp. 2d 1165 (7th Cir. 1996).

32. 126 F. 2d at 400-401.

33. In *Specht,* Internet users and a Website operator brought a putative class action, alleging that a free software program invaded their privacy by transmitting information to the software provider without users' consent.

34. 150 F. Supp. 2d 585 (S.D.N.Y.2001), *aff'd,* 306 F. 3d 17 (2d Cir. 2002).

35. 2003 WL 21406289, 2003 Copr.L.Dec. P 28,607 (C.D. Cal., Mar. 7, 2003). The first iteration of a lawsuit between the same parties ended with Ticketmaster's terms of use not being upheld by the court deciding the matter. *Ticketmaster Corp. v. Tickets.com,* Inc. 2001 WL 51509 (9th Cir. 1998).

36. This notice-sentence browsewrap presentation from around the time of the institution of the second Ticketmaster litigation can be viewed at http://web.archive.org/web/20030403073630/www.ticketmaster.com/ (last visited Aug. 30, 2004).

37. Spiders and bots are small computer applications that run in the background and send data back to their originator on an ongoing basis. For a more detailed description of spiders and bots, *see, e.g.,* The Web Robots FAQ, available at http://www.robotstxt.org/wc/faq.html (last visited Aug. 31, 2004).

38. *See infra* note 42.

39. 2003 WL 21406289 at 2.

40. *See supra* note 30.

41. *See ProCD,* 86 F. Supp. 2d.

42. A browsewrap is an agreement whose content is linked and no additional notice aside from the presence of the link is provided to the consumer regarding the existence of the agreement. *See, e.g.,* Casamiquela, *supra* note 30.

43. Characteristics of unclear browsewrap links include use of small font, gray type on gray background, and unclear labeling of the link that should alert the user to the existence of an agreement behind the link. For a discussion of browsewraps *see, e.g., Specht,* 150 F. Supp. 2d, *aff'd,* 306 F. 3d.

44. "Below the fold" means the portion of the graphical user interface that is not readily visible to a user within the confines of the user's monitor when the Website loads. Consequently, "above the fold" is the readily visible portion. *See, e.g.,* Marketingterms.com, http://www.marketingterms.com/dictionary/above_the_fold/ (last visited May 3, 2004).

45. In *Specht,* the court deemed browsewrap terms of use without a notice sentence and below-the-fold to be unenforceable. *Specht,* 150 F. Supp. 2d, *aff'd,* 306 F. 3d.

46. In *Verio,* the court deemed the defendant to have notice of the browsewrap terms of use in a notice sentence within a data entry dialog box. 126 F. 2d 238 (S.D.N.Y. 2000), *aff'd as modified,* 356 F. 3d 393 (2d Cir. 2004). In *Ticketmaster* (2003), above-the-fold browsewrap terms of use embedded in a notice sentence were deemed adequate to survive summary judgment challenge to contract claim. *Ticketmaster,* 2003 WL 21406289.

47. At this writing, Ticketmaster has changed the placement of their terms-of-use link on their home page from the time of *Ticketmaster.* However, the notice-sentence browsewrap remains. *See, e.g.,* http://www.ticketmaster.com (last visited May 3, 2006) for an example of a notice browsewrap terms-of-use presentation. *See* Yahoo! http://www.yahoo.com (last visited May 3, 2006) for an example of a traditional browsewrap terms-of-use presentation.

48. The Federal Trade Commission has arisen as the primary agency active in enforcement of privacy policies. *See* Federal Trade Commission, http://www.ftc.gov (last visited May 3, 2004).

49. The entirety of the browsewrap agreement consisted of a copyright notice in nineteen of the Websites in the sample at Time 2.

50. *See supra* note 43.

51. Another developing tension that was noted was one of contractual interpretation: browsewrap terms of use are usually not deemed enforceable, but privacy policies in the same browsewrap construction are being enforced by FTC and private actors as contracts (at least in legal approach if not explicitly).

52. Nonadaptive legal constructions are those which co-evolve with the system but push the system more toward chaos than order because they do not successfully balance content entrepreneurship with consumer protection. Nonadaptivity results in constructions without meaningful higher-level consistency that are poorly suited to the environment and the goals of the environment's actors. These constructions impede development of the system rather than facilitate it.

53. In other words, individualized contractual content must be balanced with form, standardized content.

54. Building on Lawrence Lessig's concept of architectures of control, a top-down construct, I posit the bottom-up equivalent-well-constructed legal norms emerge into architectures

of growth, which serve to guide and govern further development of the Internet marketplace. *See, e.g.,* Lessig, *supra* note 14.

55. As I use the term *adaptive* in the context of legal constructions, I mean constructions that demonstrate coevolution with the medium in an emergent manner that pushes the complex system more toward order than chaos and facilitates easier international regulatory harmonization in architectures of control.

56. Organizational code includes both market and nonmarket strategic decisions of actors within the complex adaptive system. For a discussion of nonmarket strategy, *see, e.g.,* S. L. Jarvenpaa & E. H. Tiller, Integrating Market, Technology, and Policy Opportunities in E-business Strategy, 8 *J. Strategic Info. Sys.* 235 (1999).

57. In computer security, social engineering means using offline means of human interaction to obtain critical technology security information, usually passwords; *see, e.g.,* Sarah Granger, Social Engineering Fundamentals, Hacker Tactics I, available at http://www.securityfocus.com/infocus/1527 (last visited May 3, 2004). However, here I use it to refer to processes of using offline means to "trick" certain Internet legal construction into being built to enable the system to govern itself in a more socially beneficial manner.

58. *See supra* note 54.

59. *Id.*

60. Borrowing terms from Eric Raymond, organizational code can be said to be order developing through a babbling "bazaar" that permits norms to percolate to widespread acceptance, whereas legal code and, frequently, computer code develop order through a "cathedral" style in which norms are hierarchically imposed. *See* Eric Steven Raymond, The Cathedral and the Bazaar, available at http://www.catb.org/~esr/writings/cathedral-bazaar/cathedral-bazaar/ (last visited May 3, 2004).

61. Databases of customer information are afforded significant commercial value in asset sales and bankruptcy proceedings. For a discussion of the transformation of user data into a marketable commodity, *see, e.g.,* Jessica Litman, Information Privacy/Information Property, 52 *Stan. L. Rev.* 1283 (2000).

62. Terms of use are generally written by attorneys who zealously attempt to limit their clients' liability to the greatest extent possible. However, because no negotiation of these terms occurs, they remain in their original, unnegotiated format when the Website goes live. These terms of use, meanwhile, are considered unsightly legal verbiage by the designers of Websites and are tucked away in inconspicuous places. The effect of these actions on legal enforceability generally goes uncontemplated-the lawyers have been excluded from the business decision loop. Privacy policies, on the other hand, are generally written at least in part by the public relations department of business enterprises. As such, the legally binding effect of these privacy promises are frequently not understood by the businesspeople involved in their creation. Thus terms of use and privacy policies are not necessarily thought about as being inherently interrelated by businesspeople and attorneys.

63. The standard content of terms of use, such as user indemnification provisions, may be set aside by some U.S. courts. In the United States, challenges could be brought on the basis of substantive unconscionability (*e.g.,* user indemnification provisions)—in this manner embodying offline problems of form contracts of adhesion and procedural unconscionability with

regard to formation uncertainty, as well as other formation issues arising from inadequate user notice, consent, and the absence of negotiation. Most terms of use would almost certainly be set aside in their entirety or at least in substantial part if challenged in the European Union. European Union grounds for invalidation of terms-of-use content include violation of, among other directives, the European Union Directive on Distance Contracts and the Directive on Unfair Terms. *See, e.g.,* James R. Maxeiner, Standard-Terms Contracting in the Global Electronic Age: European Alternatives, 28 *Yale J. Int'l L.* 109 (2003). Clearly, multijurisdictional unenforceability of terms of use is a suboptimal outcome from the perspective of both technologists and lawyers within an entity attempting to limit liability on a global basis.

5 THE INTERNATIONAL PRIVACY REGIME

Tim Wu

Tim Wu is professor of law, Columbia University.

If a privacy official flaps his wings in Brussels, can it set off a hurricane in San Francisco? That's the question this chapter addresses.

. . .

In the month of April 2004, back when the underlying conference was held, the state of privacy was shifting in different ways in different parts of the world. In Shanghai, China, government officials announced the installation of video cameras in each of the city's more than thirteen hundred Internet cafés. The cameras actually watch you as you read your personal email, surf Websites, or chat with friends. According to city official Yu Wenchang, the surveillance program helps protect youth from pornography and "superstitious" Websites by allowing the government to "spot illegal activities immediately." Big brother, he might well have said, is watching.[1]

At the same time, across the Pacific, Google officials announced their latest invention: "Gmail." Gmail, Google said, gives users enough storage room to keep their emails more or less forever. But there's a catch: every message you send and every message you receive is read by a highly intelligent robot, who guesses what kind of advertisements you might find interesting. Say you're discussing a trip to Spain with your secret lover: Google will sidebar advertisements for hotels and airfares. It's only a robot, not a human, reading what may be your deepest secrets. Nonetheless, some people find the whole idea unnerving.

Both stories are about private information. The first has Chinese officials reading your email, the second, Google's robots. Both flip important presumptions. In China the Internet cafés once meant freedom; they are increasingly yet another point of control. Gmail makes email, for many people a most secret place, a little less so. But both privacy concerns are countered to different degrees by consent: you don't have to frequent the Internet cafés, nor is anyone required to use Gmail. As a Gmail user myself, I find the robots harmless. Yet the consent arguments don't satisfy everyone. As Brad Templeton, chairman of the Electronic Frontier Foundation, wrote in a perceptive essay on Gmail, "the fear that computerized scanning of our e-mails (to display ads or filter out spam) will result in actual harm is largely baseless. But even irrational fears affect our freedom."[2]

That's the debate. What did the law have to say? In another twist and across another ocean, the greatest regulatory threat came from Europe, and it came to the American robots, not the Chinese officials. Within weeks of announcing Gmail, Google was surprised to find legal complaints filed against it in the European Union and various European countries. On April 19, 2004, an English group named Privacy International filed complaints in the EU, France, Germany, the Netherlands, Greece, Poland, and many other countries. It demanded that regulators "investigate the Gmail service with regard to compliance with Data Protection" and, if they found compliance wanting, "that an order may be made to prohibit the export of personal data to Google."[3]

What's going on? If Internet privacy is supposed to be primarily "self-regulating," why do privacy advocates look to Europe to police an American email service run by a private company? Conversely, isn't this all backward? Why doesn't anything or anyone protect Chinese citizens from far more unnerving invasions of their privacy?

These stories show that, today, no one can speak usefully about law and privacy without understanding the de facto international privacy system. As Peter Swire first wrote in 1998, privacy has joined one of many areas of law understandable only by reference to the results of overlapping and conflicting national agendas.[4] What has emerged since 1998 as a de facto regime is complex. Yet on the basis of a few simplifying principles, we can nonetheless do much to understand it and predict its operation.

First, the idea that self-regulation by the Internet community will be the driving force in privacy protection must be laid to rest. The experience of the past decade shows that nation-states, powerful nation-states in particular, drive the system of international privacy. The final mix of privacy protection that the world's citizens receive is disproportionately dictated by the choices and preferences of powerful nation-states and their respective effects on giant and small targets (in Swire's terminology, "elephants" and "mice").

Second, traditional conflicts analysis can help explain and predict the future course of privacy analysis. Privacy regulation can be understood as a species of information regulation to which companies and individuals will respond in predictable ways. The analysis here shows an international privacy system that has fractured into three distinct regulatory patterns. Mainstream privacy, or *transactional privacy,* has become dominated by the rule of the most restrictive state, a pattern familiar to other areas such as the world's regulation of competition (antitrust). Conversely, the problem of *information theft* has been pushed by the international system toward a kind of a race to the bottom, or to the least restrictive rule. Most akin to international piracy (the kind on boats), it is a familiar problem to international law that will nonetheless take considerable political will to reverse. And, finally, although there is a potential for the international system to influence how governments handle the privacy information of their own citizens, the direct collision of interests have limited the extent to which governments police one another.

What does this mean for Americans? First, it suggests that any normative view of privacy must take into account the descriptive fact that much of the privacy policy that affects Americans will be set overseas. Second, it suggests that those Americans who want more government privacy protection should focus their efforts on convincing significant economic units, such as countries or U.S. states, to enact strong and extraterritorial privacy legislation. Finally, it suggests that those who believe that less governmental regulation is appropriate cannot simply point to self-regulation, but must seek countervailing or "claw back" legislation.

I. THE INTERNATIONAL PRIVACY SYSTEM

Consider the following, expressed by the TRUSTe Website, a program of voluntary privacy certification: "Unless there is global harmonization of privacy laws, government oversight is seriously challenged. A Web site can easily be located outside the jurisdiction of a nation-state and thus not be bound by its laws."[5]

What is interesting is that TRUSTe has got things almost exactly backward. It is true that the ease of transferring digital information has made abuse of privacy easier, and cheaper. Cheap information has brought attention to privacy policy for the same reasons that cheap crack cocaine made drug policy an issue in the 1980s[6] and that cheap food has contributed to the American obesity epidemic.[7] Cheapness, in short, has unintended consequences.

But global information networks have also made governments more, rather than less, capable of regulating outside their borders. There are two reasons. The first and primary reason is that the targets of regulation, like the flows of information that are their business, are increasingly multinational. This is the story of .NET Passport, discussed later in this chapter. If the target of a law operates in multiple jurisdictions, a nation will sometimes influence the conduct of the multinational across jurisdictions. The second reason is slightly more legalistic: the internationalization of information flows has justified claims of extraterritorial regulation premised on domestic effect. As this paper demonstrates, the main example is well-known among scholars, if not the general public: that much online privacy policy is today influenced heavily by extraterritorial European Union regulation. But the example of the European Union is merely evidence of a broader phenomenon.

It is important to emphasize that legal internationalization is certainly not unique to privacy regulation. It follows patterns seen in other legal fields, and its consequences are not unpredictable. Antitrust law is perhaps the clearest example. When insurers in London agree on insurance policies, they need to keep American antitrust law in mind, thanks to the Supreme Court's decision finding the practices of the London insurance industry within the jurisdiction of the Sherman Act.[8] As Microsoft designs its latest operating system, it must keep in mind European, American, and probably Japanese competition law. Antitrust has been internationalized for at least the last fifty years thanks to the internationalization of commerce. And although it has certainly complicated the study of antitrust law, it has not by any means rendered the law of the nation-state irrelevant.

Yet saying that nations have seen their privacy laws enjoy greater extraterritorial effect does not answer the most important question. Will it be the country that cares least about privacy—say, China—or the country that cares most—say, Germany—that sets the default rule for the entire world? Answering this question requires the more complex model introduced next.

II. THE GOVERNANCE OF PRIVATE INFORMATION

Privacy regulation is most easily understood as a species of information regulation. Typical privacy laws are governmental rules concerning how information may be used,[9] with or without permission of a given "owner." In this respect, privacy regulation is analytically analogous to other forms of communications regulation, such as libel, copyright law, and indecency regulation.[10] It is for this reason that the rise of a universal information network, the Internet, has changed a set of questions answerable by reference simply to territory into a more complex international puzzle.

Privacy regulation is distinguished by strong, indeed fundamental, differences of opinion between nation-states. Much information regulation, like copyright, exists in a rough consensus among economically powerful nations, as embodied in international agreements such as the Trade Related Intellectual Property Agreement, TRIPS. But privacy questions seem to touch closer to the nation's psyche, and even culturally similar nations differ profoundly over what they consider "adequate" in the regulation of privacy. Americans, by reputation, see privacy as a negative freedom, that is, principally a protection from government. Americans, or at least those in Congress, are wary of government restraints on commerce practiced in the name of privacy regulation. Europeans, also by reputation, care more than anyone else in the world about the sanctity of private information and want greater policing of the abuses of the private sector. To take just another example, scholars of Chinese culture, struggling to find the meaning of privacy in the Chinese context, have gone so far as to claim that the Western conception of privacy lacks meaning altogether.[11]

Conflicts analysis arises when two or more jurisdictions share information freely, but have different privacy rules. Consider two jurisdictions, A and B, with different privacy rules, lenient and strict.

In a world where information is not shared, each exercises authority concurrent with its territorial jurisdiction. But if each state both shares information freely and wants its rules to apply (if privacy is a mandatory rule, in conflicts jargon), which law will in fact govern?

The question is whether the rule will be the rule of the lenient or strict country. The former we call the rule of the Least Restrictive, and the latter, rule by the Most Restrictive. Although a complex question, whether the default outcome will be the Least or Most Restrictive rule can be expected to depend on just a few factors.

Existing scholarship on Internet privacy has tended to focus on the *size* of the regulated entity as determinative of whether a given form of privacy regulation will be effective. This is most evident in Peter Swire's work. In 1998, he introduced the metaphors of "elephants" and "mice," predicting that privacy regulation would generally be effective against the former but not the latter.[12] In other work, Gregory Shaffer, concentrating mainly on the effects of EU regulation on large U.S. firms, predicts that the EU will generally push the United States toward more privacy protection.[13]

These authors are correct to suggest that larger entities are easier to regulate, but the observed size of firms in certain types of transactions is itself dependent on other factors. Although the international privacy system is new, it follows several dividing lines familiar from international conflicts analysis.

First, much of the international privacy system is shaped by a distinction between the behavior in the model of an international transaction, on the one hand, and that of an international crime or tort, on the other. The relevant distinction between the two is the difference between regulating *consensual* and *nonconsensual* relationships. For reasons explained further on, the elephant-mouse pattern may emerge to fit this distinction.

The transaction-tort distinction matters because it determines a factor critical to conflicts analysis: who the *initiating* party is, or who gets to choose the governing legal regime. In crimes or nonconsensual transactions, the firm initiates the transaction, and its choice dictates the relevant law. Because firms usually prefer less regulation, this drives a race to the least restrictive rule.

Conversely, for consensual relationships, it is the consumer who initiates the transaction. This puts the consumer in a position to choose the governing law, and the consumer we can assume will choose the strict regime, that which protects his or her rights. Now it may seem a mere fiction that the consumer is actively choosing a legal regime, and of course it is unlikely that the consumer is consciously doing so. But what the consumer does do is decide to trust large, well-known firms with his or her private information. This choice can amount to a choice of legal regime: for if consumers all choose large companies that are regulated by the strict rule, they have in effect made the strict rule the default rule.

From this we can conclude that the nature of the transaction will influence whether the default international privacy rule will tend toward the least or most restrictive in the first place. But from this initial default, set by the choice of the transacting parties, comes a second phase, wherein the specific will of nation-states is expressed. Nation-states, if they take an interest in the matter, may try to reverse the outcome default most or least restrictive rule.

Contests between states to alter default international rules are a familiar phenomenon to scholars of international law. Countries that resent the legal influence of other countries can and do enact legal "countermeasures" or "claw backs." For example, the United States and the rest of the world disagree profoundly on what to do about Cuba. So every time the United States has passed laws that threaten to punish foreign companies who deal with Cuba, Europeans and Canadians have reacted with reciprocal laws designed to negate the effect of the American laws.[14] Such dynamics can also shape international privacy regulation.

III. THREE PATTERNS OF INTERNATIONAL PRIVACY REGULATION

Much of the rest of this chapter is dedicated to understanding how this two-stage process has played out for privacy regulation. What we find is an emerging split among different types of privacy regulation. In what follows, consider three emerging categories of regulatory problems.

A. *Breach of Trust (Transactional Privacy).* Much information is transferred to others in consensual transactions. The unwanted behavior occurs when the other party then does things that you would prefer they not do with your information. For example, if your doctor knows you have a embarrassing disease, it might be your preference that he not tell everyone. Similarly, a bank might sell your personal information to third-party solicitors who then call day and night. In this category are laws that try to control what third parties do with information, to create a correspondence between what you want and what they do.

B. *Information Theft (Protective Privacy).* A different category of privacy problem arises when your information is taken without consent and used in abusive ways. Someone who steals your wallet might gain access to your credit card number and rack up unwanted bills. Information theft is primarily a matter of security regulation, and laws preventing information theft penalize such conduct.

C. *Governmental Abuse (Constitutional Privacy).* A final category is the misuse of private information by government entities.[15] Here, as in transactional privacy, the actor is known, yet as in information theft, the exchange of information is nonconsensual. You do not have a choice as to whether to tell the government how much money you made when paying your taxes, for example, or whether or not you want the police to listen in on your telephone conversations.

In each of these areas, recent experience has given us some guide as to what results the international privacy system will yield.

A. Transactional Privacy and the European Rule

In the spring of 2002, European Union investigators summoned America's Microsoft Corporation to Brussels. It was a familiar path for a company that had already spent years wrestling with European Competition authorities. This time, however, it was privacy investigators from the "Article 29 Data Protection Working Party" who came calling.

The European concern was Microsoft's new ".NET Passport" program.[16] Anyone who uses the Web knows that remembering dozens of different emails and passwords can be a pain. .NET Passport was designed to provide users with virtual "digital identification" to make navigation among password protected sites near automatic. But the operation of a digital ID system necessarily means the transfer of a lot of personal information. The European privacy officials in the Article 29 Party wanted to know a lot more about how Microsoft was collecting user data and what it was doing with them.[17]

Under what legal authority was the EU acting? The European Union has the world's broadest and most stringent data privacy laws. A general European Directive[18] on data protection was passed in 1995 and implemented in 1998.[19] Its breadth is remarkable. In addition to its geographic scope, discussed shortly, it regulates not individual industries piecemeal (the American approach) but *any* "data controller," that is, anyone who "processes" the data he or she collects. This has meant, for example, that the law has even reached informal social groups. For example, in 2003, a Swedish woman named Bodil Lindqvist was fined $450 for posting personal data about fellow parishioners without consent.[20] The EU directive even reaches church groups.

For all data controllers like Microsoft or Ms. Lindqvist, the Directive imposes three relatively stringent requirements: duties of notice, fidelity, and proportionality. Notice means that controllers must tell consumers why they are collecting personal data, and receive "unambiguous" consent. Fidelity means that once data are collected, they must be used for the purposes stated, and not redirected to other purposes. And proportionality requires that the data collected have a reasonable relationship to the purposes for which they are collected. They must be "adequate, relevant and not excessive in relation to the purposes for which they are collected and/or further processed."[21] To these basic requirements the Directive adds extra protection for "special information," namely, "data revealing racial or ethnic origin, political opinions, religious or philosophical beliefs, trade-union membership, and . . . data concerning health or sex life."[22] It was this latter provision that landed Ms. Lindqvist in trouble. She was fined after revealing to the world the "sensitive" information that another church member had injured her foot and would be taking time off from work.

But what really makes the European Union law controversial is its breadth of geographic scope, which can be fairly described as aggressive. Article 4 of the European Directive[23] mandates that Members' data protection laws shall apply not only to companies established in Europe, but also to any company that makes use of data processing "equipment" or "means" in Europe, and any company that may be reached by virtue of public international law. This is a broad scope that has been interpreted by European officials to reach nearly any company that collects information from European citizens.[24]

So it was under the authority of the Directive that Microsoft met the European investigators. Some of the EU's concerns would be familiar to Americans, such as Microsoft's failure to give proper notice of what the information would be used for. Others were distinctly European, such as the complaint that Microsoft was collecting more data than it needed for the purposes of the program, violating the European sense of proportionality.[25] The two sides talked, and by January 2003, Microsoft and the EU had an agreement. Microsoft agreed to make what the European Commission called "radical" changes for how .NET Passport manages user data, including much more notice and much more user control over how data are shared.[26]

Microsoft's decision reflects an economic judgment and was a foregone conclusion. The European market is obviously too large for Microsoft to decide to ignore. But perhaps most interesting of all, Microsoft decided to implement its changes to .NET Passport globally, not locally.[27] As a result, whether you're in Auckland, Timbuktu, or somewhere in between, when you use .NET Passport, you use a product ironed into shape by the European privacy authorities. .NET Passport was regulated on behalf of Europeans, but the regulations are in effect on behalf of the world.

What the .NET Passport story demonstrates is the potential for the restrictive rule to act as the effective rule of the network for individual companies. Here, Microsoft, an American company, is regulated by European privacy laws, on the basis of the fact that it serves European customers. For Microsoft, for many questions of transactional privacy, the *strictest* privacy laws become the default law of the network.

What general conditions make regulation of transactional privacy, like the example of the EU and .NET Passport, the most restrictive rule? First, and fundamentally, the regulation of transactional privacy is the regulation of known parties. Unlike the regulation of information theft, the second category, the regulation of transactional privacy, by its nature, is the regulation of a consensual relationship, usually a contractual relationship. You *know* you're giving your information to Paypal, Microsoft, the *New York Times*, or whomever. It is sometimes said that the only difference between contract and tort law is that in tort you don't know in advance who is going to crash into your car. The regulation of transactional privacy is the regulation of contract, and can advantage the European Union or any other strict jurisdiction that knows who the targets of its laws are.

Second, it is banks, airlines, and major companies, large entities, who are trusted with the most valuable personal information. These are Swire's elephants: entities likely to be responsive to the threat of European enforcement, either because of assets or a physical presence in Europe, or simply fear of being arrested when traveling to Europe. Territorial enforcement is therefore that much more likely to be effective.

B. Information Theft and Spam

In that same April 2004, yet another serious problem of privacy regulation continued its course. That's the problem of spam, and there are few problems of failed information regulation that are clearer. Spam's source is a lack of control over personal information, for if spammers weren't able to harvest millions of email addresses, there would be no spam problem. During this same month of April, spam levels reached an historic high, comprising a full 67 percent of the emails sent on the network. The statistics, while increasingly familiar, are no less depressing: $10 billion per year spent by ISPs fighting spam, and some of the first reported decisions to abandon email because of the spam problem.[28]

But that April also brought good news for those who despise spam. For the first time the power of the United States Government reached malignant spammers. Four men in Detroit were arrested for violating the brand-new CAN-SPAM Act of 2003.[29] It, among other things, makes it illegal to send an email with a fake return address,[30] which is what landed Daniel J. Lin, James J. Lin, Mark M. Sadek, and Christopher Chung in jail.

Yet whenever spammers are arrested or sued, the same question arises: What can the United States or other powerful countries do to stop spamming or any other form of information theft if it moves overseas? Although there are measures that can be taken, it remains that this category of problem—information theft—starts from a different baseline. The default rule can be the rule of the least restrictive state in the world, the state chosen by the thief. And because many countries do nothing at all to regulate junk email in particular or information theft in general, the international system exacerbates the challenge.

From the perspective of international law, however, spammers represent a familiar problem. Consider the following description: "a well-defined offense condemned by all nations, committed by private actors . . . that [takes] place . . . where enforcement is very difficult; and harm[s] the economic interests of many nations. . . ."[31] It sounds like information theft or spam, but it is Eugene Kontorovich's description of piracy, an age-old problem for the international system.

The problem of information theft has many parallels to piracy, and information thieves are probably a better successor to the label "pirate" than the copyright infringers who have inherited the title. Both follow streams of commerce and transportation, taking advantage of weak spots in nation-state power, whether the high seas or the open networks. Spammers and pirates prey on the weak, and disrupt otherwise predictable transit systems. And, in their time, they are hated by all, known as *hostis humanis generis,* or the enemy of all mankind.

Piracy was and still is a challenge for the nation-state, but there are ways of coping with pirates that can be well-adopted to the problem of information theft. Now it must be conceded that nation-states are at only the earliest stages of regulating domestic spam and information theft, as the CAN-SPAM story shows, let alone at the advanced stage of regulating international problems. The piracy model offers clear lessons for the future.

The piracy model would dictate, first, the passage of uniform and severe criminal laws among cooperating countries. Piracy, though akin to robbery, historically was punished by all nations the same way: death. This simplified administration and reduced conflict between countries. Although a death penalty for information thieves may be extreme, uniform and severe criminal laws are not.

Yet the problem of enforcement will remain, particularly given noncooperative countries. One important tool used against piracy was and is "universal jurisdiction." As *hostis humanis generis,* spammers are subject to being caught, tried, and punished on the basis only of their activity and regardless of nationality or link to the local territory. The prospect of such punishment further deterred piracy. Other efforts, consistent with the discussion in the previous section, are measures taken against countries that become havens for information thieves.

Again, nation-state action against international problems of information theft and spam is only in its earliest stages. Interestingly, some of the ideas described here are being pushed by private actors. Microsoft devotes serious resources to the international fight against spam (which shows privacy advocates that your enemy's enemy is your friend). Microsoft has filed lawsuits in the United States and the United Kingdom, and has led a campaign to enact anti-spam laws in East Asia so it can sue spammers there, too.[32] The point is that nations have in the past battled parasites who feed on international streams of commerce, and they have methods to do so again.

C. Governmental Abuse

When the Chinese Government installs cameras in Internet cafés, no one denies that it's an abuse of privacy, but nothing outside of China is done about it. We think we know why: the Chinese government is sovereign over Chinese citizens. It would be difficult if not impossible for other countries to try to pressure the Government to change how it regulates privacy. Right?

Not entirely. First, there is one international system meant to control how governments treat their own citizens, namely, human rights law. And indeed, the major human rights treaty, the International Covenant on Civil and Political Rights, signed and ratified by nearly every country in the world, contains protections for privacy. Article 17 of that Covenant reads as follows: "No one shall be subjected to arbitrary or unlawful interference with his privacy, family, home or correspondence, nor to unlawful attacks on his honour and reputation."

However, it would be fair to say that Article 17 has not had a tremendous effect on the privacy practices of nation-states. For one thing, it prohibits "unlawful" or "arbitrary" interference with privacy, presumably allowing "lawful" interference. For another, enforcement is a particularly scarce commodity in the human rights field. This provision of the Covenant is hardly an enforcement priority of any of the various entities who try to monitor human rights, given patterns of far more egregious abuse.

But if you try to take from this the general rule that states cannot or do not change how other governments treat the privacy of their own citizens, you'd be wrong. Governments do, with some success, try to change how other governments regulate their own subjects, at least when they want to.

The leading example is the notorious Article 25 of the European Directive. Article 25 is a threat: it says to other countries, either adopt adequate data privacy protection for individuals or face a ban on transfers of data from the European Union. Textually, Article 25 sets out a ban on all transfers of data to countries that fail to maintain less than "adequate" protection for privacy.[33] It shows how far countries can go when they try to push each other around.

Article 25 has much in common with other sanction regimes. When the United States blocks travel and economic transfers to Cuba or Iran premised on inadequate protection of human rights, it is doing exactly what Europe is doing for privacy rights. The approach has some similarities to an American law: the intellectual property "special 301."[34] That law obliges the U.S. administration to make an annual assessment of the legal regimes of other countries to determine whether they have been good or bad in their protection of intellectual property. Countries that have misbehaved are threatened with unilateral trade sanctions. Both Article 25 and similar U.S. unilateral regimes are efforts to set up a closed community for which entry is premised on good behavior. Both are ultimately efforts to make the laws of other countries more like the EU or the United States, respectively.

The potential consequences of Article 25 are dramatic. A ban on all data transfers between Europe and even Russia would bring economic consequences, let alone a ban on all data transfers to the United States or Japan. For that reason, when the European Directive came into force in 1998, the U.S. administration and the European Commission went into immediate, high-stakes negotiations, because neither Europe nor the United States actually wanted a ban on data transfers across the Atlantic.

What resulted was an uneasy truce that reflects the economic power of each side. The United States did not actually pass new laws that would increase privacy protection. Instead, the Commerce Department set up a voluntary program wherein companies would agree to certify their compliance with a rough approximation of the requirement of the European rules. So certified, they would, in theory, satisfy Europe's requirements and be subject to American enforcement should they fail to live up to their requirements. In 2000, the European Commission, despite reservations, agreed to find that after setting up the American safe-harbor program, the United States had successfully implemented "adequate" data privacy protection.[35] This conclusion warded off the disastrous possibility of a data embargo on the United States.

If the meaning of the safe-harbor agreements seems unclear, it is. The significance of the safe-harbor agreement, although much discussed in the privacy literature, may be greatly overrated (as Joel Reidenberg argues).[36] It is probably best understood simply as an agreement to waive Article 25 with respect to the United States. In other words, the European Union will not create an embargo on data transfers to the United States. But that doesn't mean that Europe won't influence U.S. privacy policies, as the .NET Passport and the Gmail stories show. The jurisdiction of the Directive (through Article 4, discussed earlier) still reaches many American companies. What the safe-harbor story shows is that the European Union is ready to regulate Americans, but not America.

IV. CONCLUSION

Many Americans would be surprised to learn that the first and perhaps last word on Gmail's legality will be supplied not in Washington, D.C., or Silicon Valley but in Brussels. Some, in the 1990s, expected a collapse of nation-state sovereignty with respect to privacy. It hasn't happened. Instead, there's been a complicated shift, making the European Union the most influential voice in global privacy regulation, in part because it seems to care the most.

The international privacy regime must particularly be understood by privacy advocates on every side of the debate. As the work here has shown, much can be accomplished by restrictive rules adopted by economically significant markets. In addition to the role already played by Europe, this suggests a rule for political strategies that focus on entrepreneurial U.S. states or nation-states, with an interest in setting a world rule. Conversely, those who take privacy to be already overregulated need to work to achieve claw-back, or defensive laws that protect locals from extraterritorial privacy regulation.

The consequences of international private law are sometimes surprising. It may, for example, make more sense for Americans concerned about their privacy to trust their information with Microsoft, than, say Sun, because they know that Microsoft is directly governed by European law. Such unusual results and many more will be the future of the international privacy regime.

NOTES

1. *See* China Launches Web "Big Brother," *The Australian*, Apr. 22, 2004, available at http://www.theaustralian.news.com.au/common/story_page/0,5744,9355931%255E1702,00.html.

2. Brad Templeton, Privacy Subleties of GMail, available at http://www.templetons.com/brad/gmail.html.

3. Complaint filed by Privacy International with privacy and data protection regulators of France, Germany, the Netherlands, Greece, Italy, Spain, Czech Republic, Belgium, Denmark, Sweden, Ireland, Portugal, Poland, Austria, Australia, and Canada along with the European Commission and the EU Commissioners, Internal Article 29 Data Protection Working Group (Apr. 19, 2004), available at http://www.privacyinternational.org/issues/internet/gmail-complaint.pdf.

4. *See* Peter Swire, Of Elephants, Mice, and Privacy: International Choice of Law and the Internet, 32 *Int'l Law.* 991 (1998).

5. The TRUSTe Story, Building Trust Online: TRUSTe, Privacy and Self-Governance, available at http://www.truste.org/about/truste/about_whitepaper.html.

6. *See* Edith Fairman Cooper, *The Emergence of Crack Cocaine Abuse* (2002).

7. *Cf.*, Institute for Agriculture and Trade Policy (ed.), *The Costs of Cheap Food* 2 (2003).

8. *See Hartford Fire Ins. v. California*, 509 U.S. 764 (1993).

9. For this approach, *see* Jerry Kang, Information Privacy in Cyberspace Transactions, 50 *Stan. L. Rev.* 1193 (1998); Julie E. Cohen, Examined Lives: Informational Privacy and the Subject as Object, 52 *Stan. L. Rev.* 1373 (2000).

10. *Cf.*, Timothy Wu, Copyright's Communications Policy, *Mich. L. Rev.* (2005); Yochai Benkler, Free as the Air to Common Use: First Amendment Constraints on Enclosure of the Public Domain, 74 *N.Y.U. L. Rev.* 354 (1999), available at http://www.nyu.edu/pages/lawreview/74/2/benkler.pdf.

11. *See, e.g.*, Bonnie S. McDougall, *Love-Letters and Privacy in Modern China: The Intimate Lives of Lu Xun and Xu Guangping* (2002).

12. *See* Swire, *supra* note 4.

13. *See* Gregory Shaffer, Globalization and Social Protection: The Impact of EU and International Rules in the Ratcheting Up of U.S. Privacy Standards, 25 *Yale J. Int'l L.* 1 (2000).

14. Barry E. Carter *et al.*, *International Law* 687 (4th ed. 2003).

15. *See* 5 U.S.C. § 552(a) (2004).

16. Jon Swartz & Byron Acohido, EU Scrutinizes Microsoft's Passport, *USA Today*, June 12, 2002, at B3, available at 2002 WL 4727788.

17. *See* Article 29 Data Protection Working Party, Working Document on On-line Authentication Services, adopted Jan. 29, 2003, 10054/03/EN WP 68, available at http://europa.eu.int/comm/internal_market/privacy/docs/wpdocs/2003/wp68_en.pdf.

18. A Directive is a form of European Union law that creates a set of rules and then obliges all EU member states to pass laws implementing those rules by a certain date.

19. Directive 95/46/EC of the European Parliament and of the Council of 24 October 1995 on the protection of individuals with regard to the processing of personal data and on the free movement of such data, 1995 O.J. (L 281) 31 [hereinafter European Directive].

20. *See* Press Release, The Court of Justice of the European Communities, Judgment of the Court in Case C-101/01 Bodil Lindqvist (Nov. 6, 2003, available at http://www.curia.eu.int/en/actu/communiques/cp03/aff/cp0396en.htm.

21. European Directive, *supra* note 19 at art. 6 1.(c).

22. *Id.* at art. 8. Such special data may not be shared absent "explicit" consent, *id.* art. 8 2. (a), which is understood to mean an "opt-in" scheme.

23. European Directive, *supra* note 19, Article 4, provides:

"National law applicable

"1. Each Member State shall apply the national provisions it adopts pursuant to this Directive to the processing of personal data where:

"(a) the processing is carried out in the context of the activities of an establishment of the controller on the territory of the Member State; when the same controller is established on the territory of several Member States, he must take the necessary measures to ensure that each of these establishments complies with the obligations laid down by the national law applicable;

"(b) the controller is not established on the Member State's territory, but in a place where its national law applies by virtue of international public law;

"(c) the controller is not established on Community territory and, for purposes of processing personal data makes use of equipment, automated or otherwise, situated on the territory of the said Member State, unless such equipment is used only for purposes of transit through the territory of the Community."

24. Working Paper, Privacy on the Internet—An Integrated EU Approach to On-line Data Protection 5063/00/EN/FINAL WP 37, at 28 (Article 29 Data Protection Working Party eds., 2000) (applying the substantive law of a Member State under Article 4 in the context of cookies on hard drives in a Member State), available at http://europa.eu.int/comm/internal_market/privacy/docs/wpdocs/2000/wp37en.pdf; *cf.*, Swire, *supra* note 4.

25. *See* Article 29, *supra* note 17.

26. Lisa Jucca & Tom Miles, Microsoft Fixes Passport to Meet EU Privacy Rules, *Globe & Mail*, Jan, 31, 2003, at B5.

27. Matt Loney, Microsoft Agrees to Passport Changes, CNet News, Jan. 30, 2003, available at http://news.com.com/2100-1001-982790.html.

28. Steve Stanek, Business Risks of Spam, Protiviti KnowledgeLeader, available at http://www.protiviti.com/knowledge/current_feature/071103.html.

29. Matt Hines, First Complaint Filed Under Can-Spam, CNet News, Apr. 29, 2004, at http://news.com.com/2100-7349_3-5201906.html?tag=nefd.lede.

30. *See* CAN-SPAM Act of 2003 § 5(a)(3).

31. Eugene Kontorovich, A Positive Theory of Universal Jurisdiction, 80 *Notre Dame Law Review* 33-34 (2004).

32. *See, e.g.*, Scott Charney, Trustworthy Computing 2003 Year in Review, microsoft.com, Jan. 23, 2004, at http://www.microsoft.com/mscorp/twc/yearinreview03.mspx.

33. Article 25 of the European Directive states

"The Member States shall provide that the transfer to a third country of personal data which are undergoing processing or are intended for processing after transfer may take place only if, without prejudice to compliance with the national provisions adopted pursuant to the other provisions of this Directive, the third country in question ensures an adequate level of protection."

34. Trade Act of 1974 § 301, 19 U.S.C. § 2411 (2004).

35. Commission Decision 2000/520/EC of July 26, 2000, pursuant to Directive 95/46/EC

of the European Parliament and of the Council on the adequacy of the protection provided by the safe-harbor privacy principles and related frequently asked questions issued by the U.S. Department of Commerce, 2000 O.J. (L 215) 7, available at http://europa.eu.int/eur-lex/pri/en/oj/dat/2000/l_215/l_21520000825en00070047.pdf.

36. Joel Reidenberg, Testimony before the Subcommittee on Commerce, Trade and Consumer Protection, Committee on Energy and Commerce, U.S. House of Representatives, Hearing on the EU Data Protection Directive: Implications for the U.S. Privacy Debate (Mar. 8, 2001), available at http://reidenberg.home.sprynet.com/Reidenberg_Testimony_03-08-01.htm#_ftn23.

PROMOTING PRIVACY AND SECURITY THROUGH THE COMMON LAW

Part 2

6 THE NEW VULNERABILITY
Data Security and Personal Information

Daniel J. Solove

Daniel J. Solove is associate professor, George Washington University Law School; J.D. Yale. The author would like to thank Jake Barnes for his help in the tort law discussions of this chapter. To the extent my knowledge of tort law is accurate, I accept full responsibility. As for the errors, blame Jake. Chris Hoofnagle, Ted Janger, and Paul Schwartz provided helpful comments on the manuscript. This book chapter was originally written in 2004. Subsequent to the redrafting of this chapter, in 2005, a litany of organizations announced that they had suffered massive data security breaches. I have updated this chapter slightly to discuss the 2005 data security breaches, but I am unable to add more to discuss the legal developments in the aftermath of the breaches. By and large, these developments have unfolded as I predicted back in 2004 when writing this chapter.

Data security is quickly becoming one of the major concerns of the Information Age. Computer networks are vulnerable to siege from hackers, viruses, intercepted communications, and electronic surveillance.[1] Much of the data residing in these computer networks pertains to our personal lives. Increasingly, extensive digital dossiers about us are being constructed, as businesses and the government gather pieces of personal data and assemble them in databases. Hundreds—perhaps thousands—of entities may have our personal information.[2] Our dossiers play a profound role in our lives. They are used to assess our reputation and credibility. They are examined to determine whether we receive a loan, a job, or a license—and even whether we are detained or arrested by the police. Because so many critical decisions are based on our dossiers, ensuring that they are accurate and protected from tampering is of paramount importance.

Unfortunately, our dossiers are virtually unguarded. Anybody can readily tap into our dossiers—and they do. Identity theft—the use of personal information to illegally access existing financial accounts, open fraudulent accounts, or obtain credit cards in other people's names—is the most rapidly growing type of white-collar criminal activity.[3] Complaints of identity theft in the United States rose a staggering 88 percent from 2001 to 2002.[4] According to a Federal Trade Commission (FTC) estimate in September 2003, "almost 10 million Americans have discovered that they were the victim of some form of ID Theft within the past year."[5] Collectively, victims labored for almost three hundred million hours to resolve the tribulations caused by identity theft.[6] The FTC estimates that consumers lost $5 billion due to identity theft and other information abuses.[7]

In February 2005, ChoicePoint, one of the largest database companies, announced that records containing extensive information about more than 145,000 people had been improperly accessed.[8] The number was later revised upward to encompass more than 160,000 individuals.[9] The breach sparked extensive media attention. Soon afterward, a cascade of announcements of data leaks and breaches from other companies followed. For example, another of the largest database companies, LexisNexis, announced a security breach involving personal information on more than 310,000 people.[10] Bank of America leaked data on about 1.2 million federal employees.[11] Countless other companies, government agencies, and educational institutions announced that they had leaked personal information.[12] In all, more than one hundred million records of personal information were leaked.[13]

Although abuses of personal information are becoming ubiquitous in the digital age, not enough thought has been given to how the law should understand and address these problems. Frequently, the misuse of personal information is viewed as a technology problem. Indeed, given the ease in which hackers can break into computer systems and data can be intercepted in transmission, there are bound to be significant security problems. As Helen Nissenbaum observes, "[e]xperts in computer security are worried about . . . malicious, avaricious, incompetent, or simply unauthorized outsiders who may break into our online space, damage or steal information, and destroy or compromise our systems."[14] Indeed, many companies use encryption to transmit data securely and fortify their computer systems with firewalls to prevent hackers from gaining access.[15]

However, technology is not the root cause of many abuses of personal information. The shift to a digital environment certainly facilitates information misuse, but at the core, the problem stems from a set of business and government practices. The problem is caused in significant part by the law, which has allowed the construction and use of digital dossiers without adequately regulating the practices by which companies keep them secure. Despite taking elaborate technological measures to protect their data systems, companies readily disseminate the personal information they have collected to a host of other entities and sometimes even to anyone willing to pay a small fee. Companies provide access to their record systems over the phone to anybody in possession of a few easy-to-find pieces of personal information. Even a fortress with impenetrable walls is hardly secure if the back gate is left open.

Reforming this problematic state of affairs requires a rethinking of the way the law comprehends the abuse of personal information. The law fails to focus on the causes of information abuses; it has not identified all the responsible parties; and it has not fashioned appropriate remedies to respond to these abuses. This chapter sketches a new way to think about information abuses, their causes, and the way they should be remedied. Part I examines what I call the "data abuse pyramid." The data abuse pyramid is a way to represent how and why many types of information abuses occur. At the top of the pyramid is "misuse" of our data, when information is employed to carry out identity theft, fraud, or other activities. A level below are "leaks"—when entities improperly release or provide access to personal information. And at the bottom is "insecurity," which involves the general lack of protection accorded to our personal data by the entities that hold it. The law attempts to respond at the top of the pyramid, but I contend that to stop information misuse, the law must become involved at the lower levels of the pyramid. In short, the law must address leaks and insecurity. Part II explores how the law can develop to accomplish this task. I recommend ways that existing legal concepts can be modified to more effectively redress and deter information abuses.

I. THE DATA ABUSE PYRAMID

To understand the information abuses that are occurring today, we need to understand the data abuse pyramid (Figure 6.1). The pyramid is meant to be a rather simple model, and it is not designed to represent all information abuses. But it does serve as a useful model for a large percentage of the abuses of our personal data.

There are three levels in the pyramid. I begin with the misuse of personal information, on which the law focuses most heavily, and I then work my way

Figure 6.1. The data abuse pyramid

down. It is important to distinguish between the different levels of the pyramid because the law responds differently at each level.

A. Misuse

At the top level of the pyramid is the misuse of personal information. Personal data can be misused for identity theft, fraud, stalking, abusive marketing (for example, spam or telemarketing), and spying on people. These misuses cause concrete injuries—financial losses, emotional distress, and even physical violence.

Identity theft is a nightmare for victims. The identity thief uses a victim's personal information to obtain loans, open fraudulent accounts, and loot existing accounts. As these abuses occur, the victim's dossier becomes polluted with erroneous information—unpaid debts, traffic violations, arrests, and other discrediting data. Because an identity thief impersonates the victim using the victim's personal information, law enforcement databases sometimes associate the victim's name with the thief's criminal activities.

Victims can spend years desperately attempting to fix the destruction wrought by the identity thief.[16] Victims experience great anxiety, leading to psychological harm in certain cases.[17] They have difficulty "obtaining loans, mortgages, security clearances, promotions and even gaining employment."[18] Sometimes, victims are arrested on the basis of warrants for the crimes of the identity thieves.[19] In the words of one victim, "[w]hat has taken me a lifetime to build—my trust, my integrity, and my identity—has been tainted."[20]

In addition to identity thieves, stalkers use personal information to track down people to harass or even kill them. For example, in 1989 a deranged fan brutally murdered actress Rebecca Shaeffer outside her home. He located her home address with the assistance of a private investigator who obtained it from California motor vehicles records.[21]

The law attempts to respond to actual misuses of information. This is because having one's identity stolen, being stalked, or suffering an attack or harassment are all harms that manifest themselves concretely. We can readily comprehend the damage, and we can assess financial losses, physical harm, and emotional trauma. Existing legal responses to data security problems focus on the identity thieves and other criminal miscreants who misuse our information. Indeed, the predominant approach to dealing with identity theft has been to pass new criminal laws.[22] In 1998, Congress passed the Identity Theft and Assumption Deterrence Act, making identity theft a federal crime.[23]

However, using criminal law as the main legal method to combat information abuses has thus far proven ineffective. Law enforcement officials lack enough resources to prosecute identity theft, which is seen as a minor crime when compared to violent crime and drug offenses.[24] Identity thieves are difficult to catch. An identity theft often occurs in many different locations, and law enforcement officials "sometimes tend to view identity theft as being 'someone else's problem.'"[25] Most identity theft crimes remain unsolved.[26] In one estimate, less than one in seven hundred instances of identity theft result in a conviction.[27] The focus on criminal law results in inadequate deterrence of identity theft, and it does little to help the victims whose lives are upended.

Victims can attempt to seek redress under tort law, but suing the malefactor who abuses the information will often be futile. The misuser is often too hard to track down and doesn't have deep pockets. Victims can also try to sue the companies from which the information was taken or the companies that enable the thief to set up an account in the victim's name. Although the harm is easy to understand, the law must also recognize that a duty was breached and that this breach caused the harm. These elements are more difficult to establish. The law often views the primary culprit as the thief, the hacker, or the abuser of the data. The companies from which the data is taken are perceived as victims themselves, because they often also suffer financial losses from identity theft.

Even if the law were to view companies that allow improper access to personal information to be at fault, there are still several impediments to a successful suit. It can take a very long time for a concrete injury to materialize. Personal information may be improperly disseminated yet only years later be used for identity theft.

Furthermore, it is often difficult to trace where an identity thief obtained the personal information used to commit the crime.[28] Many sources hold our personal information. Whereas a stolen piece of physical property can only exist in one location at a time, information can exist in many different hands simultaneously, all of which can spread it further. Unless we can trace where the thief gets his or her information, it will be difficult to link a concrete injury to a particular entity that failed to keep data secure. For those companies that allow the identity thief to pollute a victim's dossier—by carelessly granting credit or allowing improper access to an account—it is easier to single out the offending companies. However, there often are many participants that contribute to the harm experienced by identity theft victims: the government agencies and businesses that provide access to the personal information used by the thief, the companies that allow the thief to access and open accounts, the creditors that report the unpaid bills, and the credit reporting agencies that assemble this faulty information and then use it to report on people's reputations. Thieves may obtain information to begin the identity theft from one source; supplement it from other sources; and then go to other companies to obtain credit, open accounts, and obtain credit cards. When the bills are not paid, these companies give damaging information to credit reporting agencies. This defiles a person's credit reputation, which can harm a person who wants to obtain a mortgage, loan, or job. When the victim attempts to decontaminate her dossier, she is often stymied by uncooperative credit reporting agencies and creditors, and even after the victim manages to go through a time-consuming and lengthy process to clean out the faulty data, more pollution continues to pour into her dossier. The harms of identity theft, therefore, are created through a collaborative effort.

In its most recent attempt to address identity theft, Congress passed the Fair and Accurate Credit Transactions Act (FACTA) in 2003.[29] The FACTA contains some helpful measures to deal with identity theft. People are allowed to request a yearly free credit report from each of the three national credit reporting agencies. FACTA also allows people to opt out of offers of prescreened credit, which are direct mailings that can be intercepted by identity thieves. The Act mandates that when a person places a "fraud alert" in his or her credit file, the credit reporting agency must contact all the other credit reporting agencies to do likewise. Moreover, the FACTA allows victims to obtain records from businesses that issued credit in their name to an imposter.

Although the FACTA makes it somewhat easier for victims to ameliorate the damage caused by identity theft, this is nothing but a better band-aid. Several of the FACTA's provisions merely codify what credit reporting agencies had been doing voluntarily, such as contacting the other credit reporting agencies when a fraud alert is placed in a person's file and providing people with free copies of their credit reports. And to counterbalance these benefits, the FACTA preempts more protective state laws. In the end, the FACTA does little to make our personal information more secure. Its reforms are remedial, and it fails to proactively prevent identity theft.

How can the law respond more effectively? To do so, the law must better understand and rectify the abuses that occur earlier on before misuses such as identity theft occur.

B. Leaks

The second level of the pyramid involves instances when a company leaks personal information or allows it to be accessed improperly. I refer to this problem as "leaks" because information has been disseminated improperly and it is now somewhere beyond the control of the entity that leaked it. As discussed earlier, since 2005, scores of institutions have in combination leaked over one hundred million records. The problem existed long before 2005. For example, prior to 2005, the credit reports maintained by Ford Motor Company of about thirteen thousand people were accessed illegally.[30] A corrupt employee of a company peddled thirty thousand credit reports.[31] The University of Montana Website accidentally posted psychological records of over sixty children on the Internet.[32] Leaked information is often a precursor to a misuse such as identity theft. However, there are many instances in which information has been leaked without any resulting misuse.

With a leak, the harm consists in being exposed to the potential for being subjected to identity theft, fraud, or even physical danger. People may also suffer anxiety because there is little they can then do to recover the data and prevent downstream abuses of them. However, the law has difficulty in recognizing a harm. The law can at least recognize that a company may have done something wrong. When information is leaked, people may be exposed to a greater risk of identity theft or other abuse even though only a subset of those will actually be victimized. A harm has occurred, because a person is worse off than he or she would have been before the leak. Nevertheless, many leaks do not result in immediate injury. A concrete injury may never materialize. Or it could happen years later, far beyond any statute of limitations. Until such an injury occurs, the law will not view the situation as ripe for a remedy because the real harm is understood as being the actual misuse of the information, not the mere exposure to the possibility of such misuse. Even if a misuse such as identity theft occurs, it is often hard to trace it to the leaked information.

C. Insecurity

At the bottom of the pyramid is insecurity. Here, the data isn't leaked, but the information security is shoddy. Our digital dossiers can be insecure on numerous fronts. They can be left virtually unlocked for easy access, and they can be left inadequately protected against contamination with false data.

Insecurity is a problem of "architecture." As it is traditionally used, *architecture* refers to the design of physical structures or spaces. Information law scholars, however, have been using the term to describe information infrastructures. Lawrence Lessig and Joel Reidenberg have pointed out that computer systems have an architecture.[33] This architecture is not just a bunch of wires, memory chips, and hard drives; it also encompasses computer code.

The manner in which data is accessed and used is also an architectural matter. Information systems are designed to grant access to certain people and to deny access to others. For example, an ATM card allows access through possession of the physical card as well as a password (the PIN number). Companies often focus on improving the technological architecture to guard against unauthorized access to their computer networks, such as by using encryption and firewalls. But the security problems with our digital dossiers are often not caused by invasive technologies or by breakdowns in technological architecture. Rather, these problems are caused by certain practices of the government and businesses.

One such practice involves the degree of supervision and control that a company exercises over its own employees. According to Bruce Schneier, computer security cannot be effective unless the people who use the computers also maintain good security practices.[34] Numerous employees may have access to a database, and some unscrupulous ones may pilfer data for use in identity theft. The FTC has noted the strong growth of "insider threats," when employees funnel data to identity thieves or abscond with information.[35] Another practice that jeopardizes the security of our personal data is the selling of them to others, because all it takes is a weak link in the chain for data security to be seriously compromised.

The central security flaw is the ease by which data can be accessed from the outside through relatively low-tech means. The social security number (SSN) is at the heart of this problem. Today, SSNs are used as passwords by countless businesses, banks, hospitals, schools, and other institutions to access personal data and accounts.[36] Businesses assume that whoever knows your SSN must be you. Because the SSN is used so frequently by a wide range of institutions as an identifier, it becomes a kind of magic key to our digital dossiers. With an SSN, an identity thief can gain access to a person's existing accounts, apply for credit in the victim's name, open accounts under the name of the victim, and obtain even more information about the victim for further use.[37]

The problem is that the SSN is a terrible password. Numerous people and organizations know our SSNs: employers, government agencies, credit reporting agencies, creditors, hospitals, and schools. Because SSNs often are used on ID cards or as driver license numbers, when a person loses his or her wallet, the person's SSN is also exposed. SSNs appear on countless documents that inevitably wind their way into the trash to be plucked away by identity thieves.[38] Even if people take the time to shred their trash, thieves can still get their SSNs. The numerous employees at schools, government agencies, and businesses may discard documents with a person's SSN without shredding them. Employees might steal the documents or copy the numbers from the documents. Moreover, SSNs are routinely sold by database companies to any interested buyer.[39] In one instance, an identity thief bought from database companies the SSNs of several top corporate executives.[40] The SSNs of major government officials, including Attorney General John Ashcroft and CIA Director George Tenet, were being sold on the Internet for $26 apiece.[41] SSNs are also disclosed in certain public records.[42] As a result of the widespread use of SSNs, anybody who wants to find out a person's SSN can do so with minimal effort.

Some banks and companies also require people to supply additional information such as addresses, birth dates, or mothers' maiden names.[43] But all this information is often disclosed by the government in public record systems.[44]

Not only does insecurity allow unauthorized access to our personal information, it also results in our dossiers becoming defiled with corrupt information. Credit reporting agencies maintain detailed dossiers about people, which they provide to creditors to assess a person's creditworthiness before offering them a loan.[45] Many employers also examine the credit reports of prospective hires as part of a background check. State licensing entities, such as state bar organizations, often require applicants to submit a credit report. Because credit reporting agencies work only for the creditors and do not establish a relationship with us, we have scant participation in how they use our information, and there are not sufficient market incentives to ensure that a particular person's report is accurate.

Creditors are also to blame, as they often are careless in granting credit. By one estimate, financial institutions mail over three billion preapproved credit card mailings each year.[46] People can readily apply for instant credit in stores or over the Internet. And they can easily do this in another person's name—all they need is that person's SSN, address, and date of birth. Lynn LoPucki observes that "creditors and credit-reporting agencies often lack both the means and the incentives to correctly identify the persons who seek credit from them or on whom they report."[47]

Therefore, identity theft does not just happen. It has been constructed. The SSN was manufactured by the government. Originally not to be used for identification,[48] it began to be used almost everywhere for just this purpose.[49] Congress recognized the problem in the early 1970s, and passed the Privacy Act of 1974 to restrict the growing use of SSNs as identifiers.[50] But the Act made a critical mistake—it did nothing to restrict the use of the SSN by businesses or other nongovernment institutions.

This is an architectural system—constructed by the government and by businesses—that makes us all woefully insecure. The government has stamped us with an identification number without providing adequate regulation on its use. Companies routinely allow access to our information with the SSN as a password, which leaves our data virtually undefended. As this discussion has demonstrated, the architectural problem is not in the design of technology but in the practices for how entities use, disseminate, and provide access to our personal information.

Typically, those discussing information architectures focus on what Lessig calls "architectures of control."[51] Architectures of control are constraining; they are designed to keep people under control. In the early days of the Internet, commentators celebrated its openness and freedom. Lessig, however, saw a more ominous future: "Cyberspace does not guarantee its own freedom but instead carries an extraordinary potential for control."[52] Through computer code and legal code, the Internet can become one of the most controlled places on the planet.

Architectures of control are a serious problem, but architecture works in other troublesome ways. In particular, we are witnessing the increasing construction of what I call "architectures of vulnerability."[53] Whereas architectures of control restrict people's freedom, architectures of vulnerability expose people to a myriad of perils. They sap people of their power.

The key point is that architecture itself can cause harm. If police protection of a neighborhood were taken away, and all the locks to people's homes were removed, this would be a precarious situation to live in, even if nothing happened. Architectures of vulnerability cause harm not only by creating emotional distress and anxiety but also by increasing our risks of being victimized by identity theft, fraud, stalking, or other crimes. This increased risk is itself a harm.

Unfortunately, the law does little to redress insecurity. Insecurity seems too "soft" to be a cognizable injury. When companies provide incompetent data security, not only has a concrete injury failed to materialize, but also nothing has happened. Hackers haven't hacked it. Identity thieves haven't exploited it. Nothing has been leaked. If somebody leaves the back door ajar, but no burglars come in, then it is difficult for the law to view the situation as ripe for a remedy.

By neglecting to recognize insecurity as a harm, the law is failing in its response to the escalating abuses of personal data. The law is prepared to rectify misuses, but this is often too little, too late. The problem emerges much earlier on—with leaks and inadequate data security. Pursuing the misusers of information has proven to be ineffectual. To stop the misuse, the law must begin to focus on the locus of the problem—on leaks and insecurity.

II. RETHINKING REMEDIES

Existing legal responses to data security leave the architecture of vulnerability unchanged. They patch up the cracks in the surface, but the foundations remain shaky. The law must shift its focus from the top of the data abuse pyramid (misuse) to the lower levels (leaks, insecurity). Can the law evolve to recognize leaks and insecurity as harms?

A. Shifting the Focus to Security Practices

At the core of the problems with data security is a set of business and government practices. We need to restructure our relationships with businesses and the government with regard to how they treat us when they collect and use our personal data. Currently, the collectors and users of our personal information are frequently not accountable to us. Information is gathered and used, and we have little knowledge about and ability to control how secure it remains.

To what extent do the companies that collect and use our personal information owe duties to us? This question remains surprisingly unanswered in the law. However, there are signs that courts are beginning to recognize that the entities using our personal data do have duties to us. For example, in *Remsburg* v. *Docusearch, Inc.*,[54] a man named Liam Youens bought data about Amy

Lynn Boyer from Docusearch, a database company that maintains personal information dossiers on people. Youens requested Boyer's SSN, and Docusearch quickly provided it to him. He then asked for the address of Boyer's employer. Docusearch hired a person to find out by calling Boyer, lying to her about the reason for the call, and inducing Boyer to reveal the address. Docusearch then gave the address to Youens, who went to Boyer's workplace and murdered her. The court held that although ordinarily private parties have "no general duty to protect others from the criminal attacks of third parties," when "the defendant's conduct has created an unreasonable risk of criminal misconduct, a duty is owed to those foreseeably endangered."[55] A private investigator "owes a duty to exercise reasonable care not to subject the third person to an unreasonable risk of harm."[56] Therefore, "threats posed by stalking and identity theft lead us to conclude that the risk of criminal misconduct is sufficiently foreseeable so that an investigator has a duty to exercise reasonable care in disclosing a third person's personal information to a client."[57] *Remsburg* is an important step forward in recognizing and remedying modern information privacy harms. *Remsburg* appropriately recognizes the duty that data collectors and users have to the people whose information they maintain.

Another way to locate duties is by analogizing our relationship with the data collectors and users to a fiduciary one. A fiduciary relationship is one in which a person standing in a special position of power owes special duties to the person subjected to that power.[58] The most famous description of fiduciary duties was penned by Justice Benjamin Cardozo: "Many forms of conduct permissible in a workaday world for those acting at arm's length, are forbidden to those bound by fiduciary ties. A trustee is held to something stricter than the morals of the market place. Not honesty alone, but the punctilio of an honor the most sensitive, is then the standard of behavior."[59]

In the privacy context, suits have been brought under the tort of breach of confidentiality when personal information is leaked.[60] The virtue of the breach of fiduciary duty approach is that this tort understands the breach to be the harm. Jessica Litman proposes that the breach of confidentiality tort apply to companies that trade in personal information.[61] In particular, she contends, the "reuse, correlation, and sale of consumer transaction data is a straightforward breach of trust."[62] Litman, however, recognizes that the "payoff" of such a tort remedy would be "modest."[63] For Litman, the central problem with common law tort is that it is "gradual and slow" to develop, and "anything so slow is likely to deliver too little, too late."[64] Litman has in mind intentional transfers of data, not data insecurity. However, because fiduciary duties extend beyond a duty of confidentiality, plaintiffs may be able to sue for a breach of a duty to maintain proper data security.

The law of fiduciary relationships is an evolving one. Courts "have carefully refrained from defining instances of fiduciary relations in such a manner that other and perhaps new cases might be excluded."[65] Courts apply a multifactor analysis to determine whether a fiduciary relationship exists. These factors include "[T]he degree of kinship of the parties; the disparity in age, health, and mental condition; education and business experience between the parties; and the extent to which the allegedly subservient party entrusted the handling of . . . business affairs to the other and reposed faith and confidence in [that person or entity]."[66] Courts have likened relationships between patients and physicians as well as attorneys and clients to fiduciary relationships.[67]

The courts generally look for two basic attributes of the relationship: (1) disparities in power and (2) one party's placing trust in the other party. The first attribute is clearly present in many of our relationships with the companies that gather our personal data. We often lack an ability to bargain over the security of our information and the way it is transferred to others. Moreover, we often are not well informed of the current and potential uses of our information. The second attribute is more complicated. For the companies we do business with, the case is strong. We entrust them with our personal information with the understanding that they will keep it secure. But what about all of the companies that we never do business with that troll about gathering up our data? We don't even have a relationship with these companies. They just take our data—often secretly, without our knowledge.

But the law of fiduciary relationships is a flexible one, and it would not be too much of an expansion of the concept to apply it to the collectors and users of personal information. My argument is not that existing legal doctrine will readily work, but that it has the necessary underlying conceptions to respond to the problem of insecurity. Currently, our relationships to data collectors are perceived to be ones in which there is little accountability and responsibility. By rethinking them as more analogous to fiduciary relationships, we will recognize that the collection and use of personal data carries with it profound obligations.

What duties should data collectors and users have? Courts have held that doctors, banks, and schools have a duty to keep personal information confidential.[68] It is not a stretch to conclude that the fiduciary has a duty to keep a person's private information secure. The best source for fiduciary duties of companies that maintain our personal information are the Fair Information Practices. Originally devised in 1973 in a report by the U.S. Department of Housing, Education, and Welfare, the Fair Information Practices consist of a series of principles about rights and responsibilities pertaining to the use of personal data:

- There must be no personal-data record-keeping systems whose very existence is secret.
- There must be a way for an individual to find out what information about him is in a record and how it is used.
- There must be a way for an individual to prevent information about him obtained for one purpose from being used or made available for other purposes without his consent.
- There must be a way for an individual to correct or amend a record of identifiable information about him.
- Any organization creating, maintaining, using, or disseminating records of identifiable personal data must assure the reliability of the data for their intended use and must take reasonable precautions to prevent misuse of the data.[69]

If we recognize that the companies that keep our data owe duties to us, then the Fair Information Practices are the most coherent and well-established set of duties that have been articulated for the use of personal data.

Once we change the way we think about the harms caused by insecurity as well as the responsibility companies bear for these harms, then we can bring the law to recognize the most appropriate focal point for responding to information abuses.

B. Tort Remedies Against Businesses

Even if the law concludes that the companies maintaining our personal data bear responsibility for information abuses, it will still be difficult for individuals to pursue remedies. For actual misuses of information, the law will have the least trouble understanding the nature of the harm. As discussed earlier, however, focusing on misuses will present difficulties because it is often hard to establish a causal connection between specific companies that served as the source of the data used by an information abuser. The most effective tool in improving data security is redressing leaks and insecurity.

One option is to turn to tort law. Under existing tort law, there are at least two theories about how leaks or insecurity could be recognized as causing cognizable injury. First, leaks or insecurity can cause emotional distress. Second, leaks or insecurity can increase the risk of future harm.

1. Emotional Distress

Leaks or insecurity can cause emotional distress. Of course, the strongest case for emotional distress is when a victim suffers from an actual information misuse. Identity theft causes significant anxiety and emotional trauma when people experience the destruction of their financial reputations. But what about leaks or insecurity? Because most leaks and insecurity are the result of negligence, the tort of negligent infliction of emotional distress would be a potential remedy.

However, courts are especially reluctant to award damages when the emotional distress does not arise out of a more concrete injury, such as bodily harm.[70] Thus many courts have held that damages for negligent infliction of emotional distress cannot exist alone; they must be accompanied by other physical injuries.[71] For example, in *Doe* v. *Chao*,[72] the Department of Labor used coal mine workers' SSNs as their identifying numbers for their black lung benefits claims. Administrative law judges issued public hearing notices listing miners' names and SSNs. The judges also used the numbers in their decisions, which were made public.[73] A group of miners sued under the federal Privacy Act. Buck Doe, the lead plaintiff, testified that "[H]e was 'greatly concerned and worried' about the disclosure of his SSN; that he felt his privacy had been violated in 'words he cannot describe'; that he felt the consequences of the disclosure of his SSN could be 'devastating' for himself and his wife; and that the disclosure of his SSN had 'torn [him] all to pieces.'"[74] The court held that emotional distress damages cannot be established by a "plaintiff's own conclusory allegations that he felt 'embarrassed,' 'degraded,' or 'devastated,' and suffered a loss of self-esteem."[75] Doe "did not produce any evidence of tangible consequences stemming from his alleged angst over the disclosure of his SSN. He claimed no medical or psychological treatment, no purchase of medications (prescription or over-the-counter), no impact on his behavior, and no physical consequences."[76] The U.S. Supreme Court held that because Doe couldn't establish actual damages, he was not entitled to any liquidated damages under the Privacy Act.[77]

The reason why courts are reluctant to award damages for negligent infliction of emotional distress is that they often view emotional distress damages "with suspicion" because of "concerns over genuineness, reliability, and the specter of unlimited liability for trivial losses."[78] However, the law has made profound progress in recognizing mental and emotional injuries. Originally, the law provided no protection to such harms.[79] Later on, in what became known as the "impact rule," tort law recognized emotional distress damages when the distress arose out of physical injuries.[80] Many jurisdictions expanded the impact rule beyond requiring an initial physical injury to allowing for recovery of emotional distress when it had "physical manifestations."[81] The expansion continued when the law began to permit recovery of emotional distress that arose when a person was not physically injured but was within the "zone of physical danger."[82] The law has taken further steps, allowing recovery for bystanders not within the zone of physical impact who witness loved ones being hurt. In *Dillon v. Legg*,[83] a mother witnessed the death of her daughter in a car accident, but the mother was not in the zone of danger. The court permitted recovery based on negligent infliction of emotional distress. *Dillon* is now followed in many states,[84] but it has strict guidelines that limit recovery based on the plaintiff's observing the event and the relationship between the plaintiff and the injured party.[85] The clear trend is that the law is developing toward easing the restrictions on recovery for emotional harm. Many obstacles to recovery remain, however, and courts are still quite reluctant to recognize emotional distress alone as a cognizable injury.

The difficulty that will plague any form of tort remedy for emotional distress caused by a leak or insecurity is that damages are likely to be small. Although many people may experience some anxiety over data leaks and insecurity, it is the rare case in which the mental trauma is severe enough to warrant substantial damages. If claims are aggregated, however, a suit may have more punch, and injunctive relief could go far to rectify the problem.

2. Risk of Future Harm

Another potential tort doctrine that might be employed to remedy leaks and insecurity emerges from a growing number of cases that remedies the creation of a risk of suffering future harm. The potential future harm that a person could suffer from insecurity or leaks includes identity theft; harm to reputation; being hindered in obtaining jobs, loans, or licenses; and emotional distress. *Petriello v. Kalman*[86] involved a medical malpractice suit in which a physician used excessive suction to remove a fetus that had died in utero. As a result, damage was caused to the plaintiff's intestines, and it required repair with a bowel resection, which involved removing part of the intestine. The plaintiff produced evidence that as a result of this injury, she would have between an 8 percent to 16 percent chance that she would suffer a future bowel obstruction.[87] The court noted that under existing law "[i]f a plaintiff can prove that there exists a 51 percent chance that his injury is permanent or that future injury will result, he may receive full compensation for that injury as if it were a certainty. If, however, the plaintiff establishes only a 49 percent chance of such a consequence, he may recover nothing for the risk to which he is presently exposed."[88] The court found fault with this system, because it produced an all-or-nothing standard. The result is that "a significant number of persons receive compensation for future consequences that never occur and, conversely, a significant number of persons receive no compensation at all for consequences that later ensue from risks not arising to the level of probability."[89] Therefore the court concluded that the plaintiff should be compensated for the increased risk of developing the bowel obstruction "to the extent that the future harm is likely to occur."[90]

Courts have begun allowing people to sue for medical malpractice that results in the loss of an "opportunity to obtain a better degree of recovery."[91] Under this approach, the plaintiff "does not receive damages for the *entire* injury, but just for the lost opportunity."[92] In one case, in which the doctor argued that the damages were too difficult to calculate, the court concluded that this difficulty should not be a reason to deny recovery and "loss of opportunity is not inherently unquantifiable."[93] Allowing people to recover for potential future harm made more likely by the tortious conduct or the loss of a chance to improve one's condition is a rather new development in tort law, occurring primarily over the past twenty years.[94] Damages can include those "directly resulting from the loss of a chance of achieving a more favorable outcome," as well as damages "for the mental distress from the realization that the patient's prospects of avoiding adverse past or future harm were tortiously destroyed or reduced," and damages "for the medical costs of monitoring the condition in order to detect and respond to a recurrence or complications."[95]

Translated into the domain of information security, tort law would recognize the condition of insecurity as a breach of a duty—a fiduciary one or perhaps an ordinary duty of care. The harm of vulnerability would then be rectified by damages for the increased possibility of harm from identity theft, the mental distress caused by the increased vulnerability, and any costs needed to protect oneself against harms that could arise from the vulnerability.

A problem is that if we applied remedies for insecurity broadly, many kinds of insecurity could potentially become tortious. Suppose that a reckless driver drives aggressively and carelessly, increasing other drivers' potential to be involved in an accident. The law would certainly balk at compensating all of these other drivers for the increased risk. But in other cases the law does remedy increased risk of harm. As illustrated earlier, the law provides a remedy for increased risk of developing health complications as a result of medical malpractice. One reason for this difference is that once the reckless driver passes by, the risk has been survived and is over. In contrast, the risk of developing future complications from medical malpractice is continuing.

Security flaws fit uneasily between these two situations. Unlike medical malpractice, which produces a permanent increased risk of developing a future complication, security flaws can be patched up. This alters the risk of being victimized by data abuse. On the other hand, the risk caused by insecurity is not a once-and-done risk like the reckless driver. It continues until the security flaw is fixed. Thus, upon being sued, a company could reform its data security practices and eliminate the amount of damages a plaintiff could collect. Of course, this is not a total loss to the plaintiff, because bringing the suit can induce a company to improve its practices and the plaintiff may be able to obtain injunctive relief.

3. The Limits and Potential of Tort Law

In sum, these tort doctrines contain the necessary concepts to redress the leak and insecurity harms, but they all have significant problems and limitations that hinder their application. I do not mean to suggest that these difficulties cannot be overcome, but the road will be a rough one. The law of torts will need some creativity and development to be used as a device to induce lasting change in security practices.

In 1890, Samuel Warren and Louis Brandeis attempted to rethink privacy harms and remedies.[96] "[I]n very early times," they contended, "the law gave a remedy only for physical interference with life and property."[97] Subsequently, the law expanded to recognize incorporeal injuries: "[f]rom the action of battery grew that of assault. Much later there came a qualified protection of the individual against offensive noises and odors, against dust and smoke, and excessive vibration. The law of nuisance was developed."[98] Along this trend, the law recognized protection to people's reputations.[99] Furthermore, "[f]rom corporeal property arose the incorporeal rights issuing out of it; and then there opened the wide realm of intangible property, in the products and processes of the mind."[100] Warren and Brandeis were paving the way for the legal recognition of remedies for privacy invasions, which often involve not a physical interference but an "injury to the feelings."[101]

Since the Warren and Brandeis article, the law has come a long way in recognizing privacy harms. Among other things, people can find legal redress for disclosures of embarrassing true information about their private lives, for intrusions into their seclusion and solitude, and for a host of other types of harms.[102] Today, new abuses such as leaks and insecurity are becoming more prevalent, and they are currently not well-recognized by the law. Tort law is much more advanced than it was in Warren and Brandeis's day. Basic underlying concepts are in place, and the law even partially recognizes the kinds of harms that leaks and insecurity create. The critical question, then, is whether tort law will take the next step.

C. Constitutional Remedies Against the Government

With regard to the data practices of the government, the constitutional right to information privacy could conceivably provide a remedy. In *Whalen v. Roe*,[103] the Court concluded that the right to privacy protects not only "independence in making certain kinds of important decisions" but also the "individual interest in avoiding disclosure of personal matters."[104] The case involved a government record system of individuals who were taking prescriptions for certain medications. Although the government promised that the information was confidential and secure, the plaintiffs contended that they feared the possibility of the information leaking out. The Court concluded that because the security was adequate, the state had met its constitutional obligations. In a key passage in the case, the Court stated,

> We are not unaware of the threat to privacy implicit in the accumulation of vast amounts of personal information in computerized data banks or other massive government files. . . . The right to collect and use such data for public purposes is typically accompanied by a concomitant statutory or regulatory duty to avoid unwarranted disclosures. . . . [I]n some circumstances that duty has its roots in the Constitution.[105]

Therefore, according to the Court in *Whalen*, when the government maintains personal information, it has the responsibility to keep it secure.

The constitutional right to information privacy is a work in progress. Although the Supreme Court has done little to develop it, the right has been recognized in a majority of circuit courts.[106] Therefore, the constitutional right to information privacy has the potential to develop into a way for people to ensure that the government keep their information secure. People can bring *Bivens* or § 1983 actions for damages and injunctions. In this way, the constitutional right to information privacy can work as a tort action against the government for shoddy security. It can also limit the extent to which the government permits public access to personal information.

States that do not adequately account for privacy in their public record laws may be found to violate the constitutional right to information privacy. Because some of the personal information disclosed in public record systems can facilitate the commission of identity theft and other misuses, disclosure can compromise a person's security. For example, one court clerk in Cincinnati placed an entire county's court records on the Internet. A person whose speeding ticket was posted on the Website had his identity stolen because the ticket contained a treasure trove of personal information, including the person's SSN.[107]

At least one court has recognized that the dissemination of information in public records can implicate the constitutional right to information privacy. In *Kallstrom v. City of Columbus*,[108] a city disclosed law enforcement officials' personnel files to defense counsel of alleged drug conspirators (whom the officials had investigated). The personnel files included the officer's names, addresses, phone numbers, financial information, social security numbers, and responses to questions about their personal lives, as well as the names, addresses, and phone numbers of immediate family members.[109] The city disclosed to avert a violation of Ohio's Public Records Act, which makes records available to the public unless the record falls within an enumerated exemption. The Act did not have a privacy exemption. The court held that the disclosures created a serious risk to the "personal security and bodily integrity" of the plaintiffs and their families.[110] Applying strict scrutiny, the court held that the disclosure violated the constitutional right to information privacy because it did not further the public's understanding of law enforcement agencies.[111]

Therefore the constitutional right to information privacy imposes upon the government a responsibility to keep the data it collects secure and confidential absent an overriding consideration on the other side of the scale. However, this way of applying the constitutional right to information privacy may meet resistance in the courts, especially given the germinal and uncertain status of the right.

D. Structural Remedies

Insecurity harms are difficult to rectify with individual tort suits, because damages are harder to establish and people are often given so little information about a company's security practices that it will be difficult for them to find out enough to bring a suit. Therefore the most effective means for reforming the architecture must be more systematic than what individual remedies can provide. Although I believe individual remedies are an important tool, a system of regulation will be better able to improve security at a more global level. Information security must be regulated by a national agency with the appropriate expertise to understand information privacy issues.

Thus far, the FTC has been attempting to develop such a regulatory system. Beginning in 1998, the Federal Trade Commission has been expanding its reach by bringing actions against businesses that breach their own privacy policies. According to the FTC, such breaches are "unfair or deceptive acts or practices in or affecting commerce."[112] Armed with the power to bring civil actions and obtain injunctions, the FTC has initiated a number of cases, practically all resulting in settlements.[113] Several of these cases involved improperly disclosed or leaked data.

There are indications that the FTC is expanding its reach beyond leaks to insecurity harms. In particular, the FTC charged that Microsoft's .NET Passport, which allows Internet users to use a single username and password to log in to a variety of participating Websites, was not providing adequate security, which it had promised in its privacy policy. Microsoft settled with the FTC, and it promised to improve its security.[114] The Passport case marks a very important new development in FTC enforcement. The FTC appears to have recognized security harms as cognizable. In another recent case, *In re Guess.com, Inc.*,[115] the FTC brought an action against Guess for having shoddy security for its customers' personal data in violation of its privacy policy.

There are many reasons to remain skeptical about the FTC's ability to develop into the kind of national privacy agency needed to reform the security of our digital dossiers. The FTC's jurisdiction is limited, and the enforcement of privacy is not its primary mission.[116] Another limitation with the FTC is that it thus far only ensures that companies follow the promises they make in their privacy policies.[117] But there is a way around this limitation contained in a little-known provision of the Gramm-Leach-Bliley (GLB) Act. The GLB Act requires the various agencies that regulate financial companies to enact "administrative, technical, and physical safeguards for personal information."[118] These regulations promulgated under the GLB Act are rather vague, but they could be used to enable agencies such as the FTC to bring actions to force companies to abandon the use of SSNs and other readily available personal information as passwords. Unfortunately, this kind of insecurity has not been recognized by the FTC. The focus on information security has thus far been centered around technology, not around these basic business practices that allow easy access to personal data.

III. CONCLUSION

We are increasingly vulnerable in the Information Age, and the information abuses we are experiencing are the product of business and the government. We need to rethink information abuses by understanding insecurity as a cognizable injury and focusing more on the companies maintaining and using our personal information. The most effective approach to dealing with information abuses is to focus on the bottom of the data security pyramid, not the top.

NOTES

1. For an extensive account of security threats to computer networks, see Bruce Schneier, *Secrets and Lies: Digital Security in a Networked World* (2000).

2. Daniel J. Solove, Privacy and Power: Computer Databases and Metaphors for Information Privacy, 53 *Stan. L. Rev.* 1393, 1403–13 (2001).

3. *See* Jennifer 8. Lee, Fighting Back When Someone Steals Your Name, *N.Y. Times*, April 8, 2001; *see also* Jennifer 8. Lee, Identity Theft Victimizes Millions, Costs Billions, *N.Y. Times*, Sept. 4, 2003.

4. Tyler Hamilton, ID Theft a Click Away, *Toronto Star*, May 12, 2003.

5. Federal Trade Commission, Identity Theft Survey Report 4 (Sept. 2003).

6. *Id*. at 6.

7. *Id*. at 6.

8. Robert O'Harrow Jr., I.D. Theft Scam Hits D.C. Area Residents, *Wash. Post*, Feb. 21, 2005, at A1.

9. Tom Zeller Jr., U.S. Settles with Company on Leak of Consumers' Data, *N.Y. Times*, Jan. 27, 2006, at A3.

10. Heather Timmons, Security Breach at LexisNexis Now Appears Larger, *N.Y. Times*, Apr. 13, 2005, at C7.

11. Saul Hansell, Bank Loses Tapes of Records of 1.2 Million with Visa Cards, *N.Y. Times*, Feb. 26, 2005, at A9.

12. For a useful chart tallying the data security breaches, *see* Privacy Rights Clearinghouse, *A Chronology of Data Breaches*, available at http://www.privacyrights.org/ar/ChronData Breaches.htm.

13. Tom Zeller Jr., An Ominous Milestone: 100 Million Data Leaks, *N.Y. Times*, Dec. 18, 2006.

14. Helen Nissenbaum, Securing Trust Online: Wisdom or Oxymoron?, 81 *B.U. L. Rev.* 635, 659 (2001).

15. For a discussion of some of the technological solutions to combating certain kinds of digital security problems, *see* Neal Kumar Katyal, Digital Architecture as Crime Control, 112 *Yale L. J.* 2261 (2003).

16. *See* Janine Benner, Beth Givens, & Ed Mierzwinski, *Nowhere to Turn: Victims Speak Out on Identity Theft: A CALPIRG / Privacy Rights Clearinghouse Report* (May 2000), available at http://www.privacyrights.org/ar/idtheft2000.htm.

17. Christopher P. Couch, Commentary, Forcing the Choice Between Commerce and Consumers: Application of the FCRA to Identity Theft, 53 *Ala. L. Rev.* 583, 586 (2002).

18. Martha A. Sabol, The Identity Theft and Assumption Deterrence Act of 1998: Do Individual Victims Finally Get Their Day in Court? 11 *Loy. Consumer L. Rev.* 165, 167 (1999).

19. U.S. General Accounting Office, Report to the Honorable Sam Johnson, House of Representatives, Identity Theft: Greater Awareness and Use of Existing Data Are Needed 23 (June 2002) [hereinafter "GAO Identity Theft Report"]; Lynn M. LoPucki, Human Identification Theory and the Identity Theft Problem, 80 *Tex. L. Rev.* 89, 90 (2001); *see also* Privacy Rights Clearinghouse and Identity Theft Resource Center, *Criminal Identity Theft* (May 2002), available at http://www.privacyrights.org/fs/fs11g-CrimIdTheft.htm.

20. Robert O'Harrow Jr., Identity Thieves Thrive in the Information Age, *Wash. Post*, May 31, 2001, at A1.

21. *See* Priscilla M. Regan, *Legislating Privacy: Technology, Social Values, and Public Policy* 102 (1995). The murder of Rebecca Shaeffer led to the passage of the Driver's Privacy Protection Act of 1994, 18 U.S.C. §§ 2721-25, which restricts the ability of states to disseminate personal information in their motor vehicle records.

22. GAO Identity Theft Report, *supra* note 19, at 1.

23. 18 U.S.C. § 1028.

24. GAO Identity Theft Report, *supra* note 19, at 17.

25. *Id.* at 18.

26. Jennifer 8. Lee, Fighting Back When Someone Steals Your Name, *N.Y. Times*, Apr. 8, 2001.

27. Stephen Mihm, Dumpster Diving for Your Identity, *N.Y. Times Magazine*, Dec. 21, 2003.

28. Jeff Sovern, The Jewel of Their Souls: Preventing Identity Theft Through Loss Allocation Rules, 64 *U. Pitt. L. Rev.* 343, 398 (2003) ("[C]onsumers may face a causation issue, in that the chain of causation from the disclosure of the consumer's information to the injury to the consumer is a long one.").

29. H.R. 2622 (108th Cong, 1st Sess.) (2003).

30. Mark Truby, Ford Credit Discovers ID Theft, *Detroit News*, May 16, 2002.

31. Chris Jay Hoofnagle, Testimony Before the Subcomm. on Social Security of the Comm. on Ways and Means, U.S. House of Representatives, Hearing on Use and Misuse of the Social Security Number (July 10, 2003).

32. *See* Charles Pillar, Wee Mishap: Kids' Psychological Files Posted, *L.A. Times*, Nov. 7, 2001.

33. *See* Lawrence Lessig, *Code and Other Laws of Cyberspace* 5–6, 236 (1999); Joel R. Reidenberg, Rules of the Road for Global Electronic Highways: Merging Trade and Technical Paradigms, 6 *Harv. J. L. & Tech.* 287, 296 (1993).

34. Schneier, Secrets and Lies, *supra* note 1, at 255–69.

35. Mihm, *supra* note 27.

36. *See, e.g.,* Simson Garfinkel, *Database Nation: The Death of Privacy in the 21st Century* 33–34 (2000).

37. LoPucki, Identity Theft, *supra* note 19, at 104.

38. Mihm, *supra* note 27.

39. Robert O'Harrow Jr., Identity Thieves Thrive Online, *Wash. Post*, May 31, 2001. *See* Beth Givens, Identity Theft: How It Happens, Its Impact on Victims, and Legislative Solutions, Written Testimony for the U.S. Senate Judiciary Subcommittee on Technology, Terrorism, and Government Information 4 (July 12, 2000); Greg Gatlin, Activists Spur Action Against ID Theft; Social Security Numbers Were for Sale Online, *Boston Herald*, Sept. 26, 2003, at 38.

40. Benjamin Weiser, Identity Theft, and These Were Big Identities, *N.Y. Times*, May 29, 2002.

41. Jennifer C. Kerr, Bush Aides' Social Security Numbers Sell Cheaply on Net, *Chi. Trib.*, Aug. 28, 2003.

42. Daniel J. Solove, Access and Aggregation: Public Records, Privacy, and the Constitution, 86 *Minn. L. Rev.* 1137, 1147 (2002).

43. Robert O'Harrow Jr., Concerns for ID Theft Often Are Unheeded, *Wash. Post*, July 23, 2001, at A1.

44. *See* Solove, Access and Aggregation, *supra* note 42, at 1143–48.

45. *See* Daniel J. Solove, Identity Theft, Privacy, and the Architecture of Vulnerability, *54 Hastings L. J.* 1227, 1245 (2003).

46. Benner, Nowhere to Turn, *supra* note 16, at 13.

47. LoPucki, Human Identification Theory, *supra* note 19, at 94.

48. Robert Ellis Smith, *Ben Franklin's Web Site: Privacy and Curiosity from Plymouth Rock to the Internet* 288 (2000).

49. *See, e.g.,* United States General Accounting Office, Report to the Chairman, Subcomm. on Social Security, Comm. On Ways and Means, House of Representatives: *Social Security: Government and Commercial Use of the Social Security Number Is Widespread* (Feb. 1999).

50. *Doyle v. Wilson*, 529 F. Supp. 1343, 1348 (D. Del. 1982).

51. Lessig, Code, *supra* note 33, at 30.

52. *Id.* at 58.

53. *See* Solove, Identity Theft, *supra* note 45.

54. 816 A. 2d 1001 (N.H. 2003).

55. *Id.* at 1007.

56. *Id.* at 1007.

57. *Id.* at 1008.

58. *See Mobile Oil Corp. v. Rubenfeld*, 339 N.Y.S. 2d 623, 632 (1972) ("A fiduciary relationship is one founded on trust or confidence reposed by one person in the integrity and fidelity of another. Out of such a relation, the laws raise the rule that neither party may exert influence

or pressure upon the other, take selfish advantage of his trust[,] or deal with the subject matter of the trust in such a way as to benefit himself or prejudice the other except in the exercise of utmost good faith.").

59. *Meinhard v. Salmon*, 164 N.E. 545, 546 (N.Y. 1928).

60. *McCormick v. England*, 494 S.E. 2d 431 (S.C. Ct. App. 1997); *Biddle v. Warren General Hospital*, 715 N.E. 2d 518 (Ohio 1999).

61. *See* Jessica Litman, Information Privacy / Information Property, 52 *Stan. L. Rev.* 1283, 1304–13 (2000).

62. *Id.* at 1308.

63. *Id.* at 1312.

64. *Id.* at 1312, 1313.

65. *Swerhun v. General Motors Corp.*, 812 F. Supp. 1218, 1222 (M.D. Fla. 1993).

66. *Pottinger v. Pottinger*, 605 N.E. 2d 1130, 1137 (Ill. App. 1992).

67. *Hammonds v. Aetna Casualty & Surety Co.*, 243 F. Supp. 793 (D. Ohio 1965); *McCormick v. England*, 494 S.E. 2d 431 (S.C. Ct. App. 1997).

68. *McCormick v. England*, 494 S.E. 2d 431 (S.C. Ct. App. 1997) (doctor); *Peterson v. Idaho First National Bank*, 367 P. 2d 284 (Idaho 1961) (bank); *Blair v. Union Free School District*, 324 N.Y.S. 2d 222 (N.Y. Dist. Ct. 1971) (school).

69. U.S. Dep't of Health, Education, and Welfare, Report of the Secretary's Advisory Committee on Automated Personal Data Systems: Records, Computers, and the Rights of Citizens 41–42 (1973).

70. James M. Fischer, *Understanding Remedies* 124–25 (1999).

71. *Id.* at 133.

72. 306 F. 3d 170 (4th Cir. 2002) cert. granted (June 27, 2003).

73. *Id.* at 175.

74. *Id.* at 181.

75. *Id.* at 180.

76. *Id.* at 182.

77. *See Doe v. Chao*, 124 S. Ct. 1204 (2004).

78. Fischer, *supra* note 70.

79. Leslie Benton Sandor & Carol Berry, Recovery for Negligent Infliction of Emotional Distress Attendant to Economic Loss: A Reassessment, 37 *Ariz. L. Rev.* 1248, 1251 (1995).

80. *Id.* at 1261.

81. *Id.* at 1261.

82. *Id.* at 1262.

83. 441 P. 2d 912 (Cal. 1968); *see also Molien v. Kaiser Found. Hospitals*, 616 P. 2d 813 (Cal. 1980) (permitting recovery for emotional distress not accompanied by physical injuries).

84. Richard A. Epstein, *Torts* 276 (1999).

85. Arthur Best & David W. Barnes, *Basic Tort Law* 536 (2003).

86. 576 A. 2d 474 (Conn. 1990).

87. *Id.* at 391.

88. *Id.* at 393.

89. *Id.* at 394.

90. *Id.* at 398.

91. *Lord v. Lovett*, 770 A. 3d 1103, 1105 (N.H. 2001).

92. *Id.* at 1106.

93. *Id.* at 1108.

94. Joseph H. King Jr., "Reduction of Likelihood" Reformulation and Other Retrofitting of the Loss-of-Chance Doctrine, 28 *U. Mem. L. Rev.* 491, 502 (1998).

95. *Id.* at 505.

96. Samuel D. Warren & Louis D. Brandeis, The Right to Privacy, 4 *Harv. L. Rev.* 193 (1890).

97. *Id.* at 193.

98. *Id.* at 194.

99. *Id.* at 194.

100. *Id.* at 194.

101. *Id.* at 197.

102. *See* Restatement (Second) of Torts §§ 652B (intrusion); 652D (public disclosure).

103. 429 U.S. 589 (1977).

104. *Id.* at 599–600.

105. *Id.* at 605.

106. After *Whalen*, the Court has done little to develop the right of information privacy. As one court observed, the right "has been infrequently examined; as a result, its contours remain less than clear." *Davis v. Bucher*, 853 F. 2d 718, 720 (9th Cir. 1988). Most circuit courts have recognized the constitutional right to information privacy. *See, e.g., United States v. Westinghouse Electric Corp.*, 638 F. 2d 570, 577–580 (3d Cir. 1980); *Plante v. Gonzalez*, 575 F. 2d 1119, 1132, 1134 (5th Cir. 1978); *Barry v. City of New York*, 712 F. 2d 1554, 1559 (2d Cir. 1983); *In re Crawford*, 194 F. 3d 954, 959 (9th Cir. 1999); *J.P. v. DeSanti*, 653 F. 2d 1080, 1089 (6th Cir. 1981); *Walls v. City of Petersburg*, 895 F. 2d 188, 192 (4th Cir. 1990); *but see American Federation of Government Employees, AFL-CIO v. Department of Housing & Urban Development*, 118 F. 3d 786, 191–92 (D.C. Cir. 1997) (expressing "grave doubts" as to the existence of the right but not directly addressing the issue of the existence of the right).

107. Jennifer 8. Lee, Dirty Laundry, Online for All to See, *N.Y. Times*, Sept. 5, 2002, at G1.

108. 136 F. 3d 1055 (6th Cir. 1998).

109. *Id.* at 1059.

110. *Id.* at 1062.

111. *Id.* at 1065.

112. 15 U.S.C. § 45.

113. See Daniel J. Solove & Marc Rotenberg, *Information Privacy Law* 541–53 (2003).

114. *See* In the Matter of Microsoft Corp., No. 012-3240.

115. No. 022-3260 (July 30, 2003).

116. *See* Joel R. Reidenberg, Privacy Wrongs in Search of Remedies, 54 *Hastings L. J.* 877, 888 (2003).

117. *See* Paul M. Schwartz, Privacy and Democracy in Cyberspace, 52 *Vand. L. Rev.* 1609, 1638 (1999).

118. 15 U.S.C. §§ 6801(b); 6805(b)(2).

7 BEYOND CONTRACT

Utilizing Restitution to Reach Shadow Offenders
and Safeguard Information Privacy

Marcy E. Peek

*Marcy E. Peek is assistant professor of law, Whittier Law School. The author
would like to thank the Center for Internet and Society at Stanford Law School,
which made this project possible. The author would also like to thank Anupam
Chander, James Alton Alsup III, Hari Osofsky, Radha Pathak, and Karl Manheim
for their helpful comments and suggestions.*

PROLOGUE

Recently, the FBI discovered that an employee of a data-marketing firm
had spent two years hacking into a server owned by Acxiom.[1] The employee
"[helped] himself to unencrypted data belonging to 10% of Acxiom's customer
base—upwards of 200 large companies."[2] Acxiom, which maintains records
on 96 percent of American households, is the largest aggregator of personal
data in the world.[3] It gives its corporate customers what it calls "real-time,
360-degree views"[4] into consumers by assigning individuals a thirteen-digit
code. This code tracks us throughout life and is used to place us into one of
seventy lifestyle clusters, which changes as the information Acxiom holds on
us is updated.[5]

After the Acxiom hacking incident was reported, the FBI discovered that,
in an unrelated case, another group had hacked into Acxiom's servers for three
months, accessing records on millions of Americans.[6]

The year before, records on five million JetBlue Airways passengers were
improperly disclosed and mined without the passengers' knowledge or consent
by a company called Torch Concepts, allegedly for national defense purposes.[7]

In that case, Torch Concepts was the third-party information-mining company that obtained the passenger data from JetBlue and controlled many aspects of the project.[8] Torch Concepts also independently, and as part of the same project, purchased additional data on two million JetBlue passengers from Acxiom, including a host of sensitive information such as gender, income, number of children, social security number, occupation, and vehicle information.[9] Torch then allegedly used the aggregate data to perform a detailed customer profiling and terrorism risk-assessment study, and proceeded to present its findings at an engineering conference, including the social security number and other identifying information of one individual whom it identified as potentially high risk.[10] Later, Torch proceeded to post its profiling and risk assessment results on a publicly available Website.

I. INFORMATION ALIENATION AT THE HANDS OF SHADOW OFFENDERS

A. Introduction

Our personal data are not our own. Companies are, by and large, free to gather, aggregate, distribute, and share our personal information *ad infinitum* and as they see fit.[11] The personal information alienation that we are experiencing on a grand scale[12] has engendered a society in which our personal data are by default public and subject to outside scrutiny and disclosure. Legal scholars have struggled to find ways to give some control over personal data to the individual, and to develop an encompassing theory of privacy that includes the many interests implicated in the information privacy debate.

The concern over information privacy is, in large part, a concern with control over personal information—whether that control is in the hands of the individual or, more likely, in the hands of a corporation, a commercial information broker, or a government agency. The individual's striving toward a right to control personal data often encompasses a striving for what Louis Brandeis and Samuel D. Warren[13] called a "right to be left alone." But more profoundly, the push for personal data control is a demand for informational autonomy, human dignity, and individual freedom.[14]

What we seek is no less than a seismic shift in the cultural and economic milieu of American life. Some scholars have called for the imposition of standards of "commercial morality,"[15] but it is more than that. It is no less than the struggle between individuals and corporations;[16] between the striving for a realm of personal autonomy and the ceaseless quest for bureaucratic knowledge, surveillance, and control; and between a recognition of the significance of information power and the refusal to acknowledge that the difference between the haves and the have-nots is often a function of information access and control.[17]

A specific example of this struggle, and the dilemma addressed in this chapter, is the problem of data mishandling and misuse at the hands of what I call "shadow offenders," third-party companies that traffic in personal data yet have no direct commercial or contractual relationship with the individual. This piece argues that in cases of improper use of personal data by such companies, recovery in restitution should be available for the victims of data mishandling.

B. Data Trafficking by Third-Party Shadow Offenders

The widespread phenomenon of data handling and mishandling[18] at the hands of third-party companies offers a vivid lens on the abuse of personal data. These companies, or "shadow offenders," generally have no direct market or contractual relationship with consumers, but they have access to large amounts of personal data on millions of individuals and are largely unaccountable for their use of the data. They operate virtually outside the penumbra of legal liability not only because their access, use, and misuse of personal data goes unrecognized, but also because they are not in a direct commercial relationship or in privity of contract with the consumer. Largely because of this lack of privity, third-party entities have little incentive to protect, or even ensure the accuracy of, personal data.

These third-party actors are often information brokers and data miners; prominent examples of such companies are ChoicePoint and Acxiom.[19] Their specialty is the collection, aggregation, and analysis of personal data from a wide range of public and private sources;[20] often the information is used for profiling and marketing purposes.[21] ChoicePoint, for example, "owns an astounding 19 billion records, about 65 times as many pieces of information as there are people in the United States. As a result, ChoicePoint knows more about most people than the federal government does."[22]

The mishandling and careless treatment of our personal data at the hands of third-party offenders takes many forms, such as the unauthorized disclosures of personal information to inappropriate parties, security breaches due to hacking and insider abuse, and the cavalier sharing of information from these third-party companies to numerous companies down the line.

Such data errors and data insecurity lead to problems such as consumer fraud, identity theft, and credit nightmares for millions of individuals.[23] For example, identity theft cost individual victims $5 billion in out-of-pocket expenses in 2003.[24] There is a fundamental tension between consumers, who have a pressing interest in their private information, and private companies, which have enormous economic incentives to share and sell that private information.

II. UTILIZING RESTITUTION AS A REMEDY

A. The Restitutionary Doctrine

In these shadow offender scenarios, principles of restitution should be applied to remedy cases of unjust enrichment to third-party companies that mishandle proprietary data.

Of course, there already exist a limited number of legal methods—primarily statutory—by which to reach such third-party actors. For example, under the federal Fair Credit Reporting Act, an individual may sue a credit reporting agency such as Experian or Equifax for providing information to a party who does not have a permissible purpose for that information—a typical permissible party being an entity or individual such as a creditor, insurer, employer, or landlord.[25] Another example is Section 5 of the Federal Trade Commission Act,[26] which prohibits unfair and deceptive trade practices in commerce. Thus companies can be held liable for using personal data in ways that violate the express provisions of their privacy policies or other statements made to consumers. Finally, state laws might provide stronger information privacy protection than federal statutory or common law.[27]

Restitution, however, is particularly well-suited for the type of third-party offender cases discussed in this chapter, and it has significant advantages over the traditional legal options.

Restitution, which is properly understood both as a source of liability and a remedy,[28] looks to the value of a benefit conferred on a defendant by a plaintiff. The restitution cause of action springs from the receipt of a benefit "under circumstances such that its retention without payment would result in the unjust enrichment of the defendant at the expense of the plaintiff."[29] As a remedy, "the defendant must either restore the benefit in question (or its traceable product), or else pay money in the amount necessary to eliminate unjust enrichment."[30]

The defendant does not have to act tortiously, wrongfully, or in bad faith[31] in its acquisition of a benefit (although in such cases the remedy may be determined by reference to plaintiff's losses rather than defendant's benefit)[32] and the remedy of restitution is not punitive.[33] Indeed, "enrichment" merely requires that a person "has received a benefit. A person is unjustly enriched if the retention of the benefit would be unjust."[34] Not only is the law of restitution not tied to tortious or wrongful behavior, but also there is no requirement that a defendant dispossessed a plaintiff of property, chattels, or money[35]—or even that the plaintiff performed a service for the defendant. Rather, a person confers a benefit to another under the law of restitution if he or she "in any way adds to the other's security or advantage";[36] "the word 'benefit,' therefore, denotes any form of advantage. The advantage for which a person ordinarily must pay is pecuniary advantage; it is not, however, necessarily so limited."[37] And of course, no contractual relationship need exist for a restitutionary cause of action to arise. In fact, although contract law recognizes a remedy of restitution for breaches of contracts[38] and other situations peculiar to contractual situations (such as impossibility), the restitution cause of action is a quasi-contractual remedy; in other words, it is implied by law.

Modern restitutionary scholars have identified one of the primary conundrums inherent in restitutionary claims—namely, that although restitution is partially equitable in nature and "is the one aspect of our legal system that makes a direct appeal to standards of equitable and conscientious behavior,"[39] it is nevertheless necessary to attempt to identify the legal boundaries of restitutionary liability so that the law of restitution does not devolve into a vast category of cognizable claims based merely in morality rather than "the question of legal obligation."[40] However, the power of restitutionary theory lies precisely in its reliance on "general principles"; as commentators have noted, although such legal quandaries concerning the precise limitations of specific causes of action exist in other areas of the law, "restitution claims generate problematic cases more frequently." Certainly, a dose of legal realism requires an acceptance that such "troublesome cases will result from both the indeterminancy of rules and from the want of comprehensiveness in any set of rules—conditions from which no escape is either possible or desirable."[41] Utilizing general principles of restitution allows for recovery in cases, such as data mishandling scenarios, wherein corporate practices may otherwise generally escape public notice or accountability.

B. Imposing Restitutionary Liability on Shadow Offenders

In specific cases of imposing liability on shadow offenders for improper handling or use of private data, restitution would constitute both the source of liability and the basis of remedy. Liability in such cases would be imposed not for mere use of that data but rather for the mishandling and misuse of that data and the improper benefits that accrue. Of course, we might seek to expand the restitutionary cause of action to include the larger problem of personal data trafficking in general, particularly at the hands of shadow offenders—regardless of whether some mishandling or misuse results—but such an expansion is beyond the scope of this chapter.

Significantly, as discussed, there is no requirement that a defendant acted wrongfully or tortiously in restitution cases, because "[t]he basis of a liability in restitution is that the defendant has been enriched without legal justification at the expense of the plaintiff; it is not that defendant has necessarily done anything wrong."[42] As a practical matter, however, recovery in cases wherein data trafficking companies merely use and aggregate data in the normal course of business might prove more difficult, given the relatively wide latitude such companies are given in regard to utilizing personal data in commercial manners.[43] The challenge is in showing some benefit to defendants that a court is prepared to recognize as "unjust"; in cases of mishandling, misuse, careless use, and similar situations in which personal data can be shown to have been improperly safeguarded, a court is arguably more likely to find such unjust enrichment on the part of defendants.[44]

As recovery in these shadow offender cases, defendants would pay in restitution to the plaintiff the extent to which the defendant profited or benefited from the data of the plaintiff. In the case of the Acxiom hacking example introduced at the outset of this chapter, the hypothetical plaintiffs would argue that Acxiom's use of their personal data constituted "the receipt of an economic benefit under circumstances such that its retention without payment would result in the unjust enrichment of the defendant at the expense of the plaintiff."[45] Acxiom's failure to properly secure and safeguard the personal data of an untold number of individuals would constitute the basis of the restitutionary claim. Similarly, in the Torch Concepts case, Torch Concepts' mistreatment of the personal data of the JetBlue passengers would form the basis for a restitutionary claim. In other words, individuals whose personal data were mishandled or misused by a third-party company would argue that it would constitute unjust enrichment to allow the defendant to have created the situation that gives rise to the misuse of data, to benefit from that situation, and to leave the individuals empty handed. This is true even if the consumer was not harmed in any demonstrable manner.

Again, the focus is not merely on the fact that the defendant was enriched at the expense of the plaintiff, but specifically on the fact that the defendant was enriched under circumstances that are deemed unjust.

Crucially, it is largely irrelevant whether the "first party actor" in such cases (oftentimes the retail or service company that compiled their consumers' data in the first instance) may be held liable for improper or deceptive use of consumer data. In many cases, such actors will be in privity of contract with the consumer, and claims based on breach of contract may prove successful against such companies for using personal data in a manner that runs afoul of the contract between the company and the individual.[46] However, companies can easily escape exposure to such claims of contractual breach by, for example, simply altering their privacy policies[47] or limiting statements regarding their use of personal customer information. Moreover, a restitutionary remedy levied against third-party shadow offenders is powerful precisely because it also seeks to place accountability for improper use of personal data at the doorsteps of the broader cluster of companies involved in data mishandling, rather than myopically focusing on the obvious candidate for liability—namely, the company that originally collected the data from the individual. Liability may also be alleged against "first party" companies on the basis of a myriad of alternative claims, including unjust enrichment. Yet the power of allowing restitutionary recovery against the companies with whom the data were shared is that it allows for the possibility of redressing the problem of personal data abuse at every level of the data-trafficking industry, rather than merely reaching the usual and most obvious suspects.

C. Calculating Recovery

In these shadow offender cases, recovery should be measured by the benefit to the defendant and should take the form of monetary compensation. Generally, we would expect that recovery could be measured by the pecuniary advantage gained from use of the plaintiff's data. However, recovery need not be measured in terms of direct monetary gain,[48] and therefore could be measured by some other gain or benefit. In the Torch Concepts case, Torch arguably benefited from the use of the personal data of JetBlue passengers in ways other than direct pecuniary profit, such as its use of passenger data to build a proprietary terrorism risk-assessment model. Although Torch's ultimate benefit may have been directly monetary, its immediate and direct benefit might also be calculated by reference to the increase in the value of its intellectual property portfolio, which now encompasses the unique model generated by access to the JetBlue passenger data.

Restitutionary recovery would prove especially fruitful to plaintiffs in these data mishandling cases because they are cases in which "plaintiff's damages are hard to measure and defendant's profits are clear.[49] . . . In such cases, restitution of defendant's profits has sometimes been thought of as a proxy for plaintiff's losses. But restitution of the profits is available even when they bear no relation to plaintiff's losses."[50] Thus, for example, although a victim of identity theft may not be able to prove his or her damages, it may be easy to measure the defendant's profit from use of the plaintiff's data.

These shadow offender cases have the unique characteristic of, by and large, constituting cases wherein the plaintiff's losses and the defendant's gains will often be disproportionate.[51] In this way, they are analogous to intellectual property restitution cases, wherein "[t]he most controversial cases arise when the property produces gains to the defendant that clearly exceed plaintiff's losses. The property might change in value so that it is more valuable in defendant's hands, or simply more valuable at the time of trial, than it was in plaintiff's hands before the wrongful transfer. Or the defendant may put the fruits of his wrong to some profitable use, earning consequential gains that exceed plaintiff's consequential losses."[52] In data mishandling cases, as in these intellectual property restitution cases, "[r]estitution as a measure of recovery matters precisely when defendant's gain exceeds plaintiff's provable loss, either because plaintiff's loss is small or because it is hard to prove."[53]

On the opposite spectrum, plaintiff's losses may be high and the defendant's gains disproportionately low because the defendant's gain from that particular plaintiff's specific data is an infinitesimal portion of the benefit derived by the defendant. Of course, in a class action suit, the aggregate benefit might be quite large, but even in the case of an individual plaintiff, a jurisprudential basis for adequate recovery exists. Significantly, when "the defendant was tortious in his acquisition of the benefit,"[54] the law of restitution allows plaintiffs to recover their losses rather than the defendants' gain.[55] In addition, a defendant must also pay all profit derived from the benefit if it was "consciously tortious"[56] or intentionally acted wrongfully[57] in acquiring the benefit. Therefore, victims of data misuse and mishandling might be able to recover the amount of their losses and possibly all of defendant's profits when the defendant acted tortiously in acquiring the benefit.

However, there remains a crucial quandary in the question of recovery: Is recovery appropriate in cases wherein the defendant is not directly enriched by the mishandling of the data, for example, in cases of hacking? For instance, in the Acxiom case, Acxiom ostensibly did not receive a "benefit" from the hacking of its databases.

Data traffickers are, of course, sometimes directly enriched from mishandling of consumer data, and therefore the improper handling of the data and the defendant's enrichment go hand-in-hand.

But even when these two—the mishandling of the data, on the one hand, and the enrichment of the defendant, on the other—are *not* the foreseeable pattern of events, that is, are not the necessary cause and effect, a broader view of the proper limits of restitution is necessary. In all of these cases, the improper handling of personal data is tied to and inherently bound up with the benefit to the defendant. The personal data of an individual have directly conferred an advantage on the data-trafficking company, and because the individual's data were mishandled in a way that leaves the individual disadvantaged and in a worse position, the law of restitution should deem the retention of that advantage without payment under such circumstances to be unjust.[58]

D. The Advantages of the Restitutionary Approach

The restitutionary remedy is particularly well-suited to these third-party data offenses, and in particular, it has distinct advantages over some of the other possible approaches.

First, the restitutionary approach properly encourages third-party data traffickers to prevent mishandling of data. Restitution, in general, "seeks to punish the wrongdoer by taking his ill-gotten gains, thus removing his incentive to perform the wrongful act again."[59] In shadow offender cases, a restitutionary remedy that looks to the amount to which a company is unjustly enriched is more likely to act as a powerful disincentive vis-à-vis the counteracting profit incentive that leads to cavalier data treatment, inasmuch as it leads to corporate internalization of the costs of data mishandling.[60]

Second, a restitutionary remedy goes beyond causes of action based in a promise—such as breach of contract, fraudulent misrepresentation, or deceptive trade practices—all of which rely on a claim that a company handled one's data in a way that it said it would not do.[61] Thus it would be possible to reach one of the primary actors in the incident because there is no hurdle of finding some explicit promise made and then broken.

In contrast, a restitutionary claim is not based in promise, and therefore does not rely on the presumption that a company has made a specific set of promises before liability can be found. In many cases, of course, the contractual relationship regarding informational privacy existing between a company and its customers is governed merely by a privacy policy drafted by the company; such policies "often simply serve to notify individuals of the control that they do not have"[62] and are easily modified in order to provide an ever-increasing amount of data use by companies. To the contrary, restitutionary liability is based on the idea of unjust enrichment rather than a set of broken promises.

Third, a restitutionary remedy similarly allows us to move beyond causes of actions for personal data use based in tort—such as misappropriation of name and likeness[63]—that have met with little success in the courts. Of course, in some restitution cases, liability arises because the defendant has accrued some benefit through the commission of a tort. However, commission of a tort is not a requisite for a restitutionary claim.

Fourth, most of the harm from lapses in personal data security—which takes the practical form of societal problems such as fraud and identity theft—currently falls on the consumer. Hence, one of the added benefits of a restitutionary remedy is that it obtains a remedy for the individual victim, unlike public remedies such as the Federal Trade Commission Act, which has as its redress civil penalties collected by the FTC and public injunctions.

Fifth, a restitutionary remedy does not engender the difficulty of trying to place an inherent value on personal data or compute the precise mathematical value of one's own personal information. Rather, we are generally placing a value on what the defendant gained—for example, the extent to which the database company was unjustly enriched. And this also, interestingly, avoids the problems inherent in attempting to treat personal data as property. The leading critics of such an approach have argued that attempting to treat personal data as property is misguided, first, because it leads to jurisprudential roadblocks such as the commodification of personal data, and, second, because it encounters practical roadblocks such as the likelihood of inefficient and expensive bargaining over specific rights to personal data.[64] Restitution allows us to analyze the benefits, profits, or other advantages procured from data, rather than the precise value of individual data fragments. Indeed, the nullification of profits and ill-gotten gains is the aspect of the restitutionary remedy that could prove so powerful in the rebalancing of power in the privacy wars between consumers and corporations.

III. CONCLUSION

The restitutionary remedy argued for here is not without practical and jurisprudential limitations. It assumes some unfair quality to the nature of the relationship between the defendant and the plaintiff, such as a company profiting from use of an individual's data while, at the same time, failing to ensure adequate security measures or failing to prevent cavalier treatment of that data. It therefore does not reach those cases that do not involve improper handling of data. Similarly, although the restitutionary remedy certainly incentivizes data mishandlers to safeguard individuals' data privacy,[65] it is arguably merely a back-end measure that operates as a sort of a tax on bad actors rather than a front-end, prohibitive measure that would operate as a more complete safeguard against privacy abuses.

Nevertheless, restitution is a promising remedy because it would strongly incentivize such third-party companies to properly safeguard personal information where, traditionally, few such incentives have existed. Moreover, such a remedy allows us to move beyond the problems associated with purely public remedies, causes of action based solely in contract, and the inherent difficulties of placing monetary value on personal data.

NOTES

1. *See* Richard Behar, Never Heard Of Acxiom? Chances Are It's Heard Of You, *Fortune*, Feb. 23, 2004, at 140.

2. *Id.*

3. Acxiom handles over a billion records each day, and does over $1 billion in annual sales. *See* Behar, *supra* note 1. Acxiom has detailed and personal information on most Americans, such as social security numbers, credit card accounts, and buying patterns.

4. *See* Behar, *supra* note 1.

5. *See* Behar, *supra* note 1. Personal life events "such as marriage, the purchase of a home, the birth of a child or preparation for retirement are likely to result in a cluster change." Daily Briefing, *The Commercial Appeal*, Aug. 4, 2004, at C2 (2004 WL 84688060).

6. *See* Behar, *supra* note 1.

7. The information included, at a minimum, name, address, telephone number, and itinerary-related information. Electronic Privacy Information Center's Complaint Against JetBlue Airways and Acxiom Corporation to the Federal Trade Commission (Sept. 22, 2003), available at http://www.epic.org/privacy/airtravel/JetBlue/ftccomplaint.html [hereafter EPIC Complaint]. *See also* Consolidated Class Action Complaint, *In re JetBlue Privacy Litigation*, 2004 WL 578605, (Feb. 4, 2004).

8. Torch Concepts received the personal data directly from Acxiom, which was JetBlue's subcontractor, at JetBlue's request. *See* EPIC Complaint, *supra* note 7. *See also* Edward Alden, Protests Force Curbs on Tools of Suspicionless Surveillance, *Financial Times*, Oct. 2, 2003, at

22. Torch Concepts was a subcontractor of SRS Technologies, a California-based company, and it was allegedly "through [the contract with SRS Technologies that] Torch used [the passenger] information to perform a highly detailed passenger profile study." Consolidated Class Action Complaint, *In re JetBlue Privacy Litigation*, 2004 WL 578605 (Feb. 4, 2004).

9. Department of Homeland Security Privacy Office, *Report to the Public on Events Surrounding JetBlue Transfer* (February 20, 2004), available at http://www.cdt.org/privacy/20040220 dhsreport.pdf.

10. Consolidated Class Action Complaint, *In re JetBlue Privacy Litigation*, 2004 WL 578605 (Feb. 4, 2004).

11. This wide latitude is subject only to limited exceptions such as medical records, video rental records, student records, and cable television consumer data. The financial services industry is subject to the relatively watered-down Graham-Leach-Bliley Act of 1999. *See* CALPIRG Education Fund, Financial Privacy in the States, 4-5 (2004). *See generally* CALPIRG, Privacy Denied: A Survey of Bank Privacy Policies (Aug. 2002); Federal Trade Commission, Financial Privacy: The Gramm-Leach Bliley Act, available at http://www.ftc.gov/privacy/glbact/index .html (last accessed on Sept. 13, 2004). "Affiliate information sharing," one commentator argues, "represents a growing risk to individuals' privacy. Companies such as Citibank, with its 1,900 affiliates, or Bank of America, which has more than 1,000 entities in its corporate family, can transmit your information for cross-selling or marketing to an unlimited degree under federal law." Chris Hoofnagle, Is Your Life an Open Book? And Who's Reading It?, *Akron Beacon J.* (Sept. 8, 2003), available at http://www.ohio.com/mld/beaconjournal/news/editorial/6706395 .htm?1c. In addition, furnishers of personal credit information are subject to the Fair Credit Reporting Act, 15 U.S.C. 1681, *et seq.*

12. "Over the past few decades, there have been dramatic expansions in the quality, the breadth, and the intensity of programs that use new generations of technology for gathering, storing, sharing and using information . . . . If we add up all the frequently overlapping profiles encompassing medical records, academic and professional performance, credit ratings, consumer behavior, insurance records, driving records, law enforcement data, welfare agency information, child support enforcement programs, Internet communications, and other information systems, it is safe to say that much of the significant activity of our lives is now subject to systematic observation and analysis." Jeffrey Rosen, *The Unwanted Gaze: The Destruction of Privacy in America* 12 (2000).

13. Samuel D. Warren and Louis D. Brandeis, The Right to Privacy, 4 *Harv. L. Rev.* 193 (1890).

14. *See generally*, Julie Cohen, Examined Lives: Informational Privacy and the Subject as Object, 52 *Stan. L. Rev.* 1573 (2000).

15. Pamela Samuelson, Privacy as Intellectual Property, 52 *Stan. L. Rev.* 1125 (2000).

16. For example, in the early 1990s, "powerful financial interests, led by MasterCard, VISA and the big banks and department stores[,] trumped the efforts of [privacy groups] to enact a new federal law [protecting credit rights]. These firms, responsible for many of the mistakes in credit reports, not only sought to block proposals to make them liable for their errors, but also desired sweeping exceptions to the [Fair Credit Reporting Act]'s privacy protection." PIRG, PIRG Identity Theft II: Section II: Key Fair Credit Reporting Act Changes Effective September

30, 1997, available at http://www.pirg.org/reports/consumer/xfiles/page6.htm (last accessed on May 3, 2004).

17. *See generally* Marcy Peek, Passing Beyond Identity on the Internet: Espionage and Counterespionage in the Internet Age, 28 *Vt. L. Rev.* 91 (2003). *Cf.* John Henry Schlegel, But Pierre, If We Can't Think Normatively, What Are We to Do?, 57 *U. Miami L. Rev.* 955, 957–58 (2003) ("[T]o me, it still seems difficult to maintain, if only by silence, that violence, the exercise of power that counts, the oppressive preference for some people or activities over others, is not an integral part of the Rule of Law. . . . It is not just explicit power that I am talking about either. In many ways it is the implicit power that law conveys that is the most violent, for it requires not even the raising of a hand.").

18. *See generally* Samuelson, *supra* note 15, discussing the collection and processing of personal information in cyberspace.

19. *See* Edmund Mierzwinski, Data Dealers Seizing Control Over Our Lives, U.S. PIRG, available at http://www.pirg.org/consumer/dsefoped.htm (last accessed on Sept. 12, 2004).

20. "By drawing from . . . three sources of information—public records, internal records, and external records—profilers may have a detailed marketing dossier, which includes demographic and psychographic information. A profile available from a national-list compiler could include: name, gender, address, telephone number, age, estimated income, household size and composition, dwelling type, length of residence, car ownership, pet ownership, responsiveness to mail offers, contributor status, credit card ownership, lifestyle, hobbies, interests, and neighborhood characteristics including average education, house value, and racial composition." United States Department of Commerce, Privacy and the NII: Safeguarding Telecommunications Personal Information (Oct. 1995), available at http://www.ntia.doc.gov/ntiahome/privwhitepaper.html.

21. The data are culled from a wide variety of sources such as credit card records, motor vehicle records, court databases, magazine subscriptions, survey results, and product warranty cards. "ChoicePoint and other collectors scoop up these pieces of information and preserve them electronically. They buy the data—sometimes from each other—or obtain them from public sources, such as court and property records. Then, when their customers ask, ChoicePoint blends the pieces into a picture of you." Shane Harris, Private Eye, *Gov't Executive* (Mar. 16, 2004), available at http://www.govexec.com/features/0304/0304s1.htm.

22. Harris, *supra* note 21.

23. *See generally* CALPIRG Education Fund, *Financial Privacy in the States* (Feb. 6, 2004), available at http://calpirg.org/CA.asp?id2=12145&id3=CA& (last accessed on Sept. 13, 2004); CALPIRG Privacy Rights Clearinghouse, *Nowhere to Turn: Victims Speak Out on Identity Theft* (May 2000), available at http://www.privacyrights.org/ar/idtheft2000.htm (last accessed on Sept. 13, 2004).

24. Federal Trade Commission, *Identity Theft Survey Report* (Sept. 2003), available at http://www.ftc.gov/os/2003/09/synovatereport.pdf (last accessed on Sept. 13, 2004).

25. Federal Trade Commission, A Summary of Your Rights Under the Fair Credit Reporting Act, available at http://www.ftc.gov/bcp/conline/edcams/fcra/summary.htm (last accessed on Sept. 13, 2004).

26. 15 U.S.C. § 45(a).

27. *See, e.g,* California Constitution, art. 1 (giving individuals the "inalienable right" to privacy). However, "California is one of the few states to have a constitutional provision on privacy and is unique in the application of that provision to the private sector." Joel Reidenberg, Privacy Wrongs in Search of Remedies, 54 *Hastings L. J.* 877, 895 (2003). Also, California statutory law "requires companies and state agencies to notify California residents of certain security breaches that could result in identity theft. The law requires notice if an unauthorized person has acquired an individual's name and either Social Security number, driver's license number, or financial account number. The notice gives an individual the chance to take steps to protect against identity theft, such as putting a fraud alert on credit files." Scam-Safe: California's 2003 Law for Consumer Security, available at http://www.scamsafe.com/scamsafe/2004/03/californias_200.html (last accessed on Sept. 13, 2004) (citing Civil Code §§ 1798.29, 1798.82-1798.84 (2003)). Various state laws may also provide protection against unfair and deceptive trade practices. *See, e.g.,* Cal. Business and Profession Code § 17200, *et seq.;* New York General Business Law § 349. *See also* Revised Uniform Deceptive Trade Practices Act (1966).

28. *See* Tracy A. Thomas, Justice Scalia Reinvents Restitution, 36 *Loy. L.A. L. Rev.* 1063, 1066 (2003) ("[R]estitution as a remedy can be used with a restitution liability theory or with a regular type of contract, tort, or property claim."); David F. Partlett & Russell Weaver, Restitution; Ancient Wisdom, 36 *Loy. L.A.. L. Rev.* 975, 981 (2003) (noting the "misperception that restitution is itself just a remedy."). *See also Black's Law Dictionary* (7th ed. 1999) ("[Q]uantum meruit is . . . an equitable remedy to provide restitution for unjust enrichment. It is often pleaded as an alternative claim in a breach-of-contract case so that the plaintiff can recover even if the contract is voided.").

29. Restatement (Third) of Restitution & Unjust Enrichment § 1 (Tentative Draft 2004). *See also* Restatement (First) of Restitution § 1 (1937) ("A person who is unjustly enriched at the expense of another is liable in restitution to the other.").

30. Restatement (Third) of Restitution & Unjust Enrichment § 1 (Tentative Draft 2004). *See also Interform Co. v. Mitchell,* 575 F. 2d 1270, 1278 n. 4 (9th Cir. 1978) ("[I]n unjust enrichment [cases] . . . the recovery granted is not based upon a contract and . . . the underlying standard for the recovery is the net benefit conferred upon the defendant."); John D. Calamari & Joseph M. Perillo, *The Law of Contracts* § 9-23, at 376 (3d ed. 1987) (" 'Restitution' is an ambiguous term, sometimes referring to the disgorging of something which has been taken and at times referring to compensation for injury done.").

31. *See, e.g,. Werlin v. Reader's Digest Ass'n,* 528 F. Supp. 451, 466 (S.D.N.Y. 1981) (Defendant held liable under theory of unjust enrichment where it benefited at the expense of plaintiff yet "did not act in bad faith."); Restatement (First) of Restitution § 1, cmt. e (1937), stating that "[A] person who has been unjustly deprived of his property or its value or the value of his labor may be entitled to maintain an action for restitution against another although the other has not in fact been enriched thereby. Thus, a person who refuses to return goods for which he innocently paid full value to a thief is liable to the owner for their full value. . . . Likewise, a physician who attends and skillfully but unsuccessfully treats an unconscious woman, the victim of an accident, is entitled to recover the value of his services. . . ."

32. *See infra,* Part II, Section C of this chapter ("Calculating Recovery").

33. Restatement (First) of Restitution I, 8, 2 Intro. Note (1937). *See also 3Com Corp. v. Electronics Recovery Specialists, Inc.*, 104 F. Supp. 2d 932 (N.D. Ill. 2000) (punitive damages not recoverable in restitution cases); Andrew Kull, Restitution's Outlaws, 78 *Chi.-Kent L. Rev.* 17, 17 (2003).

34. Restatement (First) of Restitution § 1, cmt. a (1937).

35. *Cf. Werlin, supra* note 31, at 465 (In certain intellectual property cases, "the courts have held that, even if the plaintiff has no property right in an idea, and even though no express or implied—in-fact contract for the sale or use of such an idea has been established, the defendant may, in appropriate circumstances, nevertheless be found liable to the plaintiff in quasi-contract on a theory of unjust enrichment.").

36. *Olwell v. Nye & Nissen Co.*, 26 Wash. 2d 282, 285, 173 P. 2d 652, 653 (1946) (quoting Restatement (First) of Restitution § 1 (1937)).

37. Restatement (First) of Restitution § 1, cmt. b (1937).

38. Whereas the Restatement of Restitution primarily considers the benefit obtained by a defendant, the Restatement of Contracts recognizes two means of measuring restitution: first, the reasonable value of what the plaintiff gave to the defendant and second, the increase in the defendant's property or interests. *See* Restatement (Second) of Contracts § 371 (1981).

39. Restatement (Third) of Restitution & Unjust Enrichment § 1 (Tentative Draft 2004).

40. *Id.*

41. Restatement (Second) of Restitution § 1, cmt. d (Tentative Draft No. 1 1983).

42. Kull, *supra* note 33, at 17.

43. *Cf.* Douglas Laycock, The Scope and Significant of Restitution, 67 *Tex. L. Rev.* 1277, 1289 (1989) ("[T]he judicial reaction to the underlying wrong surely affects the choice of remedy.").

44. *See* Julie E. Cohen, Privacy, Ideology, and Technology: A Response to Jeffrey Rosen, 89 *Geo. L. J.* 2029, 2034 (2001) (noting that "the harvesting of private information is driven by both market and Enlightenment ideologies" but that such harvesting has limits in a society which "has determined that the common good requires limits on the profit-seeking behavior of private entities.").

45. Restatement (First) of Restitution § 1 (1937).

46. For example, in the consolidated class action suit against JetBlue, plaintiffs allege that: "JetBlue maintains on its website a clear privacy policy . . . JetBlue specifically represents that any financial and personal information collected by JetBlue 'is not shared with any third parties, and is protected by secure servers,' and also claims to have in place security measures to protect against the loss, misuse and alteration of consumer information under JetBlue's control. . . . Despite these self-imposed public assurances that created an obligation . . . not to act in derogation of JetBlue's privacy policy and to refuse to share personal and financial information it collected, in September 2002, JetBlue turned over passenger information to Torch Concepts. . . . Notably, prior to turning over such data, JetBlue failed to obtain the authorization or consent of passengers necessary under its privacy policy. . . ." Consolidated Class Action Complaint, *In re JetBlue Privacy Litigation*, 2004 WL 578605 (Feb. 4, 2004).

47. *See infra*, Part II, Section D of this chapter ("The Advantages of the Restitutionary Approach").

48. Restatement (First) of Restitution § 1, cmt. b (1937).

49. Analogously, Judge Posner has explained that in copyright infringement cases, "[b]y

preventing infringers from obtaining any net profit it makes any would-be infringer negotiate directly with the owner of a copyright that he wants to use, rather than bypass the market by stealing the copyright and forcing the owner to seek compensation from the courts for his loss. Since the infringer's gain might exceed the owner's loss, especially as loss is measured by a court, limiting damages to that loss would not effectively deter this kind of forced exchange." *Taylor v. Meirick*, 712 F. 2d 1112, 1220 (7th Cir. 1983).

50. Laycock, *supra* note 43, at 1287.

51. Indeed, as the drafters of the Restatement (Second) of Restitution explained, "[c]ases of matching gain and loss are . . . only a limited class of the applications of contemporary restitution law. The principles stated in [the Restatement] incorporate not only factors of gain and loss, but also factors of fault and mistake, of inducement and reliance, and of motivation." Restatement (Second) of Restitution, Introductory Note (Tentative Draft No. 1 1983).

52. Laycock, *supra* note 43, at 1287.

53. *Id.* Thus, for example, in *LinkCo, Inc. v. Fujitsu Ltd.*, 232 F. Supp. 2d 182 (S.D.N.Y. 2002), the court explained that in cases of misappropriation of trade secrets, recovery may be calculated by reference to plaintiff's losses or defendant's unjust enrichment; in addition, where these calculations "provide inadequate compensation to the plaintiff," recovery may be calculated based on a "reasonable royalty," *i.e.*, "what the parties would have agreed to as a fair licensing price." *Id.* at 186. The royalty measure of damages "attempts to measure a hypothetically agreed value of what the defendant wrongfully obtained from plaintiff." *Id.* at 186 (quoting *Vermont Microsystems, Inc. v. Autodesk, Inc.*, 88 F. 3d 142, 151 (2d Cir. 1996). Although this "reasonable royalty" calculation would be unavailable to plaintiffs in personal information mishandling cases because personal information is not deemed "property" subject to the laws of intellectual property, such a calculation echoes the basis of recovery in unjust enrichment, inasmuch as it seeks to recoup wrongfully obtained benefits. Indeed, in trade secret misappropriation cases, courts have determined that "the lack of actual profits does not insulate the defendants from being obliged to pay for what they have wrongfully obtained." *Id.* at 186 (quoting *University Computing Co. v. Lykes-Youngstown Corp.*, 504 F. 2d 518, 536 (5th Cir. 1974) (citing *In re Cawood Patent*, 94 U.S. 695 (1876)).

54. Restatement (First) of Restitution § 155 (1937). *See also* Restatement (First) of Restitution I, 8, 2, Intro. Note (1937); *Olwell, supra* note 36, at 287, 654.

55. *See* Restatement (First) of Restitution § 155 (1937). For example, in a case in which the plaintiff repaired the defendant's boat engines to the benefit of the defendant, the court held that although the plaintiff was "entitled to recover the benefit he bestowed under a quasi-contract theory," no evidence was shown that "any tortious conduct on the owners' part caused them to receive the benefit"; the court determined that in such cases wherein the defendant did not tortiously acquire the benefit, "the measure of recovery is the value of what was received" rather than loss or cost to the plaintiff. *Kane v. Motor Vessel Leda*, 355 F. Supp. 796, 801 (E.D.La. 1972) (quoting Restatement (First) of Restitution § 155 (1937)).

56. Restatement (First) of Restitution § 155 (1937).

57. *See* Restatement (Third) of Restitution & Unjust Enrichment § 3 (Tentative Drafts 2004).

58. As discussed earlier, although such a direct connection is not a requisite for a restitutionary cause of action, it may have an impact on the level of recovery because "the more

culpable the defendant's behavior, and the more direct the connection between the profits and the wrongdoing, the more likely that plaintiff can recover all defendant's profits." *University of Colorado Foundation, Inc. v. American Cyanamid Co.*, 342 F. 3d 1298, 1311 (Fed. Cir. 2003). *See also* Laycock, *supra* note 43, at 1289 ("The more culpable defendant's behavior, and the more direct the connection between the profits and the wrongdoing, the more likely that plaintiff can recover all defendant's profits.").

59. Am. Jur. § 35, Difference Presented When Restitution Sought—Damages (2003).

60. *Cf.* Samuelson, *supra* note 15, at 1128-29 ("[A] property rights model [of information privacy] would force companies to internalize certain social costs of the widespread collection and use of personal data now borne by others.").

61. "The unjust enrichment claim in the context of a contract implied in law does not depend in any way upon a promise or privity between the parties." University of Colorado Foundation, 342 F. 3d at 1309 (quoting *Wistrand v. Leach Realty Co.*, 364 P. 2d 396, 397 (1961)). A cause of action based in unjust enrichment "arises 'not from consent of the parties, as in the case of contracts, express or implied in fact, but from the law of natural immutable justice and equity.'" *Id.* (quoting *DCB Construction Co. v. Cent. City Dev. Co.*, 965 P. 2d 115, 119 (Colo. 1998)).

62. Cohen, *supra* note 44, at 2041.

63. *See, e.g.*, Andrew J. McClurg, A Thousand Words Are Worth a Picture: A Privacy Tort Response to Consumer Data Profiling, 98 *Nw U. L. Rev.* 63, 69 (arguing for the utilization of the tort theory of misappropriation "as one way to address invasive consumer data profiling. Appropriation provides for liability against one who appropriates the identity of another for his own benefit, which is nearly always a commercial benefit."). *See also* Reidenberg, *supra* note 27, at 877, 893-94.

64. *See* Samuelson, *supra* note 15; Jessica Litman, Privacy and E-Commerce, 7 *B.U. J. Sci. & Tech. L.* 223 (2001).

65. Commentators have similarly argued that the use, aggregation, and distribution of personal data by data-trafficking companies "create externalities, or costs borne by others. Externalities are created when a person engages in an activity that imposes costs on others but is not required to take those costs into account when deciding whether to pursue the activity. The feelings experienced by consumers whose information is sold and used against their wishes constitute just such externalities." Jeff Sovern, Opting In, Opting Out, or No Options at All: The Fight for Control of Personal Information, 74 *Wash. L. Rev.* 1033, 1106 (1999).

8 IMPROVING SOFTWARE SECURITY

A Discussion of Liability
for Unreasonably Insecure Software

Jennifer A. Chandler

Jennifer A. Chandler is assistant professor of law, University of Ottawa. The author is grateful to Anupam Chander, Margaret Jane Radin, Jennifer Stisa Granick, Lauren Gelman, and the other organizers of the excellent symposium at Stanford Law School in March 2004 for the opportunity to participate.

Cybersecurity is in poor shape. Considerable sums are lost annually as a result of the many and varied attacks on Internet-connected computer systems. Although these losses have so far been mostly monetary, some people are concerned that the increasing tendency for critical infrastructures—such as energy distribution, communications, the military, emergency services, or transportation—to be linked to or dependent upon the Internet may result in more serious losses.[1]

There are a number of causes for this problem. Software is hurriedly released to the mass market containing well-known and recurring security-related flaws. Malefactors, no longer merely the stereotypical hacker but now groups intent on creating spam relay networks,[2] extortionists running "cyber-protection rackets" and demanding payment in exchange for calling off denial of service attacks,[3] blackmailers, identity thieves, and many others, are taking advantage of these security-related flaws and of many computer users' propensity to open any and all email attachments. The Internet has also become a battleground for spammers against anti-spam organizations,[4] for factions in the battle between the open-source community and the SCO Group,[5] and for private censorship of unpopular political speech.[6] Users of the Internet fail to take basic steps to secure their computers, including applying patches to vulnerable software, running current virus-scanning software, maintaining a firewall, and refraining from opening suspect email attachments. Nevertheless, the plight of users (particularly the administrators responsible for the computer networks of large organizations) is a difficult one. They must somehow keep up with vulnerability warnings[7] and software patches[8] that are released continuously.[9]

Although the entire blame for cyber insecurity cannot be placed on the makers of insecure software, without poor software, the attacks by opportunistic criminals and the bumbling behavior of computer users would result in far less damage. In other words, a significant part of the problem can be traced to poor software quality.

The problem of cybersecurity is probably best tackled on many fronts simultaneously, including through efforts to enforce cyber crime laws,[10] measures by Internet service providers to help secure the network, improvements in the security-consciousness of end-users, and, perhaps most essential, concerted efforts to improve software security. A multipronged approach is likely necessary given that some insecurities may possibly be most efficiently addressed through modifications to user behavior.[11] Furthermore, improvements on one front may cause attackers to turn their attention to other sources of vulnerability. These options were considered in more detail in a previous article.[12] This chapter will focus on tackling the cybersecurity problem by improving software security, and, in particular, the possibility of using tort liability to do so.

Section I of this chapter will describe the problem with software security. Section II will discuss the role of tort liability and will suggest that the best plaintiff in a hypothetical lawsuit against the developer of unreasonably insecure software would be the victim of a distributed denial of service (DDOS) attack. Section III will address the hypothetical lawsuit in greater detail, discussing a theory under which certain software developers owe a duty of care to those connected to the Internet, and discussing the standard of care that should be demanded of those software developers.

I. THE PROBLEM WITH SOFTWARE SECURITY

The recurrence of security-related software flaws in common software has been identified by many as one of the key reasons for the cybersecurity problem. The National Cyber Security Partnership, launched in December 2003, and made up of security experts from the private, academic, and public sectors, has been working within five task forces, each addressing an aspect of cybersecurity improvement.[13] The Software Development Task Force,[14] which is the task force devoted to promoting security through improvements in the software development process, released its report on April 1, 2004.[15] It noted that "a primary cause is that much of the software supporting the U.S. cyber infrastructure cannot withstand security attacks. These attacks exploit vulnerabilities in software systems."[16]

The economic losses associated with software insecurity are considerable. The Software Development Task Force report estimates that tens of billions of dollars are lost annually in the United States alone as a result of software security flaws and the expense of patching critical security-related flaws.[17]

Two questions arise from these observations. First, is software really "so bad?" In other words, does software's current level of insecurity produce losses that exceed what it would cost to improve its security? The question is not whether software produces a net benefit to society despite its current level of insecurity, as most would agree that it certainly does. Instead, the issue is whether the net value of software could be increased by taking steps to improve software security. Second, if it really is "so bad," why is that? Each of these questions will now be addressed briefly.

In theory, the free market should generate an optimal balance of software price and quality attributes (in terms of both functionality and security). In this account, buyers express their acceptance of the current balance by continuing to purchase buggy software in droves.[18]

However, as is often the case, the market suffers from various imperfections that make it possible that the optimal balance of price and quality is not being achieved. Three sources of imperfection come to mind. First, the market for key pieces of software relevant to Internet-connected computers systems may not be perfectly competitive, and this may prevent the market from achieving the optimal outcome. Certain key software programs such as the Windows operating system and the Internet Explorer browser have achieved near complete market share. Reasons other than the quality of these programs, such as the existence of strong economies of scale, network externalities (particularly where interoperability with competitors' programs is impeded by the dominant incumbent), and high switching costs may contribute to this state of affairs.[19]

Second, although the market depends on the existence of perfectly informed participants in order to generate an optimal outcome, the average purchaser is incapable of assessing the security-related qualities of complex products such as modern software. The situation may be better where source code is publicly available, although this is subject to debate.[20] These "information failures" are aggravated by the efforts of some software vendors to suppress the publication of independent product reviews through "anti-benchmarking" clauses.[21]

Third, software security presents an externality problem.[22] The insecurity of one user's computer imposes costs on others, whether the computer is conscripted for later use in launching a DDOS attack[23] in a spam relay network, or whether it merely takes part in the propagation of malicious code (such as viruses or worms). In each of these examples, the user of the insecure computer may suffer consequences ranging from mild inconvenience (such as slowing of the computer or complaints from the irate recipients of spam) to major losses (for example, when malicious code destroys data or records a user's sensitive information). However, there may also be considerable harm later visited on others (particularly in the case of DDOS attacks) that is not faced by the user of the insecure computer. As a result, such users are likely to underestimate the total cost of their insecurity, and will thus be less likely to invest in security at the socially optimal level. These users will not demand the appropriate level of security in the software marketplace.

In answering the question of whether software is currently "bad" from the security perspective, it is also important to consider the hidden costs of cyber insecurity. We might benefit even more from the Internet if it were more secure. Certain applications and participants may be foreclosed from using the Internet if it remains or becomes increasingly insecure. Nevertheless, it is also important to note that improvements in software quality will be costly as well, and higher purchase prices for software may also exclude certain applications and participants. To the extent that security improvements make software less flexible or user-friendly, they may also discourage users and reduce the benefits of the Internet.

Assuming that software really is "bad" in the sense that all of the insecurity-related costs outweigh the costs of improving security, it is not immediately clear that the answer is to improve the security of software before it is released. The current approach to software vulnerabilities for mass-market software products is to develop software rapidly, albeit with some testing and attempts at quality assurance, and to "patch"[24] flaws as they come to light after the software is widely deployed. It is necessary to consider whether the patching system is a better response than investment in improved software development processes, which, as discussed later on, might impose considerable costs as well. I will not address this point further here,[25] as there appears to be a fairly solid consensus that software flaws are far cheaper to address before the software is released into the market.

Graff and van Wyk cite statistics suggesting that the cost of fixing an error with a patch after release is sixty times as much as the cost of fixing the error at the design stage.[26] Furthermore, the patch system itself causes problems. Some users fail to keep up with patch installation,[27] patches themselves contain errors[28] or interfere with existing software or system configurations,[29] and the patch delivery system may turn into another point of insecurity if hackers are able to fool users into downloading virus-laden patches.[30] The patch delivery system may also be misused by software vendors surreptitiously to alter software functions (for example, by including digital rights management technologies for copyright protection purposes) or the terms of the end-user license agreements.[31] Software engineering experts agree that the "penetrate and patch" approach to security is a poor approach to the software security problem.[32] "[A]s the Anderson report . . . noted over three decades ago, "penetrate and patch" is a fatally flawed concept: after a flaw was patched, the penetrators always found other old flaws or new flaws introduced because of or in the patch."[33]

Assuming that software really is bad, in that greater resources would efficiently be devoted to improving it, the second question arises. Why is software "so bad?"

It appears that the incentives facing software developers are such that they focus on speed to market and new features rather than on the security-related aspects of quality.[34] Buyers, for reasons already discussed, do not demand enough security.[35] From the software developer's perspective, success is achieved by capturing market share for a given application and by maintaining revenue flow by convincing buyers to upgrade to the next version. The next version must have new "bells and whistles" in order to induce users to upgrade, producing an effect known as "feature creep,"[36] (or, to be fair, "feature improvement" for those who welcome the new functions). As a result, speed to market and the introduction of new features are the key driving forces in the area of software application development for personal computers.[37] All of this generates a situation of rapid development and increasing size[38] and complexity of programs. These three factors lead to more software flaws.

II. THE ROLE OF TORT LIABILITY IN IMPROVING SOFTWARE SECURITY

If it is true, as suggested in the previous section, that one key source of cyber insecurity is the poor quality of software, and it is worthwhile to seek improvements of software security during software development, the next question is how best to encourage software developers to improve software security.

Advice from the private sector on how to improve software usually includes "market-based incentives rather than traditional regulation," and strongly leans toward "carrots" rather than "sticks" should any government action be undertaken.[39] However, the Software Development Task Force report discussed earlier contains a broader range of options. The Incentives Subgroup (one of the four subgroups within the Software Development Task Force) notes the possibility that the level of security required by national security and critical infrastructure protection may be greater than what the market will provide,[40] and suggests that, if this is so, government intervention may be needed. The Incentives Subgroup cautions that any intervention should be carefully tailored so as to disrupt security-related innovation as little as possible. The options listed by the Incentives Subgroup include "liability and liability relief, regulation and regulatory reform, tax incentives, enhanced prosecution, research and development, education, and other incentives. . . ."[41]

Lawyers[42] and nonlawyers have already suggested legal liability for insecure software. The computer security expert Bruce Schneier has argued strongly in favor of holding software vendors liable for unreasonably insecure software. He suggests that computer security is not really a technological problem but fundamentally a business problem. In his view, a rational software company would not bother with good security because implementing it is more costly than ignoring security.[43]

In Schneier's view, we already have the knowledge and means to build much more secure software, but software vendors will not do so until provided with an incentive to do so. Schneier argues that "[i]f we expect vendors to reduce the number of features, lengthen development cycles, and invest in secure software development processes, they must be liable for security vulnerabilities in their products."[44]

Although the imposition by regulation of security standards is one option, it has serious problems. Regulated standards take time to implement and to change, and are subject to lobbying pressures and industry capture. Different types of programs present different security risks, and there is a danger that regulated standards may not be appropriate for all applications. Finally, mandated security standards would have to be specified at an extremely abstract level to avoid stifling innovation in secure software engineering practices and tools.[45] Another option, and the one that will be explored in the rest of this chapter, is the option of using negligence lawsuits to encourage the development of secure software.

A. The Plaintiff

Before moving on to discuss a hypothetical lawsuit against a vendor of unreasonably insecure software, it is necessary to say a few words about the appropriate plaintiff. The immediately obvious plaintiff is the purchaser of the insecure software. Another possible plaintiff is the victim of a DDOS attack. I will address these potential plaintiffs in turn.

B. The Software Purchaser as Plaintiff

A variety of obstacles confront a lawsuit brought against a software vendor by a purchaser of defective software. These include disclaimers of liability within the software license, the problem of establishing a software vendor's responsibility when the harm is caused by the deliberate actions of an unknown third party, judicial reluctance to permit recovery of pure economic loss, and the charge of contributory negligence on the part of the plaintiff.

Mass-market consumer software of the kind we are concerned with here is normally licensed under an "end user license agreement." The licenses usually contain clauses disclaiming warranties and conditions, and clauses either limiting or excluding liability for consequential damages. The software purchaser is likely to be bound by these contractual terms, and may face a significant hurdle in convincing a court to set them aside.[46]

Even when the license does not exclude liability, additional difficulties confront a tort lawsuit. Generally, a security-related software flaw on its own causes no losses. Instead, the losses are inflicted when a third party deliberately takes advantage of the vulnerabilities. Tort law does contemplate liability in such situations in which a defendant creates an unreasonable risk that a plaintiff will be harmed by a third party. As a result, an argument can be made that a software developer may be responsible in tort for the losses caused by the deliberate wrongdoing of an unknown third party. This argument will be addressed further on, in the context of the discussion of whether the victim of a DDOS attack would be a possible plaintiff in this hypothetical lawsuit.

The negligence suit of the plaintiff-purchaser of defective software faces difficulty because the losses suffered are most likely to be pure economic losses (that is, loss that arises independent of any physical injury to person or property). An attempt to sue in tort will collide with the U.S. rule that generally precludes the recovery through tort of pure economic loss resulting from product defects.[47] Although Canadian law permits the recovery of pure economic loss in some circumstances (such as when dangerous defects exist in goods or structures[48]), it is likely that the recovery of pure economic loss would not be permitted for the nondangerous defects at issue in the case of insecure mass-market software.[49]

Three arguments might be available to the plaintiff-purchaser to try to escape from the effect of the "economic loss rule." First, a plaintiff-purchaser who is a consumer could argue that the leading U.S. case, *East River Steamship Corp. v. Transamerica Delaval*,[50] bars the recovery by commercial users of pure economic loss resulting from a product defect but leaves open the possibility of recovery by consumers.[51]

Second, the plaintiff-purchaser could attempt to establish that its losses were not pure economic losses but actual property damage if, for example, the software defect resulted in damage to hardware[52] or destroyed electronic data other than the software itself (for example, by erasing or overwriting files on the hard drive). This argument effectively characterizes the loss as property loss that is recoverable, rather than as pure economic loss, which is not. This approach is weakened by case law suggesting that electronic data are not a form of property that is susceptible to physical harm.[53] However, as our increasing reliance on the electronic storage of information becomes clear to courts, this may change.

Third, a Canadian plaintiff-purchaser could try to argue that the software security flaw is dangerous, and thus attempt to fit among the cases permitting the recovery of pure economic loss in the context of dangerous defects.[54] This is a weak argument given that the danger posed by security-related software flaws is most likely to be the infliction of pure economic loss.[55]

Finally, the vendor of defective software will likely be able to raise a strong argument that the plaintiff-purchaser who has failed to apply patches or to take other simple self-protective measures (such as using firewalls or virus-scanning software) has been contributorily negligent.[56] Pinkney suggests that software consumers should be considered negligent if they fail to apply patches that have been made available.[57] Nevertheless, the window between the discovery of new software vulnerabilities and their exploitation in attacks is narrowing.[58] This suggests that, in future, attacks could well be launched before patches are ready. In such cases, plaintiff-purchasers could not be held contributorily negligent for failing to apply patches to their software, although the failure to take other self-protective steps may still constitute contributory negligence.

In light of these difficulties, instead of depending on a purchaser of defective software to be the plaintiff in a hypothetical lawsuit against the developer of unreasonably insecure software, this chapter builds on a previous suggestion that a more promising suit could be brought by the victim of a DDOS attack.[59]

C. The Victim of a DDOS Attack as Plaintiff

A DOS (denial of service) attack is a form of cyberattack in which an attacker seeks to disable its target, usually by flooding it with an overwhelming amount of communications traffic, so that it is unable to offer the services it normally provides. In the distributed form of this attack (DDOS), the attacker launches the attack simultaneously from a large number of computers against the target. These computers have been previously conscripted into an army of "bots" by infecting them with malicious code. The attack traffic sent to the victim often contains false addresses of origin, making it difficult for the target to block illegitimate traffic or to trace the attack to the infected computers.[60]

There is little that the victim of a DDOS attack can do to avoid becoming the target of such an attack.[61] The defensive options available are largely unsatisfactory,[62] and include maintaining large excess capacity in order to absorb the attack without degrading normal services, designing the network in order to be able to shift capacity to critical services while degrading or disabling others, or shutting down. Attempts to filter out the attacking traffic may block legitimate traffic as well.[63] As a result, the victim of a DDOS attack is not open to the same charges of contributory negligence. In addition, the DDOS attack victim is also likely to be large, and, if it relies heavily on e-commerce, it might also have suffered the substantial losses that could make a tort suit worthwhile.

The plaintiff-DDOS attack victim faces the same problem as the plaintiff-purchaser of software with respect to judicial reluctance to permit the recovery of pure economic loss. As noted earlier, pure economic loss "is a financial loss which is not causally connected to physical injury to the plaintiff's own person or property."[64] In the DDOS context, the victim will have suffered an interruption in the use of its computers and computing services, with attendant loss of business, harm to goodwill, and wasted employee time and effort.

Most likely there will have been no loss of data, which might have opened the door to arguments about whether data are property of a sort that can be subject to physical injury.[65]

Although judicial reluctance to permit the recovery of pure economic loss would be an obstacle for the victim of a DDOS attack in a lawsuit against a vendor of insecure software, the victim of a DDOS attack arguably occupies a different position from the plaintiff-purchaser. In the case of a DDOS attack victim, some of the judicial concerns underlying the refusal to permit the recovery of pure economic loss when a product is defective, such as the judicial desire not to disturb a contractual bargain, are inapplicable. As a result, it is necessary to reexamine the reasons for judicial reluctance to permit the recovery of pure economic loss in this new context.

The common law courts' discomfort with permitting the recovery of negligently inflicted pure economic loss flows from certain policy concerns that are thought to be more acute in certain economic loss cases than in cases involving physical injury. These concerns include the risk of indeterminate liability,[66] the fear of a proliferation of cases that would absorb too many scarce judicial resources,[67] the need to respect and protect contractual allocations of loss, and the sense that judicial resources should not be expended on cases that involve a mere transfer of wealth rather than a net social loss.[68] In the commercial context, courts are also concerned that vigorous free-market competition might be discouraged by the prospect of liability for the negligently inflicted pure economic loss of a competitor.[69] Another explanation for the different treatment of pure economic loss and physical losses is that pure economic losses are qualitatively different from, and perhaps less important, than physical damage, particularly personal injuries.[70] Personal injuries cannot be fully repaired with money, and so it is essential to use negligence law to deter conduct that generates such injuries, whereas economic losses may be fully repaired—perhaps by non-tort methods (such as insurance or contract).[71] The distinction between pure economic loss and property damage is less clear because both would, unlike personal injury, be fully repairable in the normal course of events.[72]

Despite these concerns, courts in Canada and the United States have permitted pure economic loss to be recovered in certain circumstances.[73] Despite the differences in approach between the two jurisdictions, the courts have reached fairly similar conclusions about the principles of liability in pure economic loss cases.[74]

   The case being considered in this chapter involves a plaintiff who suffers pure economic loss flowing from business interruption because of a deliberate criminal or tortious attack by an unknown attacker. The losses could be recoverable in tort against the unknown attacker in Canada and in the United States on the basis of intentional interference with economic opportunity.[75] The attacker has marshaled an attacking army by capitalizing on weaknesses introduced into software developed and sold widely by the defendant.[76] This scenario does not fit neatly within any of the categories of pure economic loss cases already clearly addressed in the law. Although this is a case of a defective product, it is not a case in which the plaintiff can be held to the terms of the contractual bargain struck, because the DDOS victim is not a party to the license for the defective software. Another possible way of conceptualizing the scenario is as an example of "relational economic loss." Relational economic loss cases are those in which the plaintiff suffers pure economic loss as a result of some relationship with or reliance on a third party who has been negligently injured by the defendant.[77] For example, a business may suffer pure economic loss when the defendant negligently damages the upstream power line owned by the third-party power company. The analogy in the context of insecure software is that the DDOS attack victim suffers pure economic loss when the software vendor sells defective software to third-party consumers, and third-party attackers take advantage of those defects.

   U.S. and Canadian courts have mostly refused to permit the recovery of "relational economic loss," although certain exceptions are made in the United States[78] and the Supreme Court of Canada has recognized several exceptions (none of which is applicable in the present context) and has indicated that other exceptions may be possible (although they are not encouraged).[79] One situation in which a reasonable argument could be made for an exception to the rule against recovery of relational economic loss is that of economic loss resulting from damage to a public resource.[80]

   In *Union Oil Co.* v. *Oppen*, 501 F. 2d 558 (9th Cir. 1974), fishermen successfully sought compensation for lost commercial fishing profits from oil companies that had caused a major oil spill during offshore drilling operations. Feldthusen suggests that this was the correct result, as the oil companies were best situated to avoid the harm efficiently, and because there is no private party to sue for property damage in the case of damage to a public resource. If oil companies face only the cost of cleanup, rather than the full losses including business interruption, they may face too small an incentive to avoid the spill. As a result, there is a strong deterrence argument for permitting plaintiffs to sue for economic loss resulting from damage to a public resource.[81] This reasoning suggests an analogy to the present context. It could perhaps be argued that the Internet has attained the status of a public resource, which is endangered through the wide dissemination of insecure software; that there are inadequate incentives to adopt the optimal level of security (or, put another way, there is inadequate deterrence against the dissemination of unreasonably insecure software); and that software developers are best situated to avoid the harm most efficiently in this context.

One of the key policy reasons to refuse recovery of relational economic loss is the possibility of indeterminate liability (both in terms of the quantum of damages, and in terms of the number of possible plaintiffs). Although all users of the Internet could face a DDOS attack, and so could potentially be plaintiffs, only a relatively small number of prominent e-commerce businesses would be likely to be targeted in such an attack and would be likely to suffer the resulting major economic losses that would justify a lawsuit. As a result, an apparent problem of indeterminate liability might be less serious in practice than in theory. Nevertheless, this is a weakness of the hypothetical lawsuit.

III. A HYPOTHETICAL LAWSUIT:
DDOS ATTACK VICTIM V. DEVELOPER OF INSECURE SOFTWARE

Assuming it is possible to establish that the policy reasons are sufficiently compelling to overcome the rule against the recovery of relational economic loss, or to establish a new category of recoverable economic loss, I will now consider the elements of the hypothetical lawsuit by a DDOS attack victim against the vendor of unreasonably insecure software.

In making a claim of negligence, a plaintiff must establish that the defendant owed him or her a duty of care, that the defendant breached that duty in not meeting the requisite standard of reasonable care, that the breach of duty caused the plaintiff's injury, that the injury was not too remote a consequence of the breach of duty, and that damage resulted.

A. Duty of Care

Michael L. Rustad and Thomas H. Koenig have recently written an interesting article tracing the development of cyber-torts between 1992 and 2002.[82] They note that negligence claims are conspicuously underdeveloped in cyberspace, in contrast to the bricks-and-mortar world, where negligence lawsuits dominate tort litigation.[83] One reason for this is that harm in cyberspace is very often economic loss,[84] the recovery of which is limited in negligence. They also suggest that, although there are few examples from which to draw conclusions, courts are reluctant to recognize duties of care in cyberspace.

Rustad and Koenig note that modern tort law was a product of nineteenth century industrialization, and that we are experiencing a "legal lag" as tort law now fails to deal with the latest revolution, the Information Revolution.[85] They suggest that a much greater role should be played by tort in cyberspace.[86]

As noted in an earlier paper,[87] Canadian tort law recognizes situations in which a defendant owes a duty of care to protect the plaintiff from the unlawful acts of third parties over whom the defendant has no direct control or authority. In the U.S. context, the Restatement of the Law, Second, Torts, paragraph 302B indicates that "an act or omission may be negligent if the actor realizes or should realize that it involves an unreasonable risk of harm to another through the conduct of . . . a third person which is intended to cause harm, even though such conduct is criminal." Canadian cases[88] have involved landlords whose inadequate security measures exposed tenants to attack by third parties. It has also been suggested that a defendant may be held liable when he or she leaves keys in a vehicle when it is reasonably foreseeable that the vehicle may be stolen by a third party and involved in injury to the plaintiff or his property.[89]

The current case is analogous to these bricks-and-mortar duties. When a plaintiff is harmed by a third party who has taken advantage of unreasonable software security flaws in order to do so, that plaintiff should be able to pursue the software developer in negligence for having created an unreasonable risk of harm from the foreseeable deliberate cyberattacks of a third party. I have argued in a previous article that a duty of care should be found between a monopolist or near-monopolist vendor of software known to be a fundamental component of the Internet and all users of the network.[90] The foreseeability of harm to Internet-connected computer users arising from flaws in ubiquitous software should be obvious to the software developer given the frequent reporting of cyberattacks and their costliness. Furthermore, I have argued for a form of "cyber-proximity" that would recognize a sufficiently close relationship between a monopolist software vendor and each participant in the network in order to ground a duty of care.[91] Under conditions of monopoly or near-monopoly, a vendor surely knows that its software is a critical determinant of the structure of cyberspace, and that insecurities potentially expose all networked computers to attack by third parties. As with the landlords who have power and authority over the security-related characteristics of physical spaces, monopoly or near-monopoly software vendors have power over the security-related characteristics of cyberspace.[92]

B. Standard of Care

Assuming that the victim of a DDOS attack can establish that a software developer owes it a duty of care, the next issue that arises in the negligence inquiry is the requisite standard of care.

The general approach to determining the required standard of care against which a defendant's behavior is to be measured is to ask what the "reasonable person of ordinary prudence" would consider reasonable in the circumstances.[93] However, when a defendant is engaged in an expert profession or trade, the defendant's behavior is assessed according to what the reasonable practitioner of that profession or trade would have thought reasonable in the circumstances.[94] The law also requires a defendant who has special knowledge, who holds him or herself out as possessing it, or who undertakes a course of conduct that a reasonable person would recognize as requiring it, to act in accordance with that greater knowledge in assessing risk. The developer of software would likely be expected to have superior knowledge and judgment in relation to software engineering, and would be expected to recognize and avoid unreasonable security risks.

The question remains, then, what is unreasonable risk in relation to security-related software errors? The answer to this question requires "balancing the magnitude of the risk, in the light of the likelihood of an accident happening and the possible seriousness of its consequences, against the difficulty, expense or any other disadvantage of desisting from the venture or taking a particular precaution."[95]

Greater risks are usually tolerated when an activity is socially useful.[96] Some people are reluctant to view negligence in terms of economic efficiency, which requires only cost-justified safety measures.[97] However, software flaws that generate only pure economic loss seem reasonably amenable to such a dispassionate utilitarian approach. To the extent that cyber insecurity threatens health or life (for example, perhaps through the disruption of critical infrastructure), the adequacy of the cost-benefit analysis is more likely to be called into question.[98]

Clearly, software and Internet technologies are of enormous utility despite the costliness of cyberattacks, as one may deduce from the continued use of e-commerce business channels by most victims of DDOS attacks. If the current state of security were unchangeable, we would likely conclude that the Internet is highly socially useful, and we would tolerate its intrinsic risks, although we may choose not to use it for certain critical applications. However, greater security can be achieved,[99] and the relevant inquiry is whether the cost of improving security is more or less than the value of the improved security.

As already discussed, the patching system is one way in which security may be improved; however, it likely generates a smaller improvement in security at greater total expense (the expense is shared by the software developers who must develop the patches and purchasers who must apply the patches) than efforts to improve the software before it is deployed.[100] It is therefore worthwhile to explore the possibility that more rigorous software engineering practices might be adopted to ensure that software is released in a more secure state at the outset. A software developer may object that this solution would impose enormous cost (which would not be directly shared with the public as is the case with the patching system). However, the essential is the total cost of the solution, and not who will bear it initially, as the cost will likely be passed to purchasers in any event.[101]

In sum, in order to determine the appropriate standard of care with respect to the development of reasonably secure software, we must determine what security improvements a reasonable and prudent person with the knowledge, skill, and judgment of a software developer would think appropriate, taking into consideration the extent of the loss flowing from insecure software and the expense of avoiding it.

A software developer may object that everyone understands and expects that complex modern software will contain bugs, and that the "release and patch" mode of selling software is the "custom" in the mass-market software industry. It is true that the customary practice in an industry is often persuasive evidence of what is considered the reasonable standard of care.[102] As a result, conformity with custom usually suggests that the defendant has not been negligent. Nevertheless, a court may conclude that a custom is unreasonable.[103] As a result, compliance with custom is helpful but not conclusive evidence that the defendant exercised reasonable care. "Were it otherwise, an entire industry would be free, by maintaining careless methods to save time, effort or money, to set its own uncontrolled standard with no incentive to devise new and more efficient safety precautions."[104]

As discussed in more detail further on, it seems that industry custom for mass-market software leaves significant room for improvement.[105] To the extent that these improvements are cost-justified, current practices may not reflect a reasonable level of care in software development. Increasing reliance on the Internet and, therefore, the growing costs of disruption of the Internet suggest that these improvements are becoming cost-justified if they are not already.

Security experts have suggested that the vulnerability of modern software does not result from a lack of available information.[106] Indeed, the same well-known flaws arise repeatedly, and have been doing so for decades, even though it is possible to avoid them. The CERT Coordination Center statistics show that more than 90 percent of software security incidents result from the exploitation of known types of software defects.[107]

One form of software flaw, the "buffer overflow,"[108] was named the "computer vulnerability of the decade" in 1999, having been identified as the most common form of security flaw of the preceding ten years.[109] This is striking given that the problem and its solutions had been known for decades.[110] The buffer overflow flaw may be able to claim the title of "computer vulnerability of the decade" for the current decade also.[111] The authors of a recent book on developing secure software observed that

> [b]uffer-overflow disasters have been so widespread in modern software that they were the primary factor convincing us to write this book. Indeed, we could fill a good-sized volume with sad security tales on this topic alone. Go see for yourself; take a look at the security patches released by software vendors over just about any several-month period in the past few years. You will find that a huge percentage of the patches relate to vulnerabilities with buffer overflows as their root cause. We believe that every one of these implementation flaws was avoidable, and without a great deal of effort on the parts of their respective programmers.[112]

The persistence of the buffer overflow problem is remarkable, as there are known ways to avoid the introduction of the errors through careful coding and to check for errors using automated scanning tools ("static code scanning tools"). Viega and McGraw provide a list (albeit nonexhaustive) of program functions commonly used in the C programming languages that create a risk of buffer overflows.[113] In most cases, there are reasonable alternatives for the dangerous functions,[114] despite widespread failure to adopt them.[115]

The problem seems to be one of the culture and engineering practices of software developing organizations. It is worthwhile at this point to discuss briefly the discipline of software engineering, as it appears that certain types of software security issues are far more easily solved by software developers than others. The reasonable standard of care that emerges may need to reflect this.

C. Software Engineering Processes

Software engineering is a systematic procedure for "the analysis, design, implementation, testing, and maintenance of software," that is followed in order to ensure that it meets certain objectives such as efficiency, reliability, usability, and so on.[116]

A software engineering project involves a number of tasks including (1) the analysis of the problem to be solved or the function to be achieved by the software, (2) the determination and description of the specific requirements (the "specifications"), (3) the design and modeling of a solution that meets the requirements (the "design"), (4) the writing of the software code (the "implementation"), (5) the testing of the software, and (6) the preparation of documentation, including internal commenting on source code as well as manuals and guides.[117] Although the software engineering field has developed various models, known as "software life cycle models,"[118] to systematically control and describe the timing and repetition of these steps, it appears that mass-market software development actually follows a less-controlled market-driven model in which the time frames may be shorter and more steps may be conducted simultaneously.[119]

Software security problems seem to be classifiable into two broad categories: design or architectural errors, and implementation (coding) errors.[120] The Software Process Subgroup[121] distinguishes between these two forms of errors.[122] It suggests that much of the second category of implementation errors can be addressed through rigorous software engineering techniques.[123] However, "security-specific modeling, architecture, and design issues" as well as the prediction of the "emergent properties"[124] of the whole system require considerable security expertise.[125] The techniques available to address these more difficult design issues seem to consist at present of the accumulated experience and wisdom of software security experts.[126] This wisdom is presented in the form of lists of more or less abstract design principles,[127] advice to include certain procedures such as objective peer reviews,[128] and exhortations to include security experts in all stages of the software development process.[129] In fact, one of the key recommendations of the Software Process Subgroup is that security expertise must be integrated into all stages of the software development process (including specification and design) to ensure that security is formally and rigorously addressed from the beginning.[130]

Secure design seems to be more art than science at present, with design choices determined very much by context, and it is thus somewhat difficult to discuss in detail what reasonable care in design might be. Nevertheless, knowledge about the security requirements of the networked environment is maturing rapidly,[131] and it may soon be possible to identify obvious design errors. Furthermore, it is now possible to conclude that software developers should be including (and documenting the inclusion of) known security considerations from the beginning of software development, including during the specification of requirements and design. They should also be ensuring that objective security reviews and audits are being conducted at all stages of the software development lifecycle.

The Software Process Subgroup also recommended that software developers adopt one of the software development processes known to produce very low defect rates.[132] Various "formal methods" exist that can produce software with very few errors. These methods were developed to meet the needs of safety-critical (or "mission-critical") software in contexts such as military applications, power generation, aviation, trains, automatic processes in factories, and medical applications.[133] Formal methods are software engineering methods that use mathematical models and formal logic to prove the consistency and correctness of the software at some or nearly all stages of the software lifecycle, including requirements definition, design, and implementation.[134] These methods offer a means to discover and correct the contradictions, ambiguities, incomplete statements, and mixed levels of abstraction that exist in software developed using less formal approaches.[135] Although formal methods produce software with fewer defects,[136] they are more time-consuming and expensive, and fewer software developers have the background necessary to adopt them.[137] Other obstacles to the adoption of these methods may be cultural, including a sense that the methodology is too theoretical or mathematical, or that the software development industry is too immature for such strict techniques.[138] Furthermore, these formal methods cannot guarantee that a program is defect-free, as the proofs "depend on a programmer or logician to translate a program's statements into logical implications. Just as programming is prone to errors, so also is this translation."[139]

Nevertheless, formal methods have been incorporated into various processes that have produced extremely promising results.[140] Pressman suggests that there is some truth in the objections to these methods, but that the potential benefits outweigh the investment required to adopt them.[141] Pfleeger and Pfleeger note that the methods are being constantly improved, and may become a more important means to ensure security.[142] Graff and van Wyk do not recommend formal methods except for safety-critical projects, due to their costliness.[143] However, there is a case to be made that operating systems and network applications are approaching "safety-critical" status. Graff and van Wyk in fact suggest that formal methods might have been useful in designing TCP, one of the underlying protocols of the Internet. In their view, this could well have been cost-justified because of the widespread use of TCP by popular Internet applications.[144]

In the end, perhaps the strongest arguments about the reasonable standard of care in software development can be made about common implementation errors. It seems reasonable that, at a minimum, the presence of well-known, easily detectable, and easily remediable flaws should be considered negligent. Although not exactly an implementation-level error, another precaution that may qualify as reasonable would be ensuring that the default configurations for installed software are as secure as possible. Several types of errors are known to occur repeatedly, one of which is the "buffer overflow," discussed earlier. Some of these errors can be discovered using automated tools such as static code checkers. Graff and van Wyk warn that these tools are useful but have limitations, as they look only for "known and previously defined problem conditions." Nevertheless, "[t]here is no doubt that many a buffer overflow could have been avoided had more developers been using this kind of screening tool and methodology."[145] The Software Process Subgroup has suggested that static analysis of code to find known kinds of coding defects should become compulsory over time.[146]

In summary, the rule at the implementation level should be that "if you must make mistakes in your software, at least be original!"[147]

D. The Legacy Code Problem

One remaining problem is what should be done with so-called "legacy code." A large amount of software was developed before the security challenges of the networked environment became clear. Much of it will "never have good security properties without substantial redesign."[148] Some security experts strongly advocate "blanket code sweeps" at the big software companies to remove common errors,[149] although others suggest that this is simply not practical.[150]

At a minimum, it seems appropriate that a new release, including an upgraded version of a legacy system, should be judged in its entirety by the new standard of care with respect to security. Otherwise, software developers would face inadequate incentives to improve software. Furthermore, new entrants would face the cost disadvantage of having to meet higher standards than software vendors who can simply provide insecure upgrades of insecure legacy software.

E. Causation and Remoteness

A plaintiff must also establish that the defendant's breach of its duty of care owed to the plaintiff caused the plaintiff's injuries. This element of the negligence action poses certain challenges in the present context.

The victim of a DDOS attack will have to establish that the bots that attacked it were conscripted into the DDOS attack army by exploiting an unreasonable insecurity in software running on the bot computers.

In some cases, this may not be too difficult. An example is the MSBlaster worm, which circulated in August 2003. In that case, the worm exploited a vulnerability in Microsoft Windows, spread throughout the network without requiring users to open email attachments, and carried a payload designed to launch a DDOS attack on a particular URL (www.windowsupdate.com) on a particular date.[151] The victim of such a specific attack would be able to make a reasonable argument that the causal link between the harm and the software insecurity exists.

However, in other cases, it may be more complicated to establish causation. The plaintiff's problem is that the bot may have been conscripted into the DDOS attack army through a mechanism other than the exploitation of software vulnerabilities. For example, malicious code may have been introduced when the user opened an infected email attachment, and not due to the exploitation of a software vulnerability. Furthermore, a number of vulnerable programs exist on the typical computer, and it will not necessarily be clear which one was exploited in order to install the DDOS attack tools.

IV. CONCLUSION

Cybersecurity is causing increasing worry, not only about economic losses but also about possible national security implications. It is accordingly important to consider the various reasons for the current state of insecurity. One of the key reasons proffered for the poor state of cybersecurity is the poor state of mass-market software. There are reasons to believe that the market is not generating the appropriate level of investment in software security. This chapter has explored the possibility of pursuing software developers in negligence for unreasonable security flaws as a means of providing incentives to improve software.

One possible plaintiff in a hypothetical lawsuit against the developer of unreasonably insecure software is the victim of a DDOS attack. Unlike the purchaser of such software, who can use a firewall and install patches, the victim of a DDOS attack is essentially defenseless—it is instead dependent on the security status of others.

Various difficulties confront the victim of a DDOS attack as plaintiff in the hypothetical lawsuit. A key concern is that the plaintiff will likely have suffered only pure economic losses, a category of loss for which courts are reluctant to permit recovery in negligence. Nevertheless, there is a strong need to deter the release of insecure software. It would be useful to consider whether any limiting principles might be adopted to restrict the class of possible plaintiffs, or the permissible scope of recovery, in order to address the liability indeterminacy problem that often discourages courts from permitting recovery of pure economic loss.

Another important problem confronting the victim of a DDOS attack is in establishing causation, given that it may be difficult to trace the attacking computers to see if they were conscripted into the attacking computer army due to a particular software vulnerability. The problem of establishing causation will be much less acute when a very specific attack, like MSBlaster in August 2003, is being considered.

Finally, the plaintiff will need to establish the reasonable standard of care to be applied to the defendant software developer. Various classes of errors exist, ranging from well-known and relatively easily avoided coding (implementation) errors to more high-level design problems. Although the existence of the former types of errors may be argued to constitute negligence, the latter are less clear. As knowledge about secure design principles matures, it will be possible to include design errors within the scope of negligence. Nevertheless, it would be helpful for liability to serve as a spur to increase the attention paid to secure design so that better secure design techniques may be created and adopted. As a result, courts should require evidence that software developers have made a bona fide effort to include security considerations at all stages of the software development lifecycle, including independent reviews and audits.

NOTES

1. Richard D. Pethia, "Cyber Security-Growing Risk from Growing Vulnerability," June 25, 2003, Testimony before the House Select Committee on Homeland Security, Subcommittee on Cybersecurity, available at http://www.cert.org/congressional_testimony/Pethia_testimony_06-35-03.html. One recent event at an Ohio nuclear power plant offered a sobering warning about the dangers of inattention to cyber security. The nuclear plant's computer network was infected by a worm, disabling the "Safety Parameter Display System" and the plant process computer for hours. See United States Nuclear Regulatory Commission, Office of Nuclear Reactor Regulation, Information Notice 2003-14, "Potential Vulnerability of Plant Computer Network to Worm Infection," (August 29, 2003); Kevin Poulsen, U.S. Warns Nuke Plants of Worm Threat, SecurityFocus (September 3, 2003), available at http://www.securityfocus.com/news/6868.

2. See e.g., Robert Vamosi, Could You Get Caught in a Virus Gang War? CNET News.com (March 10, 2004), available at http://reviews.cnet.com/4520-3513_7-5125006-1.html .

3. John Leyden, DDoS Attacks Go Through the Roof, The Register (February 12, 2004), available at http://www.theregister.co.uk/2004/02/12/ddos_attacks_go_through/.

4. Bernhard Warner, Spammers Unleash E-mail Worm to Disable Critics, boston.com (December 2, 2003), available at http://www.boston.com/business/technology/articles/2003/12/02/spammers_unleash_e_mail_worm_to_disable_critics/ .

5. Robert Lemos, Attack on SCO's Servers Intensifies, CNET News.com (December 11, 2003), available at http://news.com.com/2100-7355-5120706.html.

6. Paul Roberts, Al Jazeera Hobbled by DDOS Attack, Infoworld (March 26, 2003) available at http://www.infoworld.com/article/03/03/26/HNjazeera_1.html.

7. Robert Lemos, Flaws Level Off, but Worms Still Squirming, CNET News.com (March 15, 2004), available at http://news.com.com/2100-1002-5173216.html, reporting that Symantec's Internet Security Threat Report indicated that 2,636 security vulnerabilities were reported in 2003, while the Computer Emergency Response Team Coordination Center reported 3,784 vulnerabilities in 2003.

8. Network World, Security Experts Form Patch Support Group, Computerworld (December 8, 2003), available at http://www.computerworld.com/securitytopics/security/story/0,10801,87950,00.html, "Patching is such a headache these days that a number of security experts have gotten together to form PatchManagement.org, a support group where network managers, systems administrators and security professionals can discuss all things patching."

9. Robert Lemos, Security Experts Bemoan Poor Patching, CNET News.com (February 24, 2004), available at http://news.com.com/2100-7355-5164650.html.

10. The enforcement of cyber crime laws is very difficult and costly. See Eugene Spafford, A Failure to Learn from the Past, Proceedings of the 19th Annual Computer Security Applications Conference (December 2003), available at http://www.acsac.org/2003/papers/classic-spafford.pdf, at § 7.4, "Laws and Professional Ethics."

11. It may be that mass-mailing worms, which are circulated as email attachments, are better addressed by modifications in user behavior, or mandatory scanning of attachments by Internet service providers, than by changes to software.

12. Jennifer A. Chandler, Security in Cyberspace: Combatting Distributed Denial of Service Attacks, 1 U. Ott. L. & Tech. J. 231 (2003-2004).

13. Robert Lemos, Programmers Told to Put Security Over Creativity, CNET News.com (April 1, 2004), available at http://news.com.com/2100-1009-5183634.html. The Website of the National Cyber Security Partnership is http://www.cyberpartnership.org.

14. The shorter form "Software Development Task Force" will be used in this chapter to designate the "Security Across the Software Development Life Cycle Task Force."

15. Improving Security Across the Software Development Lifecycle Task Force Report (April 1, 2004), available at http://www.cyberpartnership.org/SDLCFULL.pdf.

16. *Id.* Software Process Subgroup Summary, at p. 6.

17. *Supra* note 15, Education Subgroup Summary, at p. 3.

18. Mark G. Graff & Kenneth R. van Wyk, *Secure Coding: Principles & Practices* 25 (2003). The authors write that "[a] friend of ours was 'security coordinator' for one of the major Internet software producers. Often buttonholed by customers at security conferences and asked questions like, 'When are you guys going to stop shipping this crap?' he claims the answer he is proudest of was, 'Sometime soon after you folks stop buying it.'"

19. Chandler, *supra* note 12, at 251.

20. Thomas C. Greene, Does Open Source Software Enhance Security? *The Register*, (March 5, 2004), available at http://theregister.co.uk/content/55/36033.html; John Viega & Gary McGraw, *Building Secure Software: How to Avoid Security Problems the Right Way* 89 (2002).

21. An "anti-benchmarking clause" is a software license that bars licensees from publishing product reviews or disclosing the results of benchmark tests without the licensor's prior consent. See People v. Network Associates, Inc. dba McAfee Software 195 Misc. 2d 384, 758 N.Y.S. 2d 466 (N.Y.S.C., 2003).

22. A negative externality exists when a person's actions in the market impose costs on third parties, for which the person does not have to pay.

23. For a description of DDOS attacks, please *see* the discussion, *infra* section IIC.

24. Patches are small pieces of software that are developed to fix errors in software programs.

25. For discussion of this point, *see* Chandler, *supra* note 12 at 248-49.

26. Graff & van Wyk, *supra* note 18 at 56. Another estimate, cited by *The Economist*, is more dramatic: "One rule of thumb, says Djenana Campara, chief technology officer of Klocwork, a young firm based in Ottawa, Canada, is that a bug which costs $1 to fix on the programmer's desktop costs $100 to fix once it is incorporated into a complete program, and many thousands of dollars if it is identified only after the software has been deployed in the field." Building a Better Bug-Trap, *The Economist* (June 19, 2003), available at www.economist.com/science/tq/PrinterFriendly.cfm?Story_ID=1841081; Roger S. Pressman, Software Engineering: A Practitioner's Approach 13-14 (2001), indicates that it is far more efficient to make changes to software before it is released.

27. Lemos, *supra* note 9; Stephen Hinde, Compsec 2002: The Complete Security Circle, 21 IEEE Computers & Security 689-93 (2002), (noting that IT departments are suffering from "patch overload.").

28. Graff and van Wyk estimate that 10 to 15 percent of security patches themselves introduce security vulnerabilities. Graff & van Wyk, *supra* note 18 at 5-6.

29. Jay Wrolstad, Industrious Worm vs. Lazy IT? *NewsFactor Network* (September 10,

2003), available at http://www.newsfactor.com/perl/story/22253.html; Paul Roberts, Microsoft SSL Patch Creating SSLowdown: Some Systems That Use Security Update MS04-011 Stop Responding, Computerworld.com (April 29, 2004), available at http://www.computerworld .com/ securitytopics/security/story/0,10801,92757,00.html; Patrick Gray, Security Firm: IE Patch Does Not Work, CNET News.com (September 8, 2003), available at http://news.com.om/2100 -1009-5072672.html.

30. Elias Levy, Poisoning the Software Supply Chain, *IEEE Security and Privacy* 70 (May-June 2003); Robert Vamosi, Swen Prevention and Cure: Swen Virus Masquerades as a New Microsoft Patch, CNET Reviews (September 18, 2003), available at http://reviews.cnet .com/4520-6600_7-5078675.html.

31. Andrew Orlowski, Microsoft EULA Asks for Root Rights-Again, *The Register* (August 2, 2002), available at http://www.theregister.co.uk/content/4/26517.html; Thomas C. Greene, MS Security Patch EULA Gives Billg Admin Privileges on Your Box, *The Register* (June 30, 2002), available at http://www.theregister.co.uk/content/4/25956.html.

32. Graff & van Wyk, *supra* note 18 at 6, note that "[a]pplying patches over and over-as though system operators had nothing else to do-is never going to give us a secure Internet-based infrastructure."

33. Charles P. Pfleeger and Shari Lawrence Pfleeger, *Security in Computing* 583 (3rd ed., 2003). *See also* discussion of the dangers and inadequacies of the patching approach at 96-97; and Viega & McGraw, *supra* note 20 at 16.

34. Bruce Schneier, "Preface," in Viega & McGraw, *supra* note 20 at xix-xx: "It's the software development system that causes bad software. Security is not something that can be bolted on at the end of a development process. It has to be designed in correctly from the beginning. Unfortunately, those who are in charge of a product's security are not in charge of the software development process. Those who call for increased security don't win against those who call for increased functionality. Those who champion principles of secure software design are not in charge of the software release schedule. The rallying cry of software companies is 'more and faster,' not 'less, slower, and more secure'."

35. Mary Ann Davidson, chief security officer for Oracle, has said that people should "get out their pitchforks and firebrands" to demand better software. She is quoted in Lemos, *supra* note 9.

36. Charles C. Palmer, Can We Win the Security Game? 10 IEEE Security & Privacy 10-11 (Jan.-Feb. 2004) (suggesting that three key problems have been identified as contributing to the sorry state of software: a focus on speed to market above quality, the tendency to approach security as an afterthought rather than as a consideration at the specification and design stages of software development, and the increasing complexity of systems driven by "feature creep.").

37. Ronald J. Leach, *Introduction to Software Engineering* 26 (2000).

38. Paul Festa, The Root of the Problem: Bad Software, CNET News.com (November 28, 2001), available at http://news.com.com/2008-1082-276316.html, quoting Gary McGraw: "It turns out that software is way more complicated than it used to be. For example, in 1990, Windows 3.1 was two and a half million lines of code. Today Windows XP is 40 million lines of code. And the best way to determine how many problems are going to be in a piece of software is to count how many lines of code it has. The simple metric goes like this: More lines, more bugs."

39. ISAlliance, ISAlliance Board Approves Menu of Market Incentives for Cyber Security (November 14, 2003), available at http://www.isalliance.org/ISAlliance_Board_Approves.doc.

40. *Supra* note 15, Appendix D, Incentives Subgroup Report .

41. *Supra* note 15, chart, third proposal under "Incentives for Software Development Organizations."

42. Kevin R. Pinkney, Putting Blame Where Blame Is Due: Software Manufacturer and Customer Liability for Security-Related Software Failure,13 *Alb. L. J. Sci. & Tech.* 43 (2002).

43. Bruce Schneier, Hacking the Business Climate for Network Security, 87 *IEEE Computer* 87-88 (April 2004).

44. *Id*. at 88.

45. Nancy Eickelmann & Jane Huffman Hayes, eds., New Year's Resolutions for Software Quality, *IEEE Software*, 12-13 (Jan.-Feb. 2004), quoting Professor Nancy Leveson of MIT, at 13. "The misguided actions of some government agencies in requiring the use of a particular design, specification method, or process is setting back software development decades. Quality is achieved by building it in from the beginning, using methods and processes that fit the application and the development context, and making it clear to the developers that quality is the highest priority."

46. *See, e.g.,* Dean F. Edgell, *Product Liability Law in Canada* 149 (2000); Dan B. Dobbs, *The Law of Torts* 1030 (2000).

47. Herbert Bernstein, Civil Liability for Pure Economic Loss Under American Tort Law, 46 *Am. J. Comp. L.* 111, 118-22 (1988); Bruce Feldthusen, *Economic Negligence* 166, 178 (4th ed., 2000); Dobbs, *supra* note 46 at 972.

48. Feldthusen, *supra* note 47 at 162-63; *M. Hasegawa & Co. v. Pepsi Bottling Group Co.* (Canada), 213 D.L.R. (4th) 663 (B.C.C.A. 2002); *Hughes v. Sunbeam Corp.* (Canada), 61 O.R. (3d) 433 (Ont. C.A. 2002).

49. *See* Feldthusen, *supra* note 47 at 171 for a discussion of the Canadian approach to the recovery of pure economic loss involving dangerous and nondangerous defects.

50. 476 U.S. 858, 106 S. Ct. 260 (1986). *See* Bernstein, *supra* note 47 at 120 and Feldthusen, *supra* note 47 at 167.

51. Bernstein, *supra* note 47 at 120-21.

52. The "Chernobyl" virus, released in 1998, caused damage when its destructive payload was triggered on April 16, 1999. The virus was able to destroy data and to cause physical damage to BIOS chips and motherboards. Mitch Tulloch, *Microsoft Encyclopedia of Security* 57 (2003).

53. *Seaboard Life Insurance Co. v. Babich* B.C.J. NO. 1868 (B.C.S.C. 1995).

54. As already discussed, this exception is established in Canada. Similar public safety considerations may also operate in U.S. law (*see* Bernstein, *supra* note 47 at 121-22).

55. Nevertheless, there may be situations in which the flaws may threaten critical infrastructures whose interruption would generate physical injuries.

56. Stephen E. Henderson & Matthew E. Yarbrough, Suing the Insecure? A Duty of Care in Cyberspace, 11 *N. M.L. Rev.* 15 (2002), suggesting that those whose insecure computers are hacked and later used in a DDOS attack against a third party should be liable to that third party; David L. Gripman, The Doors Are Locked but the Thieves and Vandals Are Still Getting In: A Proposal in Tort to Alleviate Corporate America's Cyber-Crime Problem, 16 *J. Marshall*

J. Computer & Info. L. 167 (1997), suggesting that corporations that do not adequately maintain the security of their systems should be responsible to third parties harmed by misuse of the corporate networks.

57. Pinkney, *supra* note 42 at 76.

58. Robert Lemos, Flaws Quickly Spawn Net Attacks, CNET News.com (October 1, 2003), available at http://news.com.com/2100-7349-5084992.html.

59. Chandler, *supra* note 12.

60. *See generally,* Allen Householder *et al., Managing the Threat of Denial-of-Service Attacks,* v. 10.0, CERT Coordination Center (October 2001, Carnegie Mellon University), available at http://www.cert.org/archive/pdf/Managing_DoS.pdf at 21-22; Kevin J. Houle & George M. Weaver, *Trends in Denial of Service Attack Technology,* v. 1.0 CERT Coordination Center (October, 2001, Carnegie Mellon University), available at http://www.cert.org/archive/pdf/DoS_trends.pdf at 18-19; Chandler, *supra* note 12.

61. Richard D. Pethia, "Computer Security," Testimony before the Committee on Government Reform, Subcommittee on Government Management, Information and Technology (March 9, 2000), available at http://www.cert.org/congressional_testimonyPethia_testimony_Mar9.html.

62. Householder, *supra* note 60 at 5.

63. *Id.* at 13.

64. Allen Linden, *Canadian Tort Law* 405 (7th ed., 2001).

65. Some commentators draw a distinction between lost profits due to system crashes, which would clearly be pure economic losses, and the corruption of data and hardware damage, for which "there is a strong argument that property has been damaged." Suzanne R. Eschrich, The Year 2000-Delight or Disaster: Vendor Liability and the Year 2000 Bug in Computer Software, 4 *B. U. J. Sci. & Tech. L.* 8 at para. 48 (1997). Sprague also suggests that the destruction of electronic data could be treated as property damage. Robert D. Sprague, Software Products Liability: Has Its Time Arrived? 137 *W. St. U.L. Rev.* 159-62 (1991). For contrary judicial authority, *see Seaboard Life Insurance Co. v. Babich* B.C.J. NO. 1868 (B.C.S.C. 1995).

66. This concern with the imposition of ruinous and open-ended liability "in an indeterminate amount for an indeterminate time to an indeterminate class" was stated by Justice Cardozo in *Ultramares Corp. v. Touche,* 174 N.E. 441, 255 N.Y. 170 (C.A. 1931).

67. Feldthusen, *supra* note 47 at 11.

68. *Id.* at 14. For example, a factory whose business is interrupted due to negligent damage to a power line owned by the power company will suffer losses, but a competitor may expand production and gain business, resulting in a transfer of wealth rather than a net social loss. Feldthusen notes that, from society's perspective, such transfers may not necessarily be objectionable and deserving of the judicial resources required to undo them.

69. John G. Fleming, *The Law of Torts* 193 (9th ed., 1998).

70. Lewis Klar, *Tort Law* 173 (3d ed., 2003); Linden, *supra* note 64 at 408.

71. Klar, *supra* note 70 at 173.

72. Feldthusen discusses the historical and policy reasons why property damage is subject to the negligence rules applicable to personal injury, rather than the more restrictive rules applicable to the recovery of pure economic loss (*supra* note 47 at 13-15).

73. Dobbs, *supra* note 46 at 1287; Feldthusen, *supra* note 47 at 1-2.

74. Feldthusen, *supra* note 47 at 8; Dobbs, *supra* note 46 at 1282-87.

75. W. Page Keeton, General Ed., Prosser and Keeton on Torts para. 130 (5th ed., 1984). Dobbs, *supra* note 46 at 1257 *et seq*. Klar, *supra* note 70, at 637 discussing the possible emergence of the tort of interference with economic interests by unlawful means.

76. This may not necessarily be the case, as some computers may have been infected by another means (*e.g.*, the computer's owner may have downloaded infected files). The difficulty of establishing that a particular bot was created by taking advantage of a particular software vulnerability will be addressed later within the discussion at the causation stage of the negligence inquiry.

77. The terminology *relational economic loss* is Canadian, but the same problem is discussed in U.S. law. *See, e.g.*, Dobbs, *supra* note 46 at 1283.

78. Feldthusen, *supra* note 47 at 195; Dobbs, *supra* note 46 at 1284-87.

79. Feldthusen, *supra* note 47 at 198; *Bow Valley Husky (Bermuda) Ltd. v. Saint John Shipbuilding Ltd.*, 3 S.C.R. 1210 (S.C.C. 1997).

80. *See* Bernstein, *supra* note 47 at 122-25; Feldthusen, *supra* note 47 at 249: "When the plaintiff's complaint is that he has suffered pure economic loss consequent upon physical damage to a public resource there may be policy factors favouring recovery which are absent in the various cases discussed previously."

81. Feldthusen, *supra* note 47 at 252.

82. Michael L. Rustad & Thomas H. Koenig, Cybertorts and Legal Lag: An Empirical Analysis, 13 *S. Cal. Interdis. L. J.* 77 (2003).

83. *Id.* at 122.

84. *Id.* at 93.

85. *Id.* at 139.

86. *Id.* at 140.

87. Chandler, *supra* note 12.

88. *See* the examples listed in Robert M. Solomon, R. W. Kostal, & Mitchell McInnes, *Cases and Materials on the Law of Torts* 288-90 (6th ed., 2003).

89. *Hewson v. Red Deer*, 63 D.L.R. (3d) 168 (Alta. T.D. 1976), rev'd, 146 D.L.R. (3d) 32 (Alta.C.A. 1997); *Werbeniuk v. Maynard*, 7 W.W.R. 704 (Man. Q.B. 1994).

90. Chandler, *supra* note 12 at 256-59.

91. *Id.*

92. *Id.* at 257-58.

93. Fleming, *supra* note 69 at 117; The Restatement of the Law, Second, Torts, para. 283.

94. Restatement of the Law, Second, Torts, para 299A; G.H.L. Fridman, *The Law of Torts in Canada* 396-97 (2d ed., 2002).

95. Fleming, *supra* note 69 at 127.

96. Linden, *supra* note 64 at 125; Restatement of the Law, Second, Torts, para. 291.

97. Fleming, *supra* note 69 at 131-32.

98. This is because of the difficulty of quantifying the losses to health and life, as well as to the sense that unlucky individuals should not bear the total losses even if this optimizes general social welfare.

99. The existence of "mission-critical" software and software engineering procedures designed to produce it make it clear that highly secure software can be generated, albeit at relatively high cost. For a discussion of "mission-critical" software development see Leach, *supra* note 37 at 28; Sara Baase, *A Gift of Fire: Social, Legal and Ethical Issues for Computers and the Internet* 148 (2nd ed., 2003).

100. This point was discussed in more detail in footnotes 26 to 33 and the accompanying text.

101. Fleming, *supra* note 69 at 131. "[I]n so far as the cost factor is raised, it may lose weight if the cost need not be absorbed by the defendant personally but can (and even should) be passed on to the beneficiaries of the enterprise."

102. "[Custom] tends to show what others in the same 'business' considered sufficient, that the defendant could not have learnt how to avoid the accident by the example of others, that most probably no other practical precautions could have been taken . . ." Fleming, *supra* note 69 at 133; Linden, *supra* note 64 at 183-84, 190.

103. *Waldick v. Malcolm*, 2 S.C.R. 456 (S.C.C. 1991); *See* the examples cited by Linden, *supra* note 64 at 193-99. The Restatement of the Law, Second, Torts, para. 295A, comment (c).

104. Fleming, *supra* note 69 at 133.

105. Richard C. Linger & Stacy J. Prowell, *Developing Secure Software with Cleanroom Software Engineering*, at 1., paper submitted to the Improving Security Across the Software Development Lifecycle Task Force, available at http://www.cyberpartnership.org/Software%20 Pro.pdf.

106. Lauren Heinz, *Preventing Security-Related Defects* (2002, Security Engineering Institute, Carnegie Mellon University), available at http://interactive.sei.cmu.edu/news@sei/ features/2002/2q02/pdf/feature-1-2q02.pdf, at 2: "The problem, Hernan and Davis agree, is not a lack of available data, knowledge, training, or support regarding security practices. Incident response centers (such as SEI's CERT Coordination Center), guidelines, checklists, best practices, and other useful materials are widely available."

107. Heinz, *supra* note 106.

108. The "buffer overflow" error is described by Pinkney, *supra* note 42 at 53.

109. Paul Festa, Study Says "Buffer Overflow" Is Most Common Security Bug, CNET News. com (November 23, 1999), available at http://news.com.com/2100-1001-233483.html. Viega & McGraw, *supra* note 20 at 135, write that buffer overflows accounted for over 50 percent of the major security bugs described in CERT/CC advisories in 1999.

110. *Supra* note 109, Festa citing Matt Bishop, U.C. Davis, "We're not learning the lessons of the past. . . . We knew how to handle buffer overflows in the 1960s and '70s. But the solutions that were required typically either used hardware or were implemented within the program itself. Some felt it made the program go too slow, so a lot of programs went out there without buffer checks, and now we're paying the price." *See also* Viega & McGraw, *supra* note 20 at 135.

111. For observations on the ubiquity of "buffer overflows," *see* James A. Whittaker & Herbert H. Thompson, *How to Break Software Security: Effective Techniques for Security Testing* 42 (2004) (noting that "[b]uffer overflows are by far the most notorious security problems in software"); S. W. Smith & Eugene H. Spafford, Grand Challenges in Information Security: Process and Output, 69 *IEEE Security & Privacy* 69 (Jan.-Feb. 2004); Pfleeger & Pfleeger, *supra* note 33

at 104; Spafford, *supra* note 10 at section 7.2, "Software Flaws" (writing that a review of vulnerability databases such as the CERIAS Cassandra Service, or the NIST ICAT database, reveals that more than 25 percent of reported flaws can be traced to buffer overflows); Susan C. Lee & Lauren B. Davis, Learning from Experience: Operating System Vulnerability Trends, *IEEE IT Professional* 17-24 (Jan.-Feb. 2003).

112. Graff & van Wyk, *supra* note 18 at 101.

113. Viega & McGraw, *supra* note 20 at 141-42, 152-53.

114. *Id*. at 143.

115. *Supra* note 15, Appendix B, Software Process Subgroup Report, at 2.

116. Leach, *supra* note 37 at 9.

117. *Id*. at 11-12. Leach includes several other tasks such as installation and delivery, post-release activities such as maintenance, and so on. *See also* Pfleeger & Pfleeger, *supra* note 33 at 151.

118. One example is the "waterfall mode," which usually follows a systematic, sequential approach to software development that progresses through problem analysis, design, coding, testing, and support. (Pressman, *supra* note 26 at 28.) Another example is the "spiral" software development model that takes an iterative approach.

119. Leach, *supra* note 37 at 21-22.

120. Viega & McGraw, *supra* note 20 at 24.

121. The Software Process Subgroup was one of the subgroups within the Task Force on Security Across the Software Development Lifecycle, which, in turn, was one of the Task Forces established in December 2003 as part of the National Cyber Security Partnership. *See* note 14 and accompanying text.

122. *Supra* note 15, Appendix B, Software Process Subgroup Report, at 47.

123. Graff & van Wyk, *supra* note 18, at 145, also note that implementation flaws are generally far easier to detect and remedy than design flaws. They write that "[v]arious tools-both commercial and open source-simplify the process of testing software code for the most common flaws (including buffer overflows) before the software is deployed into production environments."

124. *Supra* note 15, Appendix B, Software Process Subgroup Report, at 37. The overall security of a system is difficult to predict by looking at its subparts. High-level security attributes such as confidentiality and integrity are generally emergent properties.

125. *Supra* note 15, Appendix B, Software Process Subgroup Report, at 21.

126. Viega & McGraw, *supra* note 20 at 33: "Right now, there is no substitute for direct experience. . . . Identifying security risks (and other software risks for that matter) requires experience with real risks in the real world. As more software security resources become available, and as software security becomes better understood by developers, more people will be able to practice it with confidence."

127. *See* Peter G. Neumann, *Principles for Assuredly Trustworthy Composable Architectures* (2004), paper submitted to the Improving Security Across the Software Development Lifecycle Task Force. The paper is available at http://www.cyberpartnership.org/Software%20Pro .pdf. Neumann identifies the key lists of secure design principles since the "classic" 1975 Saltzer-Schroeder principles. The Saltzer-Schroeder Principles are (1) economy of mechanism: keep the design as simple and small as possible; (2) fail-safe defaults: base access decisions on permission

rather than exclusion; (3) complete mediation: every access to every object must be checked for authority; (4) open design: the design should not be secret; (5) separation of privilege: where feasible, a protection mechanism that requires two keys to unlock it is more robust and flexible than one that allows access to the presenter of only a single key; (6) least privilege: every program and every user of the system should operate using the least set of privileges necessary to complete the job; (7) least common mechanism: minimize the amount of mechanism common to more than one user and depended on by all users; and (8) psychological acceptability: it is essential that the human interface be designed for ease of use, so that users routinely and automatically apply the protection mechanisms correctly. (Jerry Saltzer & Mike Schroeder, The Protection of Information in Computer Systems, 63 *Proceedings of the IEEE* 1278-1308 (Sept. 1975).

128. Graff & van Wyk, *supra* note 18 at 159; Viega & McGraw, *supra* note 20 at 117; Pfleeger & Pfleeger, *supra* note 33 at 155-56.

129. Viega & McGraw, *supra* note 20 at 32-40. *Supra* note 15, Appendix B, Software Process Subgroup Report, at 21.

130. *Supra* note 15, Appendix B, Software Process Subgroup Report, at 47, 52.

131. *See* for example, the recent books by Viega & McGraw, *supra* note 20, Graff & van Wyk, *supra* note 18, Pfleeger & Pfleeger, *supra* note 33, and the "how-to" description of common attacks by Whittaker & Thompson, *supra* note 111.

132. *Supra* note 15, Appendix B, Software Process Subgroup Report, at 47, 52. Software producers should "use a process that can predictably produce software with very low specification, design, and implementation defects-less than 0.1 . . . defects per thousand lines of new and changed code delivered."

133. Leach, *supra* note 37 at 28; Baase, *supra* note 99 at 148.

134. *Supra* note 15, Appendix B, Software Process Subgroup Report, at 16.; Pressman, *supra* note 26 at 673; Pfleeger & Pfleeger, *supra* note 33 at 167. "The notion 'formal methods' means many things to many people, and many types of formal methods are proffered for use in software development. Each formal technique involves the use of mathematically precise specification and design notations. In its purest form, formal development is based on refinement and proof of correctness at each stage in the life cycle. But all formal methods are not created equal."

135. Pressman, *supra* note 26 at 675.

136. *Supra* note 15, Appendix B, Software Process Subgroup Report, at 17; Pfleeger & Pfleeger, *supra* note 33 at 167. Studies examining the effectiveness of formal methods have generated mixed results, although they do tend to suggest a positive influence on software quality. Pfleeger & Pfleeger conclude that anecdotal support for formal methods has been growing, but more evaluation is needed to understand how they contribute to quality and how to choose between the many competing formal methods.

137. Pressman, *supra* note 26 at 44.

138. Pressman, *supra* note 26 at 700, referring to J. Henderson, Why Isn't Cleanroom the Universal Software Development Methodology? 8 *Crosstalk* 11-14 (May 1995).

139. Pfleeger & Pfleeger, *supra* note 33 at 166.

140. *Supra* note 15, Appendix B, Software Process Subgroup Report, at 17-18.

141. Pressman, *supra* note 26 at 700.

142. Pfleeger & Pfleeger, *supra* note 33 at 168.

143. Graff & van Wyk, *supra* note 18 at 158.

144. Graff & van Wyk, *supra* note 18 at 160.

145. Graff & van Wyk, *supra* note 18 at 164.

146. *Supra* note 15, Appendix B, Software Process Subgroup Report, at 48.

147. Graff & van Wyk, *supra* note 18 at 122.

148. *Supra* note 15, Appendix B, Software Process Subgroup Report, at 49.

149. Graff & van Wyk, *supra* note 18 at 26.

150. *Supra* note 15, Appendix B, Software Process Subgroup Report, at 36.

151. *See* Internet Storm Center, SANS Institute, RPC DCOM Worm (MSBlaster) (August 14, 2003), available at http://isc.sans.org/diary.php?date=2003-08-11.

9 CURING CYBERSECURITY BREACHES THROUGH STRICT PRODUCTS LIABILITY

Shubha Ghosh and Vikram Mangalmurti

Shubha Ghosh is professor of law, The University of Wisconsin Law School. Vikram Mangalmurti is research fellow, Carnegie Mellon University, Heinz School of Public Policy.

Computer security and information privacy traditionally have been viewed as matters of private right to be protected either through contract, property, or technological measures.[1] We argue in this chapter that computer security and information privacy can be more effectively understood by analogy to the regulation of hazardous activities, workplace accidents, and defective products through common law and statutes.[2] For example, Professor Edward Lazowska, of the University of Washington Department of Computer Science, has analogized computer security to auto safety, "where a set of government regulations has caused automobiles to become far more safe over the course of 35 years."[3] Regulation of health and safety has served to create assurance in new technological developments such as the automobile. We propose a similar approach to the regulation of cybersecurity breaches leading to compromises of privacy. Our approach is grounded in what we will refer to as the "social assurance" perspective.

We use the term *social assurance* in contrast with *social insurance*, which has negative associations with failed or troubled social welfare programs. Instead, *social assurance* parallels *social capital*, a term that acknowledges the role of nonmarket and nongovernmental institutions as a means to regulate conduct through the creation of norms and trust.[4] *Social assurance* is preferable to *social capital* for our purposes, however, because of our concerns with the hazards posed by information security breaches. Instead of framing security and privacy as matters of private harms and private law, our approach highlights the role of regulation in establishing the social foundation of trust necessary for cyberspace transactions.

The patchwork of current regulation, ranging from privacy default rules in contracts to criminalization of attacks on data storage devices, can best be understood as mechanisms for allocating and distributing the risk and uncertainty associated with breaches in critical information systems.[5] The social assurance perspective provides a template to understand regulatory measures and reform them. Furthermore, the social assurance perspective provides the means to assess the use of products liability theories to address computer security and information privacy issues. Although the existing legal and economic literature has hinted at the use of products liability theory,[6] there has not been systematic study of the use of the products liability model as a means to regulating security and privacy.

Our argument is structured as follows. In Section I, we present the social assurance model of security and privacy and develop a legal theory based on products liability doctrine. In Section II we show how the social assurance model incorporates traditional contract, property, and technological approaches by developing a legal theory that mimics the theory of products liability while avoiding some of its pitfalls. In Section III we conclude.

I. THE SOCIAL ASSURANCE MODEL

The social assurance perspective assumes that breaches of security and information privacy are a matter of social regulation. Although individuals are the immediate victims of data losses and leakages of private information that arise from the hacking of security systems, social institutions and systems are harmed as well. The analogy can be made to highway systems. When two vehicles collide, the individual drivers and passengers are the immediate victims. But the particular accident can cause backups in traffic flow that affect other users of the highway indirectly. Moreover, the threat of such accidents with both direct and indirect harms can affect people's perceptions of a particular highway and its surrounding geography. Put simply, our analysis of breaches of security and information privacy focuses attention on the social cost of such breaches. The social cost is not simply the aggregation of individual costs associated with harms such as identity theft, improper bank transfers, data loss, and so on. It also includes the costs that stem from the resulting risks that are faced by all users, actual or potential, whether or not they are the victim of an accident. In other words, the social costs include the costs associated with a loss of faith in the system.[7] Such costs may include a lag in the adoption of Internet use by end users due to fear, and the resulting lag in business and efficiencies by providers of Internet content and services. Our focus is on the systemic effects of Internet security breaches, particularly as they affect liability and accountability.

A. Liability

An offshoot of the theory often contrasted with property rights, liability means the imposition of a payment obligation on a person to compensate an injured party. We use *liability* here in a broader sense to mean an obligation to make someone whole for an imposed injury. The injured party can be made whole through injunctive relief or through damages. The form of remedy is of less concern to us here than the nature of the obligation. Put simply, liability centers on the question of how we should determine when person A is "liable" to person B for certain injuries that B has suffered.

The scholarly analysis of liability is well-known, and we summarize here the analysis that can be traced to Ronald Coase's writing on social cost.[8] According to Coase, the notion of injury was indeterminate. In most situations, to say that A's actions legally caused B's harms is to make a statement of A's rights to engage in certain activities vis-à-vis B. In his classic example of the railroad and the farmer, the conclusion that the sparks from the train caused a fire on the farmer's land is to make an assumption about the railroad's rights to build the railway next to the farmer's land. The dispute is really a matter of conflicting rights, and there needs to be a basis for concluding whose rights claim is stronger. Coase rejected a moral or deontological way to resolve the claim of conflicting rights. Instead, his focus was on how the conflict could be resolved through private bargaining. In other words, the problem of external cost could be best understood as a matter of negotiation between the conflicted parties over the allocation of an entitlement, defined and secured by legal institutions.

Our characterization of the standard Coasean story of liability highlights two problems with its application to the type of Internet transactions that is the subject of this chapter. First, despite the reference in the title of his paper to "social cost," Coase's analysis transforms social costs into an aggregate of private costs. The fire in the railroad-farmer hypothetical is assumed to harm only the crops owned by the farmer. But the fire hazard would also affect the railroad, because an out-of-control fire would hinder rail service along the farmer's land. It could also affect the neighboring farmers and other economic and social actors. Under Coase's view, all of these affected parties would have to be allowed to enter into negotiation. Here the concept of transaction costs becomes salient, because the number of interested parties would clearly impose large transaction costs on private negotiation. But more than individual harm is at stake. The fear of the railroad causing fire as a fact in the world, rather than as a proposition of legal liability, may influence people's perceptions and trust in the railroad itself. One need only think of the crash of the Hindenberg, an incident that, for many reasons, put an end to the age of the zeppelin, to recognize that the types of costs identified by Coase cannot readily be made private: hence the impossibility of creating efficient market mechanisms.

A response to this argument is that much of what we have described is really a matter of accounting. If the hazards we isolate can be quantified, then insurance and other markets can be created to deal with the hazards. Clearly, the structure of these markets will depend on the structure of entitlements. The rule of legal liability will simply determine whether it is the farmer or the railroad that must buy insurance.[9] But this response is too simplistic because it fails to distinguish between risk and uncertainty. Certainly, some aspects of the relationship between the railroad and the farmer can be described by a probabilistic model. But others cannot. For matters of uncertainty, for questions such as "Is this airline safe?" or "Is rail transportation more dangerous than other means?" market answers may not be feasible. Some other regulatory structure, for example, the Federal Aviation Administration or the National Highway Traffic Safety Administration, may be needed to ensure safety and guarantee trust in the system.[10] Such regulatory structures need to exist in addition to the market institutions to manage risk in order to govern the full range of hazards. Because of the complications of risk and uncertainty, liability is not simply a matter of private right and negotiation, but a question of systemic regulation.

B. Accountability

The second building block of the social assurance perspective is the concept of accountability. Liability is, of course, a type of accountability.[11] If A is liable to B, then in some sense A is accountable to B, even if it is only in the narrow sense of A having to compensate B through the payment of money damages. But our sense of accountability is much broader than that. First, our notion of accountability recognizes that there will also be an element of uncertainty in a system. A complex array of regulatory structures and insurance markets might create the nagging doubt that the agencies and firms may be corrupted in some way. This nagging doubt may be impossible to quantify, meaning that it would be impossible to insure against political or market uncertainties. Institutions need to be designed to ensure that accountability is present in order to reduce these nagging doubts. Second, unlike liability, accountability has a process dimension and is not a matter purely of entitlement definition. Transparency in regulatory structures and market institutions is required either directly or through learned intermediaries, such as lawyers or journalists, in order to ensure that governing institutions do not become corrupted. The creation and maintenance of transparency require some degree of participation by individuals other than insiders. Accountability can be structured in many ways, for example, through a combination of disclosure rules, meta-rules of liability, and participatory rules. Whatever institutional arrangements are adopted, the goal of accountability is to create trust in a governance system.

We have presented the blueprint for the cathedral of the legal regulation of information security breaches. In the next section, we present one version of the cathedral based on the doctrine of products liability. Our goal is not to suggest that a products liability approach is the solution to the problems of information security and privacy, but to illustrate one way in which the social assurance perspective can be made operational. Our analysis in the next section should be viewed as a thought experiment, helpful in illustrating the strengths and identifying the weaknesses of the social assurance perspective presented here.

II. PRODUCTS LIABILITY AND INFORMATION SECURITY BREACHES: AN ANALYSIS OF A POSSIBLE SOCIAL ASSURANCE APPROACH

The historical dimensions of products liability law are key to understanding the social assurance perspective on information security breaches. Two specific transformations in products liability make it particularly appropriate to regulating information security breaches. The first is products liability's roots in contract law. As several scholars have pointed out, the development of contractual warranties made it possible to impose liability on manufacturers and vendors for injuries caused by products that failed to operate as promised.[12]

Once the bars of contractual privity were removed, it was a small step to conceptualize this promise into a duty not to cause harm from defective products. The second relevant transformation was the conception of defect, which originally was defined in terms of deviations from standard manufacturing of a product.[13] However, the concept of defect extended to design choices, including choices of how to market the product and how to inform the consumer about latent and other hazards through warnings.

To the extent that arms-length, anonymous market relations are becoming the norm in cyberspace, tort law, judiciously applied, can be used to respond to the resulting risk and uncertainty and impose liability and restore accountability. The difficulty in this argument has been the reluctance of tort law to embrace the notion of economic harms as a form of personal harm.[14] The commodification of information and the resulting loss of privacy are unlikely to result in physical harm to an individual or an individual's tangible property. Products liability law, if it is to keep pace with the times and continue to provide an adequate measure of risk management and social assurance, must broaden the definition of personal harm to include damage to privacy. As transactions are increasingly conducted via remote means, personal identity and privacy are increasingly becoming the currency of trade. A disintegration in the faith of the integrity of personal information will hamper future growth.

To explore these issues, and to assess the appropriateness of products liability as a form of social assurance, we analyze how information security breaches would be addressed in light of traditional products liability doctrine. We focus on three doctrinal issues: (1) the product-service distinction in products liability; (2) the concept of privity; and (3) the legal standard for determining defect.

A. Information Security as Product or Service?

An important distinction for strict products liability law is the distinction between products and services. Defective products are judged under a strict liability standard, whereas defective services are judged only under a negligence standard.[15] Several policy reasons are given for this distinction.

First, services are not standardized to the same extent as products. Haircuts, real estate services, and legal services, to take some cases in which the issue of strict liability has arisen, are individualized and highly specialized, varying from client to client. Because services, unlike products, are not standardized, it becomes difficult to craft a standard for defect based on strict liability. Instead, the more appropriate standard is one of negligence, which applies a utilitarian cost-benefit analysis that is highly contextualized. Second, the cost shifting imposed by strict liability may be difficult for many service professionals to absorb through insurance. The high costs of strict liability would impose disincentives to enter certain professional fields, creating potential shortages in areas such as medicine, law, and accounting and shifting access to the wealthy and away from poor clients. Related to the cost-shifting issue is the "shallow pockets" of certain services, such as hair styling, to refer to an earlier example. Because of the shallower pockets in certain service industries, the costs cannot effectively be internalized by the industry. Finally, many services are self-regulated by professional associations, and the self-regulation is developed with the expertise of professionals who better understand the field than courts. The negligence standard can incorporate industry self-regulation into the standard of care more effectively than strict liability. To the extent that strict liability can incorporate industry self-regulation, for example through the standard for defect, strict liability may effectively be equivalent to the negligence standard.

If information security systems are classified as a service, liability for harms arising from defective information security would be scrutinized under the negligence standard. The case for liability under negligence, however, is more than likely unsuccessful for two reasons.[16] First, if an industry standard applies, it is exceedingly difficult for a plaintiff to show what reasonable alternative conduct by the creator or vendor of the information security system would have been available. Second, if a more general, nonindustry specific standard applied, a showing of negligence will depend upon a comparison of the magnitude of the resulting harm, its probability of occurring, and the cost of avoidance. As under the industry standard, the problem is one of demonstrating the cost of avoidance, which arguably might be quite high if no feasible alternative is readily available to prevent the harm. Because of the service-product distinction, imposing tort liability on information security has been difficult.

There are several arguments to challenge the characterization of information security as a service rather than as a product. First, unlike typical services, information security, provided in the form of proprietary software or hardware, is standardized. As software has become more commodified, what seems to be a mere list of instructions or automated acts of labor is really a good bought and sold in the marketplace. An analogy can be made to the more "physical" world. A service vendor that monitors the traffic of a corporate Internet site for suspicious activity by specifically tailoring algorithms for that company and manning a service desk to actively pursue possible illicit conduct is a service, analogous in many ways to a security guard at the front desk of an office building or a guard that roams the grounds of a warehouse. Firewalls that are designed to be implemented on home PCs, or an antivirus software, or even the security features inherent to most Internet browsers, are products, not much different than a lock. Several jurisdictions treat software transactions as falling under UCC Article 2, and as discussed earlier, strict products liability has a direct lineage from the introduction of warranties under the UCC.[17]

Second, large software companies, ones that dominate the industry like Microsoft, are deep pockets, and so the problem of deterring the entry of service professionals is mitigated. Although it is not correct to generalize to the entire industry from the example of a company such as Microsoft, there are reasons to think that the imposition of strict liability would not impose severe costs on the software industry. Most smaller software companies have adopted the strategy of creating one strong application with the hopes of being bought out by a company like Microsoft. If strict liability is imposed, much of the liability for defective software will be shifted to larger entities with little negative effect on smaller companies. Effectively, the deep pockets will absorb the cost of liability while small companies will still have incentives to enter the killer application lottery. In addition, the liability associated with the development of insecure software should create an incentive for small software companies to pay special attention to quality controls.

Further support for treating defective information security, including both software and hardware, as a product is accorded by the Restatement Third of Torts (Products Liability), which states a definition of "product" to include "tangible personal property distributed commercially for use or consumption" and "other items . . . when the context of their distribution is sufficiently analogous to the distribution and use of tangible property."[18] The notes to the Restatement definition of "product" state that the electricity when it enters a consumer's home (as opposed to being transmitted through a grid) is treated as a product under products liability law. The authors of the Restatement explain the distinction as follows: "Plaintiffs in the post-delivery cases typically complain of unexpected drops or surges in voltage, resulting in personal injury or property damage. Those claims seem better governed by principles of strict liability for physical deviations from intended design."[19] We would argue that the treatment of "electricity flowing inside a consumer's home" is the appropriate model for tort treatment of information security systems that are implemented by the end users on their computer systems. Whether downloaded from the Internet or installed via disk, information security systems should be treated as products, and not services, under products liability law.

B. Who Should Be Liable?

Strict products liability expanded the scope of liability to include anyone in the distribution chain of a product, starting with the manufacturer and ending with the retailer from whom the product is purchased. The breakdown of the privity requirement was a key move for the expansion of liability. The shift from negligence to strict liability eased the proof problems in establishing liability of distant manufacturers and distributors. In the shadow of tort rules, contractual provisions facilitate risk sharing and risk spreading and transform the distribution chain that connects the manufacturer with the consumer into a means of providing social assurance for the harms imposed by defective products.

In one respect, the conceptual framework of the distribution chain at the heart of strict products liability lends itself to the imposition of strict products liability for defective information security systems. Software in the box or hardware bought either through bricks-and-mortar outlets or through the Internet fall readily into the traditional framework of distribution. The challenge is raised by software downloaded through the Internet or software systems that are integrated features of either Internet service providers (ISPs) or browsers. Each of these cases poses interesting questions for how to conceptualize manufacturing and distribution of information security systems. Equally challenging questions are posed by the case of programmers who independently create software that may be distributed as part of a proprietary system or as part of an open source arrangement. We discuss each of these issues in turn.

In the case of downloaded software, the distribution chain needs to be analyzed more contextually. If the software is downloaded directly from the manufacturer's Website, then the manufacturer is acting like a distributor, and usual strict liability principles would apply. It is as if the customer had obtained the software through mail order. If the customer has to go through several links to obtain the software, the question arises as to liability of the owner of the linking site. Strict product liability would require that the linking site be viewed as a distributor so that the full internalization and allocation of liability occurs within the chain of distribution. But there may be reasons not to impose such liability on the linker. If the linker does not have a deep pocket, is simply an aficionado of a certain piece of software, and is providing the link as a generous service, then it may be preferable not to impose liability for its enthusiasm. An added complication to the analysis arises with the use of peer-to-peer services to share software. Should the peer-to-peer service and its participants be viewed as distributors of software for the purposes of strict liability? The answer, we contend, should rest ultimately on tort principles of risk allocation and avoidance rather than on the legality of the conduct, which is better handled through copyright law. There is a risk, however, that if product liability is expanded to include peer-to-peer services, the threat of tort liability may impose a burden on the development of this technology.

The case of ISP liability in many ways fits squarely in the chain-of-production model that informs strict products liability law. To the extent that the ISP creates and promises a secure interface as part of its Web portal or other communication device, the ISP is acting as a manufacturer and should be held liable for any defects in the interface. To the extent the ISP facilitates the distribution of defective software, it should be held liable in the same way as the linker discussed in the previous paragraph. If the ISP is a mere passive conduit, however, for the downloading of defective software, the case can be made that liability should not be imposed. The case against liability rests in part on the omission-commission distinction and in part on the looser connection between the transmission of defective software and any profit that the ISP is earning on the transaction. As a passive conduit, the ISP presumably is not directly profiting from the transmission of the defective software any more than it profits from general usage of the system.

Programmer liability is the last issue we will discuss in addressing the question of who should be liable for defective software. If the programmer is an employee of the manufacturing company, then usual *respondeat superior* doctrine applies, and the manufacturer should be liable under strict product liability theory. As in many cases, the programmer may be an independent contractor or the program may have been purchased as part of an acquisition of a software company. We would argue that the independent contractor case should be treated in the same way as the employee case, with liability shifting entirely to the company with no liability imposed on the programmer if the software company can internalize the liability better than can the independent programmer. In the case of an acquisition, the usual principles of successor liability should apply.

The harder question is what to do with open source software. If a company distributes software as open source, and one of the users programs what turns out to be defective software that is subsequently distributed, who should be liable? We argued earlier, and will argue later in this chapter, that our model of products liability is favorable toward open source. But the allocation of liability in the chain of distribution of open source software may severely deter the usage of open source systems. As a matter of consistent and fair application of the law, the rules should be devised so that they are neutral between open and proprietary systems. Imposition of strict liability on the vendor of open source software for defects introduced later, however, seems unfair, especially if the introduction of the defect could not be detected or prevented. At the same time, imposition of strict liability on the party that introduced the defect and anyone who subsequently distributed the software may deter experimentation and open access and usage. Part of the conceptual problem is that the traditional chain of distribution is not applicable to the open source situation. In other words, each link in the chain is in some sense both a manufacturer and a distributor. Because of this discrepancy between the open source model and the traditional distribution model, the argument could be made that a more appropriate standard is one of negligence. Such an argument can be reconciled with a consistent and fair application of the law. Comparing open source and proprietary systems in terms of the traditional distribution model is an invalid comparison and the difference would warrant different treatment for liability.

C. What Is a Defect?

Originally, products liability protected against defects in the manufacturing of a product. A manufacturing defect was, and continues to be, defined with respect to consumers' expectations of how a product was supposed to function. These expectations may have been created by advertising or promises, whether expressed or implied, made by the manufacturer or distributor of the product. Often, these expectations are based on the standards associated with a particular product. For example, cola bottles are not expected to explode in one's hand. Even if no promises were made by the seller that a coke bottle would not explode, an exploding bottle would not be standard issue for the product coming off the assembly line. Consumer expectations would be frustrated, and a defect would be found.[20]

Manufacturing defects follow almost neatly from products liability's roots in the law of consumer warranties in contract. Although the law of contract, through the Uniform Commercial Code, talks about express and implied warranties based on representations by the seller and warranties based on promises of merchantability and fitness of purpose, the tort notion of manufacturing defects expanded the set of promises about the way in which a product could be expected to function. This expansion of expectations became the basis for liability in tort.[21]

Design defects expanded the set of expectations even further. Whereas manufacturing defects assumed a particular standard for a product, the deviation from which would be the basis for liability, the concept of design defects questioned the choice of the standard itself. Liability on the theory of design defect rested on a showing that the seller's choices of product standards fell below some general, legal standard. The determination of this standard has two dimensions. First, there is the traditional tort question of whether the standard should be one of negligence or strict liability. For some products, such as pharmaceuticals, courts rejected strict liability for design defects in favor of a standard of negligence. The requirement of negligence meant that a plaintiff would have to show not only that the design was defective but that the defendant was unreasonable in the choice of design.[22]

The second dimension of determining the standard for design defect focuses on the definition of design defect itself. Mimicking the approach to manufacturing defects, some early courts applied a consumer expectations test to the determination of design defect. Such an approach was criticized for being too consumer friendly and for potentially conflating manufacturing and design defects. More critically, the consumer expectation standard blurred the line between consumer and producer. Although the consumer may have expectations about the standards for a specific product coming out of the product, it stretches reality to think that consumers have any expectations about the standard for an entire product line.[23]

The alternative, and more favored approach, for determining design defects developed by courts is the risk-utility analysis.[24] Under this approach, the court weighs the benefits of a particular design choice with the risks posed by the choice. A design defect would exist if the risks outweighed the utility. Different courts elaborated on the risk-utility analysis with the introduction of detailed factors. Some courts and commentators suggested that the risk-utility analysis was a disguised form of negligence that rested liability, implicitly, on a finding of unreasonable choices in the design of a product. For these latter courts, the risk-utility analysis blurred the distinction between the standard of care, which focused on the conduct of the defendant, with the definition of defect, which focused on the product. In effect, liability for design defect was strict in name, but based on negligence in fact.[25]

Springing from the design defect theory was the theory of liability based on failure to warn, a theory that marked a shift away from strict products liability to negligence.[26] Inclusion of warnings may, in certain situations, defeat the finding of a design or manufacturing defect by providing the basis for a defense of assumption of risk. But mere inclusion of a warning is not sufficient to avoid liability. The nature of the risk, the customary and possible uses of the product, and the obviousness of the danger all aid in gauging the adequacy of the warning. The Restatement Third describes the duty to warn as a question of foreseeability, and in general, negligence is the standard for determining when a warning is adequate.[27] What is interesting about the duty-to-warn theory is its relationship to products liability's roots in the law of warranties. Both duty-to-warn and warranties theories rest on the notion that information disclosure is an important aspect of the marketing of products. For warranties, the disclosure is of promises about the quality of a product, its merchantability, and its fitness of purpose. For defect warnings, the disclosure is of inherent dangers in the product. The parallel between the two theories should not be surprising. The similarities illustrate how products liability theory has served to expand the set of expectations that a consumer has in entering the marketplace beyond the simple set of promises and representations made by a seller with whom the consumer contracts.

Two lessons can be gleaned from the development of the understanding of "defect" for regulation of information security systems. The first is the role of products liability law in creating a system of trust in particular marketplaces by expanding consumers' expectations about the quality, reliability, and safety of products. The second lesson concerns the details of how products liability law can be applied to information security systems. We are not by any means suggesting that the products liability system is perfect. Instead, our goal is to distill what is good about the products liability system and to avoid the system's defects, so to speak. The extension of the definition of defect to information security systems is a case in point.

An assumption of our analysis is that manufacturing defects in information security systems, based on software, will be rare. The reason for this assumption is that software can be copied without alteration in the code or standard. In other words, downloading or uploading software results in a perfect assembly-line replica. Of course, problems can arise in the process of downloading or uploading, such as the transmission or introduction of viruses. For example, downloading software on a nonconventional browser may not result in an exact replica and may introduce what could be described as defects, arguably analogous to the defects introduced in a manufacturing process such as the failure to adequately secure a bolt. The question is whether such a defect should be treated as a conventional manufacturing defect. The problem, once again, is that traditional categories seem inapplicable. When an end user downloads or uploads software, he or she is arguably not a manufacturer, but no different from a consumer using a product. Conceptually, however, what the end user is doing is making a copy of the product, an act that seems very similar to manufacturing. One way to avoid this quandary is to recognize that the problem arises from the failure of the original software to be interoperable with different browsers or operating systems. This failure seems more analogous to a design defect than to a manufacturing defect. For this reason, we maintain the assumption that manufacturing defects will be rare for information security systems and shift to the question of what should constitute a design defect.

The concept of design defect applies beyond the situation described in the previous paragraph. If an information security system fails to adequately ensure against viruses and other security threats, then the problem could also be addressed as one of a design defect. Whether the failure is actually the result of a defect depends on the standard for defect. We acknowledge the problems with a pure consumer expectations test for design defects. The determination of a design defect purely on the grounds of a breach of consumer expectations ignores the business and engineering decisions that are necessary for product design. Such expertise should not be ignored. Consequently, we propose that the risk-utility standard would be the appropriate standard to determine defect. By advocating this standard, we are implicitly introducing negligence principles into the determination of liability. Negligence principles may undermine the strong deterrence of strict liability, but they also permit more nuanced judgments about when liability should apply.[28]

Having adopted the risk-utility approach, we need next to address the problem of after-the-fact design decisions, specifically by a less-than-qualified judiciary or jury. The most salient problem is that the risk-utility balance may vary from individual to individual. This problem extends beyond the problem of software. For some users, no amount of risk is satisfactory. Such users may want very strong protections built into a product at the expense of the functionality of that product. Others may tolerate more risk. The problem with the risk-utility approach is one of choosing the appropriate degree of risk tolerance.[29] In the context of software design, the question can be seen as one of how much interactivity should be allowed in the use of a particular application or system. Should, for example, a user be able to set the sensitivity of a virus filter or should the filter always be set high? Should the user be able to turn off the filter or should the filter run automatically without the possibility of cancellation by the user?

Determining the appropriate standard for design is a familiar problem for products liability law. In the area of information security, the question is particularly compelling because of the adverse selection problem. If the risk tolerance is set low, the entire system may be threatened because of the weakest link. Alternatively, if the risk tolerance is set high, the functionality of the system is compromised. Furthermore, too high a risk tolerance may create disincentives for a system to adapt to different security risks, posing the problem of greater threats in the future. Judicial creation of a standard is far from a perfect resolution.

One argument in favor of judicial design decisions is the inadequacy of the market in determining the appropriate design.[30] If the market for computer standards has been monopolized, and the threat of security increased because of the integration and uniformity of code, then judicial oversight may serve as a check on poor market design choices.

Warnings play an important role in the determination of design defects of software. Warnings of a certain sort, however, are simply ineffective. The disclosure that an application may be subject to bugs or virus attacks seems gratuitous; after all, all consumers know that software is not perfect and may crash and be corrupted. A requirement that companies release patches to protect against potential breaches would be an important complement to the statutory disclosure obligation. Of course, companies already do engage in such warnings and do provide patches and other protection. The argument could be made that the market has resolved the problem by providing adequate disclosure. Once again, however, we should not assume that the market is perfect, and more careful study of how well the market functions in providing warnings of and protection against breaches is warranted in determining the exact scope of the duty to warn.

An additional complicating factor in the issue of defining defect in the context of the Internet is that what is a "defect" for some is a "feature" for others.[31] For example, it is possible to increase the security of your Internet browser by turning on all of its security features. The result, however, is also a browser that is significantly limited in the number of features supported and tasks capable of completing. From a products liability perspective, this raises significant questions on the issue of whether or not a design defect has occurred. In essence, the very things that cause a security risk are often what makes the product valuable. A sharp knife can do harm but a dull knife is pretty much useless. To a significant degree, the issue is a matter of the sophistication of the end user. Sophisticated users may be able to navigate through security pitfalls without disabling the most powerful features of a browser; unsophisticated users may not. In such cases, the defect may be based on failure to warn the unsophisticated buyers. The treatment of defects and features illustrates the way in which products liability law shapes consumer expectations in the marketplace.

III. CONCLUDING THOUGHTS

The social assurance perspective provides a means to think more creatively and pointedly about preventing and curing information security breaches. Common law products liability, though not a perfect model, offers a template for statutorily addressing the harms caused by security breaches. A well-designed products liability system that can aid in defining compensable harms and the forms of compensation will also aid in spurring on the development of private and public insurance systems to govern these hazards. In addition, it may be worth considering a state-sponsored system of immunization, much like the one that is used for polio, to limit the spread of known viruses and to secure existing systems. The last proposal is worthy of a separate discussion.[32] Whatever concrete proposals are eventually debated and chosen, the social assurance approach is instrumental in expanding our regulatory toolkit beyond property and contract.

NOTES

1. *See, e.g.,* Jerry Kang, Information Privacy in Cyberspace Transactions, 50 *Stan. L. Rev.* 1193 (1998). *See also* Symposium on Cyberspace and Privacy: A New Legal Paradigm, 52 *Stan. L. Rev.* 1201 (2000).

2. For a discussion of social assurance, *see* Tom R. Tyler & Roderick M. Kramer, Whither Trust? in Trust in *Organizations: Frontiers of Theory and Research* 10-12 (Roderick M. Kramer & Tom R. Tyler, eds., 1996). For a discussion of these issues using the term *social insurance*, see David A. Moss, *When All Else Fails: Government as the Ultimate Risk Manager* 152-79 (2002); Hal R. Varian, Redistributive Taxation as Social Insurance, 14. *J. Pub. Econ.* 49-68 (1980).

3. Steve Lohr, Fixing Flaws, Microsoft Invites Attack, *N.Y. Times*, Sept. 29, 2003, at C1, C5.

4. *See* Francis Fukuyama, *Trust: The Social Virtues and the Creation of Prosperity* 26 (1995) (defining social capital); Mark Granovetter, Economic Action and Social Structure: The Problem of Embeddedness, 91 *Am. J. Soc.* 481, 487-93 (1985) (discussing the role of trust in market transactions).

5. For an overview, *see* Daniel J. Solove & Marc Rotenberg, *Information Privacy Law* 1-61 (2003); Robert A. Pikowsky, An Overview of the Law of Electronic Surveillance Post September 11, 2001, *94 Libr. L. J.* 601-620 (2002).

6. *See* Helen Nissenbaum, Accountability in a Computerized Society, in *Human Values and the Design of Computer Technology* 41-64 (Batya Friedman, ed. 1997); Jeffrey H. Matsura, *Security, Rights and Liabilities in e-Commerce* 55-57 (2002); H. Varian, Economic Science Column, Managing Online Security Risks, *N.Y. Times*, June 1, 2000.

7. *See* Rino Falcone & Christiano Castelfranchi, A Belief-Based Model of Trust, in *Trust in Knowledge Management and Systems in Organizations* 306-43 (Maija-Leena Huotari & Mirja Iivonen, eds., 2004); Fukuyama, *supra* note 4 at 5-7.

8. *See* R. H. Coase, *The Problem of Social Cost in the Firm, the Market, and the Law* (R. H. Coase, ed., 1988).

9. *See* Steven Shavell, *Economic Analysis of Accident Law* 243-45 (1987).

10. *See* Neal Komesar, *Imperfect Alternatives* 90-97 (1995).

11. *See* Nissenbaum, *supra* note 6 at 57-62.

12. *See, e.g.,* Shavell , *supra* note 9 at 239-41.

13. *See id.* at 245-46.

14. *See Saratoga Fishing Co. v. J.M. Martinac & Co.*, 117 S. Ct. 1783 (1997); *East River S.S. Corp. v. Transamerica Delaval Inc.*, 106 S. Ct. 2295 (1986).

15. *See, e.g., Johnson v. William C. Ellis & Sons Iron Works, Inc.*, 604 F. 2d 950 (5th Cir. 1979).

16. For a different perspective on the application of a negligence standard to information security breach, *see* Jennifer Chandler, Improving Software Security: A Discussion of Liability for Unreasonably Insecure Software, Chapter 8 in this volume.

17. *See* discussion in *Specht v. Netscape Communications Corp.*, 306 F. 3d 13 (2d Cir. 2002).

18. Restatement (Third) of Torts: Products Liability § 19 (1998).

19. *See id.* at cmt. d.

20. *See id.* § 7.

21. *See* William Powers, A Modest Proposal to Abandon Strict Products Liability, 1991 *U. Ill. L. Rev.* 639, 653-54 (1991).

22. *See Brown v. Superior Court*, 44 Cal. 3d 1049 (1988).

23. *See* Paul D. Rheingold, What Are the Consumer's "Reasonable Expectations?" 22 *Bus. Law.* 589 (1967).

24. *See, e.g., Turner v. General Motors Corp.*, 584 S.W. 2d 844 (1979).

25. *See* Sheila Birnbaum, Unmasking the Test for Design Defect: From Negligence [to Warranty] to Strict Liability to Negligence, 33 *Vand. L. Rev.* 593 (1980).

26. *See, e.g., McDonald v. Ortho Pharmaceutical Corp.*, 475 N.E. 2d 65 (Mass. 1985).

27. *See* Restatement (Third) of Torts: Products Liability § 2, cmt. i-l (1998).

28. *See* John E. Calfee & Richard Craswell, Some Effects of Uncertainty on Compliance with Legal Standards, 70 *Va. L. Rev.* 965 (1984).

29. *See* Alan Schwartz, Proposals for Products Liability Reform: A Theoretical Synthesis, 97 *Yale L. J.* 353 (1988).

30. *See* William Landes & Richard Posner, A Positive Economic Analysis of Products Liability, 14 *J. Legal Stud.* 535, 555-56 (1985); Ross Anderson, *Why Information Security Is Hard: An Economic Perspective*, unpublished manuscript.

31. *See* James Henderson, Judicial Review of Manufacturers' Conscious Design Choices: The Limits of Adjudication, 73 *Colum. L. Rev.* 1531 (1973).

32. For an interesting analysis of vaccination that has implications for cybersecurity, *see* Pierre-Yves Geoffard & Thomas Philipson, Disease Eradication: Private Versus Public Vaccination, 87 *Am. Econ. Rev.* 222-30 (1997) (showing why privately provided vaccination will not lead to disease eradication because of demand-driven price effects).

Part 3

PROMOTING PRIVACY AND SECURITY
THROUGH STATUTORY REFORMS

10 PUTTING IDENTITY THEFT ON ICE

Freezing Credit Reports to Prevent
Lending to Impostors

Chris Jay Hoofnagle

Chris Jay Hoofnagle is now senior staff attorney to the Samuelson Law, Technology & Public Policy Clinic, and senior fellow to the Berkeley Center for Law & Technology. At the time this manuscript was written, Hoofnagle was associate director of the Electronic Privacy Information Center (EPIC); his positions addressing identity theft have evolved somewhat, and in a recent article, he advanced an alternative, lightweight, nonregulatory approach to the one articulated in this article; see Identity Theft: Making the Known Unknowns Known, 21 Harv. J. of Law & Tech. 97 (2007), available at http://jolt.law.harvard.edu/articles/pdf/v21/HOOFNAGLE_Identity_Theft.pdf. The author is indebted to Professor Daniel Solove and to Woodrow Neal Harzog, a candidate for L.L.M. at the George Washington Law School, for their insightful comments on this manuscript.

Identity theft is a growing problem. It occurs when an individual uses another person's personal information to commit fraud.[1] Most identity theft cases involve the acquisition of the victim's social security number for the purpose of opening new credit accounts known as "tradelines."[2] The impostor may obtain credit cards, begin wireless phone service, or even establish utilities in a victim's name.

In 2003, in a nationally representative telephone survey of one thousand Americans, the Federal Trade Commission (FTC) found that 12 percent of respondents were victims of some form of identity theft in the previous five years.[3] The crime affects millions of individuals and imposes billions of dollars of costs on the economy: the FTC found that approximately 9.9 million individuals were victims of identity theft in 2002, that the crime cost businesses

$47 billion, and that victims incurred $5 billion in losses and 297 million hours in wasted time recovering from the crime.[4]

Prior legislative and regulatory efforts to address identity theft have centered on remedial measures, including the creation of "identity theft affidavits," which assist victims in reporting the crime to creditors and credit reporting agencies.[5] These remedial measures do little to prevent the crime. In fact, even formally criminalizing identity theft has not been effective in curbing its incidence.[6]

Instead of remedial measures, we need deeper changes in the system to prevent impostors from opening tradelines. As Professor Daniel Solove has argued, "many modern privacy problems are systemic in nature. They are the product of information flows. . . ."[7] Identity theft is such a problem, as the availability of personal data under current information architectures makes it simple for impostors to obtain the identifiers needed to apply for credit. Solove argues that to address these "problems that are architectural, the solutions should also be architectural."[8] By creating an architecture that secures personal information and by establishing rights for individuals and responsibilities on data collectors, we can reduce the risk of misuse of personal information. Such an architecture would encourage more involvement from the individual with respect to data, and could provide incentives for companies and governments to reduce the amount of information they collect.

But even if the general information architecture were revamped to create greater protection for data, identity theft may continue to occur because of lax credit-granting practices, such as giving a new credit card to an impostor who has made obvious errors on the credit application. Lax granting practices have continued because the credit reporting system law treats credit issuers, such as retailers and credit card issuers, as trusted insiders. As trusted insiders, credit issuers can easily gain access to reports with or without legal justification. Furthermore, these trusted credit issuers have not adopted sound measures for determining the actual identity of credit applicants. Such protocols allow identity thieves to open new accounts in others' names.

This chapter proposes a fix to address these weaknesses in the credit-granting system. It takes the form of a change in the default state of credit reports from their current "liquid" state to a "frozen" one. That is, our current credit system allows our personal information to flow like water to almost anyone who requests it. Once credit information is released, credit grantors who are operating in an extremely competitive market race to issue new tradelines. This makes it simple for impostors to commit identity theft by obtaining new credit accounts.

Under the proposed system, credit reports would be sealed or "frozen," available only when the individual "thaws" his or her file and specifies to whom, when, or in what contexts it should be released. Creditors will not extend tradelines without a credit report, and thus under a frozen credit report system, impostors would have great difficulty in obtaining new accounts. The frozen system would also prevent businesses and others from obtaining credit reports without consumers' full consent, thereby limiting marketing and other impermissible uses of the report.

I begin this chapter by explaining that identity theft is exacerbated by credit grantors who irresponsibly issue tradelines to impostors. Three factors in irresponsible lending are explained, and examples are presented of these activities in practice. I then explain the remedial and preventative measures in place, and argue that they are deployed too late or otherwise fail to counter the forces that drive irresponsible lending activity. Next, I describe the shift to a frozen system in greater detail, and argue that building in simple barriers to obtaining a credit report will provide a shield for all individuals against most identity thieves. Finally, the last section responds to anticipated objections to a shift to frozen credit.

I. CLIFFORD J. DAWG: CANINE CARD MEMBER SINCE 2004 AND OTHER EXAMPLES OF IRRESPONSIBLE CREDIT PRACTICES

Clifford J. Dawg is one of the newest holders of a Chase Manhattan Platinum Visa Card. Mr. Dawg enjoys the freedom of a $1,500 credit limit that is accepted worldwide. The problem is that Mr. Dawg is a dog, a four-legged domestic animal that lacks the ability to pay credit card bills or even enter into a credit contract.[9]

In this instance, the owner of the dog had signed up for a free e-mail account in his pet's name and later received a preapproved offer of credit for "Clifford J. Dawg." The owner found this humorous and responded to the preapproved offer, listing nine zeros for the dog's social security number, the "Pupperoni Factory" as employer, and "Pugsy Malone" as the mother's maiden name. The owner also wrote on the approval: "You are sending an application to a dog! Ha ha ha." The card arrived three weeks later.[10]

Mr. Dawg's owner contacted the issuing bank to cancel the card. According to the owner, the issuing bank explained that Mr. Dawg's name had been acquired from a marketing list.[11] The issuing bank's representative joked that the incident could be used as a commercial with the slogan "Dogs don't chase us, we chase them."[12] Mr. Dawg's Visa card illustrates some of the problems with credit granting. All systems, especially complex ones that are used millions of times, can fail and occasionally produce errors. But Mr. Dawg's case suggests that there is a more systemic problem in the credit application approval process.

The financial services industry might argue that this is an isolated event. Like General "Buck" Turgidson defending the military's unauthorized nuclear attack on Russia in the classic movie *Dr. Strangelove*, a financial services lawyer might say, "I don't think it's quite fair to condemn a whole program because of a single slip-up."[13] But it is not a single slip-up. Credit has been offered and issued to other dogs, including Monty, a Shih-Tzu who was extended a $24,600 credit line.[14] The slip-ups also occur with humans. Credit has been granted to children and babies and young teenagers.[15] These events suggest that the credit issuers are lax in their marketing and authentication efforts. It suggests that the applications are processed by a computer, and that no human reviews them to prevent fraudulent or improper credit granting.

Three factors lead to lax lending practices and inadequate protection of the credit report. First is that under the Fair Credit Reporting Act (FCRA), credit reporting agencies only are required to "maintain reasonable procedures designed" to prevent unauthorized release of consumer information.[16] In practice, this means that credit reporting agencies must take some action to ensure that individuals with access to credit information use it only for permissible purposes enumerated in the Act. The Federal Trade Commission Commentary on the FCRA specifies that this standard can be met in some circumstances with a blanket certification from credit issuers that they will use reports legally.[17]

This certification standard is too weak. It allows a vast network of companies to gain access to credit reports with little oversight. It treats credit issuers and other users of credit reports as trusted insiders, and their use of credit reports and ultimate extension of credit as legitimate. The problem is that insiders can pose a serious risk to security of personal information.[18] For instance, in a high-profile case, criminals relied on the relationship between Ford Motor Credit Company and credit reporting agency Experian to steal credit reports for identity theft purposes.[19] The criminals used passwords for terminals that gave Ford access to the Experian database. To create this relationship as a trusted user of the credit system, Ford Motor Credit Company would have had to certify that it only obtained and used credit reports for permissible purposes. Despite this certification standard, the criminals were still able to order thirty-thousand reports using Ford's account before they were caught.[20] Because this fraud occurred over a three-year period, it suggests that a mere certification does not include monitoring or auditing of access to the credit database.

The second factor in lax issuance is that credit grantors do not have adequate standards for verifying the true identity of credit applicants. Credit issuers sometimes open tradelines to individuals who leave obvious errors on the application, such as incorrect dates of birth or fudged social security numbers.[21] Identity theft expert Beth Givens has argued that many incidences of identity theft could be prevented by simply requiring grantors to more carefully review credit applications for obviously incorrect personal information.[22]

TRW Inc. v. *Andrews* illustrates the problems with poor standards for customer identification.[23] In that case, Adelaide Andrews visited a doctor's office in Santa Monica, California, and completed a new patient's information form that requested her name, birthdate, and social security number.[24] The doctor's receptionist, an unrelated woman named Andrea Andrews, copied the information and used Adelaide's social security number and her own name to apply for credit in Las Vegas, Nevada. On four occasions, Trans Union released Adelaide's credit report because the social security number, last name, and first initial matched. Once Trans Union released the credit reports, it made it possible for creditors to issue new tradelines. Three of the four creditors that obtained a credit report issued tradelines to the impostor based on Adelaide's file, despite the fact that the first name, birthdate, and address did not match.[25]

California has attempted to address the customer identification problem by requiring certain credit grantors to comply with heightened authentication procedures. California Civil Code § 1785.14 requires credit grantors to actually match identifying information on the credit application to the report held at the credit reporting agency. Credit cannot be granted unless three identifiers from the application match those on file at the credit bureau. However, this protection only applies when an individual applies for credit at a retailer.[26] Thus Internet, telephone, and mail credit granting is not covered. Furthermore, the categories of information to be matched could probably be found in public records, the white pages, or other readily available tools. The categories to be matched include "first and last name, month and date of birth, driver's license number, place of employment, current residence address, previous residence address, or social security number."[27]

The last factor leading to irresponsible credit granting is competition to obtain new customers. Grantors have flooded the market with "prescreened" credit offers, preapproved solicitations of credit made to individuals who meet certain criteria. These offers are sent in the mail, giving thieves the opportunity to intercept them and accept credit in the victim's name.[28] Once credit is granted, the thief changes the address on the account in order to obtain the physical card and to prevent the victim from learning of the fraud.[29] The industry sends out billions of these prescreened offers a year; in 1998, it was reported that 3.4 billion were sent.[30] In 2003, the number increased to an estimated 5 billion.[31]

Competition also drives grantors to quickly extend credit. Once a consumer (or impostor) expresses acceptance of a credit offer, issuers approve the transaction with great speed. Experian, one of the "big three" credit reporting agencies, performs this task in a "magic two seconds."[32] In a scenario published in an Experian white paper titled "Customer Data Integration," an individual receives a line of credit in two seconds after supplying only his name and address.[33] Such a quick response heightens the damage to business and victims alike, because thieves will generally make many applications for new credit in hopes that a fraction of them will be granted.

II. THE INADEQUACY OF EXISTING PROTECTIONS AGAINST IDENTITY THEFT

A. The Fraud Alert: Too Little, Too Late

A fraud alert is a notice filed at a credit reporting agency by a consumer who suspects that credit fraud may have, or has, occurred. When a credit issuer pulls a report from the agency, the alert is designed to warn a creditor that the applicant may be an impostor.

This protection is only triggered when an individual suspects fraud, when the individual is aware that he or she can file the alert, and when the individual actually does file the alert. But many identity theft victims never experience any indication of fraud until it is too late. A recent study found that 85 percent of victims discovered the crime in a "negative manner."[34] That is, a denial of credit, a refusal of employment, or a notice from a creditor alerted the victim to a credit problem. The Federal Trade Commission found that when identity fraud involves the creation of a new account in the victim's name, 33 percent of victims discover the fraud between one and five months after it occurred.[35] 24 percent don't discover the fraud for over six months.[36]

Once the individual does suspect wrongdoing and triggers an alert, new protections in the Fair and Accurate Credit Transactions Act (FACTA) require that creditors use "reasonable policies and procedures to form a reasonable belief that the user [creditor] knows the identity of the person making the request."[37] This suggests that in the absence of a fraud report, a tradeline can be extended without at least "reasonable policies and procedures" to verify the credit applicant's identity. Such protections should be in place by default, rather than only when fraud is actually expected.

The fraud alert also allows the consumer to leave a phone number on file at the credit reporting agency. If the phone number is present, the creditor must call it to check whether the credit applicant is an impostor.[38]

B. Credit Monitoring:
Alerting Victims to Fraud That Has Already Occurred

Credit monitoring is a service that can alert an individual electronically when the credit report is accessed or when some other credit-relevant event occurs. Monitoring does not prevent impostors from acquiring credit in the victim's name. Instead, it allows victims to discover the crime and act quickly to mitigate harm.

Not only is credit monitoring merely reactive to identity theft, it is also expensive. Experian offers "Credit Expert" monitoring for $89.95 a year.[39] Instead of paying that amount, individuals could instead periodically request a credit report every three or four months at the rate set by the Federal Trade Commission, which is currently $9 per report. In 2004, as a result of changes to the FCRA, individuals became able to request a free report from each of the credit reporting agencies once a year.[40] With that price change in effect, monitoring service makes sense only for people who have more money than time.

C. Failed Attempts to Curb Identity Theft Through Negligence Actions

Attorneys have attempted to curb identity theft by bringing negligence actions against sloppy credit grantors. The goal of the cases is to establish a duty of care between the credit issuer and the identity theft victim, and thus give the issuers a stronger incentive to make decisions more responsibly. However, the courts have been reluctant to assign liability to the credit-granting companies.

In *Huggins* v. *Citibank*, the South Carolina Supreme Court rejected the tort of "negligent enablement of imposter fraud."[41] In that case, the plaintiff identity theft victim alleged that banks owe a duty to identity theft victims when they negligently extend credit in their name. The defendants argued that no such duty existed because the victim was not actually a customer of the bank. Focusing on the requirement that an actual relationship exist between victim and tortfeasor before a legal duty arises, the court rejected the proposed cause of action:

> We are greatly concerned about the rampant growth of identity theft and financial fraud in this country. Moreover, we are certain that some identity theft could be prevented if credit card issuers carefully scrutinized credit card applications. Nevertheless, we . . . decline to recognize a legal duty of care between credit card issuers and those individuals whose identities may be stolen. The relationship, if any, between credit card issuers and potential victims of identity theft is far too attenuated to rise to the level of a duty between them.[42]

Other suits have failed as well.[43]

An array of credit-industry groups wrote briefs as amici in cases that followed *Huggins*. These included the American Bankers Association, American Financial Services Association, America's Community Bankers, Consumer Bankers Association, the Financial Services Roundtable, MasterCard International, Inc., and Visa U.S.A., Inc.[44] These groups must be concerned about liability because periodically, absurd errors in the credit business come to light, such as the situations described earlier in which dogs and babies received new credit cards. The errors are severe enough that if they were more widely known, policymakers might legislatively create a tort to address negligent credit issuance or amend the FCRA to require heightened consumer authentication standards to prevent identity theft.

III. PUTTING ID THEFT ON ICE BY FREEZING CREDIT REPORTS

Because it is too easy for impostors to open new accounts in victims' names, and because existing protections are ineffective in preventing identity theft, we need to change the default status of credit report availability. Credit is in a liquid state by default, one in which credit reports are available to networks of certified credit, resellers of reports, and other businesses. It's simply too easy to obtain a credit report and extend instant credit under the current architecture. For instance, in February 2004, a Massachusetts Attorney General investigation found that for only $320, an investigator was able to purchase a credit report, social security number, and bank statement illegally.[45]

In other words, by default, we are continuously open to new credit accounts. This offers great convenience—it allows one to walk through a shopping mall and, on a whim, buy an expensive item from a complete stranger. This has been referred to as the "miracle of instant credit."[46] But that miracle is accompanied by the miracle of instant identity theft. It allows identity thieves to conveniently apply for credit in victim's names and rely on the alacrity of creditors to obtain a new account.

After the change in the default status of credit reports, access to the credit would be frozen by default. Before credit could be granted, individuals would have to "thaw" their credit by contacting a credit reporting agency and requesting release of the report.

A frozen credit system would require the consumer to establish a business relationship with the credit reporting agency in which an authentication procedure is chosen. For instance, an individual could specify that credit should only be unfrozen when the request to the credit reporting agency is made from a specified work, home, or wireless phone number. Agreed-upon passwords could be employed. Or the credit reporting agencies could employ newly developed "out of wallet" authentication systems. These systems ask individuals questions that a mugger or someone who has just stolen a wallet could not answer. Instead of asking, "what is your social security number," the system would give a series of multiple choice questions such as "Do you have an IRA with Fidelity?" or "Which of the following companies holds your home mortgage?" These bits of information are in credit reports but aren't readily available to someone who has stolen a victim's wallet.

This system could be highly customized to individuals' comfort levels regarding the risk of identity theft and to their spending behavior. The thaw could be limited for a certain amount of time, say a weekend of shopping, or to certain creditors when the individual knows where he or she is going to purchase an item.

Finally, spendthrifts and others who simply don't wish to use the thawing process could opt out of the system, and keep their credit liquid at all times. This could be done by directing the credit reporting agency to release the report to any creditor unless the individual revokes the authorization.

A frozen credit report system would address the three factors in sloppy credit granting described in Section II. Trusted insiders and grantors with poor authentication systems could not obtain a report unless the consumer had specifically thawed the file. Similarly, grantors who send out prescreened offers and those that grant credit quickly would pose less of a threat in enabling identity theft.

A frozen system also solves a long-standing problem with authorized access to credit reports, the "impermissible pull." This occurs when someone with access to the credit reporting system obtains a report on a consumer without a credit application or existing relationship with the consumer. Impermissible pulls sometimes occur in the context of automobile purchasing.[47] Some automobile salespersons will greet a window-shopping customer and obtain the customer's name. The salesperson then leaves and "pulls" a report using the name only in order to evaluate the seriousness of the shopper or to increase bargaining power. This practice is illegal under the FCRA, but is still common enough that at least one state has addressed it by statute.[48] A frozen system would stop these impermissible pulls unless the consumer had thawed the credit report prior to window shopping.

IV. OBJECTIONS TO AND LIMITATIONS OF A FROZEN CREDIT REPORT SYSTEM

The financial services industry and retailers are likely to have many objections to a frozen credit system. Consumers may object to some aspects as well. These objections are analyzed in this section.

A. Cost

Objections may be raised that a frozen credit system would add unnecessary costs to credit granting. Credit reporting agencies would have to bear the burden of establishing more formal relationships with all credit-active individuals. Call centers and other infrastructure would have to be improved to accommodate requests for credit freezes and thaws.

This is a valid objection, and certainly a frozen system would entail costs to retailers, credit reporting agencies, and financial services institutions. Objections to the shift to frozen credit, however, must be weighed against the costs of the current liquid system. The current system leads to over $50 billion in costs transferred to individuals and businesses annually.[49] Implementation of a frozen system would prevent a large amount of identity theft, and though costly, it would likely be a fraction of the annual cost of the current system.

Viewed from a different perspective, cost may be an argument supporting a shift in credit. A frozen credit system could be less costly in money and time to businesses and individuals than the current liquid system of credit.

It would also transfer costs from identity theft victims to those who run and maintain the credit system.

The costs with implementing the proposed system have already been incurred to some extent. California law already allows individuals to exercise a prophylactic freeze on their credit reports. The California law requires individuals to specifically request the freeze rather than keeping it in place by default under the system proposed in this chapter.[50] Once in place, the California freeze prevents almost all releases of the credit report. Consumers can lift the freeze by first contacting the credit reporting agency with identification information, a freeze identity number, and password.[51] Unlike the shift proposed in this chapter, the California law allows but does not require the credit reporting agency to develop telephone, Internet, or other systems to thaw credit.[52] Nevertheless, the presence of the optional freeze system in California suggests that systems are in place that could be scaled to the entire nation.

B. Inconvenience

The financial services industry and consumers alike may find a frozen system inconvenient. That is, by changing the default state of credit, it will delay purchasing decisions. Individuals will no longer be able to buy an expensive item without some forethought. A major benefit of the "miracle of instant credit" will be jeopardized, resulting in lost sales.

First, the point of a frozen system is to change the relationships among credit reporting agencies, credit issuers, and consumers. By changing these relationships, costs of identity theft are more properly allocated to those who control the system-the credit reporting agencies and creditors. The current system is maximally convenient for credit grantors, but not for consumers. The average consumer may go a year or longer without applying for credit, but the current liquid system is prepared for daily credit granting.

Second, a consumer who wishes to take advantage of discounts associated with opening up a new credit card can still do so. Such consumers could direct the credit reporting agencies to keep their credit in a liquid state permanently, or allow the credit report to be released with weak authentication procedures. This burden can be set to a minimal level so that individuals who, for instance, wish to take advantage of a discount for obtaining a departmental credit card can do so quickly.

Third, a frozen system does not eliminate the benefits of the miracle of instant credit. Rather, the miracle, if it can be termed as such, lies in the ability of the system to determine an applicant's credit risk. The miracle is the ability of businesses to grant credit reliably to complete strangers. Creditworthiness reporting would be unaffected. It is only the process of formally granting credit that will be affected.

Last, the miracle of instant credit has been accompanied by not only the miracle of instant identity theft, but also by the miracle of instant bankruptcy. Consumer bankruptcy is at its highest rate ever at over 1,600,000 households in 2003.[53] Consumer credit debt topped $2 trillion in 2003.[54] Delinquency in credit card payments, accounts that are more than thirty days past due, is at an all-time high as well.[55] Slowing down purchasing decisions may be a good thing. It might lead to more fiscal responsibility and fewer bankruptcies.[56]

C. Authentication Problems

A frozen system would require credit reporting agencies to develop authentication systems in order to verify the identity of consumers attempting to release their report. Implementing these systems for over one hundred million Americans would be difficult. There will be errors in this implementation, resulting in individuals being prevented from legitimately accessing credit. Identity thieves will attempt to crack the system, too.

This is a serious, but surmountable challenge. The shift in credit is intended to change the relationship between consumers and credit reporting agencies so that individuals are more involved in the dissemination of personal information. This will require credit reporting agencies to establish more formal relationships with consumers. With existing consumers, credit reporting agencies can use the out-of-wallet authentication procedures (questions are posed to the consumer about facts that are unlikely to be in a wallet, such as "What was the amount of your last deposit"). Credit reporting agencies already use this form of heightened authentication when consumers request their own credit reports. But they do not use it when credit grantors request individuals' reports.

With individuals who are new to the credit system, implementing an authentication system is more difficult. New applicants may be introduced into the system by trusted members who are already enrolled, such as the parents of the applicant. New applicants without friends or family members in the system may have to establish a relationship by mail, which may cause some delay.

In the worst-case scenario of when authentication procedures fail, individuals would have to establish their identities in person with some trusted third party. Already, this infrastructure exists for identification verification in other contexts. For instance, individuals initiate application for a U.S. passport by visiting a post office, presenting identification documents, and completing an application that is eventually processed by the State Department. A similar process could be established using the post office, or a trusted private-sector party, such as a money wire service or a bank.

D. Businesses Needing Reports Outside the Credit-Granting Process

Businesses normally pull credit reports for "account review" purposes. That is, a mortgagor or credit card company regularly requests credit reports on their customers to keep track of their debt burdens. If their debt burdens increase, the companies may change the terms of a loan, cancel a tradeline, or sometimes grant more credit.

This objection is easily addressed. An exemption would be available to any company with a live credit relationship with the consumer. That would allow businesses to engage in account review, maintenance, and upgrades or credit increases.

V. CONCLUSION

With the increasing incidence and severity of identity theft, we need to seek architectural changes to the credit system to protect personal information. Existing proposals have focused on establishing Fair Information Practices, rights, and responsibilities in the use of personal information. But this challenge also requires specific changes to the credit reporting system. Freezing credit information from its current liquid state to a frozen one is one such protection. A system that is frozen by default will act as a strong shield against identity thieves who are trying to open new lines of credit in others' names. It will also protect individuals against the thousands of companies with access to the credit system who currently can obtain their credit report with little oversight. Freezing access to credit reports addresses the factors that lead to irresponsible credit granting and identity theft. Some challenges, including cost, inefficiency, and customer authentication would have to be surmounted. Overall, a frozen system places more power over personal information in consumers' control, and is more consistent with privacy norms.

NOTES

1. Identity Theft: How It Happens, Its Impact on Victims, and Legislative Solutions, Hearing Before the Senate Judiciary Subcommittee on Technology, Terrorism, and Government Information, July 12, 2000 (testimony of Beth Givens, director, Privacy Rights Clearinghouse), available at http://www.privacyrights.org/ar/id_theft.htm.

2. *Id.*

3. Federal Trade Commission, Identity Theft Survey Report 4-5 (Sept. 2003), available at http://www.ftc.gov/os/2003/09/synovatereport.pdf.

4. *Id.* at 7.

5. Federal Trade Commission, Identity Theft Affidavit, available at http://www.ftc.gov/bcp/conline/pubs/credit/affidavit.pdf.

6. Congress formally criminalized identity theft in 1998, but reports of the crime continue to rise. *See* Identity Theft and Assumption Deterrence Act of 1998, Pub. Law. No. 105-318, 112 Stat. 3007 (1998); Federal Trade Commission, *Overview Report and Timeline of the IDT Program,* fig. 1 (Sept. 2003), available at http://www.ftc.gov/os/2003/09/timelinereport.pdf. In 2004, Congress increased the penalties for using personal information in connection with fraud, terrorism, and numerous federal felonies. Identity Theft Penalty Enhancement Act, Pub. L. 108-275 (Jul. 15, 2004).

7. Daniel J. Solove, Identity Theft, Privacy, and the Architecture of Vulnerability, 54 *Hastings L. J.* 1227, 1232 (2003).

8. *Id.* at 1241. One generally accepted architectural framework is "Fair Information Practices" as specified by the Organization for Economic Cooperation and Development. *See* Marc Rotenberg, What Larry Doesn't Get: Fair Information Practices and the Architecture of Privacy, 2001 *Stan. Tech. L. Rev.* 1 (2001); Will Thomas DeVries, Protecting Privacy in the Digital Age, 18 *Berk. Tech. L. J.* 283 (2003).

9. Dog Gets Carded, *Wash. Times* (Jan. 30, 2004); Dog Issued Credit Card, Owner Sends in Pre-Approved Application as Joke, NBC San Diego (Jan. 28, 2004), available at http://www.nbcsandiego.com/money/2800173/detail.html.

10. Dog Gets Carded, *supra* note 9.

11. *Id.*

12. *Id.*

13. *Doctor Strangelove, or How I Learned to Stop Worrying and Love the Bomb* (Warner, 1964).

14. Identity Thieves Feed on Credit Firms' Lax Practices, *USA Today,* Sept. 12, 2003, at 11A; Kevin Hoffman, Lerner's Legacy: MBNA's Customers Wouldn't Write Such Flattering Obituaries, *Cleveland Scene,* Dec. 18, 2002; Scott Barancik, A Week in Bankruptcy Court, *St. Petersburg Times,* Mar. 18, 2002, at 8E.

15. Identity Theft Resource Center, *Fact Sheet 120: Identity Theft and Children* (February 2007), available at http://www.idtheftcenter.org/artman2/publish/v_fact_sheets/Fact_Sheet_120.shtml.

16. 15 U.S.C. § 1681e(a).

17. The Federal Trade Commission is statutorily barred from promulgating regulations on the FCRA. 15 U.S.C. § 1681s(a)(4). The agency issues a nonbinding commentary on the Act. Credit, Trade Practices, 16 CFR § 600, 607 (1995).

18. Brooke A. Masters & Caroline E. Mayer, Identity Theft More Often an Inside Job, Old Precautions Less Likely to Avert Costly Crime, Experts Say, *Wash. Post,* Dec. 3, 2002, at A1.

19. Benjamin Weiser, Identity Ring Said to Victimize 30,000, *N.Y. Times,* Nov. 26, 2002, at A1.

20. *Id.*

21. *See Nelski v. Pelland*, U.S. App. LEXIS 663 (6th Cir. 2004) (phone company issued credit to impostor using victim's name but slightly different social security number); *United States v. Peyton*, 353 F. 3d 1080 (9th Cir. 2003) (impostors obtained six American Express cards using correct name and social security number but directed all six to be sent to the impostors' home); *Aylward v. Fleet Bank*, 122 F. 3d 616 (8th Cir. 1997) (bank issued two credit cards based on matching name and social security number but incorrect address); *Vazquez-Garcia v. Trans Union De P.R., Inc.*, 222 F. Supp. 2d 150 (D.P.R. 2002) (impostor successfully obtained credit with matching social security number but incorrect date of birth and address); *Dimezza v. First USA Bank, Inc.*, 103 F. Supp. 2d 1296 (D.N.M. 2000) (impostor obtained credit with social security number match but incorrect address).

22. The Fair and Accurate Credit Transactions Act of 2003: Hearing on H.R. 2622 Before the Committee on Financial Services (2003) (testimony of Chris Jay Hoofnagle, deputy counsel, Electronic Privacy Information Center).

23. 534 U.S. 19 (2001); Erin Shoudt, Identity Theft: Victims "Cry Out" for Reform, 52 *Am. U. L. Rev.* 339, 346-47 (2002).

24. *Id.* at 23-25.

25. *Id.*

26. Cal. Civ. Code § 1785.14(a)(1).

27. *Id.*

28. Identity Crises—Millions of Americans Paying Price, *Chi. Tribune*, Sept. 11, 2003, at 2.

29. *Id.*

30. Identity Theft: How It Happens, Its Impact on Victims, and Legislative Solutions, Hearing Before the Senate Judiciary Subcommittee on Technology, Terrorism, and Government Information (2000) (testimony of Beth Givens, director, Privacy Rights Clearinghouse) (citing Edmund Sanders, Charges Are Flying Over Credit Card Pitches, *L.A. Times*, June 15, 1999, at D-1), available at http://www.privacyrights.org/ar/id_theft.htm.

31. Rob Reuteman, Statistics Sum Up Our Past, Augur Our Future, *Rocky Mountain News*, Sept. 27, 2003, at 2C; Robert O'Harrow Jr., Identity Crisis; Meet Michael Berry: Political Activist, Cancer Survivor, Creditor's Dream. Meet Michael Berry: Scam Artist, Killer, the Real Michael Berry's Worst Nightmare, *Wash. Post Mag.*, Aug. 10, 2003, at W14.

32. Experian, Inc., *Customer Data Integration: The Essential Link for Customer Relationship Management*, white paper 15, (2000), available at http://www.experian.com/whitepapers/cdi_white_paper.pdf.

33. *Id.*

34. Identity Theft Resource Center, *Identity Theft: The Aftermath* 15-16 (Summer 2003), available at http://www.idtheftcenter.org/idaftermath.pdf.

35. Federal Trade Commission, *Identity Theft Survey Report* 20-21 (Sept. 2003), available at http://www.ftc.gov/os/2003/09/synovatereport.pdf.

36. *Id.*

37. Pub. L. No. 108-159 § 112 (h)(1)(b)(i). FACTA amended the Fair Credit Reporting Act, 15 U.S.C. § 1681.

38. *Id.* at § 112 (h)(1)(b)(ii).

39. Experian, Inc., Credit Expert, available at https://www.creditexpert.com/creditexpert/orderpage1.aspx?sc=623000&bcd=productdetail&pkg=DCZ1Y.

40. 15 U.S.C. 1681j.

41. 355 S.C. 329 (SC 2003).

42. *Id.* at 334.

43. *Garay v. U.S. Bancorp*, U.S. Dist. LEXIS 1331 (E.D.N.Y. 2004); *Smith v. Citibank*, U.S. Dist. LEXIS 25047, (W.D. Mo. 2001); *Polzer v. TRW, Inc.*, 256 A.D. 2d 248 (N.Y. App. Div. 1998).

44. 355 S.C. 329 (SC 2003).

45. Bruce Mohl, Firm Barred from Selling, Collecting Financial Data, Order Protects Mass. Residents, *Boston Globe* (Feb. 6, 2004), available at http://www.boston.com/business/personal-finance/articles/2004/02/06/firm_barred_from_selling_collecting_financial_data/.

46. How the FTC Is Policing Privacy: Chairman Timothy Muris Explains the Commission's Strategy for Trying to Protect Individuals and How They Can Help Themselves, *Business Week* (June 5, 2002), available at http://www.businessweek.com/technology/content/jun2002/tc2002065_9287.htm.

47. National Consumer Law Center, *Fair Credit Reporting* (Anthony Rodriguez, Carolyn L. Carter, & Willard P. Ogburn, eds., 5th ed., 2003).

48. La. R.S. § 9:3571.2 (2003).

49. Federal Trade Commission, *Identity Theft Survey Report* 7 (Sept. 2003), available at http://www.ftc.gov/os/2003/09/synovatereport.pdf.

50. Cal. Civ. Code § 1785.11.2(a).

51. *Id.*

52. Cal. Civ. Code § 1785.11.2(f).

53. William Branigin, U.S. Consumer Debt Grows at Alarming Rate, Debt Burden Will Intensify When Interest Rates Rise, *Wash. Post* (Jan. 12, 2004), available at http://www.washingtonpost.com/ac2/wp-dyn/A10011-2004Jan12?.

54. The Federal Reserve Board, *Consumer Credit* (Feb. 6, 2004), available at http://www.federalreserve.gov/releases/g19/Current/.

55. Card Delinquents, Cardtrak Online (Mar. 28, 2003), available at http://www.cardweb.com/cardtrak/news/2003/march/28a.html.

56. *See, e.g.,* Michele Singletary, *Money Mantras for a Richer Life : How to Live Well with the Money You Have* 7 (2003).

11 ANONYMOUS DISCLOSURE OF SECURITY BREACHES
Mitigating Harm and Facilitating Coordinated Response

Edward J. Janger and Paul M. Schwartz

Edward J. Janger is professor of law, Brooklyn Law School. Paul M. Schwartz is professor of law, U.C. Berkeley Law School.

Reputational sanctions are often offered as a substitute for law. Robert Ellickson has shown how social norms and gossip allow Shasta County ranchers to order their affairs and resolve disputes without resort to, or regard for, legal sanctions.[1] In business regulation, particularly in the post-Sarbanes-Oxley world, disclosure is king. On eBay, feedback fora allow participants to choose trading partners based on the number of positive and negative experiences others have had with the proposed counterparty.[2] The emerging regime for regulating data security is no exception, with recent state statutes and federal regulations mandating customer notice of security breaches involving personally identifiable data.[3] In all of these contexts, information about reputation benefits the public.

Behavior is changed, transactions happen, and markets work because information is made publicly available. It is also assumed (1) that the desire for a good reputation will produce desirable conduct and that information about behavior will be disseminated (Shasta County and eBay) or (2) that where information is likely to be concealed or undersupplied, disclosure should be mandated (securities regulation). When disclosure is mandated, anonymity is impermissible, and notice must be particularized. After all, reputational sanctions only work if they relate to an identifiable person or company.

In this chapter, we examine the evolving rules for protecting personal financial data of the sort that would facilitate identity theft and question the conventional wisdom about the importance of reputational sanctions in ensuring data security.[4] We focus on recent regulations promulgated pursuant to the Gramm-Leach-Bliley Act of 1999 that mandate customer notice about security breaches at financial institutions. Such disclosure, it is thought, will allow consumers to choose the financial institutions with the "best" security practices. We also discuss recently enacted state disclosure statutes. In our view, a disclosure-focused regime has both strengths and weaknesses. Fear of reputational sanction may lead, notwithstanding the legal mandates, to excessive secrecy about security breaches involving sensitive customer information.

In an attempt to think through the role of reputational sanctions, we explore what may seem like a paradoxical approach: limiting, or even eliminating, the reputational sanction associated with customer notices through the use of an *anonymizing disclosure intermediary.* We suggest that anonymous disclosure of security breaches may reduce any disincentive to discover and share data about security breaches. The resulting increased information flows in turn may increase the ability of consumers, financial institutions, and government agencies to mitigate the harm caused by disclosures of sensitive personal information. Our particular concerns are identity theft and cyberfraud, when poor security at one financial institution may allow an impostor to use stolen information to open an account under an assumed identity at another institution, or to otherwise engage in fraud. When we talk about "sensitive information" our focus is, therefore, limited to data that would facilitate identity theft, such as personal identification numbers (PINs), social security numbers (SSNs), account numbers, security questions, and other personal information that is useful for two purposes: (1) completing authorized financial transactions by the account holder and (2) theft by malefactors.[5]

Our proposed anonymizing disclosure intermediary takes the form of a public or private intermediary that acts as a clearinghouse for information about customers whose personal data have been compromised. The information about security breaches would be shared with the financial institutions and the general public *without identifying the location of or entity subject to the suspected security breach.* We conclude that anonymization is likely to be useful, but only under limited circumstances.

The critical question, when choosing between particularized and anonymous breach notices, is whether the principal value of the information about security breaches is prospective or retrospective. When security breach information has prospective value, the focus of disclosure is on altering consumer behavior and financial institution behavior through the threat of reputational sanctions. In this context, particularized notice is required. By contrast, when the value of the information is retrospective, the focus is on mitigating the harm caused to consumers and financial institutions by breaches that have already occurred. Under such circumstances, information about the source of the breach may not be as valuable, and notice may not need to be particularized.

In the first part of this chapter, we consider the legal landscape for protecting the security of sensitive financial data in the payment system. This section identifies legal and technological influences on data security. First, a new legal regime is emerging that focuses on notifying customers about data security breaches. We examine recently promulgated regulations for data security (the "Interagency Guidance") under section 501 of the Graham-Leach-Bliley Act (GLB Act), and state breach notice statutes recently enacted in California and numerous other states. Second, we seek to show how this interaction of law and technology raises further concerns: (1) financial institutions' fear of reputational sanction appears likely to restrict the flow of information about security breaches, even under the proposed regulations; and (2) at the same time, the rise of financial intermediaries and the outsourcing of data-related functions raise the stakes by creating new types of systemic risk and undercutting the payment system's traditional allocation of incentives to take care.

In the second part of this chapter, we note that the regulations in the Interagency Guidance and state disclosure statutes often operate exclusively based on a model of mandatory disclosure coupled with statutory or regulatory sanction. The apparent goal of these regulations is to create a regime of mandatory disclosure that will allow the reputational sanction to work. This is a typical regulatory response when information is a public good and undersupplied by the market. Such regulation seeks to spread reputational information and is designed to influence commercial behavior *ex ante*. We consider a second approach—often overlooked—that focuses on enforcement and mitigation. Such a regulation would focus on gathering information to help minimize harm related to acts that have already occurred. Along these lines, we examine the likely impact of sharing nonparticularized information about a security breach. We consider the strengths and weaknesses of a public or private anonymizing disclosure intermediary. The third part develops the concept of the anonymizing disclosure intermediary and considers its benefits and costs, and how it might be integrated with other remedies. Although in this piece we limit our focus to security breaches in the payment system, our discussion has implications for repositories of other types, which we explore elsewhere.[6]

I. PROTECTING PERSONAL FINANCIAL INFORMATION IN THE PAYMENT SYSTEM: THE CURRENT LEGAL REGIME, THE STAKES, AND THE CASE FOR REGULATION

Increasingly, the financial institutions and intermediaries that play a role in the payment system are repositories of huge amounts of personal financial information. Credit reporting agencies have files on a significant majority of the population.[7] Banks and payment intermediaries such as Quicken or Pay-Pal maintain information about their customers. These data include SSNs, PINs, and other account information that, if compromised, could facilitate widespread fraud.

Unauthorized access to personal data in the control of financial entities already contributes to the problem of identity theft that financial institutions and government regulators are struggling to contain.[8] Both federal and state statutes at present protect the security of personal information. Of particular interest are Section 501 of the GLB Act that regulates data practices at financial institutions, and state statutes, such as the security breach notice statutes enacted in California and at least forty-three other states that mandate customer notice of security breaches.

A. The Evolving Legal Regime-GLB Section 501, and the Proposed Interagency Guidance

Section 501 of the GLB Act obligates financial institutions to protect certain kinds of customer information. Its chief mechanism for doing so is a requirement that the Federal Deposit Insurance Corporation, Office of the Comptroller of the Currency, the Federal Reserve, the Federal Trade Commission, and other regulatory agencies promulgate regulations to ensure the "privacy, security and confidentiality" of customer data.[9]

Pursuant to Section 501(b), the relevant agencies have issued a set of common interagency security guidelines (the "Security Guidelines"), which require financial institutions covered by GLB to develop and implement procedures to protect the personal information of their customers and to ensure that their subcontractors have similar protections in place.[10] The Security Guidelines do not, however, require that financial institutions report security breaches to their supervising agency.

More recently, the Office of the Comptroller of the Currency, Federal Deposit Insurance Corporation, Federal Trade Commission, Federal Reserve Board, and Office of Thrift Supervision have promulgated a set of regulations known as the Interagency Guidance.[11] The Interagency Guidance proposes a distinction between general customer information and "sensitive" information. According to the Interagency Guidance, customer information is the broader category; it is the kind of personally identifiable information that is frequently used in telemarketing and shared by affiliated and nonaffiliated entities. The second type of personal information at stake in the Interagency Guidance is so-called "sensitive" information. By this term, the agencies refer to data such as PINs, SSNs, user names, account numbers, passwords, and any other information that might either give unauthorized people access to customer accounts or facilitate identity theft. It is important to note here that the sensitivity of data does not necessarily turn on whether the data are of the sort that the customer might want to keep private. Rather, sensitivity depends only on the potential of the data for leading to fraud or identity theft.

The Guidance's approach to protecting sensitive customer data is to focus on both prospective and retrospective measures. The prospective measures regulate *internal* procedures regarding information protection by requiring financial institutions to (1) *conduct a risk assessment* to ascertain reasonably foreseeable risks to customer information and customer information systems, the likelihood of damage, and the sufficiency of existing policies; (2) *implement access controls* on customer information systems; and (3) *conduct background checks* on employees with access to customer information. These data-security measures apply to both sensitive and nonsensitive customer data, but the need for security obviously increases as the sensitivity of the data grows. Note as well that these prospective measures are aimed at ensuring that data are kept secure and security breaches are prevented.

The *retrospective* component of the Guidance is contained in its requirement that an institution establish a "response program" to react to incidents of "unauthorized access to" or "use of" customer information. The requirements of the "response program" are aimed at "cure" rather than "prevention." As part of the "response program," the financial institution must (1) *assess* the situation; (2) *notify* the institution's primary federal regulator of the incident; (3) *take steps to contain* and *control* the situation; (4) *take corrective measures* such as flagging and securing accounts; and (5) under certain circumstances, give *notice* to customers.

For the purposes of this chapter, the Guidance's key provisions are its external notice requirements. These provisions take a two-tiered approach, applying a stringent standard requiring government notification of security breaches and a more permissive standard regarding customer notification. Agency notification is required when the financial institution "becomes aware of an incident involving unauthorized access to or use of customer information that could result in substantial harm or inconvenience to its customers." By contrast, customer notification is required when the institution "becomes aware of unauthorized access to *sensitive* customer information unless the institution, after an appropriate investigation, reasonably concludes that misuse of the information is unlikely to occur and takes appropriate steps to safeguard customers."[12] Thus all security breaches involving potentially harmful or inconvenient customer information must be reported to the regulating agency, but only security breaches involving sensitive customer data must be reported to customers, and then only after the financial institution has conducted an investigation and perceives a risk of disclosure or misuse.

B. The Evolving Legal Regime-State
Security Breach Notification Statutes

State security breach notification statutes are another important kind of regulation for data security. Many of these statutes are modeled on a statute enacted by California, though there are sometimes significant differences.[13] The California statute contains a one-tier trigger: "reasonable likelihood" that an unauthorized party has "acquired" personally identifiable information. The trigger is higher than the agency notification standard under the Guidance, but lower than that regulation's threshold for customer notification, which is whether a "reasonable likelihood" of "misuse" exists. Unlike the Guidance, the California notice statute and its progeny focus only on notice and do not establish standards for data security, or internal procedures. These laws rely for their effectiveness solely on publicizing the fact of a security breach.

C. The Critics

The Guidance has managed to become the target of complaints from both privacy advocates and financial institutions. Privacy advocates at EPIC and the U.S. Public Interest Group criticize the Guidance on two grounds. They argue that the required notice should extend to threats to the "customer information system" as well as the "customer information" itself. They further criticize the customer notice provisions because the definition of "appropriate investigation" is vague and because the risks of unauthorized use go beyond the institution from which the information was stolen.[14] By contrast, representatives of financial institutions have criticized the Guidance because of its lower threshold for reporting all security breaches to regulators, rather than just those that, after investigation, seem likely to lead to misuse of the information. They take the position that the reporting of security breaches, even to the agency, should be required only *after* an investigation is conducted and the financial institution has concluded that a risk of misuse exists.

One industry critic, the Securities Industry Association, opined as follows:

> We believe that the customer notice requirement is the more appropriate standard because it allows the institution to assess the potential injury to its customer, and if injury is unlikely, to avoid the burden of notice provided the institution safeguard customer interests appropriately. If the regulatory and customer notice provisions are not harmonized, institutions would be required to provide innumerable notices to regulators which would be burdensome and overbroad.[15]

Fleet Bank's comments are even blunter, and suggest that fear of reputational sanction will lead to footdragging by financial institutions:

> FleetBoston recommends that the notification requirement in the Proposed Guidance be narrowed to situations where substantial harm to customers *has* occurred, or is *likely* to occur, instead of a possibility of occurring. . . .
>
> We believe that a response program that unnecessarily mandates notification of customers and other entities, such as law enforcement and regulatory agencies, of security breaches that do not rise to the appropriate "threat level" will tend to discourage service providers from disclosing security breaches because of potential liability and reputational risk.[16]

The fear, in brief, is that institutions will be overwhelmed with reporting requirements. The industry representatives would prefer, where possible, to keep information about security breaches to themselves.

We are intrigued by these industry comments for two reasons. First, financial institutions do not wish to make disclosures about security breaches. This reluctance may create a perverse dynamic, which is hinted at by Fleet's comments: if discovery of a security breach leads to a requirement to disclose, financial institutions face a perverse incentive *not* to discover security breaches.

Second, by applying the same standard to agency notification and customer notification, an important check will be eliminated. The more liberal agency notification standard provides a check on the financial institution because the agency will know about the security breach even when the institution concludes that no customer notification is necessary. Financial institutions have a strong incentive not to announce security breaches to the public. The market, they fear, will sanction a financial institution with a reputation for poor security. They may even be subject to legal liability. The Federal Reserve Bank of Chicago in its comments on the Guidance suggests that this disincentive has caused financial institutions to resist disclosure:

> [R]ecent experiences involving the compromise of sensitive customer information indicate that some financial institutions may resist proactive notification of customers for a variety of reasons, including the cost of notification and the potential for adverse public response and resultant competitive disadvantage. These issues may discourage some financial institutions from notifying customers and an on-going investigation could serve as a justification for the decision not to notify.[17]

Data, once leaked, may be misused quite quickly, or they may sit for a while before causing harm. We therefore worry that the investigation preceding notice to the agency and customers will take precious time while the stolen information is already in circulation. At the same time, we are also concerned that financial institutions may conclude that because no use has been made of the information after four to six weeks, the risks of use are small. This ignores the possibility that the information may be used many months or even years later.

The contrasting comments from privacy advocates, EPIC and the U.S. Public Interest Group, and from industry, the Securities Industry Association and Fleet Bank, on the Interagency Guidance highlight two competing considerations. As we will discuss, financial institutions have a strong incentive to safeguard sensitive information even in the absence of regulations. The questions then are (1) Does the disclosure disincentive impose significant costs on customers? and (2) Is there anything that can be done about it? To put it another way, is there a need for regulation of disclosure, and if so, is there a way to craft that regulation to maximize the benefit to the public without imposing undue costs on financial institutions?

D. The Rationale for Regulation

Fear of liability may chill disclosure. Therefore compelling disclosure may help to remedy this resistance. Nonetheless, requiring customer notice is not a panacea. It ignores the need for a culture of compliance within the financial institutions, and the effect that a notice requirement may have on a financial institution's internal dynamics. As for market incentives on financial institutions, the impact might be positive or negative. The positive impact occurs when the market causes financial institutions to safeguard personal financial data. On the other hand, market forces can make financial institutions nervous about notifying customers about security breaches. In this section, we explore these dynamics.

1. Distinguishing Information Privacy from Data Security

In an earlier piece, we explained that mandatory rules were likely necessary with regard to nonsensitive, nonpublic, personally identifiable information, such as that found on customer lists, and that opt-out rules like those contained in GLB for nonsensitive customer data were inadequate.[18] In our view, opt-out rules created incentives for financial institutions to provide obscure notices that conceal opt-out rights. Curiously, the rationale for regulating the process of disclosing leaks of such nonsensitive data is different from the rationale for regulating the security of sensitive personal data, at least where financial institutions are concerned.

There is an important distinction between information privacy and data security. The debate over information privacy has focused on secondary use of information, in which the harm caused by disclosure, although important, is dignitary and not always easy to measure in financial terms. In the usual information privacy scenario in the financial sector, a financial institution, such as a bank, may want to share customer information such as purchase history, credit rating, or salary information with an affiliated company for a reason unrelated to that for which the information was originally provided. The financial institution may also wish to generate profits by selling the information to a nonaffiliated company.

When the security of sensitive financial information is involved, however, the dynamic is different. Unlike in the privacy context, financial institutions want their customers' data (such as PINs or SSNs) to be secure. They do not want to make secondary use of information, or to allow others to do so. Unlike in the situation for customer information, in which the current default is no liability, or limited liability, for disclosure, financial institutions bear significant financial risk in the event of security failures. There is a tight link between failure to protect sensitive personal data and financial liability.[19] Financial institutions don't want to "sell" access to their customers' accounts, and would face liability if they did so, because they bear the full risk of unauthorized checks and charges. They do not suffer the inconvenience associated with identity theft, but they do absorb the financial cost of unauthorized charges. Yet there are also important externalities involved with leaks of information—and these costs are not all absorbed by the financial institution where a data leak takes place.

2. Externalities Associated with Data Leaks

Financial institutions do not bear the full risk associated with information stolen from their information systems.[20] Information stolen from one financial institution can be used to commit fraud against another financial institution, through identity theft or otherwise. When compromised information is used for identity theft, the new accounts may not be opened at the same institution.[21] The harm will be to a different financial institution that extends credit on the basis of the stolen information. This harm will also be borne by the individual whose information was stolen, in the form of damaged credit, unauthorized charges, and so on. The externality of cyberfraud has a direct effect on disclosure incentives. Just as financial institutions do not bear the full cost associated with lax security practices, they will not bear the full risk associated with failure to disclose those security breaches. We call this phenomenon the "disclosure externality." Because of this externality, and because financial institutions *do* suffer from any reputational sanction and fear liability as a result of such disclosure, they have a strong disincentive to avoid disclosure.

To continue this parade of horribles, when considering cyberfraud in the checking system, it is also necessary to consider risks to (1) banks in the payment system and (2) the payment system itself. If one or a number of financial institutions fail, the fraud may harm the payment backbone. The payment system is a complex web of banks and clearinghouses that rely on each other's credit to move trillions of dollars each day. We have come a long way from the scene in the movie *Mary Poppins* in which a child complaining that the bank won't give him back his "tuppence" can start a run on the bank.[22] Nonetheless, the Federal Reserve's mission to preserve the stability of the payment system operates against the still valid recognition that bank failures can cause chain reactions. A fraud that puts one or a number of banks at risk of failing might endanger the stability of the payment system.

Increasingly, checks are moving to the background as payment devices. Payment intermediaries such as Quicken and PayPal are emerging as the payment devices of choice. These intermediaries make some use of the checking system, but often they operate through the Automated Clearinghouse (ACH) and wire transfer systems instead. In addition, electronic bill payment sites, where bills are paid directly to credit card companies, also make use of ACH technology rather than paper checks. As Ronald Mann has noted in a recent article, the increased use of payment intermediaries deemphasizes the role of banks in the payment system, and this development has risks. As Mann puts it:

> [T]he regulatory regimes directed to the activities of the new payment intermediaries depend in part for their effectiveness on the background regulatory supervision of the banks governed by those regimes. Because nonbank payment intermediaries are not generally subject to that supervision, there is a cognizable risk that they will show less care in complying with those regimes than conventional depository institutions.[23]

Mann's focus is on protection of consumers from fraud resulting from these new intermediaries, but security of sensitive information may be an even greater concern. Not all payment intermediaries, however, will be putting as much at risk, and many, particularly at the startup stage, are likely to be thinly capitalized. Indeed, the potential risk associated with a security breach at a data aggregator might significantly exceed the value of its assets.[24]

II. REGULATING TO REMEDY THE DISCLOSURE DISINCENTIVE

The preceding discussion identifies two reasons why public regulation of data security may be justified. Banks, financial institutions, and payment intermediaries may not fully internalize the costs associated with lax security practices. Furthermore, financial institutions have an incentive to conceal, or indeed not to discover, information about security breaches.

The current proposed Interagency Guidance is organized around remedying both the "externality" and "incentive" problems through a single approach: mandatory disclosure. This approach makes sense when the principal purpose of information is to provide reputational information to a marketplace of consumers who shop on the basis of data security. Yet our view is that an exclusive focus on reputation may be a mistake. Indeed, it may reflect a misunderstanding of the retrospective purpose of disclosure in this context. Paradoxically, more useful information may be obtained if the regulatory focus is placed on using information to mitigate or prevent harm, *ex post*, rather than to influence market behavior *ex ante*.

A. The Disclosure Disincentive

Information about security breaches benefits the public in two ways. First, it helps the market to function properly by assisting customers when choosing whether to deal with (or stop dealing with) a particular financial institution. Second, it allows financial institutions to respond effectively to security breaches.

Such information is a type of "public good" in the sense that it is likely to be undersupplied if the market is left entirely to itself. First, disclosure of information about security breaches has costs to the financial institution. Such disclosure may harm its reputation, and, by calling attention to the financial institution's role in a security breach, it may cause the institution to become a target for lawsuits. As a result, the institution may prefer not to disclose information about security breaches. Second, sensitive data, once in the public domain, do not carry with them their own provenance. Although it may be possible to tell that information was stolen, the original source of the data may be impossible to identify. As a result, a financial institution with lax security will not bear the full reputational sanction associated with any harm, provided it does not call attention to its own role in the security breach.

A rational financial institution that discovers a security breach will therefore have strong incentives both to take steps necessary to insulate itself from any fraud losses and to keep silent about the breach. Fear of reputational sanction and the absence of any other sanctions create a disclosure disincentive that is likely to encourage financial institutions to hide information about security breaches.

In addition to the disclosure disincentive, there is also a disincentive to discover security breaches. To the extent that discovery of a security breach leads to an obligation to publicize the fact of the breach, mandatory disclosure regimes may create a strong incentive for an institution to hide its head in the sand. This concern is mitigated somewhat by a financial institution's desire to avoid fraud losses. Nonetheless, market forces are unlikely to provide the optimal amount of information about security breaches because of the interaction of the data security externality, the disclosure disincentive, and the discovery disincentive.

B. Remedying the Disclosure Disincentive

1. Mandatory Disclosure

The Interagency Guidance recognizes the existence of the disclosure disincentive. Its mandatory rules for disclosure of security breaches to agency officials and to customers manifest this concern. By setting different standards for disclosure to regulatory agencies and customers, the Guidance appears to recognize that this notice can serve two different functions. Disclosure to customers allows customers to protect themselves from identity theft and provides information to the marketplace. Disclosure to regulatory agencies provides information about possible hackers as well as bank security practices to regulators, promotes an opportunity for coordinated response among agencies and financial institutions, and may also allow the aggregation and generation of comparative information among institutions about the effectiveness of various security practices. The information flows envisioned in the Interagency Guidance are depicted in Figure 11.1.

At least in partial recognition of these different functions, the Interagency Guidance applies different standards for reporting security breaches to the government and reporting them to customers. There is a category of information that would be useful to the regulators and law enforcement officials that might not be useful to consumers, or in which reputational sanction may not

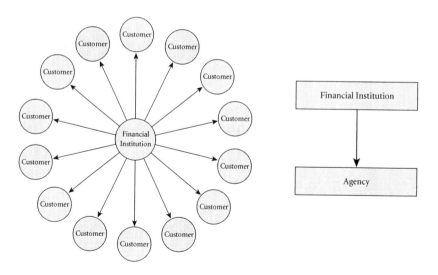

Figure 11.1. Particularized customer notice versus notice to agency

be warranted. The Federal Reserve Bank of Chicago proposes a novel solution to increasing the flow of necessary information about data incidents. The Chicago Fed notes both the existence of the disclosure disincentive and the disclosure externality:

> We recognize that notifying customers that their sensitive information has been compromised may lead to adverse consequences for financial institutions. In particular, financial institutions may face negative public reaction and potentially significant losses, if customers take their business elsewhere following notification that their sensitive information has been breached. The resulting financial institution reluctance to notify customers may be exacerbated in cases where multiple financial institutions have been affected by the compromise of sensitive customer information aggregated by a service provider or other third party. In this situation, customer notification may be delayed because no affected institution wants to be the first to notify customers.[25]

A breach may affect multiple institutions, but none wants to take responsibility and incur reputational sanction. In response, the Chicago FRB proposes an intermediary to solve this incentive problem:

> In order to deal with this situation, we suggest that financial institutions develop a means to coordinate customer notification through a trusted, neutral third party such as the Financial and Banking Information Infrastructure Committee (FBIIC) or the Financial Services Information Sharing and Analysis Center (FS/ISAC). In the event of a widespread compromise of customer information, financial institutions could leverage the ability of these or similar organizations to facilitate anonymous information sharing among financial institutions and to coordinate a timely response to customers. This approach has the potential to minimize the public perception of differences in institutional response and to promote proactive, unified notification of affected customers.[26]

They advocate what might be called an "anonymizing disclosure intermediary" (Figure 11.2). Instead of requiring the financial institution to notify customers, responsibility should be given to a trusted third-party intermediary, which could be public[27] or private.[28] That intermediary could provide notification on behalf of multiple institutions, could give notice without disclosing the name of the compromised institution, or could coordinate the response of multiple institutions.

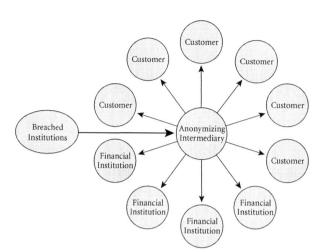

Figure 11.2. Anonymizing disclosure intermediary

Instead of relying on a reputation-based approach, which seeks to influence customers *ex ante*, the FRB's proposed anonymizing disclosure intermediary focuses on mitigation *ex post*-seeking to minimize the harm caused by a security breach. When mitigation is the goal, the source of disclosure is virtually irrelevant, and reputational information is, almost by definition, too late to do any good.

III. THE ANONYMIZING DISCLOSURE INTERMEDIARY: FLESHING OUT THE CONCEPT

In our view, an anonymizing intermediary, by allowing a financial institution to disclose the fact of a security breach to the intermediary without risking publicity, might make a financial institution more willing to disclose, and less reluctant to investigate and discover, any security breaches. The intermediary might then be able to do a number of things with that information that would help to mitigate the harm caused by the security breach. To fully appreciate these benefits, however, we must shift our focus from reputational sanction, which influences behavior *ex ante* to mitigation of harm, *ex post*.

A. The Benefits of Mitigation

First, the intermediary should notify other institutions about the breach. In turn, these institutions could (1) flag accounts held by the affected person at their own institution and (2) watch out for impostors using that person's name to open accounts that might be used for identity theft. Availability of this information helps limit two externalities. Most directly, this action eliminates the nondisclosure externality. Financial institutions are given information about security breaches in order to protect themselves from impostors. But this action has a positive spillover effect.

In addition to eliminating the nondisclosure externality, it mitigates the data security externality. As we noted earlier, financial institutions do not bear the full risk of harm associated with security breaches and may take suboptimal precautions. Enhanced disclosure limits the harm these lax practices may cause. Note, however, that none of the externality-limiting effect is lost if the intermediary does not disclose the name of the institution where the security breach occurred.

Second, the intermediary could give the customer notice of the security breach. With this information, the customer might change PINs and passwords and watch his or her own accounts for unusual activity. The customer might also request credit checks in order to detect identity theft. Again, the key point to note here is that none of these precautions require the customer to know the source of the security breach. The only behavior that requires knowledge of the source of the security breach is the customer's desire to cease doing business with the institution that suffered the attack. In other words, the trade-off is that the customer gets more information to allow him or her to protect against disclosures that actually happen, and loses some ability to modify his or her behavior going forward by altering marketplace behavior. The critical question is whether the lost benefits of any reputational sanction are outweighed by an enhanced ability to mitigate the harm of a security breach by eliminating the disclosure disincentive.

B. Cataloguing the Costs of Anonymity

The anonymizing intermediary might eliminate the incentive for financial institutions to take reasonable care to safeguard information. However, at least in the first instance, the concept of the anonymizer operates without reference to, and without limiting, the types of liability that might be available to those affected by the security breach. For example, nothing about the anonymizer would limit the liability of a financial institution for improperly honoring fraudulent checks. Similarly, to the extent that the security breach might give rise to tort liability, disclosure to the anonymizer need not limit that liability. The incentive to take care is only affected if disclosure to the intermediary confers immunity from liability. Immunity is not, however, a precondition for our proposal. The anonymizer *could* be implemented without altering the existing liability regime.

The anonymizer, at least in the first iteration, treats the tort system as exogenous. It is a device for *ex post* mitigation, and need not be linked to a shield from *ex ante* liability.

A second concern is that the anonymizer may deprive customers of information about the security practices of financial institutions. Here it is crucial to ask how customers use information about security breaches. First, they might use the information retrospectively to protect against harm, by changing PINs, monitoring their accounts, alerting other financial institutions, and obtaining credit reports. Second, they may choose to change financial institutions with whom they do business, or may choose not to do business with institutions that have bad reputations. The first group of behaviors focuses on mitigation; the second focuses on reputation.

Behavioral economics has cast severe doubt on whether consumers are good at comparing nonprice terms such as privacy. For example, empirical work on the used-car market suggests that information asymmetries between buyers and sellers may lead to a so-called "lemons equilibrium," in which good sales practices do not develop and used-car purchasers are forced to choose among dealers that all use bad sales practices. As we discussed in our earlier article, there is also reason to believe that such a "lemons equilibrium" may exist where privacy is involved.[29] If this is true with regard to data security as well, the ability to mitigate would be much more important than the importance of reputational information.[30] Nonetheless, as we discuss elsewhere, noneconomic dignitary concerns and consumer opposition may make anonymous disclosure to consumers impracticable as a political matter.[31]

Finally, even with the benefit of the anonymizer, a disclosure to customers by the anonymizer about a security breach might lead to a discovery of the source of the breach, or worse yet, to inaccurate rumors about the source of the breach. These rumors may arise because customers think that they have only given their information to a limited subset of institutions. They are likely to be inaccurate, however, because customers often have little sense of who has their information, and with whom it has been shared. To a certain extent, this concern can be met through the nature of the disclosure. Few people's commercial relations are limited to one financial institution. Although a person may only bank at one institution, he or she may have a credit card from another institution, and a mortgage from another, and a student loan from yet another. Sensitive information is also held by insurers, employers, and others. Nevertheless, there is some risk that anonymous disclosure may cause false positives through misallocation of guilt by inference.[32] Most individuals will be likely to blame their bank or credit card issuer rather than some unseen entity, such as a data aggregator, payment processor, or data storage company, or a lower-profile entity, such as a typical bricks-and-mortar retailer.

In sum, anonymity has both costs and some important benefits. If it is to be considered as an alternative, its use will be where the importance of preventing future harm outweighs the benefit of reputational sanctions, or where the disincentives to discovery and disclosure seem likely to limit the flow of information about security breaches flowing from repositories to regulators.

IV. CONCLUSION

Disclosure about security breaches is important, not just to the institution where the security breach occurs but to other financial institutions and to consumers. Customers need to take steps to guard against identity theft, and other institutions need to be on the lookout for impostors seeking to use stolen information to commit fraud. Information about whose information was stolen and what information was stolen is important to both customers and other financial institutions. Information about the source of the breach will often have less analytical significance. Reputational sanction is unlikely to influence customer behavior *ex post*, and knowledge about the source of a breach does not change the steps a customer should take when seeking to safeguard him or herself against future harm. Therefore policymakers should consider when and whether the benefits of anonymity outweigh its costs.

NOTES

1. Robert C. Ellickson, *Order Without Law: How Neighbors Settle Disputes* (1991).

2. Clayton P. Gillette, Reputation and Intermediaries in Electronic Commerce, 62 *La. L. Rev.* 1165 (2002); Susan Block-Lieb, E-reputation: Building Trust in Electronic Commerce, 62 *La. L. Rev.* 1199 (2002).

3. Such state statutes have now been enacted in at least forty-four states. Paul M. Schwartz & Edward J. Janger, Notification of Data Security Breaches, 105 *Mich. L. Rev.* 913 (2007). As an international example, Japan is the first nation to include a breach notification requirement in a national law. For a discussion, *see* Miriam Wugmeister *et al.*, *What You Need to Know About Japan's New Law Concerning the Protection of Personal Information* (Apr. 2005), available at http://www.mofo.com/news/updates/files/update02019.html.

4. We are not the first recent scholars to suggest that anonymity, rather than accountability, may further certain public policies. Bruce Ackerman and Ian Ayres have recently suggested that requiring political contributions to be made anonymously may limit the ability of donors to influence public policy debates. Bruce Ackerman & Ian Ayres, *Voting with Dollars* (2004).

5. We are not, here, concerned with other types of sensitive information, such as medical information that is sensitive for traditional privacy reasons, and as we will discuss further, we therefore sidestep much of the traditional privacy debate.

6. Schwartz & Janger, *supra* note 3, at 913.

7. *In re Trans Union Corp. Privacy Litig.*, No. 00 C 4729, 2002 WL 31028234, at *19-*23 (N.D. Ill. Sept. 10, 2002). *Cf. Washington v. CSC Credit Serv.*, 199 F. 3d 263, 268 (5th Cir. 2000).

8. As an example, *see* the Fair and Accurate Credit Transactions Act of 2003 (FACTA), Pub. L. No. 108-159, H.R. 2622, §§ 202, 205, and 501, 108th Cong. (2003). *See also* FACTA, §§ 112, 152, and 211, which enhances the ability of consumers to gain access to their credit reports. Other examples are discussed further on.

9. Gramm-Leach-Bliley Act of 1999, Pub. L. No. 106-102, 113 Stat. 1338 (1999) (codified in scattered sections of 12 and 15 U.S.C.).

10. The FDIC's Security Guideline is set forth at Appendix A. The other agencies have adopted similar guidelines tailored to the scope of their respective agency. The Office of the Comptroller of the Currency's Security Guidelines can be found at 12 CFR 30 App. B, available at http://frwebgate.access.gpo.gov/cgi-bin/get-cfr.cgi?TITLE=12&PART=30&SECTION=6&TYPE=TEXT. The Federal Reserve Board's Guidelines are at 12 CFR part 208, app D-2 and part 225 app. F, available at http://frwebgate.access.gpo.gov/cgi-bin/get-cfr.cgi?TITLE=12&PART=208&SECTION=101&TYPE=TEXT , and http://ecfr.gpoaccess.gov/cgi/t/text/text-idx?c=ecfr&sid=29d3f6cf5a1e329e0154ecc9efc5e921&rgn=div9&view=text&node=12:3.0.1.1.6.10.8.10.11&idno=12. The Guidelines for the FDIC are at 12 CFR part 264 app. B, and are available at http://ecfr.gpoaccess.gov/cgi/t/text/text-idx?c=ecfr&tpl=/ecfrbrowse/Title12/12cfr264_main_02.tpl. The Guidelines for the Office of Thrift Supervision can be found at 12 CFR part 570 app. B, and are available at http://a257.g.akamaitech.net/7/257/2422/01jan20081500/edocket.access.gpo.gov/cfr_2008/janqtr/12cfr570.5.htm.

11. [Proposed] Interagency Guidance on Response Programs for Unauthorized Access to Customer Information and Customer Notice (August 12, 2003), Federal Register 47954.

12. "Sensitive customer information" is defined as: "a customer's social security number, personal identification number, password or account number, in conjunction with a personal identifier such as the customer's name, address, or telephone number."

13. Schwartz & Janger, *supra* note 3.

14. In the Matter of Notice Regarding Unauthorized Access to Customer Information, Comments of the Electronic Privacy Information Center and The United States Public Interest Research Group, Oct. 14, 2003.

15. Regarding Interagency Guidance on Response Programs for Unauthorized Access to Customer Information, Comments of the Securities Industry Association, October 14, 2003, available at http://www.ots.treas.gov/docs/9/96020.pdf , at p. 2 (last visited Mar. 5, 2008).

16. Comment Regarding Interagency Guidance on Response Programs for Unauthorized Access to Customer Information and Customer Notice, FleetBank Boston (October 14, 2003), available at http://www.ots.treas.gov/docs/9/95992.pdf (last visited Mar. 5, 2008).

17. Letter dated October 10, 2003, from Michael Moskow, president of the Federal Reserve Bank of Chicago, to Jennifer Johnson, secretary of the board of governors of the Federal Reserve System (hereinafter, "Moskow Letter").

18. Edward J. Janger & Paul M. Schwartz, The Gramm-Leach-Bliley Act, Information Privacy and the Limits of Default Rules, 86 *Minn. L. Rev.* 1219 (2002).

19. The UCC places forged check liability on the payor's bank and forged endorsement liability on the first solvent person to trust the forger (usually the depositary bank). 3-404-406, 4-401, 4-207, 4-208. TILA 133(a)(1)(B) limits liability for unauthorized use to a maximum of $50. Visa and Mastercard voluntarily absolve customers of all liability so long as the cardholder reports the lost card within two days. Ronald Mann, *Payment Systems and Other Financial Transactions* 132 (2003).

20. When checks are involved, Articles 3 and 4 of the Uniform Commercial Code govern. The basic rules are (1) when a drawer's signature is forged, and the check is honored, the bank on which the check is drawn bears the risk of loss, UCC §3-401; (2) when an endorser's signature is forged, the risk of loss is born by the first solvent party to trust the forger (*i.e.*, the bank where the check is deposited), UCC § 3-416, 417, 4-216, 217; and (3) if the account holder's negligence somehow contributes to the forgery, the customer bears the risk of loss. UCC § 3-404, 405, 406, 4-406.

21. Fed. Res. Bank of Chicago Comments at 5 ("For example, many loan applications request credit information from applicants which may be stored in physical and logical form within a financial institution. If this information is compromised, the information could be used for identity theft purposes. Under the proposed Guidelines, it is not clear whether a financial institution would be required to notify a customer if sensitive customer information associated with accounts at another financial institution or another entity were compromised. Moreover, it would be very difficult for the financial institution that was the subject of the security breach to monitor whether or not the compromised customer information was used for identity theft purposes.").

22. Or, for that matter, Frank Capra's *It's a Wonderful Life*, in which Uncle Billy's misplaced check for $10,000 brings the Bailey Building and Loan to near collapse.

23. Ronald J. Mann, Regulating Internet Payment Intermediaries, 82 *Tex. L. Rev.* 681, 702 (2004).

24. Mann notes this risk as well: "At the most basic level, the direct purpose of much of federal banking regulation-federal supervision of capital maintenance and lending practices-is to ensure the solvency and fiscal prudence of the institutions. If that regulation is even marginally effective, it increases the likelihood that banks will have the assets necessary to comply with their obligations under those statutes. That might seem like a small thing, but the likelihood that a major Internet payment fraud could create a regulatory responsibility beyond the assets of a small dotcom P2P provider is plausible. That is particularly true given the likelihood that those providers will be targets for fraudulent activity, as PayPal has been." *Id.* at 701.

25. *Moskow Letter, supra* note 17.

26. *Id.*

27. Such as the Financial and Banking Information Infrastructure Committee (http://www.ncua.gov/FBIIC/).

28. Such as the Financial Services Information Sharing and Analysis Center (http://www .fsisac.com/).

29. Janger & Schwartz, *supra* note 18.

30. This intuition has not been empirically tested, however, and there is reason to believe that a security breach directly affecting a customer might have more impact than information about privacy practices generally.

31. Schwartz & Janger, *supra* note 3.

32. Individuals who receive nonparticularized breach disclosure letters will be likely to draw conclusions about the culprit's identity.

12 RFID AND PRIVACY

Jonathan Weinberg

Jonathan Weinberg is professor of law, Wayne State University. The author is indebted to the participants in the Cyberlaw Summer Camp sponsored by Harvard Law School's Center for Internet and Society on August 4–8, 2003; the participants in the Conference on Comparative IP and Cyberlaw, held at the University of Ottawa on October 4, 2003; and most of all to the organizers of, and the participants in, the Conference on Securing Privacy in the Internet Age, held at Stanford Law School on March 13, 2004. The author owes special thanks to Jessica Litman for her insightful comments. A substantially updated (and longer) version of this chapter has been published as Jonathan Weinberg, Tracking RFID, 3 ISJLP 777 (2007–2008).

When I came to Stanford Law School in 2004 for its *Conference on Securing Privacy in the Internet Age*, Wal-Mart and other large retailers were pushing to get RFID implementations in place. U.S. government officials were contemplating RFID tags on passports, on airline boarding passes, and on every package of prescription drugs. One company had announced a "secure, subdermal RFID payment technology for cash and credit transactions." Consumers would have the chip implanted in the triceps area, and make payments by passing a scanner over their arms. After all, the company urged, this way the payment device would be impossible to lose.[1]

Two years later, commercial RFID implementation has slowed. Potential adopters are having a hard time seeing how RFID will save more money than it will cost. But growth in a different set of uses is booming. Governments are increasingly turning to RFID, for identification documents and otherwise. A couple of years past the hype, I will look at RFID technology, its trajectory and diffusion, the privacy threats it might pose, and some possible responses.

I. INTRODUCTION

The term *RFID* (or Radio Frequency IDentification) describes a family of technologies in which (1) a "tag" contains an integrated circuit storing data that identifies or describes the tag itself, or the item it is attached to, or the person carrying it; and (2) the data can be read, wirelessly, by a separate device called a "reader." The reader, in turn, is part of a system of networked computers that can take action based on the tag data they receive.[2]

The distance at which RFID information can be read varies according to operating frequency, tag design, reader design, and the level of external interference. In "passive" tag implementations, in which the tag itself has no internal battery and gets its power from the reader's signal, the limiting factors include the size of the tag antenna and the power the tag's integrated circuit needs in order to operate, as well as the reader's transmission power, antenna gain, and receiver sensitivity. Inexpensive passive tag systems using the frequency bands now contemplated appear to have a theoretical maximum distance of about twenty meters between tag and reader.[3] Distances actually achievable in the field for these tags are typically much shorter; one industry expert describes ten meters as the "best case scenario today," and suggests that a typical operating environment features a read range of three to five meters.[4] Other tags are engineered for shorter read ranges, but those ranges can vary widely: smart cards bearing the ISO 14443 chip are designed to operate at a range of two to four inches, but are vulnerable to attack from considerably farther.

Beginning in 1999, the Auto-ID Center at the Massachusetts Institute of Technology led a major technology development and standardization effort, now housed under the EPCglobal organizational structure, aimed at RFID's most commercially important implementation: inventory management. The EPCglobal architecture contemplates that each pallet or case of consumer goods—indeed, each individual retail item—can have affixed a passive RFID tag holding a globally unique Electronic Product Code (EPC) that in turn points to an entry in a worldwide distributed database called the Object Name Service. The EPC is designed to serve the same function in the inventory supply chain as a traditional bar code. It extends the bar code's functionality, though, in two ways.

First, because readers can detect the EPC wirelessly, tags need not be scanned manually. The reader does not need a line-of-sight connection with a tag, and can read multiple tags at one time. In theory, if each widget were tagged with an EPC, one could place a reader near any of the billion sealed boxes of widgets a retailer receives each year and instantly know exactly what was inside and how many of them there were, without unpacking, handling, or manual scanning. A shelf wired with a reader would always know, in real time, what it held.

Second, the EPC can uniquely identify each individual item of merchandise rather than simply identifying a product line. Each tag can serve as a pointer to a particular database entry, with each database entry describing a *particular* television set, or automobile transmission, or can of beans.

What specific characteristics of RFID give rise to privacy concerns? First, RFID-equipped goods and documents will blab information about themselves, and hence about the people carrying them, wirelessly to people whom the subjects might not have chosen to inform. If an ordinary citizen is carrying items or documents equipped with RFID tags, then complete strangers can read information from those tags without any current or prior relationship with the person carrying them, indeed without having known anything about that person at all before cranking up the tag reader. The subject need not be aware that the information is being collected.

Moreover, that capability follows the target through space, and reveals to data collectors how the target moves through space. RFID allows observers to learn something about a target that most other privacy-invasive technologies don't—and that's *where* she is physically. It's thus, quite directly, a surveillance technology. And there's more: not only does the profile that RFID technology helps construct contain information about where the subject is and has been, but RFID signifiers travel *with* the subject in the physical world, conveying information to devices that otherwise wouldn't recognize her, and that can take actions based on that information.

II. RFID DEPLOYMENT

Starting in 2003, Wal-Mart and several other large retailers began pushing hard to implement RFID tagging in their supply chains on the case and pallet level.[5] They had a strong case for implementing RFID. They urged that the ability to track cases and pallets wirelessly and automatically would give them a better picture of where manufactured items were in the supply chain, so that they could be more efficient in moving goods through the distribution process. Wal-Mart's project has hit some snags; although the benefits of RFID tagging in this context accrue to retailers, the costs are borne by suppliers. Many suppliers have reluctantly made only the minimum expenditures necessary to comply with Wal-Mart mandates. Nonetheless, Wal-Mart argues that in pilot stores it has reduced out-of-stocks significantly, and has been able to replenish empty shelves three times faster.

A variety of companies have experimented with the placement of RFID tags on individual consumer items. The most prominent retailer committed to item-level RFID as a stock control system is Marks & Spencer, which emphasizes that its tags are large, visible, and easily removed by the consumer. Levi Strauss conducted a small pilot program in which certain of its men's jeans sold at a single (undisclosed) U.S. store carried external RFID hang tags; Gap and Abercrombie also conducted small pilots. With a few exceptions, though, these initiatives don't seem to be going anywhere. Few early adopters, their pilot programs over and done with, seem to be investing in item-level tagging.

There's reason to doubt the business case for item-level tagging. It's hard to imagine widespread distribution of item-level tags unless the price per tag drops below five cents, and harder to imagine tags on really cheap consumer items—say, boxes of cereal and bars of soap—unless the price per tag drops to below a penny. But the cost of the least expensive tag in 2004 was more than ten cents by some accounts, and forty cents by others. Those cost numbers haven't changed much. Even if tag costs come down substantially, taking advantage of item-level tagging will require retailers to incur the costs of purchasing and installing reader networks, training reader operators, and putting in place back-end data systems to manage the information. Some observers estimate that hardware costs for RFID will amount to only 3 percent of the total, with software to process the huge amounts of data generated by the network making up 75 percent.

If item-level tagging is to justify its costs, it will have to be markedly more convenient and reliable than currently available technologies such as bar-code scanning. But early adopters wrestled with the fact that RFID tags are subject to considerable interference from items in the retail environment such as fluids and metal, not to mention nylon conveyor belts and dense materials such as frozen meat and chicken parts. Even in environments that could be optimized for RFID, firms have had difficulty achieving adequate read rates. It's more difficult still to get satisfactory read rates for RFID tags on the retail store floor. Although reports indicate better read rates with tags conforming to EPC's new Gen2 specification, the problem is still significant.

All this suggests that there are major obstacles in the way of the industry's dream of "put[ting] a radio frequency ID tag on everything that moves in the North American supply chain."[6] Some predict that we will see mass adoption of RFID on the item level, but not until the 2020s or later. With a time frame twenty years or more in the future, though, no prediction is reliable.

RFID has made important inroads in specific applications. Michelin, for example, began fleet testing RFID in tires in 2003. The tags are too expensive for passenger-car use, but are in production now for airplanes and fleet trucks. Tire-industry engineers are developing specifications to combine that functionality with sensors monitoring temperature and pressure.

A variety of automobile manufacturers incorporate RFID into the ignition key, so that the key can identify itself to the anti-theft system. So far, indeed, transportation-related uses—also including cards and tickets for buses and trains—have accounted for more than 40 percent of the 2.4 billion RFID tags that one source estimates have been sold to date. RFID tags have been extensively deployed in library books, and used to track livestock and pets.

There has been a move under way for some time in the pharmaceutical industry to tag shipments of drugs to pharmacies with unique serial numbers on RFID tags. Concerns about privacy, the security of confidential business transaction data, the accuracy and speed of RFID reader systems, and the effect of RFID on sensitive products, though, all present substantial obstacles to the RFID use in this context. Only a small number of high-value and heavily counterfeited medications, such as Viagra, are likely to see extensive RFID tagging in the near future.

There's been considerable publicity associated with implanting RFID tags into people subcutaneously. Mexico's attorney general announced in 2004 that he and his staff had chips implanted in their arms to authenticate their access to secure areas and to enable them to be found "anywhere inside Mexico" in the event of assault or kidnapping. (How a chip with a read range of a few inches would allow the wearer to be found anywhere in the country was left unexplained.) More recently, the FDA approved the implantation into human subjects of RFID tags referencing the subjects' medical records. Yet actual instances of human implantation have been flaky and isolated (and sometimes, as in the case of the Mexico attorney general's office, silly). There would be huge market resistance to any such private-sector initiative.

More generally, for many RFID implementations—this includes most item-level tagging—the business case has not yet materialized in which tagging would generate the return on investment that would make the project worthwhile. Focus on RFID hardware—on tags and readers—has led to a heavily populated hardware supplier sector in which the "hardware folks are desperately trying to differentiate themselves" and "a lot of blood is running" but prospective buyers are holding back, unconvinced that RFID can actually make money for them.[7] The complexity and costliness of deployment, as well as the entrenched nature of existing bar-code-based tracking systems, have left many firms unenthusiastic about adopting the technology.

So is RFID adoption at a standstill? Hardly. While not too many for-profit firms have been eager to embrace the technology, RFID has secured a different, enthusiastic, and growing market: government. Thirteen agencies of the U.S. government have implemented, or plan to implement, a specific RFID deployment plan.[8] Some of those relate straightforwardly to logistics support, tracking the movement of shipments or other materials. Others are less innocuous from a privacy perspective: Department of Health and Human Services (HHS) and the Treasury Department plan to use RFID for physical access control, and the Department of Transportation, for "screening." The State Department has already begun issuing passports equipped with RFID, and Homeland Security intends to use RFID-equipped documents for border control. The U.S. General Services Administration (GSA) is procuring government ID cards that identify themselves wirelessly (although GSA insists that because these contactless cards encrypt communications from tag to reader, they are not "RFID").

The U.S. Department of Defense (DoD) was an initial key adopter of RFID for the logistics chain. Full-scale deployment is now under way; DoD expected all twenty-six of its Defense Distribution Centers to be ready to accept RFID-tagged product by the end of 2007.

The State Department has moved successfully to embed RFID in passports. The United States was closely involved in the formulation of an International Civil Aviation Organization committee recommendation that all passports and other travel documents store electronic data on "contactless integrated circuit" chips (which is to say, RFID technology or a close relation). The U.S. government then moved quickly to implement that recommendation. New U.S. passports now have RFID embedded. The passport electronically stores the bearer's picture and the other information physically printed on the passport. In response to pressure, the State Department has incorporated some important privacy protections in its technology. The passport cover incorporates shielding, so that the digital material cannot be read when the cover is closed. Further, the digital information on the passport is encrypted; the key is printed on the passport and is gained by swiping the passport through an optical reader. Thus no attacker can pull unencrypted data from the card without physical access to it.

There appear, though, still to be security shortcomings in the passport design. An attacker may be able to read data broadcast by an opened passport (as much as ten feet away and perhaps farther) and associate with it a string of data that is unique to it and consistent over time. The attacker could use that persistent unique identifier to track the passport holder. The State Department has introduced a randomized unique ID feature that the agency says will "mitigate" this attack, but it makes no claim that the feature will eliminate it.

The Department of Homeland Security (DHS) plans to issue other RFID-enabled travel documents. The first of those is the PASS travel document. Recently enacted U.S. law requires citizens to have passports to enter this country from Canada, Mexico, or the Caribbean; because it costs nearly a hundred dollars to get a passport, the PASS card was conceived as a cheaper alternative. DHS intends to incorporate a ninety-six-digit unique serial number into each card, using technology essentially identical to that used on EPC tags. The serial number would be broadcast promiscuously, and could be read under the right circumstances as far away as twenty-five to forty feet. The card would not incorporate passport security features. DHS contemplates that travelers approaching the U.S.-Canadian border will remove their PASS cards from their protective sleeves and place them on their car dashboards. About thirty feet before the border kiosk, they will pass under a portal containing a card reader; the reader will extract the PASS card IDs and display the associated information on a computer screen for the border control official.

From a privacy and security standpoint, this is problematic. It would be easy for third parties to pick up and track the unique ID on the card. Without access to the DHS database, the attackers could not immediately learn the personal information associated with the card,[9] but they would be able to use the card's output as a persistent unique identifier. Indeed, having done so, they could use that information to clone the card—to program an inventory-control tag so that it "looks," electronically, like somebody else's PASS card. At that point, it would be relatively easy to forge a PASS card for anybody who looked somewhat like the target, and all of the electronic traces it would leave would be the target's.

Another major DHS RFID project relates to I-94s, the documents that all "nonimmigrants" (that is, noncitizens admitted into the United States other than for permanent residence) must carry at all times. The agency is seeking to use I-94s to match up nonimmigrants' entry records with their exit records, and thus to have a complete image of which nonimmigrants are in the country at any time. To effectuate that task, DHS has decided, the I-94 should include an RFID chip similar to that contemplated for the PASS card. The chip would contain a unique serial number pointing to a database entry containing the traveler's biographic and biometric information. It would broadcast that unique serial number, promiscuously, via RFID; DHS would read the tags at U.S. exit and entry points without the participation of the person carrying the document. In the Department's words, this would allow it to compile a "complete travel history" for each visitor.

The program has been the subject of vigorous criticism on several fronts. As one critic put the point, "this is the first case in which anyone in the USA (even non-citizens), other than convicted criminals or those subject to specific restrictive court orders issued following adversary and evidentiary legal proceedings, will have been required by law to carry remote radio tracking devices."[10] Privacy advocates urge that the RFID tag serial number will both serve as a persistent unique identifier and identify the carrier to anyone with an RFID reader as a nonimmigrant visitor. At the same time, technology experts (perhaps providing some reassurance to the privacy advocates) suggest it's questionable whether agency RFID devices will be able to read the tag information on a sufficiently reliable basis.

A variety of other United States government RFID initiatives are also in the works. The Transportation Security Administration and Coast Guard are planning a Transportation Worker Identification Credential program, under which various workers in the transportation industry will be required to apply for and receive RFID-enabled identification cards. The GSA is planning an RFID-enabled Personal Identity Verification card for identifying federal employees and contractors. The Department of Homeland Security is looking at an RFID-enabled First Responder Authentication Card (FRAC), for use in emergency response coordination efforts among first responder categories within federal, state, and local agencies.

The United States, of course, is not the only country planning RFID initiatives. In the People's Republic of China, government plans to issue more than 1.3 billion RFID "resident identification" cards, directly storing—and broadcasting—personal identifying information including the holders' names and birthdates. The cards will not be able to be read from as great a distance as those of the DHS; it appears that the tags' reliable range will be in the neighborhood of a foot. But the fact that the entire population, apparently, will be required to carry the RFID-equipped card, identifying themselves wirelessly, without demand, is an order of magnitude beyond anywhere DHS has gone so far.[11]

Not to be outdone, in the United States, the CEO of the company manufacturing the implantable Verichip has sought to leapfrog the PRC in privacy-invasive technology. He has lobbied in Washington in favor of injecting chips directly into the bodies of foreign workers allowed into the United States, to be used "at the border . . . [and] for enforcement purposes at the employer level."[12]

Even as State Department and DHS plans for incorporating RFID into identity documents have gone forward, we are seeing some backlash in this country against other comparable government implementations. Two years ago, the state of Virginia was exploring proposals for RFID-equipped driver's licenses. A year ago, some analysts believed that the Department of Homeland Security would mandate RFID for all driver's licenses under its REAL ID Act[13] authority. The political landscape, however, has now changed. State agencies have examined RFID in the context of their driver's license programs and found it unsuited to their needs. This year, a house of the California legislature voted preemptively to ban RFID in driver's licenses. A house of the New Hampshire legislature voted not to comply with the REAL ID Act at all. Analysts now seem confident that DHS will not include an RFID mandate to appear in its REAL ID regulations; the issue is too politically volatile.

In the wake of all this, a DHS advisory subcommittee recently issued a report urging that in general, the government should not use RFID for human identification.[14] RFID, the report argues, does not increase the speed or efficiency of identification processes. The RFID transmission by itself provides no assurance that the person holding an RFID-equipped document is the person described in it. To get reliable identification, a government verifier must compare biometric identifiers on the document with the bearer's own characteristics. But RFID provides little help in that process. RFID is helpful in reducing forgery and tampering with identification documents, the report continues, but no more so than any other means of digitizing and storing the relevant information. On the other side of the ledger, the report urges, the use of RFID for human identification poses privacy and security risks out of proportion to its benefits.[15] As of this writing, the report—which drew fierce opposition from such organizations as the American Electronics Association and the Smart Card Alliance—is before the full DHS advisory committee on Data Privacy and Integrity, where its fate is uncertain (and given DHS's current full-throated support for RFID, dubious).

III. ANALYZING RFID THREATS

It's hard to predict the future. Tags may never become widespread on consumer goods; they may become commonplace in connection with some application I haven't discussed in this chapter, such as access badges or credit cards. It may be that all the barriers to item-level tagging of retail goods will be overcome in the next fifteen years.

Two years ago, many of us paying attention to RFID were most interested in commercial applications. Privacy scholars know the importance of commercial privacy threats, given the industry's huge ability and incentive to monetize information about potential purchasers. Moreover, it was hard to ignore the science-fictional flair of the image of one's underwear broadcasting one's identity. But commercial businesses will implement privacy-invasive (or any other) technologies only to the extent they see return on investment. Further, at least some commercial businesses have shown themselves to be sensitive to public concerns about RFID technology. All this has limited the commercial RFID privacy threat.

Government has different incentives and constraints. If federal government decision makers decide that a particular technology is desirable, especially in the homeland security arena, they can deploy it even where industry would see no return on investment. And not all government entities are equally sensitive to public privacy concerns. The Department of Homeland Security, in particular, has seemed to view privacy (and public perceptions of privacy) as low priority.

RFID technology seems likely to become widespread, although not necessarily pervasive, in everyday life. We're seeing the beginnings of widespread government adoption. We may or may not see widespread business adoption in realms that directly touch consumers' lives; it may be that government uses will cross-fertilize business uses, as volume purchases in one area bring down the price in the other. We need to consider how to think about all that from a privacy standpoint.

Let's start by distinguishing among different sorts of RFID implementations. First, consider an RFID tag that directly stores, and makes available to anyone with a reader, the holder's personal identifying information. Data on the RFID tag can be read either by the responsible entity or by an unrelated (and unauthorized) third party, and either way the person carrying the tag may not be aware of the privacy invasion. The twenty-meter read range I referred to earlier as a theoretical maximum for inexpensive passive tags leaves room for substantial surveillance capabilities. Other tag implementations have shorter read ranges, but readers can effectively invade privacy even with shorter read ranges. One can embed an RFID reader, invisibly, in floor tiles, or carpeting, or a doorway. A read range of only a few feet is entirely adequate to track people coming through a door. So the opportunities for surveillance are extensive.

This sort of RFID implementation presents three related privacy threats. The first is surveillance. Any person with access to a reader will know the identity of each person carrying a tag (and in the PRC example just noted, all residents would be required to carry one by law). The ability to read names off RFID tags, given that RFID situates its data subjects in space, means that every reader network is a Panopticon geolocator. A listener seeking to compile a database with the identities of all of the people attending an event in a building would merely have to station readers at the building entrance. The rest of the data collection and analysis would be automatic.

The second threat is profiling. The data collector can maintain a profile on the target, and include in that profile not only the results of the surveillance but also any other information gleaned at a distance from the tag. In the case of a passport, say, this would include identifying numbers, address, and physical characteristics. (Recall that the data collector may be a third party, not the government entity that created the tag in the first place.)

The third is the "action threat."[16] After learning a person's identity via RFID, people or devices associated with the reader network can take actions regarding that person (ranging from further surveillance and arrest on the one hand, to displaying targeted ads on the other) based on their knowledge of who she is and what she is like.

Next, let's consider an implementation in which RFID tags do not broadcast personal identifying information directly. Instead, as with the Department of Homeland Security's proposed PASS card and I-94, they broadcast pointers to entries in a limited-access database containing the holders' personal identifying information. How does that change the privacy calculus?

It does not change the calculus at all, of course, when it comes to privacy threats from the entity responsible for the tag and in control of the database. A U.S. citizen carrying a PASS card (at least so long as the card is out of its protective sleeve), is still subject to surveillance, profiling, and action threats from the Department of Homeland Security and from anyone else that has gotten database access from DHS.

To the extent that third parties cannot gain access to the database, an important privacy-related concern remains: the data on the tag can serve as a persistent unique identifier of the person carrying it. Without knowing anything about the *meaning* of the serial number on a particular tag, a person with a reader can use that serial number to aggregate data about a particular subject over time—if only on the level of "this is the same guy who was here making trouble last week." The person carrying the tag is still subject to the surveillance, profiling, and action threats, except that those threats will be directed at the nameless (for now) holder of the particular unique tag, not at her as a named person. Moreover, if the link between the tag number and the subject's identity makes its way later on into an information broker's database, the privacy threats become identical to those posed in our first scenario.

What if an RFID tag neither points to, nor carries, personal identifying information? An item-level retail inventory control tag, after all, does not contain the name or address of the person carrying it; it merely points to a database entry revealing that it is a sweater (say), from a particular manufacturer, of a particular style and color, with a given unique serial number. Where are the privacy threats there?

The first question we need to answer is whether third parties will know the meaning of the tag serial numbers. Let's assume that an item-level inventory control tag conforms to the EPCglobal architecture. This system was designed for easy and transparent access to tag data in the Object Name Service (ONS) by actors up and down the supply chain, to promote supply-chain visibility and coordination. Recently, though, it's come to seem likely that manufacturers will restrict access to portions of the ONS under their own control, or avoid the ONS entirely, so that RFID scanning will not reveal sensitive competitive information.[17] If a manufacturer restricts access to portions of the ONS under its own control, then the distributed database might inform the casual requester that the Electronic Product Code on a particular tag referenced a product made by shoe manufacturer Mephisto, but that the rest of the information referenced by the EPC was stored in a limited-access database on Mephisto's servers. This will ameliorate some of the privacy threat.

On the other hand, the meaning of common tag "object classes," identifying the type and model of goods supplied by a given manufacturer, will likely not stay secret long. Different manufacturers' policies will vary; and as manufacturers embrace the modern reality that they can monetize consumer information by selling it to aggregators, it's by no means clear that the information associated with tag data will remain closely held. It's at least possible, therefore, that a tag on the shoe you purchase in the near future will tell anyone who asks, as you walk around town, that it's a Mephisto shoe style 17, size 40, in black, serial #139421386. In that way, a wide range of strangers to you could learn, automatically and without direct contact, the data on the tags you're wearing or carrying.

That casts the profiling threat in a new light. When I presented the profiling threat earlier, it was fairly straightforward: a data collector could enter in a profile, say, a person's address, lifted from his driver's license or resident identification card. Item-level tags on retail goods make this threat more interesting. Consumers may find themselves carrying a variety of different tags, on different occasions. Profiling may incorporate data signaled by all of those tags—not (only) on identification documents, but on clothing, vehicles, and portable possessions. When an entity reads new information about the target from a different tag or tags, it can add to the profile associated with that name any new characteristics associated with that new RFID information (as well as the unique tag numbers themselves).

One might object that this is not much of a privacy threat, because information that readers will collect from retail tags will likely be visible to the naked eye. Yet RFID is important from a privacy standpoint even when it only facilitates the collection of information that could otherwise be collected by analog means. Imagine, after all, the movement of automobiles down a highway. There's nothing stopping a government from posting an employee to copy down license plate numbers, or a camera to photograph them. That information, though, comes into being in analog format; it would be time-consuming and expensive to enter it into a digital database. As a result, the information won't in fact be entered digitally except on particular occasions when it's important and cost-effective to do so. By contrast, if a reader were positioned in the highway collecting data from RFID tags in automobile tires (with the tag data linked to automobile VINs in a separate database), then the collection of the data and its inclusion in a searchable digital database would be automated, cheap, and easy. RFID readers automate their information collection, and collect the information in a format that makes its inclusion in networked databases trivial. That's important, because the cheaper it is to collect, store, and analyze information, the more information will in fact be collected, stored, and analyzed.

It's already become clear from this discussion that although strangers can collect RFID data from tags on goods or documents in my possession, that data isn't *necessarily* linked to my name or other personally identifying information. In some situations, it will be easy for a data collector to draw a link between my name (or other personally identifying information) and data on an RFID tag. If I go into the Gap and buy a tagged sweater, then the Gap can link the sweater EPC with my name and other information in its database. Assuming that the tag isn't disabled at point of sale or after, then every time I walk into the Gap wearing that sweater, store personnel will be able to know who I am without having to ask. If the Gap sells or trades the data linking my tag information with my personally identifiable info, then wherever I go *anyone* in possession of that data can read my tag and accordingly know who I am, and my profile, without having to ask. In other situations, by contrast, RFID tag information, while attached to the geographic location or the physical person of the target, will not necessarily be attached to anyone's name or personally identifying information. The data collector may know what type of sweater I wear, but still may not know my name.

When a target's tags themselves broadcast personally identifying information or can be linked to such information, the target is subject to a strong form of the profiling threat. A reader network can cheaply and seamlessly collect RFID information from her belongings and documents, and easily add it to her profile. When an entity reads information from her tags, it will be able to add to the profile associated with her name any new characteristics associated with that RFID information (as well as the unique tag numbers themselves). She would also be subject to a strong form of the surveillance threat, because the devices attached to the reader network will know who the person carrying the tags is. Finally, she would be subject to an equally strong form of the action threat.

By contrast, when a target's tags do not themselves broadcast personally identifying information (directly or through pointers to a database the reader has access to), then a stranger who knows nothing about the target other than what it can pull from her tags will not necessarily be able to make a connection between the target's RFID data and her name or other personally identifying information. This largely eliminates the profiling and surveillance threats. The target is still subject to a version of the action threat. Even without knowing the target's name, the listener can associate information with her physical being in a particular location and take action based on that association—displaying particular advertisements to the target, steering her to particular goods the seller thinks may be of interest, offering her differential rates, imposing obstacles to her admission to a mall. Moreover, the tag numbers can serve as unique and semi-persistent identifiers.[18] Any listener with an RFID reader situated near a place I go can collect information over time about me (the individual, located intermittently or long term in a particular geographic space, who is associated with given unique tag numbers). This information collection over time can inform the actions I've just described. And once those dossiers exist, they may be linked to my name at a later point.

How robust is this distinction between linked and nonlinked tag information? As profiling accelerates in the modern world, aided by the automatic, networked collection of information through technologies such as RFID, information compiled by one data collector likely will increasingly be available to others as well; the economic (and homeland security) forces pushing in that direction are powerful. As a result, information linking tag data to my personal identity may well move easily into the hands of actors who are strangers to me in any meaningful sense. Further, when a target carries both a "linked" and an "unlinked" tag (say, a PASS card and a commercial tag), it becomes trivial for the data collector to associate the (heretofore) unlinked card with the linked identity.

Linking persistent identifiers to personally identifying information thus may turn out to be quite easy. As John Gilmore has put the point, the fact that an RFID payment tag supplying persistent ID does not directly broadcast the identity of its carrier will be privacy—protective "only . . . once"—until "anyone who wants to"

> correlates that token ID "blob" with your photo on the security camera, your license plate number (and the RFIDs in each of your Michelin tires), the other RFIDs you're carrying, your mobile phone number, the driver's license they asked you to show, the shipping address of the thing you just bought, and the

big database on the Internet where Equifax will turn a token ID into an SSN (or vice verse) for 3c in bulk.[19]

That suggests that the privacy provided by tags (such as DHS's PASS card) that broadcast only serial numbers pointing to database entries is elusive; it may be all too easy for outsiders such as information brokers to link each serial number with the target's identity sometime after her profile is created. From the other direction, it would be easy for a government entity maintaining a database keyed to PASS, I-94, or federal employee RFID numbers to add in the information gleaned from commercial tags.

So far, I have discussed RFID implementations that promiscuously broadcast tag data to third parties. That's not an inherent characteristic of RFID technology. One can manufacture RFID tags with sophisticated access controls, which won't release their information unless the reader establishes through a cryptographic handshake that the tags' programmer has authorized it. That technology is expensive; for an authorized reader to securely authenticate a tag via public key cryptography is well beyond the resources of the sort of low-cost tag used in retail applications. Nonetheless, if one is willing to pay for more expensive tags, one can supplement cryptography with other technical protections aiming at the ability of RFID tags to supply globally unique identity. More sophisticated RFID architecture allows tags to emit not a single, unchanging, unique ID but a series of random pseudonyms that can only be understood by authorized verifiers.

There's been no movement by device manufacturers or standards bodies to incorporate these approaches into ordinary inventory-control tags, and one would hardly expect there to be. For a tag to implement access controls, it needs to add logic gates, and that increases its size and cost. But the Personal Identity Verification card mentioned earlier, planned for identifying federal employees and contractors; the Transportation Worker Identification Credential (TWIC), issued in prototype by the Transportation Security Administration; and the First Responder Authentication Card (FRAC), being issued in Department of Homeland Security pilots, will all use RFID chips meeting ISO 14443 smart card specifications. Those cards incorporate more sophisticated access control, designed to deny third parties the opportunity to read the data on the cards. Do they ameliorate the privacy threats discussed earlier?

It is surely the case that less availability of personal information to third parties is better than more. As before, though, the security against third-party eavesdropping does nothing to mitigate privacy invasions by the card issuer. Moreover, even with more sophisticated technology, security problems remain; recall the concern about whether attackers can get persistent ID from passports using the ISO 14443 chip. At best, the more sophisticated technology presents an arms race between RFID card designers and third parties seeking to hack that technology. In the words of one informed analyst, "a passport has a ten-year lifetime. It's sheer folly to believe the passport security won't be hacked in that time."[20]

IV. POLICIES FOR RFID DEPLOYMENT

We thus can sketch two broad classes of RFID implementations presenting privacy threats. The first is represented by government identification documents. These documents incorporate personally identifying information and either broadcast that information directly to reader devices or broadcast pointers to database entries containing the information. Usually, but not always, the RFID technology used in these documents incorporates relatively sophisticated protections against third-party access. The potential these documents present for surveillance and tracking means that the wireless availability of the information to *authorized* government readers, without more, is worrisome from a privacy standpoint. And the possibility of attack or interception by unauthorized readers, even if it consists only of the interception of a persistent unique ID, is always present.

The second class is represented by item-level inventory control tags. Here the information stored on the tag, apart from its possible use as a persistent identifier, is less sensitive (perhaps a pointer to a database revealing that the tag is attached to a particular model and color of sweater). Data security, on the other hand, is essentially nonexistent. Some of the privacy threat here comes from the possibility that individuals may find themselves, at one time or another, carrying a variety of tags, and thus at the center of a buzzing swarm of small information transfers that can be aggregated into a much larger whole. The remaining privacy threat comes from the possibility that, once a unique ID on a tag is linked to an individual's personal identifying information, the tag for surveillance purposes is equivalent to a device transmitting the identifying information directly.

What public policy response is appropriate for each? With respect to any RFID implementation—indeed, any implementation of privacy-invasive technology—it's useful to ask two questions to frame the public-policy analysis.

The first is whether it makes sense to use RFID for this purpose at all; the second, assuming that RFID will be used, is how it can be implemented to avoid unacceptable privacy threats.

With respect to government ID documents, the most salient question is the first. If one takes as a given that a passport should incorporate RFID, then the State Department's technological approach seems a reasonable attempt to mitigate privacy risks. The more important question, though, is why a passport should incorporate RFID at all. It's useful, from a security standpoint, to have digitized information on a passport; it makes the passport harder to forge or modify. But other forms of reading a passport's digitized information, such as contact chips, 2D barcodes, and optical memory stripe technology, would be more secure and less vulnerable to eavesdropping and skimming.[21]

The relevant International Civil Aeronautics Organization subcommittee (ICAO) (on which the United States played an active and supportive role) excluded contact chip technology for passports because there were no established standards for fabricating or reading passports with contact chips, and because of fears that they would be insufficiently durable.[22] But it does not appear that the agency or the ICAO focused adequately on privacy risks. In consequence, it gave inadequate attention to RFID alternatives. With respect to other government documents, the key question is the same. Absent any good reason why driver's licenses should incorporate RFID, we need not worry about finding the most privacy-friendly RFID implementation.[23] The privacy risks mean that RFID should not be in driver's licenses at all.

When it comes to private-sector RFID, various actors have suggested privacy solutions short of banning RFID technology in the retail supply chain. Early on, EPCglobal endorsed the "kill command." Under EPCglobal's specifications, RFID tags will respond to a password-protected command directing the tag's integrated circuit to disable itself. Retailers can give consumers the option to have RFID tags on their purchases disabled before they leave the store.

There's appeal to the "kill command." The option of killing retail tags at point of sale recognizes the different trade-offs the technology presents at different points in the retail-good lifecycle. While goods are moving through the retail sales chain, RFID tagging can offer important inventory-control benefits, with essentially no cost in terms of consumer privacy. Once the good is sold to the consumer, by contrast, there is no further need for inventory control. Moreover, the approach EPCglobal contemplates—that at point of sale the consumer would have the option to ask that a tag be disabled—allows the consumer to maintain the functioning tag if she sees benefit in that course.

EPCglobal's approach, however, has at least one important flaw: it seems unlikely to do a very good job of actually keeping live tags off the streets. Retailers are unlikely to want to incur the additional expense associated with allowing customers to kill tags. Small retailers in particular, who may find it cheaper to continue counting inventory by hand than to invest in smart shelves or a reader network, will be reluctant to buy expensive equipment to disable the RFID tags they'll be receiving, uninvited, on their consumer packaged goods. Even if the law should require that consumers be offered a kill option, consumers may not exercise that option if disabling the tag requires more time at checkout or other inconvenience. That's all the more true if retailers or manufacturers offer consumers any sort of incentive to forgo disabling their tags, such as a more convenient return policy.

So we're brought to the question of what other restraints on information use and sharing might be appropriate in the commercial RFID context. Our starting point is the guidelines known as Fair Information Practice principles, which, though only sporadically reflected in U.S. law, play an important role in U.S. and European information privacy thinking. I'll paraphrase a version here: (1) Consumers should get notice of an entity's privacy policies before that entity collects any personal information from them. (2) Consumers should be able to choose whether to convey the information, and how it can be used or transferred. (3) Consumers should be able to see the information collected about them, and to contest its accuracy or completeness. (4) The collector must take reasonable care that the information it maintains is accurate and secure. (5) There must be some mechanism, other than the data collector's good intentions, to bring about compliance.[24]

Fair information practice principles are not obviously well-suited to data-collection systems such as RFID. The architecture of unsophisticated RFID systems allows anyone, including persons entirely unrelated to the tag's manufacturer or its intended users, to be a data collector. Reading is undetectable, and nothing will cause the consumer to know that a reader is collecting data about her. Data collection may be the basis of privacy threats even though the information is never linked to the subject's name. Fair information practices work best in systems with clearly identified data collectors, who have the information in the first place because the consumer has voluntarily given it to them in order to facilitate some transaction the consumer wants, and who are subject to meaningful restraints on information reuse and sharing. They work less well in systems in which devices blab information indiscriminately, so that there's no way to identify a class of information collectors who can be made subject to the rules.

Nonetheless, a variety of actors have developed best practices and privacy guidelines based on fair information practice principles.[25] A working group assembled by the Center for Democracy and Technology, including industry actors such as Procter & Gamble, Intel, Verisign, and Microsoft, developed a set of best practices stating that consumers should be provided with notice when information is collected through an RFID system and is linked, or is intended by a commercial entity to become linked, to an individual's personal information. The notice should specify why the linked information is being collected, and how it will be used; consumers should be given the choice to refuse consent for uses other than enabling the functioning or delivery of a purchased device or contracted service, or facilitating the completion of the business transaction. On the other hand, businesses need not give notice if, in their "judicious discretion," they determine that the ease and likelihood of linkage is sufficiently attenuated as to lower the privacy risk.[26]

The European Commission (EC) has launched an ongoing consultation on RFID policy; it issued a communication in 2007 setting out general initial steps toward a policy framework.[27] An earlier EC Working Party published a document in 2005 taking the position that existing European data protection law covers the collection of RFID data whenever that information either contains personal information or is reasonably likely to be linked to it. In those situations, the report continues, data controllers are obligated to comply with European data protection principles: information must be used only for the purposes for which it was collected, must not be excessive for that purpose, and must be kept no longer than necessary. In most circumstances, it can be collected only on the basis of specific, unambiguous informed consent. Data subjects must have notice of the identity of the data collector, and the purposes of the collection, and they must have access to any information being kept about them.[28]

The EC document notes that RFID technology may make some of these limitations illusory. It may be difficult to monitor the purposes for which linked data is used, or even to know which parties are maintaining data about a subject.[29] Therefore, beyond a focus on linked data, a second general approach to privacy protection would impose restrictions on tag data collection to minimize the respects in which RFID makes fair information practice principles problematic. To that end, the EC working party concluded that data subjects must have notice of the presence of RFID tags and readers, as well as the consequences of that presence in terms of information gathering, and must be told how to remove or disable RFID tags.[30] The Electronic Privacy Information Center once suggested guidelines that would prohibit the use of tag readers except where individuals have been warned that they are present, and require that readers emit a tone or light, or some other easily recognizable indicator, when they draw information from RFID tags.[31]

This last set of rules is simpler than the first; it's worth thinking, though, whether the rules could be simpler still. In particular, it's hard to see a reason why EPC-compliant item-level tags should not have to be clearly labeled and easily removable.[32] That shouldn't pose an insuperable barrier for industry; EPCglobal's own "best practice" guidelines for RFID tags on consumer products "anticipate[] that for most products," tags will be "part of disposable packaging or . . . otherwise discardable."[33] Alternatively, retailers could rely on technology such as the IBM Clipped Tag.[34] The Clipped Tag is perforated. After purchasing a tagged item, a consumer can tear the tag along the perforations to remove part of its antenna, reducing its read range from tens of feet to a few inches. This provides an easy and visible way of disabling most remote read capability, while still preserving the serialized ID for uses such as returns (so that, say, a consumer could return an item without proof-of-purchase by virtue of the store's having associated the sale price and buyer's name with the tag ID in its database at point of sale).[35]

If manufacturers eschewed technology like the Clipped Tag and simply made tags visible and easily removable, then consumers would have to choose between privacy protection and post-sale tag functionality. A consumer who discarded a tag wouldn't get the benefit of a retailer's use of RFID to facilitate returns. Recycling centers wouldn't be able to rely on EPCs to categorize recycled items. Consumer items such as stoves and washing machines wouldn't be able to read tag information to get cooking or washing instructions. Yet that result should not be too distressing. Consumers would be able to retain tags when they chose. Manufacturers would remain free, if they chose, to incorporate information more permanently into consumer goods via a non-wireless bar code, or a generic tag not carrying a globally unique identifier.

It's by no means clear that item-level retail RFID tags will ever see substantial deployment. If they do, I suspect that their cool and valuable post-sale uses will be few, in part because manufacturers' reluctance to expose tag data to the world via the ONS will make it harder for third parties to offer post-sale functionality. The privacy-invasive uses of such tags once goods are sold, by contrast, will be many—that's the direction that economic incentives push in. It makes sense, therefore, to allow consumers to opt out easily, by tearing off RFID tags and dropping them in the trash.

V. CONCLUSION

In the business sector, the most important driver for RFID deployment has been the push for better inventory control. In the government sector, it has been security. The Department of Homeland Security has embraced RFID as a means of increasing security and has pushed for its deployment in a wide (and ever-increasing) range of identification documents. Given wireless communication's comparative vulnerability to interception and attacks, this is ironic.

RFID can be seen as a tool for better security in two ways. The first is that identification documents are harder to forge when they incorporate digitized information, and by necessity there must be some way for a government actor to read that information; the State Department has championed broadcast technology as the most practical and convenient way of communicating digitized passport information to a border control officer. The second is the idea that government actors can make us more secure against evildoers when their surveillance capacities are increased, and widespread deployment of RFID-enabled identification documents will increase the reach of government surveillance. This rationale seems all too close to that motivating the Department of Homeland Security.

DHS's strong support for RFID may well enable other RFID implementations in both government and business sectors by establishing standards, increasing public acceptance of the technology, and bringing price down through volume purchases. So one would be wrong, two years after the 2004 hype, with business implementation of RFID lagging outside of certain limited environments, to think that privacy advocates now can worry less about this technology. Substantial privacy threats from business implementation of RFID may or may not materialize. If they do, it may or may not be possible to address them with legislative or self-regulatory solutions. But the sector to watch, right now, is a determined government and the new privacy threats it is engendering.

NOTES

1. Press Release, Applied Digital Solutions' CEO Announces "Veripay(tm)" Secure, Subdermal Solution for Payment and Credit Transactions, at ID World 2003 in Paris (Nov. 21, 2003), available at http://www.adsx.com/news/2003/112103.html (internal quotation marks omitted).

2. For purposes of this paper, I will include in the RFID category both less expensive technology such as EPC Gen2 inventory control tags (see *infra* Part I) and more expensive, more sophisticated technologies. Some vendors of more sophisticated technologies urge that only simple and unsophisticated implementations should be referred to as "RFID." *See, e.g.,* SMART Card Alliance, *Contactless Smart Cards v. EPC Gen 2 RFID Tags: Frequently Asked Questions* (July 2006), available at http://www.smartcardalliance.org/alliance_activities/epc_gen2_faq.cfm.

3. *See* Matt Reynolds, *The Physics of RFID* (Nov. 15, 2003), available at http://www.rfid privacy.org/papers/physicsofrfid.pdf.

4. Radio Frequency Identification Applications and Implications for Consumers. Hearing before the Federal Trade Commission (June 21, 2004) [hereafter FTC RFID Workshop] 23-34 (testimony of Daniel Engels, executive and research director, Auto-ID Labs); *see also id.* at 35 (testimony of Manuel Albers, Phillips Semiconductor); *id.* at 247 (testimony of Jim Waldo, Sun Microsystems Laboratories).

5. For more background on commercial RFID deployment, *see* FTC RFID Workshop, *supra* n. 4; Simson Garfinkel & Beth Rosenberg, *RFID: Applications, Security and Privacy* (2006).

6. Lori Valigra, Smart Tags: Shopping Will Never Be the Same, *Christian Science Monitor* (Mar. 29, 2001), available at http://search.csmonitor.com/durable/2001/03/29/fp13s1-csm.shtml (quoting Steven Van Fleet, program director, International Paper).

7. Sandra Gittlen, The Failure of RFID, *Computerworld* (June 15, 2006), available at cwflyris.computerworld.com/t/601111/1423078/22956/0/.

8. General Accounting Office, *Information Security: Radio Frequency Identification in the Federal Government* (May 2005), available at http://www.gao.gov/new.items/d05551.pdf. In response to a GAO questionnaire, only one of the thirteen agencies answered that it believed there were legal issues associated with RFID use, and only six responded that they were concerned with security issues.

9. But *see infra* text accompanying note 19.

10. Edward Hasbrouck, *The Practical Nomad: Update on RFID Passports and Traveller Tracking* (Aug. 19, 2005), available at http://www.hasbrouck.org/blog/archives/000735.html.

11. Like U.S. passports, the tags will broadcast their holders' identifying information directly, rather than just displaying a serial number pointing to a database entry. It's not immediately clear what level of access control the card technology will support, and thus the extent to which the information will be available to anyone with a reader, not just authorized government agents.

12. Fox & Friends interview with Scott Silverman, chairman of the board of VeriChip Corporation (May 16, 2006), transcript available at http://www.spychips.com/press-releases/silverman-foxnews.html.

13. P.L. No. 109-13, §§ 201-07 (2005).

14. *The Use of RFID for Human Identification: A Draft Report from the DHS Emerging Applications and Technology Subcommittee*, v. 1.0 (May 2006), available at http://www.dhs.gov/dhspublic/interweb/assetlibrary/privacy_advcom_rpt_rfid_draft.pdf.

15. *See id.*

16. Ravi Pappu, *Privacy and Security in the EPC Network* (Nov. 15, 2003), available at http://www.rfidprivacy.us/2003/papers/pappu.pdf.

17. *See* Ross Stapleton-Gray, *Scanning the Horizon: A Skeptical View of Rfids on the Shelves* (Nov. 13, 2003), available at http://www.stapleton-gray.com/papers/sk-20031113.PDF; FTC RFID Workshop, *supra* n. 4, at 38 (testimony of Sue Hutchinson, product manager, EPCglobal); *id.* at 222-23 (testimony of Christopher Boone, program manager, IDC).

18. I'll describe them here as semi-persistent because, after all, if a tag is attached to a retail good I'm carrying, I may end up carrying or wearing the good only some of the time.

19. Email from John Gilmore to the Cryptology Mailing List (Sept. 18, 2005), disseminated by David Farber on the IP list (Sept. 19, 2005), available at http://www.interesting-people.org/archives/interesting-people/200509/msg00288.html.

20. Bruce Schneier, *Hackers Clone RFID Passports* (Aug. 3, 2006), available at http://www.schneier.com/blog/archives/2006/08/hackers_clone_r.html.

21. *See* Comments of EFF *et al.* in the Department of State's Electronic Passport proceeding (Apr. 4, 2005), available at http://www.epic.org/privacy/rfid/rfid_passports-0405.pdf#search=%22passport%20%22contact%20technology%22%22.

22. *See* 70 Fed. Reg. 61,553-61,555 (Oct. 5, 2005) (Department of State final rule on electronic passports); Bruce Schneier, *Hackers Clone RFID Passports* (Aug. 3, 2006) (quoting Randy Vanderhoof, executive director, Smart Card Alliance), available at http://www.schneier.com/blog/archives/2006/08/hackers_clone_r.html#c99421.

23. *See* Testimony Before the Virginia Legislature on House Joint Resolution 162, Considering the Creation of Smart Driver's Licenses (Chris Calabrese, ACLU) (Oct. 6, 2004), available at http://www.aclu.org/Privacy/Privacy.cfm?ID=16658&c=39.

24. *See* U.S. Federal Trade Commission, *Privacy Online: A Report to Congress*, at § III.A (1998), available at http://www.ftc.gov/reports/privacy3/fairinfo.htm#Fair%20Information%20Practice%20Principles; *see also* FTC RFID Workshop, *supra* n. 4, at 275-76 (testimony of Cedric Laurant, policy counsel, Electronic Privacy Information Center).

25. The first of these, to my knowledge, was Simson Garfinkel, *Adopting Fair Information Practices to Low Cost RFID Systems* (2002), available at http://www.simson.net/clips/academic/2002_Ubicomp_RFID.pdf. *See also* Comments of the Electronic Privacy Information Center to the Federal Trade Commission (July 9, 2004), in connection with the FTC Workshop on Radio Frequency Identification Applications and Implications for Consumers, available at http://www.epic.org/privacy/rfid/ftc-comts-070904.pdf, at 17-18.

26. CDT Working Group on RFID, *Privacy Best Practices for Deployment of RFID Technology* (Interim Draft May 1, 2006), available at http://www.cdt.org/privacy/20060501rfid-best-practices.php.

27. *See* RFID ConsultationWebsite, available at http://www.rfidconsultation.eu/.

28. *See* Article 29 Data Protection Working Party, *Working Document on Data Protection Issues Related to RFID Technology* (Jan. 19, 2005), available at http://ec.europa.eu/justice_home/fsj/privacy/docs/wpdocs/2005/wp104_en.pdf, at 8-11. The RFID Privacy Guidelines published by Ontario's Information and Privacy Commissioner run along similar lines. *See Privacy Guidelines for RFID Information Systems* (June 2006), available at http://www.ipc.on.ca/docs/

rfidgdlines.pdf#search=%22cavoukian%20rfid%20privacy%20guidelines%22.

29. *See* Article 29 Data Protection Working Party, *supra* n. 28, at 13.

30. *Id.* at 10.

31. *See* Comments of the Electronic Privacy Information Center to the Federal Trade Commission, *supra* n. 25, at 17.

32. *See id.* at 14; *see also* FTC RFID Workshop, *supra* n. 4, at 190 (testimony of Beth Givens, director, Privacy Rights Clearinghouse).

33. EPCGlobal, *Guidelines on EPC for Consumer Products*, available at http://www.epc globalinc.org/public_policy/public_policy_guidelines.html (last modified Sept. 13, 2004).

34. *See* Ann Bednarz, *IBM Demos RFID Tag with Privacy-Protecting Features* (May 1, 2006), available at http://www.networkworld.com/news/2006/050106-ibm-rfid-privacy.html?fsrc=rss-rfid.

35. *See id.*

13 SHOULD CRIMINAL LIABILITY BE USED TO SECURE DATA PRIVACY?

Susan W. Brenner

Susan W. Brenner is NCR Distinguished Professor of Law, University of Dayton School of Law.

The persistent evolution and proliferation of computer and related technologies has generated concerns about "data privacy." One, so far seldom-invoked, alternative for protecting the privacy of personal data is the use of criminal liability; because law is generally parsimonious with criminal liability, one wonders why it should be necessary to resort to criminal sanctions to protect the privacy of personal data. Warren and Brandeis, after all, were content to use tort law to establish their right to privacy.[1]

Logically, there are two reasons to use criminal liability: (1) civil liability (alone) is not sufficient to ensure data privacy and (2) data privacy is an interest significant enough to justify defining violations as an affront to the state. This chapter considers whether either justifies resort to the criminal sanction. Because both assume that data privacy is a legally cognizable interest, Section I examines the concept, analyzing the extent to which various types of data can be said to be private and therefore protectable under a criminal or civil enforcement scheme. Section II then considers the extent to which criminal liability can, and should, be used for this purpose.

I. DATA PRIVACY

U.S. law currently takes a piecemeal approach to privacy; statutory and constitutional provisions protect various aspects of privacy, but there is no overarching "right to privacy."

A. Constitutional and Statutory Standards

The Bill of Rights protects certain aspects of privacy: the First Amendment creates a right to speak anonymously and to preserve the confidentiality of one's associations, and, under modern Supreme Court interpretations,[2] the Fifth Amendment protects the privacy of one's thoughts by barring the state from compelling incriminating testimony.[3] The Fourth Amendment comes the closest to providing a general right to privacy, at least as to state actors.[4]

In *Katz* v. *United States*, the Supreme Court outlined the current Fourth Amendment conception of privacy, explaining that what "a person knowingly exposes to the public . . . is not a subject of Fourth Amendment protection. . . . But what he seeks to preserve as private . . . may be constitutionally protected."[5] In his concurring opinion, Justice Harlan set out the test that has been used to operationalize the decision: "[T]here is a twofold requirement, first that a person have exhibited an actual (subjective) expectation of privacy and, second, that the expectation be one that society is prepared to recognize as 'reasonable.'"[6]

Katz dealt with wiretapping.[7] In a series of subsequent decisions, the Court dealt with the Fourth Amendment's applicability to various types of data.

In *Smith* v. *Maryland*, 442 U.S. 735 (1979), the Court held that the state's use of a pen register to capture the numbers Smith dialed on his home telephone did not violate the Fourth Amendment because Smith had no "reasonable" expectation of privacy in them.[8] The *Smith* Court relied on the fact that the dialed numbers were "conveyed" to the telephone company for its use in placing calls and keeping account records; from this, it concluded that "telephone subscribers" could not reasonably believe that the numbers they dialed, even from their homes, would "remain secret."[9] A few years earlier, in *United States* v. *Miller*, 425 U.S. 435 (1976), the Court had held that bank customers have no Fourth Amendment expectation of privacy in records created and maintained by their bank.[10] The *Miller* Court relied on *Katz*'s "assumption of the risk principle":[11] "The depositor takes the risk, in revealing his affairs to another, that the information will be conveyed by that person to the Government."[12]

There is therefore no constitutional right to privacy in the contents of third-party records, that is, data one generates by engaging in transactions with other individuals or entities. Unsettled by the *Miller* decision, Congress established a statutory right to privacy by adopting the Right to Financial Privacy Act of 1978,[13] which declared that the government could not obtain individuals' financial records unless (1) the customer consented or (2) the records were obtained pursuant to a subpoena, search warrant, or "formal written request."[14] This approach was later replicated in other legislation.[15] These enactments established a delimited right to privacy as to state action that is secured by protections that are comparable to, but in some instances less than, those required by the Fourth Amendment.

Currently, therefore, the protection of data privacy in the United States rests not upon constitutional principles but upon the rather fragile reeds of statutes that create a disjointed and often uncertain right to privacy in specific types of data. This brings us to the critical question: Should a generalized concept of data privacy be a free-standing interest in American law?

B. Varieties of *Data Privacy*

To answer that question, it is first necessary to define *data privacy*. One apparently generally accepted definition is that it denotes our "ability to control the dissemination of personal information."[16] Implicit in this definition is the premise that the data in question are in the hands of third parties, who have either exclusive or shared access to them.[17] This premise is relevant for two reasons. First, it focuses our discussion: I have a constitutional right to privacy in data that concerns me and as to which I have exclusive access. Under *Katz*, as long as I do not share information about myself with others— do not "knowingly expose" it to public view—it is protected by the Fourth Amendment,[18] and law enforcement cannot lawfully gain access to it except with a search warrant, with my consent, or pursuant to another exception to the warrant requirement.[19] State law provides similar protection in the form of civil remedies (invasion of privacy, trespass) and criminal liability (theft, criminal trespass) in the unlikely event a private citizen invades my home or office and takes personal information I have sequestered there.[20]

These guarantees are relevant because they are predicated upon and consequently reveal traditional assumptions about "privacy." Privacy has been an oppositional concept, an antonym; my activities, my thoughts, and my predilections have been regarded as private only to the extent I have taken steps to shield them from others.[21] For centuries, this concept was spatially based. The *Katz* Court abandoned the spatially based conception of privacy and forced us to grapple with how we can implement a normative-based conception of privacy in a world made increasingly transparent by technology.[22] This brings us to the second reason why the premise noted earlier is relevant to this discussion: How can we conclude, even under *Katz*'s nonspatially based conception of privacy, that information I have shared with others is private?[23]

The notion seems hopelessly contradictory: I share my information with others, thereby surrendering control over it and assuming the risk that the recipients will further disseminate it, but insist that it somehow remains "private."[24] The process of answering the posed question is further complicated by the fact that personal information is not a unitary construct; the conditions and circumstances under which various types of data are generated differentiate them in ways that bear upon the privacy issue and can bring a countervailing force into play—the First Amendment. To understand the variegated nature of personal data and the extent to which their dissemination can implicate the First Amendment, it is helpful to divide personal data into three broad categories: (1) tool data, (2) biographical data, and (3) transactional data.

1. Tool Data

Tool data encompass personal information that is valued not for its content but for its utility. That information includes social security numbers, dates of birth, driver's license numbers, and other data; it will no doubt come to include biometric identifiers such as DNA. Tool data are a given; they are not the product of my will or effort but are assigned, more or less arbitrarily, to me. Tool data have "value" because they are an implement that can be used for good or evil: my social security number, for example, is a tool I can use to identify myself for various benign purposes (positive value) and one a criminal can use to steal my identity (negative value).[25]

Though tool data are something I "receive," they are not inherently "public;" unlike biographical and transactional data, they are not protected by the First Amendment and are therefore more easily controlled.[26] My social security number and date of birth may be "public," in that I have shared them with others, but that is not inevitable; like the other types of tool data in current circulation, they are "public" because we have not conceptualized tool data as commodities that have "value" and must therefore be protected. The need for, and use of, tool data is a historical accident, an ad hoc solution to the complexity of modern society; we use tool data to identify ("I am Susan Brenner") and authenticate ("Here is proof I am Susan Brenner") ourselves.[27] For most of human history, these functions were relational; people were born, were raised, and lived their lives in the same community, where everyone knew and recognized them.[28] As populations became increasingly mobile and urbanized, relational identification and authentication no longer sufficed; it became necessary to find some surrogate, and that is what social security numbers, driver's licenses, and other personal data became.[29] It is because they have become tool data that we are concerned about keeping them private; as long as my driver's license was simply my authorization to operate a motor vehicle, my license number had little "value" in the identification sense. Once it— along with my social security number and other data—became my de facto identifiers, they took on "value" and became a source of concern.

How can we secure tool data? One option is to continue to rely on ad hoc tool data but adopt federal legislation that defines them as private and imposes sanctions, like those discussed in Section II, for unauthorized disclosures. Another option is to eliminate our reliance on ad hoc tool data and adopt a national identifier; because such an instrument would be used only to identify and authenticate, it could consist of a limited, neutral data set. Such an instrument would have "value" in the same sense as current types of tool data, so it, too, would have to be protected by a legislative privacy regime secured by sanctions such as those discussed in Section II. It should, however, be easier to maintain the integrity of a single, federally issued standard, and its federal status would let us use federal criminal sanctions against those who violate its integrity.

2. Biographical Data

Biographical data are not a given. They derive from my activities in real and cyberspace; they include where I live and where I have lived, where I work and where I have worked, the car I drive, the routines I follow, and the places and people I visit. Biographical data are inevitably and intrinsically "public" because they are the product of my behavior in "public" places, where what I do can be observed by anyone who shares that space with me.[30] We cannot close our eyes and ears to what is around us: "Complete privacy does not exist in this world except in a desert, and anyone who is not a hermit must expect and endure the ordinary incidents of the community life of which he is a part."[31] Consequently, biographical data, defined as information that was or could have been obtained by observing activity in a "public" place,[32] are not private under *Katz* or under cognate tests used to implement civil privacy protections.[33] And because courts have held that biographical data are speech protected by the First Amendment, their dissemination cannot be enjoined absent compelling circumstances.[34]

Technology introduces a complicating factor into this analysis. Assume that a New York City police officer, who works undercover in the department's drug task force, jogs on a track at a Brooklyn high school. His jogging on the track is not private because it occurs in public and can be observed by anyone nearby. Now assume that someone creates a Website and posts photographs of the officer jogging on the track, along with specific information about where the track is located and how often the officer jogs there.[35] Arguably, posting this information on the Website in no way violates the officer's privacy; it merely documents what anyone who was at the track when the officer was jogging could have observed. Intuitively, however, we feel some discomfort with what the Website does; even if it does not identify the jogger as a police officer, it seems to go beyond the type of exposure we all expect to assume in the course of our everyday activities. The Website captures information that can be observed by anyone present when the officer is jogging on the track, preserves the information, and disseminates it so it is available to individuals who were not, and could not have been, present when the officer jogged. Capturing and disseminating the information seem, somehow, to constitute an incremental invasion, one that exceeds the intrusiveness of merely looking at someone who is jogging around a track.[36]

This issue can arise as to tool data, but because they are not considered speech, tool data can be defined as private and their dissemination prohibited without violating the First Amendment.[37] As Section I(B)(3) will explain, the same issue arises in an even more compelling fashion with regard to transactional data, which are also protected by the First Amendment; Section I(C) considers how we can resolve the issue with regard both to transactional and biographical data.[38]

3. Transactional Data

Transactional data are generated by our interactions with others. In analyzing the privacy of transactional data, it is useful to divide them into two types: (1) professional transactional data, which result from interactions with attorneys, physicians, religious advisors, psychiatrists, accountants, and other professionals; and (2) commercial transactional data, which result from interactions with those who provide commercial goods or services offline or online. There are certain constants across these categories: each generates data that establish (1) that I interacted with a particular professional or commercial resource on one or more occasions; (2) the nature of that interaction (seeking legal advice, making a purchase); and (3) the details of that interaction (seeking legal advice about an estate, purchasing vitamins or electronics or clothing). None of these data are private under the *Katz* test or cognate civil standards because by interacting with external entities (human or auto-mated) I have knowingly exposed 1 through 3 to public view; I assumed the risk that those with whom I interact will reveal the details of that interaction to others.[39]

Despite these constants, the law has treated the categories differently. Professional interactions are usually encompassed by privileges that bar the professional from revealing details of the interaction without the client's permission; the purpose is to provide confidentiality when it is "essential to the full and satisfactory maintenance of the relationship between the par-ties."[40] For commercial interactions, the general rule is that "the facts of a transaction belong jointly and severally to the participants. If Alice buys a chattel from Bob, ordinarily both Alice and Bob are free to disclose this fact."[41] As noted earlier, neither type of transactional data is private in the constitutional-common law sense, but the evidentiary and other constraints American law places on the dissemination of data resulting from profes-sional interactions limit it to those involved in the professional consultation; therefore, although professional transactional data are not private, they are secured. And these constraints do not violate the First Amendment.[42]

This leaves commercial transactional data, which are also not private in the constitutional-common law sense but are protected by the First Amend-ment.[43] The latter can certainly impede efforts to restrict the dissemination of commercial transactional data, but it is the underlying issue—whether data one shares with others can be private—that is the focus of this discussion. We could employ the approach we use for professional transactional data, that is, concede that the information is not private but secure it by establishing a "commercial data privilege" that bars individuals and entities from disclos-ing information about their customers. This may be a logical option but it is not a desirable one; such a privilege would remove information that can be used "to start new companies, charities, grassroots political groups, to de-velop new products, to establish new markets, to dramatically lower the costs of distributing products, and to control fraud" from the public domain.[44] It would also be difficult to implement. Unlike professional privileges, which attach to transactions that are not routine and involve a one-to-one relation-ship, a commercial transactional data privilege would attach to an astonishing array of routine transactions, many involving multiple parties. My dealings with grocers, clothing and other stores, automotive repair shops, electricians, gardeners, and a host of other commercial goods and service providers would become privileged; and that, in turn, would require (1) determining whether and to what extent the privilege applied or had been breached in particular circumstances and (2) enforcing the privilege by sanctioning violators. It would all prove quite unworkable.

This brings us back to the question posed earlier: Should data generated by commercial transactions be considered "private?" With perhaps one exception, they should not, for the same reasons biographical data are not considered private; both involve activities I knowingly expose to public view because they are "ordinary incidents of the community life of which" I am a part.[45] It would be empirically absurd for me to claim my visits to the local grocery are private, so that the employees must maintain absolute confidentiality as to my purchases; I necessarily assume the risk that they will observe, discuss, and even exploit my buying habits. These interactions are an unavoidable incident of social life; actually, we enjoy more privacy in this regard than did any of our ancestors. Historically, most people lived in, or conducted their commercial transactions in, very small communities. If I had lived in Bates, Ohio, in the nineteenth century, I would have purchased all my necessities at the (only) general store; the clerk(s) would have known my tastes and my interests intimately and could have shared tidbits about them with others in the community. Shopping today still reveals information to those who staff and frequent the shops I patronize, but I can dilute the amount of information available to them by patronizing many stores, offline and online.

The point is that—perhaps with one exception—information about our commercial transactions is not and cannot be regarded as private, at least not in the traditional sense. The next section argues that the concept of data privacy derives not from the traditional notion of privacy—which goes to my ability to shield myself and my activities from observation by others—but from principles more analogous to those that govern the acquisition and use of property.

The possible exception to the principle that commercial transactional data are not private concerns the process of paying for the goods or services at issue in the transaction.[46] If I pay in cash, that is not private for the reasons given above, that is, I knowingly expose my use of cash to public view; but if I pay by credit card or check, the issue becomes more complex. Unlike cash, credit cards and checks contain what are in effect tool data; that is, unlike cash, which is a neutral instrument that has no utility beyond tendering it for a debt, both credit cards and checks contain information that has negative value, in other words, can be used for unlawful purposes.[47] The question is whether I assume the risk that this information will be disseminated to those who are not parties to the transaction. If I use my credit card to pay for dinner and the waiter skims the numbers,[48] how can I say my privacy has been violated? I knowingly gave him the card and thereby surrendered any expectation that he would not be able to access the data it contains. As the next section explains, the issue, here, too, is one that goes more to property than to privacy.

C. Data Property?

The real problem we confront for the three categories of data discussed in the previous section is not privacy, in the sense of being able to *prevent* others from gaining access to data, it is *control*.[49] The police officer who jogs on the track at a nearby high school knows his activity is not private but he assumes it results in a controlled disclosure of information; that is, he assumes that only those in the immediate area when he jogs are able to observe his activity. The same is true when I give my credit card to the waiter to pay for dinner; I know I have given him access to the information that (1) I have a Visa card, (2) the card numbers are 3333 4444 5555 6666, and (3) the expiration date is 07/2006. But, again, I assume I am making a controlled disclosure of that information; I assume the waiter will use it only to process the credit that will pay my debt. And the same is true if I give the sponsor of a conference at which I spoke my social security number so the institution can reimburse me for my expenses; here, too, I assume I am making a controlled disclosure of the information in which it will be used for the intended purpose and no others. This expectation of controlled disclosure is an unarticulated, perhaps unrealized, but essential component of the commercial transactions and other activities we pursue in our everyday lives; it is a historical artifact, a product of a world in which the clerks at the general store where I might once have shopped could note my purchases and predilections but had no way, aside from provincial gossip, to distribute that information to others.

As we all know, things have changed. Data have become implements we employ for various purposes, including identification, authorization, and payment; I can use cash to pay my debts, but it will be extraordinarily inconvenient for me to use it to buy a new laptop or new car. And I cannot use cash for certain types of transactions; I must use data, in the form of a credit card, and other types of data, such as my social security number, to identify myself. Routine aspects of my life, such as my purchases, become data, and my activities, such as jogging, can be transformed into data. None of these data are private, in the sense of being accessible only by myself; I understand others have access to them, but I expect, somehow, that their access will be limited, that I am making, as noted earlier, controlled disclosures of information about myself.

The problem is that, except for the professional privileges discussed earlier,[50] we have no conceptual basis for structuring disclosures; we have bailments for property but not for information.[51] And this, really, is what is at issue. We are grappling with the commodification of personal data; our activities can be tracked, documented, quantified, and disseminated. Because these activities occur in public, we cannot object to their being observed, just as the jogging officer cannot object to being observed by others at the track. What we object to is the incremental intrusion that results from having others track our activities and use those data for various purposes. Our objection goes more to a loss of control than to a loss of privacy; because the data concern me, I feel I should be able to control how they are compiled and used.[52] That notion of control implicates principles we use to deal with property, especially intangible property;[53] there are proposals to establish intellectual or equivalent property rights in personal property so I can control the use of my personal data and perhaps even receive royalties for their use.[54] The particulars of those solutions are quite outside the ambit and aspirations of this chapter; the issue of personal-data-as-property is relevant here only insofar as it has an impact on the use of the criminal sanction to enforce limitations on the compilation and utilization of personal data.

The concept of property is one of the oldest notions in human culture, and one of the first to be protected by rules that evolved into criminal law.[55] The concept of privacy as an interest to be protected by criminal sanctions is a relatively new notion in American law; and the crimes so far tend to require that the defendant violate an expectation of privacy in the *Katz* sense by, say, videotaping someone in a bathroom.[56] It seems, then, that criminal sanctions which target the unauthorized collection and dissemination of the types of data considered in Section I(B) would more properly be predicated on property analogies, because the conduct at issue does not itself violate an expectation of privacy.[57] This could, as is explained in the next section, provide a basis for implementing such sanctions under the traditional approach to criminal liability.

II. CRIMINAL LIABILITY

There are two justifications for using criminal liability to enforce data privacy.

One is that civil liability is insufficient; this "true crime"[58] rationale is based on the premise that a violation of data privacy inflicts personal "harm" of the type society cannot tolerate. The "public welfare" rationale is based on the premise that data privacy is a systemic interest significant enough to justify defining violations as an affront to the state.

A. "True Crime"

Criminal law is concerned with "mak[ing] people do what society regards as desirable and . . . prevent[ing] them from doing what society considers to be undesirable."[59] It maintains order, which is essential if a society is to carry out the processes necessary for its survival. The traditional model of criminal law targets "true crime," which consists of one individual's inflicting a proscribed type of "harm" upon another. A society's "crimes" each target a specific "harm." The "harms" encompass conduct a society cannot tolerate; every society therefore criminalizes "harms" against persons (murder, rape) and against property (theft, arson) because a society cannot survive if its members are free to prey upon each other and each other's property. Societies also outlaw "harms" against morality (for example, adultery or blasphemy) and against the state (for example, riot or treason) but crimes against persons and property have been the core of criminal law.

The effectiveness of these prohibitions lies in their enforcement, which takes place after a crime has been committed. "True" crime requires that a prohibited type of "harm" has been inflicted upon a victim.[60] Law enforcement reacts to the crime by investigating and apprehending the offender, who is, ideally, prosecuted, convicted, and sanctioned. The operating assumption is that sanctioning this offender works to prevent the commission of future crimes and to maintain order by (1) incapacitating and discouraging him or her from re-offending and (2) using the offender's experience as an example to deter others from engaging in similar conduct.[61]

1. "Harm"

The first step in applying this model to data privacy is identifying the "harm" that warrants the use of criminal sanctions. The use of such sanctions does not have to be the only avenue of recourse against a perpetrator; victims of such traditional crimes as murder and fraud can sue their victimizers.[62] But if we are to authorize the use of criminal sanctions to secure data privacy, we must identify a "harm" of sufficient severity to justify such a measure, one that cannot be adequately addressed by the use of civil liability.[63]

So we need a "harm" that, when inflicted upon individuals, "disturbs the community's sense of security" in some exceptional way. As Section I(C) explained, one option is to use a property analogy and develop a "misuse of personal data" offense. The gravamen of the offense would be that the offender used data falling into any of the categories discussed in Section I(B) in ways that I, the "person" whom it concerns, did not authorize. The rationale would be that personal data are intangible property that "belong" to the person whom they concern in the same way intellectual property "belongs" to its author; the theory is that although personal data are not a commodity over which I can exercise exclusive possession and control, they "belong" to me in the sense that I can dictate with whom they are to be shared and how those persons can utilize them.[64]

A misuse-of-personal-data crime is to some extent analogous to the privilege postulated in the discussion of commercial transactional data.[65] Like the postulated privilege, a misuse-of-personal-data offense would mean that those who obtain commercial transactional data (and biographical data and tool data) are not free to disseminate them or use them except as authorized by the "owner" of the data. The two differ, however, in certain respects. The essence of a privilege is that information will *not* be disclosed; the essence of a misuse-of-personal-data offense would be that personal data will not be disclosed *except as authorized*. I might, for example, authorize the collection and use of my biographical data and my commercial transactional data, restricting the use only of tool data.

Another difference goes to enforcement: if we approach data privacy as a privilege, I will have a privileged relationship with all the individuals and entities with whom I interact on a commercial basis.[66] Professional privileges are enforced by professional bodies that are charged with maintaining clearly identified standards of behavior and have the authority to suspend or bar violators from engaging in their profession.[67] Who could enforce a data privilege that applied to essentially anyone with whom I engaged in a commercial transaction? The enforcement structure we use for professional privileges simply cannot be adapted for this purpose; the virtue of a misuse-of-personal-data offense is that enforcement is consigned to law enforcement agencies, which have the expertise and resources to undertake the task.

2. Elements

The second step in using the approach just outlined to apply the traditional model of criminal law to data privacy is designing a misuse-of-personal-data offense. Traditional offenses have three basic elements: (1) conduct, (2) mental state, and (3) a prohibited result.

The first issue we need to address, then, is the conduct that constitutes a "misuse" of data. This seems relatively simple, because concerns about data being misused focus on two activities: (1) collecting personal data and (2) using them. The "conduct" element of the offense will therefore encompass collecting or using personal data; and we will assume "personal data" includes the categories of data discussed in Section I(B). But we still need to define other terms. What does it mean to "collect" personal data? It does not encompass "observation"; when my neighbor sees me come home, he has not "collected" data establishing that I live at 555 Lamont Terrace, Dayton, Ohio. Collection requires that the data become a commodity, something that can be preserved, manipulated, and distributed; under this definition, photographing the officer jogging on the high school track or noting the officer's jogging there and posting that information on a Website would seem to constitute "collecting" personal data.[68] The waiter's skimming my credit card numbers would clearly constitute "collecting" data, as defined, and the same is true for Websites or real-world establishments that record and compile customer information.[69]

What about "using" data—how should we define that? In criminal statutes, "using" has been defined as "[t]aking or exercising control over property; or . . . [m]aking any . . . disposition, or transfer of property."[70] The waiter who skims my credit card numbers would be "exercising control over property," as defined earlier, and by the same token, commercial establishments' logging and compiling data about my buying habits would be "taking control over property," and their selling the information to other commercial entities would clearly qualify as transferring that property. As to the jogging officer, photographing him might be considered "taking" his property (that is, his likeness), and posting the image on a Website might be considered exercising control over it or disposing of it; one can make a similar argument if all the observer does is to note the officer's name and the track where he jogs and post that information on a Website.[71] The real problem here may be constitutional, not definitional; except for the credit card numbers,[72] the data described above all qualify as speech under current First Amendment interpretations, and their dissemination cannot be prohibited except in accordance with First Amendment principles.[73] If such an objection were raised, we could argue that this is not a speech crime, it is a property crime; because we conceptualize the data as "property," the offense is focused not on restricting the dissemination of speech but on preventing the misuse of property.[74]

The next offense element we need to define is *mens rea*. Because the traditional model of criminal law tends to limit liability to advertent conduct, we will do the same.[75] Under the influence of the Model Penal Code, American criminal law relies on two advertent mental states: purposefully and knowingly.[76] One commits an offense *purposefully* when it is her conscious objective to cause the "harm" constituting the crime; one does so *knowingly* when he is aware it is practically certain his conduct will cause such "harm."[77] When a statute makes it a crime "knowingly" to inflict a proscribed harm, an offender can be convicted even though he or she acted purposefully.[78] Using purposefulness as the required mental state for the misuse-of-personal-data offense would circumscribe its reach because it could only be used to prosecute those whose *goal* it was to engage in the unauthorized collection and use of personal data. When the "harm" an offense addresses is conduct, it is reasonable to use the purposefulness standard because the object is to sanction only those who deliberately engage in that conduct.[79] But when an offense addresses a "harm" consisting of a specific result,[80] there is a strong argument for expanding the requisite culpability level to include knowing, as well as purposeful, conduct; this allows the prosecution of those who are aware that their conduct will almost certainly produce the proscribed result, as well as of those whose goal it is to cause that result. Therefore, because the misuse of personal data is concerned with results, not with conduct, the appropriate level of culpability should be "knowing" misuse.[81]

The final offense element is the result, the "misuse" of personal data as defined earlier. The only issue we need to consider is whether to limit the scope of the offense to instances in which misuse actually occurred (substantive offense) or extend it by including an "attempt to misuse personal data" offense (inchoate offense).[82] Pragmatically, it seems an attempt offense would seldom be used, because it is unlikely law enforcement officers would successfully frustrate the efforts of those bent on misusing other's personal data with any degree of frequency. On the other hand, such an option would allow prosecution when such efforts were interrupted.

B. "Public Welfare" Offenses

"Public welfare" offenses are the product of a very different approach to the imposition of criminal liability. To understand this approach, it is helpful to consider a specific offense, antitrust. Antitrust prosecutions differ from traditional prosecutions in that they are predicated on the infliction of a systemic "harm," whereas traditional criminal proceedings are predicated on the infliction of "harm" to individual victims.[83] In a traditional criminal proceeding, the state acts to vindicate its obligation to protect the individual members of the social system it represents;[84] in a criminal antitrust proceeding, the state acts to vindicate its obligation to ensure the viability of an essential component of a social system.[85] The "harm" at issue is an erosion of the principle of competition; criminal antitrust proceedings target "systemic" crimes—in other words, crimes that have an impact on a nation's infrastructure—instead of "individual" crimes.

1. United States v. Park

"Public welfare" offenses emerged at the beginning of the twentieth century.[86] They were the product of a "shift in emphasis from the protection of individual interests that marked nineteenth-century criminal administration to the protection of public and social interests."[87] They differed from "true crimes" in that (1) the *actus reus* of the offense "was not intrinsically wrong"[88] and (2) they did not require *mens rea*.

The Supreme Court's opinion *United States* v. *Park*[89] illustrates how "public welfare" offenses are used. John Park was CEO of a grocery chain that had "36,000 employees, 874 retail outlets, 12 general warehouses, and four special warehouses."[90] Its headquarters, and Park's office, were in Philadelphia.[91] Park was prosecuted for violating 21 U.S. Code Section 331(k), which makes it a crime to let food that is being held for sale become adulterated.[92] Federal inspectors found that rodents were contaminating food stored in a Baltimore warehouse; such contamination constituted adulteration under Section 331(k).[93] Park argued that although all of Acme's employees were "under his general direction," the responsibility for ensuring sanitary conditions at the warehouse belonged to the Baltimore division vice president, who had told Park he was taking care of the problem.[94] Park was convicted and appealed to the Supreme Court; it upheld his conviction, concluding that his "responsible" position in the company's corporate structure justified holding him liable for not preventing the contamination.[95]

In *Park*, the Supreme Court upheld the imposition of criminal liability in the absence both of culpability (strict liability) and personal participation in unlawful conduct (vicarious liability).[96] The rationale for eliminating these otherwise fundamental requisites of Anglo-American criminal liability is that "public welfare" offenses target systemic "harms" that are important enough to justify placing the risk of preventing a particular "harm" on those who are in a position to do so.[97] The need to do this results from the fact that "public welfare" offenses target conduct that occurs in a business setting in which it can be difficult, if not impossible, to prove personal moral fault on the part of specific employees.[98] To eliminate the potential unfairness inherent in this approach, liability cannot be imposed if someone was "powerless" to prevent the harm.[99]

2. Data Crime

If we decide the interest in controlling the collection and dissemination of one's personal data is a systemic interest sufficient to warrant the creation of a "public welfare" offense, we can use the approach just outlined to protect that interest. This approach offers certain advantages. One is that prosecutions can proceed without the government having to prove that an individual "harm" occurred; it is enough to prove that conditions were in place that *could have resulted* in such a "harm." In *Park*, after all, the government did not have to prove that the contamination of the food in the Baltimore warehouse actually "harmed" anyone; it only needed to prove that the conditions created the proscribed systemic "harm," in other words, a default in the company's duty to ensure the integrity of the food it held for sale. In this regard, "public welfare" offenses are similar to inchoate offenses; that is, they allow the government to intercede, and impose liability, without having to wait until an individual "harm" occurs.[100]

Under the "true crime" approach, prosecutors can do nothing unless and until they are approached by a victim who has suffered an actual, individual "harm" of the type proscribed by the-misuse-of-data offense described in Section II(A). Once they are approached by such a victim, the prosecutors must investigate the case, file charges, assemble evidence, and assume the risk of persuading a jury (typically) beyond a reasonable doubt that the defendant "knowingly" engaged in the unauthorized collection or use of the victim's personal data. The defendant, in turn, can present evidence showing that (1) no such misuse occurred and (2) if it did, it was not due to "knowing" conduct on his or her part. In so doing, the defense, of course, does not have to actually prove anything; all the defense has to do is raise a reasonable doubt in the jury's mind. Consequently, even if the prosecutors believe in their case, they may lose, or they may find it advisable to engage in a plea bargain for a lesser crime, instead of going to trial.

This brings us to another advantage of the "public welfare" approach: "public welfare" offenses put the risk of failing to discharge a statutorily prescribed obligation on the entities and individuals who have chosen to engage in the activity targets by the statute(s) at issue. In "true crime" prosecutions, defendants can challenge the prosecution's claims of unlawful conduct and motives and may gain an acquittal; in "public welfare" prosecutions, they can challenge neither, which means, as the *Park* case demonstrates, they are very likely to be convicted if prosecuted. The only viable defense in a "public welfare" prosecution is for the defendant to prove that he or she simply did not have the power to prevent the conditions that give rise to the charges. Since this will no doubt be impossible to do, it creates incentives to ensure that an organization does not default on the statutorily prescribed obligations to which it is subject.

What might a "public welfare" data offense look like? It would not include *mens rea*, but it would have to identify the individuals and entities to which the offense applied and the types of data it protected. The latter would drive the former, because the offense's restrictions would be imposed only on those who deal with the types of data it encompassed. As to that, one can argue that a "public welfare" data offense should apply only to tool data and transactional data (presumably, only to commercial transactional data) because these are the only types of data that can reasonably be said to constitute a systemic interest sufficient to support the imposition of *Park*-style liability. They, unlike biographical data, are routinely generated by, used in, and sought for use in commercial and other endeavors, and the focus of "public welfare" offenses is on collective, not individual, activity. Biographical data could be protected separately, if that is deemed necessary, by creating a "true crime" offense; this should be sufficient because, as with the hypothetical jogging officer discussed earlier, it is likely that the misuse of biographical data will involve intentional conduct.

A "public welfare" data offense would therefore target the activities of commercial and other entities that generate, collect, use, and disseminate personal data within the constraints set out in the previous paragraph. The gravamen of the offense would be doing any of these things except in accordance with authorization provided by the person to whom particular data pertained. A violation could take either of two nonexclusive forms: it could consist of allowing data actually to be collected, used, and disseminated without authorization, or, adhering more closely to *Park*, a violation could (also) occur when an entity's systems and procedures were found to be inadequate to prevent such an unauthorized collection, use, and disclosure. The first option resuscitates the "true crime" element of actual, individual "harm", but this is not uncommon in "public welfare" offenses; the advantage here is that someone (the victim) is likely to bring the violation to law enforcement's attention. The second option has the advantage of letting law enforcement intervene before an actual, individual "harm" has occurred, but it would require providing law enforcement with investigators who can identify these inchoate violations, just as the *Park* investigators identified the contamination in the Baltimore warehouse.[101] The advantage of combining these options is that dedicated investigators can identify actual "harms" that have gone unnoticed by the victims or that they were unable or unwilling to pursue.[102]

III. CONCLUSION

This chapter has analyzed how two varieties of criminal liability—the "true crime" and "public welfare" offense approaches—*could* be used to secure data privacy, which is not to say that either *should* be used for this purpose. Criminal sanctions have always been and should continue to be extraordinary measures that are invoked only when recurring conduct inflicts a type of "harm" that is egregious enough to warrant the creation of a new offense and cannot be adequately addressed by the use of civil liability.

Having said that, *Park*-style criminal liability seems a promising strategy for protecting data privacy (or data property). A "true crime" approach to this issue suffers from some of the same problems as a civil liability approach. Both are reactive strategies; neither is available unless and until an individual "harm" to data privacy or property has occurred. Both rely on the individual victim to discover that such a "harm" has occurred and to seek redress for it; in civil context, the victim seeks redress by bringing private litigation, whereas in the criminal context he or she reports the matter to the authorities and cooperates in their investigation and in the prosecution of the offender. And both require that the party pursuing redress, whether the plaintiff in a civil suit or the prosecution in a "true crime" proceeding, establish culpable conduct on the part of the violators. The violators, in turn, are free to raise evidentiary and other issues to convince a trier of fact that the "harm," if one occurred, is not their responsibility.

Park-style criminal liability implements a preventative, not a reactive, strategy. If it were applied to data privacy or property, law enforcement investigators could monitor the procedures those who "handle" personal data have in place to secure the data and prevent their unlawful collection or use. Having identified actual or potential violations, the investigators could employ criminal liability to sanction those responsible; an essential component of such sanctions would be remediation, that is, requiring the violator(s) to implement procedures that will prevent further violations. The imposition of such sanctions should encourage other, similarly situated entities to monitor their procedures to ensure they are adequate to prevent such violations.

"Public welfare" offenses emerged a century ago to protect tangible items and activities. Given the increasingly critical role intangible items, including personal data, play in defining the "public welfare" in twenty-first-century America, it seems both reasonable and prudent to use this approach to protect them, as well.

NOTES

1. *See* Samuel Warren & Louis D. Brandeis, The Right to Privacy, 4 *Harv. L. Rev.* 193 (1890).
2. *See, e.g.,* Susan W. Brenner, The Privacy Privilege: Law Enforcement, Technology and the Constitution, 7 *U. Fl. J. Tech. L. & Pol'y* 124, 136-37 (2002).
3. *See, e.g., id.* at 182.
4. *See, e.g., City of Indianapolis v. Edmond,* 531 U.S. 32, 52 (2000).
5. 389 U.S. 347, 351 (1967) (citations omitted).
6. *Id.* at 361.
7. *See* 389 U.S. at 348-49.
8. *See* 442 U.S. at 742-43.
9. *See id.* at 743.
10. *See* 425 U.S. at 440.
11. *See supra* note 5 and accompanying text.
12. *Id.* at 443 (citation omitted).
13. Pub. L. No. 95-630, tit. 11, 92 Stat. 3697 (1978).
14. *See* 12 U.S. Code § 3402(2).
15. Pub. L. No. 99-508, 100 Stat. 1848 (1986). *See* 18 U.S. Code §§ 2702, 2703; S. Rep. No. 541, 1986 WL 31929.
16. William McGeveran, Mrs. Mcintyre's Checkbook: Privacy Costs of Political Contribution Disclosure, 6 *U. Pa. J. Const. L.* 1, 14 (2003). *See, e.g., U.S. Dep't. of Justice v. Reporters Comm. for Freedom of the Press,* 489 U.S. 749, 763 (1989).
17. *See, e.g.,* 489 U.S. at 763.
18. Information is also protected by the Fifth Amendment if it has not been memorialized. *See, e.g., Garner v. United States,* 424 U.S. 648, 650 (1976).

19. *See supra* Section I(A) of this chapter.

20. *See, e.g.*, Restatement (Second) of Torts §§ 158 (trespass) & 652A (invasion of privacy); Model Penal Code §§ 223.2 (theft) & 221.2 (criminal trespass).

21. *See, e.g.*, 489 U.S. at 763.

22. *See, e.g.*, Brenner, The Privacy Privilege, *supra* note 2 at 164-82.

23. The *Katz* test is utilized as the benchmark for "privacy" because it can fairly be said to capture the generalized assumptions about privacy that hold at any given time. *See, e.g.*, Amitai Etzioni, *The Limits of Privacy* 203-207 (1999).

24. We might analogize this process to the "sale" of software. When I buy software, I do not actually "own" it; I purchase a license to use it. *See, e.g.*, Victor F. Calaba, Quibbles 'n Bits: Making a Digital First Sale Doctrine Feasible, 9 *Mich. Telecomm. & Tech. L. Rev.* 1, 9-10 (2002). This transaction is both analogous to and different from the process outlined earlier: it is analogous in the sense that the software manufacturer is at once surrendering control over the product while retaining the right to prevent its being copied. It is different in the sense that the software manufacturer structures the transaction so as to reserve this residual control over the property being transferred; in the outlined scenario, the individual makes no comparable effort with regard to his or her personal information.

25. *See, e.g.*, *Bowen v. Roy*, 476 U.S. 693, 710-11 (1986).

26. *See City of Kirkland v. Sheehan*, 2001 WL 1751590, at *6-*7 (Wash. Super. 2001).

27. *See, e.g.*, Bruce Schneier, *Beyond Fear* 182-95 (2003).

28. *See generally id.* at 184.

29. *See, e.g.*, Matt Sundeen, License to Drive = Proof of Identity, 29 *State Legislatures* (April 1, 2003).

30. *See Remsburg v. Docusearch, Inc.*, 149 N.H. 148, 816 A. 2d 1001 (N.H. 2003).

31. Restatement (Second) of Torts § 652D cmt. c.

32. *See U.S. v. Knotts*, 460 U.S. 276, 282-85 (1983).

33. *See Remsburg v. Docusearch, Inc.*, 149 N.H. at 157, 816 A. 2d at 1009.

34. *See City of Kirkland v. Sheehan*, 2001 WL 1751590 at *6-*7; *Sheehan v. Gregoire*, 272 F. Supp. 1135, 1142 (W.D. Wash. 2003). *See also infra* Section II(A)(2) of this chapter.

35. *See* Jackson Heights Man Accused of Revealing Cop Info Online, *Domains Magazine*, March 18, 2004, available at http://domainsmagazine.com/managearticle.asp?c=1269&a=4974.

36. *See, e.g.*, Susan W. Brenner, Complicit Publication: When Should the Dissemination of Ideas and Data Be Criminalized?, 13 *Alb. L.J. Sci. & Tech.* 273, 381-401 (2003). The same is true as to collecting or aggregating and storing data.

37. *See City of Kirkland v. Sheehan*, 2001 WL 1751590 at *6-*7.

38. *See also infra* Section II(A)(2) of this chapter.

39. *See supra* note 33 and accompanying text. *See also supra* notes 11-12 and accompanying text.

There can be some overlap between transactional data and biographical data. To understand why, it is useful to consider two real-world transactions. In the first, I consult with an attorney whose office is in my neighborhood; in the second, I purchase a prescription from a pharmacist at my local drug store. My traveling to the law office and to the drug store takes place in "public," and so can be considered biographical data. They are also transactional data insofar as they show that I interacted with the lawyer and with the pharmacist. These respective encounters differ somewhat in the extent to which the nature and details of the interactions are biographical. My purchasing a prescription from the pharmacist takes place in "public," and so the nature of the transaction tends toward the biographical; but the details of the purchase will remain confidential unless I choose to share them or unless the pharmacist is indiscreet enough to announce the nature and uses of the medication I buy. Because it is reasonable to infer that I went to a law office to obtain legal advice, the nature of that transaction also tends toward the biographical; but because the transaction itself does not take place in "public," the details do not constitute biographical data.

40. Paul F. Rothstein & Susan W. Crump, *Federal Testimonial Privileges* § 1.1 (2004).

41. A. Michael Froomkin, The Death of Privacy? 52 *Stan. L. Rev.* 1461, 1521-22 (2000).

42. *See American Motors Corp. v. Huffstutler*, 61 Ohio St. 3d 343, 347, 575 N.E. 2d 116, 120 (Ohio 1991). *See also In re Sawyer*, 360 U.S. 622, 646-47 (1959) (Stewart, J., concurring in result).

43. *See, e.g.*, Solveig Singleton, Privacy Versus the First Amendment: A Skeptical Approach, 11 *Fordham Intell. Prop. Media & Ent. L. J.* 97, 134-41 (2000).

44. *Id.* at 137.

45. *See supra* note 40, § I(B)(2).

46. The analysis presented here also applies to professional transactions because payment data are not encompassed by the privileges that protect professional consultations. *See, e.g., Seventh Elect Church in Israel v. Rogers*, 102 Wash. 2d 527, 531 688 P. 2d 506, 509 (Wash. 1984).

47. *See supra* note 40, § I(B)(1).

48. *See, e.g.*, David B. Caruso, Two Men Charged with Using "Skimmer" to Clone Diners' Credit Cards, *SecurityFocus* (June 6, 2003), available at http://www.securityfocus.org/news/5546.

49. *See*, Brenner, Complicit Publication, *supra* note 36, at 398-402. This may seem obvious, because the concept of privacy implicitly encompasses the ability to control (1) who can access information and (2) the purposes for which they can use information to which they have access. The first involves prevention, *i.e.*, foreclosing access, while the second concerns the type of structured disclosure discussed earlier.

Prevention, of course, is a type of control: by securing my bicycle with a chain and lock, I prevent it from being stolen and thereby retain control over it; for tangible property, prevention and control tend to be synonymous because tangible property is a zero-sum commodity, *i.e.*, one person has it and others do not. That is not true of non-zero-sum property: I buy a CD issued by my favorite recording artist and thereby gain limited access to the intangible property it contains. I can listen to the music and copy it for my own use, but I cannot sell or otherwise distribute copies of the CD; the artist has given me access to her property but retained control over how I use it. Our conceptualization of privacy is analogous to our approach to tangible property-we assume something is either private or not-private. We have not defined degrees of privacy because, as was explained earlier, until recently privacy was a state, an absolute, not a commodity. *See, e.g., State v. Valenzuela*, 130 N.H. 175, 187-88, 536 A. 2d 1252, 1261 (N.H. 1987). *See also* Kathryn R. Urbonya, A Fourth Amendment "Search" In the Age of Technology: Postmodern Perspectives, 72 *Miss. L. J.* 447, 498-99 (2002).

50. *See supra* note 41, § I(B)(3).

51. *Cf. Liddle v. Salem School* Dist. No. 600, 249 Ill.App. 3d 768, 769-73, 619 N.E. 2d 530, 531-33 (Ill. App. 1993).

52. *See, e.g.,* Brenner, *Complicit Publication, supra* note 36, at 400-05.

53. *See id.*

54. *See, e.g.,* Vera Bergelson, It's Personal But Is It Mine? Toward Property Rights in Personal Information, 37 *U.C. Davis L. Rev.* 379 (2003); Robert W. Hahn & Anne Layne-Farrar, The Benefits and Costs of Online Privacy Legislation, 54 *Admin. L. Rev.* 85, 102-03 (2002).

55. *See, e.g.,* Code of Hammurabi ¶¶ 6-12, 23-24; Salic Law Tit.II-III, XI-XII.

56. *See, e.g.,* 11 Del. Code. Ann. § 1335(a); Haw. Rev. Stat. Ann. § 711-1111; Or. Rev. Stat. Ann. § 163.700; Wis. Stat. Ann. § 942.08. *See also* Brenner, *Complicit Publication, supra* note 36, at 384 n. 542.

57. *See supra* note 40, §§ I(B)(1)-(3). Property analogies are appropriate for other reasons, as well. Rights are zero-sum commodities: the First Amendment, for example, gives me the right to free speech. The default position is that I can speak and write freely (free speech); I can surrender my right to do so by signing a confidentiality agreement as part of my employment (no free speech). In signing the agreement, I am in a sense bartering my right to free speech for employment and remuneration; but the transaction is more properly characterized as a waiver. I am not transferring my right to free speech to my employer; I am, instead, knowingly and voluntarily giving up that right.

Zero-sum analysis is not suitable for the issues outlined in this text, which go to our ability to control the use of data that results from surrendering our right to privacy by, *e.g.,* jogging in public or engaging in online transactions with commercial or other entities. *See supra* note 40, §§ I(B), I(C). Property analogies are more appropriate for structuring how transferred data can be used by those to whom they are transferred. *See, e.g., supra* note 24. Over the millennia, we have developed a repertoire of constructs and principles that govern property transfers; we can utilize extrapolations from these constructs and principles to structure the permissible uses of transferred data, as well. *See supra notes* 53, 54, and accompanying text. This approach has the added advantage of giving individuals the ability to barter away as much or as little of their personal information as they desire.

58. *See* Francis B. Sayre, Public Welfare Offenses, 33 *Colum. L. Rev.* 55, 84 (1933).

59. Wayne R. LaFave, *Substantive Criminal Law* § 1.5 (2nd ed., 2003). The discussion that follows is drawn from Susan W. Brenner, Toward a Criminal Law for Cyberspace: Distributed Security, 10 *B.U. J. Sci. & Tech. L.* 1 (2004).

60. Modern criminal law also encompasses attempts to inflict "harm." *See, e.g.,* LaFave, *Substantive Criminal Law, supra* note 59, at § 11.2.

61. *See* Brenner, Toward a Criminal Law for Cyberspace, *supra* note 59.

62. *See, e.g., Bernoskie v. Zarinsky,* 344 N.J. Super., 160 781 A. 2d 52, 53-45 (N.J. Super. 2001).

63. There are several reasons why a "harm" cannot be adequately addressed by the use of civil liability. Some are practical: the person who "harms" an individual victim may be judgment-proof. Other "harms"-such as operating a vehicle under the influence of alcohol-target systemic injury and consequently do not encompass individual victimization. Other reasons go to the nature and magnitude of the "harm" inflicted. Civil liability, alone, is considered

inadequate for the "harms" produced by murder and terrorism, both because the likelihood of deterrence is low and because of the symbolic need to denounce the conduct at issue.

64. *See supra* note 40, § I(C).

65. *See id.* § I(B)(3).

66. *See id.*

67. *See, e.g.,* New York State Office of Professional Medical Conduct, http://www.health.state.ny.us/nysdoh/opmc/main.htm.

68. *See* Brenner, Complicit Publication, *supra* note 36, at 398-402.

69. As noted earlier, "collecting" requires the commodification of data. Therefore, if my neighbor sees me come home, he has observed my activity but has not "collected" data. But if he notes the times I leave for and return from work, this would constitute "collecting" data, at a minimal level, because the information has taken tangible form and can be manipulated and transferred.

70. Fla. Stat. Ann. § 825.101 (10).

71. *See* Brenner, Complicit Publication, *supra* note 36, at 396-400.

72. *See supra* note 40, §§ I(B)(1) & I(B)(3).

73. *See* Brenner, Complicit Publication, *supra* note 36, at 381-401.

74. *See, e.g., id. See also* Julie E. Cohen, Examined Lives: Informational Privacy and the Subject as Object, 52 *Stan. L. Rev.* 1373, 1417 (2000).

75. Liability for inadvertent violations is discussed in Section II(B) of this chapter, *infra.*

76. *See* Model Penal Code § 2.02(2) (Tentative Draft No. 13, 1961).

77. *See id.*

78. *See id.* § 2.02(5).

79. *See, e.g.,* Ark. Code Ann. § 12-63-209(a) (trespass on military reservation).

80. *See, e.g.,* LaFave, *Substantive Criminal Law, supra* note 59 at § 1.4(b): (arson as a result crime).

81. *See, e.g.,* 42 U.S.C. § 1320d-6(a).

82. *See, e.g.,* LaFave, *Substantive Criminal Law, supra* note 59 at § 11.2 (attempts).

83. *See supra* note 40, § II(A).

84. *See* American Bar Association Standards for Criminal Justice 3-2.1, cmt .

85. *See, e.g.,* U.S. Dept. of Justice, *United States Attorneys' Manual,* § 7-1.100 (1997), available at http://www.usdoj.gov/usao/eousa/foia_reading_room/usam/title7/1mant.htm.

86. *See* Francis B. Sayre, Public Welfare Offenses, *supra* note 58, at 67-68.

87. M. Diane Barber, Fair Warning: The Deterioration of Scienter under Environmental Criminal Statutes, 26 *Loy. L.A. L. Rev.* 105, 110 (1992).

88. *Id.* at 111 (notes omitted).

89. 421 U.S. 658 (1975).

90. *Id.* at 660.

91. *Id.*

92. *See id.*

93. *See id.*

94. *See id.*

95. *See id.* at 668-70.

96. *See, e.g.*, LaFave, *Substantive Criminal Law, supra* note 59, § 13.4(c).

97. *See generally id.*

98. *See id. See also id.* § 5.5(c).

99. *See* 421 U.S. at 673.

100. *See id.*

101. In the given scenario, the violation is choate in the sense that the proscribed activity-*i.e.*, not having procedures in place to prevent the unauthorized collection, use, and disclosure of data-has occurred. This violation, like all "public welfare" offenses, is inchoate in the sense that it targets an unrealized "harm"; that is, the offense encompasses creating conditions from which an actual "harm" can result. *See supra* note 100 and accompanying text.

102. *See, e.g.*, David A. Dana, Rethinking the Puzzle of Escalating Penalties for Repeat Offenders, 110 *Yale L. J.* 733, 743-44 (2001).

14 THE UNEASY CASE FOR NATIONAL ID CARDS

A. Michael Froomkin

A. Michael Froomkin is a professor at the University of Miami School of Law in Coral Gables, Florida, specializing in Internet law and administrative law. He is a founder-editor of ICANNWatch, and serves on the editorial boards of Information, Communication & Society *and* I/S: A Journal of Law and Policy for the Information Society. *He is on the advisory boards of several organizations, including the Electronic Freedom Foundation and BNA Electronic Information Policy & Law Report. Froomkin is a member of the Royal Institute of International Affairs in London. He is also active in several technology-related projects in the greater Miami area.*

I. NATIONAL ID CARDS: THE COMING DEBATE

Proposals abound for the introduction of a national identification system, a computer-based record system in which a unique identifier (a national ID) would be associated with every U.S. citizen and permanent resident.[1] Opponents of national ID cards or national identification numbering systems[2] see them as threats to privacy and liberty. Whatever one's opinion of the merits, it is undeniable that a substantial and powerful community advocates national ID cards.[3] Here in the United States, we will have a national debate on ID cards, if we are lucky; if we're unlucky, we'll dispense with the debate and go straight to the cards and the databases.

The U.S. Supreme Court's decision in *Hiibel* v. *Sixth Judicial District Court of Nevada, Humboldt County*[4] hints, but does not hold, that a requirement that people carrying ID cards show them to police might be constitutional. Although holding that a state may impose a duty on citizens to identify themselves orally to police officers during a *Terry* stop[5] (at least in the absence of "any articulated real and appreciable fear that his name would be used to incriminate him, or that it 'would furnish a link in the chain of evidence needed to prosecute' him"[6]), the Court noted that "the statute does not require a suspect to give the officer a driver's license or any other document."[7] Furthermore, whether Congress could constitutionally require that all citizens obtain or carry ID remains an open question.

Despite its limited legal reach, *Hiibel* could forever change the fundamental psychological relationship between the citizen and the state's front-line symbol of authority, the police officer. More important, the *Hiibel* decision increases the chance that the United States will adopt a mandatory national ID card regime in the near future. In time, an identification requirement might even affect the political process, as it might have a chilling effect on some forms of political action.

Yet viewed from another perspective, *Hiibel* may not be that significant. No result in *Hiibel* would have slowed the growth of our de facto national ID regime, which is maturing into a virtual ID card. A hybrid of formally public and formally private systems of identification, data-retention, and correlation, this developing virtual national ID card regime needs no federal legislation to become a reality. It is time, therefore, to reexamine the benefits and consequences of ID cards.

The ID card question immediately invokes larger issues: the utility of ID cards and also their dangers depend directly on the extent to which the cards link the data subject to databases and sensors. Similarly, the benefits—and especially the dangers—of ID cards are acutely sensitive to the technical architecture of any ID card system and to the design of legal rules that will constrain misuses. This chapter is primarily concerned with national identification systems in which a unique identifier is associated with every U.S. citizen and permanent resident. That unique identifier may reside in a database and be linked to the individual holder by means of a token such as a national ID card. The token may have just the ID number, or it may carry other information. In principle, a national ID system can function without a token, for example, using biometric linking. And, whether or not there is a physical token, the master database may contain authenticating and additional information about the holder, raising questions about transparency and access.

A national ID card that uses reliable data[8] and is sufficiently tamper-proof and secure[9] to reliably identify and authenticate the holder would be valuable in public and private transactions. People who control resources—admittance to a building or permission to play online music—want or need to know who you really are in order to allow the interaction or transaction, and they want or need to keep a record of it.

Many people—including me—have an initial negative reaction to government-sponsored national ID systems. Yet the *marginal* harms that could be caused by a well-designed national ID system are fewer than one might initially believe given the ways in which invasive technology are reducing personal privacy. Nevertheless, ID cards present genuine dangers to civil liberty and to privacy that we should be wary of. Whether or not one supports the basic idea, it may be profitable to consider what rules might be crafted to minimize harms and maximize benefits.

A fair evaluation of the likely privacy costs of a national ID regime requires a proper understanding of the privacy baseline. The growth of distributed databases and the ease with which they can be linked means that this baseline is already low. As a result, the marginal cost to privacy of national ID cards is much less than it would be if we were starting from a high-privacy regime. If the privacy baseline is as poor as I suggest, then there is a (perhaps unlikely) scenario in which national ID cards could be used to enhance privacy. Somewhat counterintuitively, most persons' privacy rights against the government could be greater if ID cards are legally required than if they are formally optional because due process and other constitutional rights are difficult to assert when enmeshed in formally "voluntary" systems. Ensuring that the data subject retains a property interest in government-held data about him or her will further enhance personal privacy and other protections against misuse. Similarly, a government-mandated scheme in which the government retained ownership of the ID number would allow the government to condition use of that number on businesses' adoption of privacy principles. The carrot of easy, secure, and reliable identification might suffice to create market-based incentives to get businesses to accept the stick of adherence to substantive privacy conditions.

A mandatory national ID card regime could also form the basis for a political strategy aimed at creating at least a national dialog on privacy issues. Putting a piece of plastic in everyone's pocket would be a stark reminder that privacy is in play. Centralizing the debate at a national level would not necessarily result in the adoption of the best privacy principles, as it would also provide a single target for those lobbying for anti-privacy and data sharing, but it might.

II. BENEFITS OF NATIONAL ID:
LINKING PERSONS TO FACTS (AND FACTS TO PERSONS)

The value of real and virtual national ID cards depends on many technical and organizational factors. Chief among these factors are the quality of the data used to establish identity; the security of the system (as regards both forgery of the card and authenticity of the data, wherever they reside); and the information it stores or is linked to. An ID card system, if linked to extensive databases with biometric information and near-real-time activity monitoring, can form the anchor of a wide-ranging system of surveillance, authorization, and, optionally, control.

Although touted as a means of preventing or deterring terrorism, the real benefits of a national ID system probably lie elsewhere. The security benefit from an ID card regime depends first on the quality of the data input into the system, and secondarily on how secure and difficult to forge the cards are. The first problem alone is enormous, as current U.S. identification data are notoriously poor.[10] Similarly, unless there are very substantial improvements in data quality, an ID card regime will provide little additional security against competent foreign terrorists. The greatest near-term benefits of a national ID card regime are likely to be in more routine law enforcement, benefit and tax administration, streamlining of some paperwork such as proof of authorization to work, and the enhanced ability it will give firms that use the ID number as an index to organize their data about their customers.

In the most general terms, any identification document or system links persons to facts, and facts to persons. The facts that an ID, whether real or virtual, links to persons fall into four broad and overlapping categories: permanent personal attributes, data about past activities, data about the person's present, and authorizations, which are a type of future-oriented information. ID cards arguably provide benefits in managing and using data in each category.

Permanent personal attributes are things a person is born with and is unable to change. A national ID card can store or link to information about the data subject's body. The biometric information can also serve as the identifying or authenticating information that links the person to the card. As technologies for distinguishing body parts improve, it seems increasingly attractive to use the body as password.[11]

Biometric identifiers enhance privacy when they prevent information from being stolen or improperly disclosed. Even so, biometrics have disadvantages as a personal identifier and are an imperfect basis for authenticating a person's access to data. First, a biometric provides a unique identifier that can serve as a high-quality index for all information available about an individual. The more reliable the biometric identifier, the more it is likely to be used, and the greater the amount of data likely to be linked to it.[12] But because a biometric is a part of the person, that index is hard to change if needed. Second, some biometrics, particularly those that involve DNA typing, could disclose extraneous information about the data subject, such as race, sex, ethnicity, and propensity for certain diseases.[13]

Past attributes are facts about a person's life activities such as medical data, employment and criminal history, and legal or economic facts such as insurance claims, civil litigation, bankruptcies, and transaction history. These types of facts differ from permanent attributes in that they are not congenital, and ordinarily not biometric either.[14] Allowing others access to these facts can be beneficial; for example, emergency medical personnel can access life-saving information. Centralizing employment and criminal records would facilitate common background checks, improving their quality but at the cost of creating a single point of failure that might make someone unemployable.

Present facts are a hybrid category made up of persistent facts and transitory facts. Persistent facts are past facts that remain true today. Transitory facts are things that can be detected in real time such as a person's current location, the goods the person is bringing to the checkout counter, or the speed at which he or she is driving.

Unlike past facts, present facts can be changed. For example, home ownership is a present fact, subject to change if the home is sold. In contrast, last year's purchase of that real property or of a chattel is a fact that cannot be changed.[15] Present facts about a person include citizenship, current employment, marital status, religion, residence, salary, and visas.

Accurate information about persistent and transitory present facts is of obvious interest to the government and to many private parties. The extent to which present facts can be linked in real time (or near real time) to a national ID depends on the efficacy and deployment of sensors and other data-capture devices. In the case of point-of-sale information, the presentation of an ID card may facilitate linking the transaction data to the holder's file. Linking CCTV and other camera data to a person would require more sophisticated facial recognition techniques than currently exist or some other means to identify people at a distance.

Location information is especially valuable to law enforcement: current location information allows police to locate a suspect, and stored location information makes new enforcement techniques possible. At its most benign, full location information would make it relatively easy to investigate street crime. If the mugging happened at 10:05 p.m. at the intersection of Elm and Main streets, and stored location data allow the police to identify everyone who was within a block of there during a ten-minute period, producing a list of suspects may be as simple as requesting a printout and calling up current location. The availability of other biographical information (such as age or employment) may also allow the police to prioritize their investigation.

Authorizations are a special type of future-oriented information, as they permit but do not require, some type of activity. Identity confirmations are a common means of determining whether a person is authorized to do something. For example, a debit card's PIN number provides a limited assurance that the person holding the card is entitled to it. The card's most important function, however, is to authorize two parts of the transaction: payment and exchange of goods when the merchant queries the bank to ensure that there are sufficient funds in the account to pay for the purchase.

Authorizations, even more than identification, are likely to be a prime function of a robust national ID card scheme. ID cards can authenticate registered voters and prevent double voting. They can identify a jury pool. Alcohol, cigarettes, and other restricted goods and services can only be sold to persons over a given age; a card can verify precise age, or just the binary over or under twenty-one. A card can confirm eligibility for government benefits. Standardizing identification with a single national ID card that is difficult to forge would also make it easier to identify benefit fraud.[16]

Eligibility for employment is an example of an authorization that could usefully be keyed to a national ID card. Federal law currently requires that employers verify the identity and right to work of all new employees.[17] Critics of this rule argue that the employer sanctions for hiring undocumented aliens create an incentive for employers to discriminate against legal Hispanic workers and others whom employers fear are not citizens.[18] A national system of employee identification would put all legal workers on an even footing, thus reducing potential discrimination; would reduce any paperwork burden that might be worrying employers; and would also make it easier to ensure that employees receive the social security and other benefits to which they are entitled. Reliable and easy verification of eligibility to work would make life more difficult for illegal aliens, reducing the attractiveness of illegal immigration—

an outcome that must be treated as a social benefit so long as the U.S. retains its immigration laws.

Not all uses of a national ID card are necessarily desirable. A strong and ubiquitous system of personal identification would ease the deployment of new technologies designed to maximize revenue for intellectual property at the expense of file sharing and fair use. In particular, intellectual rights holders seek, via digital rights management (DRM) technologies,[19] to enforce licenses that allow copyrighted (or even public domain) content they provide to be viewed only by paying customers. "Trusted computing"[20] initiatives will prevent computers and other devices from making copies, or even displaying information, without permissions set by the rights holders, trumping the wishes of the operator or owner of the hardware. If ID cards are unique, secure, and too necessary to daily life to share with others, then the "trusted" computer or other device can refuse to display the information unless the card is present, greatly reducing the current risk that authorizations such as passcodes will be shared between users.

Using a single national identification system to establish the right to do something (such as work) also creates leverage over most people's economic affairs that could be used to achieve social goals that may not always be directly relevant to the activity itself.[21] The "deadbeat dad" statute requires the federal government to maintain a database with the social security numbers, addresses, and wages of every new hire in the nation so that persons owing child support can more easily be located.[22] In theory, any social policy could be enforced in a similar manner, an outcome with potentially Orwellian overtones.[23]

III. DANGERS TO LIBERTY ARISING FROM A NATIONAL ID SYSTEM

Along with their economic and other benefits, ID cards pose many risks to liberty: (1) risks from the legal use of accurate information; (2) risk of reliance on false information; (3) risk of intentional creation of false information; (4) risks from illegal use of accurate information; (5) risk of overdependance on some feature of the system (completeness of database, ubiquity of card or other token).[24] Most of these classes of risk pose somewhat different dangers in the public and private sectors; in this chapter, I will concentrate on the public-sector risks, but the private-sector risks, which include price discrimination, illegal discrimination, and the enhanced enforcement of fair-use-destroying digital rights management systems, are also substantial.

A. Risks from the Legal Use of Accurate Information

It may seem counterintuitive, but a national ID system poses substantial risks to personal freedom even if the information it contains is accurate and the uses made of it are legal. Part of this seeming paradox comes from the fairly weak privacy protections found in U.S. law, and the weaker protections in the U.S. Constitution.

The least quantifiable, but undoubtedly significant, danger of a national ID system is the moral or psychological cost, especially if the system uses national ID cards. Many people find value in being able to move through life without an obligation to identify themselves, just as there is a value in the right not to be stopped or searched without cause. Correlatively, there may be at least as great a value in having a system of law enforcement in which the enforcers understand that people have that freedom. An ID embedded in a token, such as a card, that might have to be displayed on demand, undermines whatever value we place in being free(ish) from the demand to show our papers at the street corner, a freedom already badly eroded in airports, other places of mass transit, courthouses, and other public buildings.[25]

Although the question is not entirely free from doubt, the Constitution almost certainly imposes at best limited controls on the government's ability to do data mining and conduct law-enforcement-related virtual "general searches" on data under its control. Although some uses of a database are unproblematic, even desirable,[26] many are not.[27] And the more varied and detailed the information in the database, the greater the risks of profiling, of false positives, of efficient stigmatization, and of function creep. Currently, the Privacy Act prevents some of these dangers at the federal level, but it is impossible to imagine that the nation would go to the trouble and expense of setting up a national ID system if it were not going to use it. Even without a formal national ID, the increasing amount of data held by the government, or available to it from the private sector, will make data searching seem more and more attractive.

The Privacy Act states that non-law-enforcement agencies generally may not collect information about First Amendment activities,[28] but it imposes few other limits. Data must be limited to "such information about an individual as is relevant and necessary to accomplish a purpose of the agency required to be accomplished by statute or by executive order of the President"[29] and the agency must not release information before making a reasonable effort to assure itself "that such records are accurate, complete, timely, and relevant for agency purposes."[30] Given the natural bureaucratic desire to amass information "just in case," a tendency that can only have been strengthened by the terrorist attacks of 9/11, these do not seem like very broad protections.

Even with the Privacy Act in place, government law enforcement agencies and intelligence agencies are allowed to amass dossiers that they can mine to create profiles. Indeed, it's alleged that "a federal agency involved in espionage actually did a rating of almost every citizen in this country . . . based on all sorts of information."[31] And here the issue becomes almost metaphysical. One could say that the act of "searching" through a database of personal information, much of it furnished voluntarily either in private commercial transactions or in formally voluntary transactions with a government agency (for example, a driver's license application[32]), is nothing like a search. The data have been alienated before the search, they are no longer the subject's, and their new owner, the government, can do with it as it sees fit. Unless there is some constitutional principle to the contrary, whether there is a reasonable expectation of privacy depends on the legal rights one has over the data, and the law defines what our reasonable expectations are. Thus, unless the subject has a property right in the data that the government holds about him or her, or unless some special form of privacy legislation creates a due-process-like right to protect the data, or unless some privacy or due process right preventing such searches exists in the Constitution, the government may "search" data it owns about us for law-enforcement purposes.[33]

At present, virtual profiling is somewhat constrained by the Privacy Act of 1974,[34] which imposes some limits on the ability of the federal government—especially the parts not involved in law enforcement—to run database searches and conduct profiling in the absence of a particularized suspicion of an individual. Statutes change; enduring and reliable protection, if it exists, must lie in the Constitution.

The Fourth Amendment protects against unreasonable "searches" without a warrant. Courts grant search warrants only on a showing of particularized suspicion. A trawl of a database to find potential suspects by definition does not involve a particularized suspicion of anyone, and it is highly unlikely that a request for such a search would meet the standard needed to get a court to issue a warrant. Indeed, a database search more closely resembles a "general search," one of the evils that the Fourth Amendment was designed to prevent.[35]

On the other hand, because the subjects of the virtual search are unaware of any intrusion, some of the values the Fourth Amendment protects—the sanctity of the person, the home, and of one's property—suffer less intrusion than with a physical search. Indeed, it has been argued that courts might treat many searches over a database as being the sort of reasonable search that does not require a warrant.[36] And, as noted, if the government owns or leases the data, courts for constitutional purposes might not treat a database trawl as a "search" at all, because there is no intrusion onto the property of the subject.

A national ID database (or any national ID card) without Fourth Amendment and property-like due process protections for its data risks many undesirable outcomes. Vesting title over the data in the subject would prevent many of them. Alternatively, legislation could leave title in the government but give an easement-like right over the use of the data. Any later attempt to remove this propertized protection would constitute a "takings," entitling every subject in the database to financial compensation—providing a strong disincentive to any Congress contemplating changing the database's status.

Property rights alone, however, do not suffice, especially if they do not attach to law enforcement's investigatory files. Currently, there is no official mechanism by which unproved denunciations to the local police, or to the FBI, become part of a file that is communicated widely among government officials. A national ID system and its associated databases—fueled perhaps by something such as Attorney General John Ashcroft's Terrorist Information and Prevention System (TIPS) proposal[37]—would create a mechanism by which unverified derogatory information could circulate widely, at least among government agencies. It might be objected that because the denunciation is unproved, and stands a good chance of being false, it belongs in the category of "uses of false information." But it is the fact *of the denunciation* that is recorded and searchable, and (absent police fabrication) it is true that there was such a communication from the public.

In addition to the obvious possible harms of having law enforcement use these tips as the "reasonable" basis for traffic stops and searches, there is the more fundamental harm to the body politic of developing an informer and dossier culture.[38] Because law enforcement, not to mention intelligence, agencies will resist any rules that require giving persons (suspects) access to data collected about them, or even notice that such an investigation has taken place, any privacy rules will be difficult to enforce. Some nations have created privacy commissioners or privacy ombudspersons charged with monitoring government data collection, retention, and sharing. Though worth trying—it can't hurt—it is not altogether clear how successful these officials have been.[39]

A large and rich database invites predictive profiling,[40] in which data mining is used in an attempt to predict who is likely to be dangerous. Inevitably, predictive profiling creates false positives, and stigmatizing.[41] Indeed, even without profiling, a rich database of accurate conviction information that is made available to the public invites a regime of stigmatization. Already some conviction information is sent to neighbors of released felons whether those neighbors ask for it or not.[42] This may only be the tip of the iceberg; a publicly available database might, for example, contain current addresses and all conviction histories, creating a class of "social leper."[43] Whether the loss of "social forgiveness, the principle that over time a citizen's crimes are forgiven," is a good thing or not may be debatable.[44] But any change of that magnitude should be debated, rather than be a side-effect of technology.

B. Risks from Reliance on (or Creation of) False Information

A fundamental problem with any national ID system is its vulnerability to GIGO, the old computer adage of "Garbage In, Garbage Out." We do not today have in the United States a particularly reliable system of formal identification. Major pieces of ID such as passports, social security numbers, driver's licenses, and credit cards frequently trace back to birth certificates. But the highly decentralized network of birth certificate issuers—hospitals—is notorious for its porousness and unreliability.[45]

A new centralized system would not only build on old risks of reliance on false information but introduce new ones: if IDs are linked to a centralized database relied on by government agencies this creates a particularly powerful place for someone to plant false information. Planted evidence is nothing new, and the possibility that a new system could be abused in the same manner as old ones is not necessarily a reason to fear a new system. Nevertheless, unless the system is engineered very carefully, the danger of virtual planted evidence is very serious. Today, planting evidence requires physical presence, and contact with the crime scene or with the evidence removed from it. Tomorrow, changing the contents of a record to incriminate someone may be as easy, or as hard, as accessing a file. No system is perfect, but the extent of a national ID system's vulnerability to this sort of "inside job" illicit modification will depend in large part on the extent to which the system is designed with this danger in mind. A separate, and perhaps greater, risk is that if the government and the public rely on the system, there is one centralized target for anyone trying to get a false ID—and if they succeed, the ID is too likely to be trusted.

Proper design of information systems can reduce risk of intentional inaccuracy, although no system is foolproof. If the information resides in a central location, then the danger of intentional and accidental inaccuracies can be reduced by *transparency*—ensuring that the data subjects have access to records about themselves. The more dispersed the records are, the less meaningful this protection becomes. ID card systems centralize; thus they make meaningful transparency that much easier.

Centralization of data in a single national system means that large numbers of people will be able to access those data for a wide variety of purposes. The more accesses there are, the greater the chance that inaccurate information will damage the data subject. However, the same centralization that creates this danger also may make it easier to correct inaccuracies in a manner calculated to reach people who previously were exposed to the erroneous datum. A big database is a big target. One would expect the incidence of identity theft to increase—but also that once detected, it should be easier to stop the thief from continuing to profit from it, and the victim from continuing to be charged with the thief's bad acts. Unfortunately, however, if the ID system relies on a biometric and the thief found a way to counterfeit it, the subject may have a problem. Even if it is easy to change ID numbers, it is hard to change corneas.

C. Risk of Illegal Use of Accurate Information

A national ID system also creates new opportunities for the illegal use of accurate information. Here, the problem is primarily one of increased opportunity, rather than of new classes of dangers.

Public-sector dangers from the illegal use of accurate information include the familiar problems of both organized and unauthorized snooping into public records. The prospect of a J. Edgar Hoover with a computer and a national ID database is not an attractive one—but neither is the prospect of J. Edgar Hoover's successors forced to operate without those tools. Similarly, unless audit tools are carefully built into the system and used properly, the existence of a database makes it likely that employees will sometimes misuse it for private purposes; although similar dangers exist currently, any increase in the quantity and scope of the data available will only make the database a more attractive place to snoop.

One argument often made against a national ID system is that were there ever to be a totalitarian government,[46] the database would make roundups of disfavored classes easier.[47] Certainly recent efforts to find and interview immigrants and student-visa holders from the Middle East in the wake of 9/11—combined with the Bush administration's arguments that the government has the legal right to detain U.S. citizens without trial or counsel for indefinite periods upon a government official's unsupported declaration that the citizen is an "enemy combatant"[48]—give this concern a new saliency. It can be argued that a national ID database would make a difference because data about people, such as their addresses, would be updated continuously, rather than once every ten years with the census. Census data on residence date quickly, given that 16 percent of the U.S. population moves to a new residence every year.[49] Personally, I find this argument unpersuasive given the existence of massive private databases. A government prepared to build internment camps is prepared to buy, or take, the privately held data it believes it needs.

D. Risk of Over-Dependence

One of the greatest risks of a national ID system, with or without cards, is success. One of the most obvious dangers is that dossier inspection might become a routine part of major transactions such as employment and credit.[50] General reliance on a national ID card or on a centralized dossier creates at least three sorts of risks. Unless the system is more secure than is likely with current technology it may, by creating an unjustified sense of security, make users more vulnerable to identity theft. Identity theft or impersonation will be especially problematic if there is a biometric component to the authentication mechanism because we may lack a means to generate a replacement ID once the theft of the original is discovered. Routinized credentialing also destroys the ability of people to move and transact anonymously, undermining an important privacy right with implications for political and civil liberty.[51]

But perhaps the greatest danger if a national ID system really takes off is that people will become dependent on it for ordinary life, creating an attractive chokepoint for all sorts of regulation. If an enhanced national ID card[52] becomes ubiquitous, and is routinely presented for purchases, proof of age, transport, payment of tolls, and perhaps to cut off stop-and-frisk-upon-reasonable-suspicion *Terry* stops,[53] then anything that makes the ID harder to use becomes a powerful sanction. If the card or the data are government property, then many of the constitutional protections one might expect could be missing. If no taking of private property is involved, the only possible grounds for a due-process-based objection to government interference with one's use and enjoyment of the ID is an objection based on a liberty interest. Although such arguments sometimes swayed the courts in the context of passport denials, it was easy to show that without a passport, foreign travel was next to impossible. It is doubtful whether such a showing would be as easy in cases about a national ID card (or number), especially in its early days when the precedents are being set.

Even if there are difficulties in actively sanctioning people for information in their dossiers, there will be considerably fewer barriers to making a "clean" record a precondition for some permits or benefits. Lest this seem far-fetched, consider that "[f]ifteen states now link driver's licenses with school attendance and performance."[54] A significant feature of a national ID system is that it creates a whole new avenue of leverage that can be applied by government to encourage and discourage behaviors. How one feels about this may depend on the goals it serves, or on one's more general beliefs about the propriety of social engineering.

IV. BETTERING THE PRIVACY BASELINE:
THE (VERY?) UNEASY CASE FOR MANDATORY
FEDERAL NATIONAL ID CARDS

To understand how a national ID system could be designed to achieve limited privacy gains, it is important first to understand the current privacy landscape. Indeed, the argument in this chapter relies on one key factual assertion: the enormous growth of the ability to link distributed databases means that we already have, or will soon have, a "virtual" national identification system, in effect "virtual ID cards." Today, the virtual system is sufficiently pervasive that it includes background data on almost every legal resident, and a very large quantity of transaction data. In the near future, this virtual system will expand to include substantial quantities of medical information, and positional and movement information.[55]

A. The Virtual National ID System

The collection and use of personal data is the key privacy issue[56]; the ID card is only the surface phenomenon. Indeed, the primary importance of a *physical* national ID card is its symbolic effect and its political consequences. As we have seen, the dangers of a national ID *system* are serious. Unfortunately, most of these dangers are equally real whether or not the national ID system includes a physical *card*. Any national database system, combined with any method of authentication, be it a card or other token, a biometric, or even a challenge-response, has most of the same dangers with only a small difference in degree. The only substantial exception to this rule may be the psychological effects. If it is the case that introducing an identity document that would have to be produced on demand would really work a psychological change on citizens or law enforcement, then a system that relied only on virtual IDs might escape this danger—although why a system that relied on, say, facial recognition scans would be less pernicious is a little difficult to imagine. Psychology, however, works two ways, and the very visibility of a system that relied on a physical card might also have a salutary effect on the average consumer-citizen's privacy awareness.

Whether or not actual national ID cards are introduced, the United States has, or will very soon have, a privatized, de facto, national ID system capable of providing relatively detailed information about almost every resident. At present neither data collection, collation, nor disclosure in the private sector are subject to anything more than limited, patchwork regulation.[57] Government data practices are regulated by the Privacy Act, but these limits do not apply to law enforcement,[58] and as a practical matter, the government can always purchase access to private databases, meaning that information gathered in the private sector is available to the government. The reverse is sometimes true also, as governments sometimes seek to use their databases as a source of revenue,[59] subject to a possible backlash from the public.[60]

Four synergistic sets of changes are creating a virtual national ID system. First, a number of legislative initiatives have required the creation of (ostensibly) special-purpose databases, each of which covers a substantial fraction of the population. Second, increased use of credit and debit cards, store loyalty cards, Web-based marketing, and other private initiatives have collectively allowed retailers and financial intermediaries to amass great amounts of data on consumers. Third, both private and government actors have taken advantage of decreasing costs in camera and other sensor technology to install an expanding base of monitoring equipment on both public and private property. Fourth, advances in computer storage and networking technology have made it vastly cheaper to store, search, and share the gigabytes of data resulting from these developments. The result is a hybrid public-private system in which a very great amount of information about almost every U.S. resident is available for a small fee. Much of this information is currently distributed on separate networks, but the technology to tie them together exists.[61]

It should be possible to design a national ID system that would enhance privacy rights above those enjoyed in the "virtual" national ID system— although these rights would not necessarily be superior to the "no ID at all" world we have lost. The first part of the strategy is to take half a leaf from the legal treatment of passports and have the government own the national ID numbers themselves. Due process rights regarding an individual's use of his or her own number would need to be substantially better than the very limited rights to a passport, and they would be because the ID number would be used in ways that strike closer to core constitutional rights than the right to have government documentation to facilitate travel abroad. The architectural safeguards needed to blunt the dangers of a national ID card system include security, transparency, individual control over personal information, support for multiple IDs (and perhaps even anonymity), and good error handling. Some of these are difficult to engineer. Others have faced, and likely will continue to face, political opposition that makes any broad legislation mandating good practices in the private sector unlikely. Even good design safeguards, however, do only a little to protect against a political decision to misuse the system. Design can reduce the risk of harmful unlawful uses; it is far less potent against a decision to make bad uses lawful.

The government would condition the use of the new national index number by both the public and private sectors on adherence to national data protection and privacy rules. Additional protection against government abuses could be achieved by giving the individual a property right in at least some of the data held in government files. The ownership and dissemination of private sector data would remain a matter of contract, but constrained by the third party's duty to adhere to government-defined data protection rules when using the federally owned ID number to index data, or even when using any data that had been so indexed.[62]

The privacy rules restricting the use of indexed information would be set nationally. Although this creates a focal point for regulation, it also inevitably creates a single point of policy failure, and a large target waiting for capture by industries that will want the minimum restrictions on their ability to process and share personal information. This is undoubtedly a risk, but it is one that should be weighed against the virtual ID card world currently being built, one in which the locations at which privacy-destroying decisions occur are scattered and often invisible. Centralizing the debate at least raises the visibility and salience of the issues. It makes it easier for public-interest coalitions to form, and reduces the cost of organization for already stretched pro-privacy organizations.

Another major goal of the centralized rules should be transparency—ensuring that the data subject knows what is being recorded about him or her, who has permission to access the data and for what purposes, and (at least for non-law-enforcement access) who actually accesses the data. Transparency as to the data content is essential if persons are to be able to contest and correct errors. Transparency as to access is essential if persons are to be able to monitor against abusive profiling, data-based discrimination, and unsanctioned snooping.

A national ID system threatens anonymous and pseudonymous speech and commerce. The threat to anonymous speech affects a valuable constitutional right—one needed most by persons least able to speak out for it, as they are the ones who have a legitimate fear of retaliation.[63] Anonymous reading is threatened by DRM, which becomes much easier to enforce in a world of strong identification. All of these problems but the last can be greatly ameliorated if the system allows anonymity or multiple pseudonyms[64]—artificial, selectable personae that can be presented to the world and are capable of transacting, reading, and writing. In order not to undermine the binding of identity to person that justifies the ID card system, all pseudonyms would have to be distinguished from primary identities. Setting a 'nym bit would give fair notice to the world that the true identity of the user is masked. A cleverly designed system could permit the passing on of appropriate characteristics and authorizations (such as age) to the user's 'nym if he or she so chooses.

The "OECD Guidelines" or, more formally, the 1980 Organization for Economic Co-operation and Development *Guidelines on the Protection of Privacy and Transborder Flows of Personal Data*,[65] set out recommendations for nations concerned about data privacy to "take into account in their domestic legislation," subject only to the minimum limits necessary to preserve national security. Many privacy advocates see the OECD Guidelines as central to fair information practices;[66] others see the Guidelines as insufficient.[67] I am uncertain myself about the relative efficacy of legal protections as opposed to technological ones. But at the dawn of the twenty-first century, what we have in the United States is far too little of either,[68] with relatively little prospect of improvement. Of the federal privacy laws, only the federal Privacy Act of 1974[69] could be accused of having a wide application, and it applies only to records collected by the federal government. Federal privacy regulation of the private sector is spotty at best.[70]

New privacy rules will successfully piggyback on a national ID system only if private-sector data users decide that it is in their economic interest to use the new number. Otherwise, presumably, they can keep on building an alternative system that relies on whatever other identifiers they choose. A single reliable identifier should be of considerable interest to most private-sector data users, as the alternatives that exist today are unreliable due to data quality problems and also because the data are difficult to sort reliably, at least without expense. The carrot of lower transactions costs dangled by easy, secure, reliable, and cheap identification might suffice to create market-based incentives to get businesses to accept the stick of adherence to substantive privacy conditions. The private sector already makes routine use of the SSN despite its known security and uniqueness flaws; a new number that promised uniqueness, full coverage, and greater security would, one hopes, be very popular for e-commerce and even ordinary commerce. Given this attractive carrot, there is scope for some stick, for making adherence to a set of fair information practices rules implementing the OECD guidelines a condition precedent to commercial use of the new ID number.

An even better privacy rule would copy one aspect of the European Data Protection Directive and make obligations to follow privacy principles run with the data subject to the rule regardless of privity. In this version, once a firm chose to use the national ID number to organize or index its data, it would be forbidden to sell parts of the data set to other firms unless they, too, adhered to the same privacy principles. Without this extra provision, the weaker rule, which only imposed these obligations on firms if they used the actual ID number, might be subject to evasions.

B. Optimizing Ownership of Data

Ensuring that data subjects retain an ownership right in data held about them by other private actors is frequently suggested as a way of enhancing personal privacy. The theory is that if each data user must buy the right to share information on a per-transaction basis, this will put the subject on notice as to how data about him or her is being used, and also create an opportunity for the subject to veto unwanted uses. If nothing else, the argument goes, it will allow data subjects to share in the profits accruing from uses of their data.[71] But, as Jessica Litman notes, we usually create property rights in things we want to allow to be sold, not in things we want to keep from being traded.[72] In addition, it seems very implausible that Congress would adopt a sort of moral right for personal data that would run with it no matter who acquired it and under whatever circumstances.[73] And, if instead the new data property regime only requires a special form of words to allow full alienation of the personal interest in data, then it seems certain that this formulation will quickly find its way into every standard form consumer contract.[74]

Changing default rules for the ownership of privately held data is unlikely to do much to increase personal control over data if people are likely to contract around it without much thought. In contrast, a reliance on property law makes much more sense in the context of public law relating to government-controlled information because it invokes the Constitution.[75] If the federal government retains ownership of the ID number, then government can impose conditions on the use of the number. As the number becomes routinely essential, and as the amount of data subject to privacy rules that run with the index number grows, the private sector will find the number too valuable to avoid. Conversely, giving citizens a property right in noninvestigatory data[76] about themselves held by the government ensures that uses of the data will be subject to constitutional constraints including limits on search and alienation. Firms would be unable to contract around the ID number ownership rule because they would be mere licensees. Whether citizens should ever be allowed to surrender their property interest in their government-held data may be a hard question to answer in the abstract, but in practice, few would choose to waive their protection against government data trawling in the absence of improper pressure.[77]

The simplest way of conditioning the use of a new ID number by third parties on adherence to fair information practices would be to have the government retain ownership of the ID number and any associated card, following the passport model,[78] and to issue rules making data protection run with the use of the number or the data. But, as the legal history of the passport teaches us, this strategy is dangerous because it also opens the door to subsequent changes in law or in the regulations that might substantially affect the freedom of anyone who used the number or card.[79]

Indeed, the right—if right it be—to a passport carries conditions. The passport regulations provide for denying a passport for various grounds that might reasonably suggest the person seeks to leave the country to avoid unpleasant legal consequences.[80] But there is also the political test: the passport can be denied if the "Secretary determines that the national's activities abroad are causing or are likely to cause serious damage to the national security or the foreign policy of the United States."[81]

A national ID system that allows the government to suspend the ID card or make it difficult to use would easily become oppressive unless the citizen had clear rights to the card and also a right to a pre-deprivation hearing. If the card is required for work and for most transactions, it becomes the cornerstone of a citizen's economic identity. If the ID card is routinely required by common carriers and toll authorities, it will function as a de facto internal passport, making any governmental interference with it an assault on the right to travel. Something this important cannot be left to the uncertainties of a legal regime that might or might not distinguish it from the regime contemplated by *Haig v. Agee*. Vesting ownership of both the ID card and the number in the person whom they identify would ensure that the due process the Court associates with property rights attaches to governmental attempts to regulate the use and enjoyment of the card. Alas, vesting ownership of the number in individuals revives the scenario in which individuals likely will be invited to sign away their data privacy rights in merchants' standard form contracts.[82] Achieving the best of both worlds may not be possible without a new form of information property ownership, akin to joint (but not several) ownership of real property for both the card and number. Otherwise, one must choose between potential evils: the danger that the government might change the rules, or the danger that the private sector will attempt to contract around them. The first is more dangerous; the second is more certain.

Whether or not citizens have a property right in their ID number, they ought to own at least part of the data the government holds about them. Personal ownership of government-held data would limit the government's ability to share the data with third parties without the subject's consent. And it would more clearly invoke the warrant requirement before the government "searched" the data as part of a data-mining operation. To be most effective, however, the property right would have to extend not only to data acquired directly from the citizen but also to data the government acquired from commercial databases. At the very least, the government should be subject to the same viral data protection rules as would any other buyer of the data.[83]

V. CONCLUSION

A fair evaluation of the likely privacy costs of a national ID regime requires a proper understanding of the privacy baseline. The current data privacy picture is worse than most people realize, and the odds are it will continue to get worse. In that light, the marginal harms caused by a well-designed national

ID system may be fewer than one might initially believe, although there are genuine dangers to civil liberty and to privacy. In particular, there are possible psychological and moral costs to liberty that are hard to quantify, and serious risks to civil liberties unless some constitutional means can be found to ensure that the government cannot simply revoke or burden the use of the ID without substantial pre-deprivation due process hearings.

There is a (politically unlikely) scenario in which national ID cards could be used as a means to enhance privacy: use of the ID number by third parties could be conditioned on those third parties adhering to fair information practices modeled on the 1980 OECD guidelines. Because using a ubiquitous and reliable numbering system should be very attractive to businesses, they would have an incentive to adopt it, and might accept the bargain that they take the fair information practices obligations with it. Defining the ID number as the property of the government, or as jointly but not severally owned with the citizen, would cut off private-sector attempts to demand that citizens waive their data protection rights.

If an ID card were widely adopted by both government and business, it could become a daily necessity for most residents. If the card becomes a routine requirement for work, transactions, and travel, then it also becomes a target of opportunity for regulation and for law enforcement. Although some of these uses are likely to prove valuable, there is a serious risk of abuse. These dangers can be reduced by giving the data subject a property interest in information the government collects about him or her. If the information is private property, it will enjoy greater, although still bounded, protections under the Fourth and Fifth Amendments, and the government's ability to search it, to construct predictive profiles using it, and especially to sell it to third parties, will all be constrained.

In the thirty years since the relatively far-reaching success of the Privacy Act of 1974, privacy advocates in the United States have enjoyed only sectoral, and sometimes limited, achievements in their attempt to secure federal protection for data privacy, especially as regards data in private hands.[84] The privacy provisions of the Gramm-Leach-Bliley Financial Modernization Act of 1999 are a case in point: they are, in practice, quite weak.[85] Had the HIPPA rules proposed by the Clinton administration taken effect, the story might be different, but the regulations that replace them are also fairly anodyne.

Although there have been successes, the last two decades' explosion of privacy-destroying technologies suggest pretty strongly that standards and practices unfriendly to data privacy are being set more quickly and in more places than the privacy community can cope with. A perverse advantage of centralized national ID regime would be that it would create a very visible, single target for debate about privacy regulation. Again, this is only a mixed blessing, for although allowing privacy campaigners to focus on one debate, it also allows the interests that tend to oppose restrictions on the use of personal data to unite their lobbying efforts in one massive push for the goldfish bowl society.[86]

Even with such protections in place, an ID card regime is likely to contribute to the continued erosion of personal privacy. Although their adoption is not likely, an ideal set of national ID card rules might actually benefit privacy compared to the rather unappetizing alternative, not least because it would move the debate over privacy rules out of the widely dispersed arenas where it now occurs and where pro-privacy forces tend to be outnumbered, if they are even at the table.

This political calculation may be absurdly optimistic, but the mechanics of ID card implementation nonetheless merit careful thought because there is a real possibility that Congress may enact a national ID card program for reasons of its own, and indeed with REAL ID may have taken the first two steps in that direction. Ironically, the political justification for national ID cards is likely to be their supposed virtues as an anti-terrorism measure, although the cards' true merits probably lie elsewhere in both the short and medium run. Yet if we are to have a national ID card program, it makes sense to work out how it could best be structured to do the least harm to personal privacy—and maybe do some good as well.

NOTES

1. The interesting question of how legitimate foreign visitors acquire temporary ID numbers, or function without them, is beyond the scope of this chapter. *Cf.* Computer Science and Telecommunications Board, National Research Council, *IDs Not That Easy: Questions About Nationwide Identity Systems* (2002) [hereinafter NRC Report].

2. For the seminal formal definition, *see* Roger A. Clarke, *Human Identification in Record Systems* (June 1989); Roger A. Clarke, The Resistible Rise of the National Personal Data System, 5 *Software L. J.* 29, 33-36 (1992).

3. Polling data suggest that, at least in times of crisis, "the public strongly favors a national ID card 'to bolster anti-terrorism defenses.'" *Wired* (Sept. 25, 2001), available at http://www.wired.com/news/conflict/0,2100,47073,00.html (quoting question asked by Pew Research Center poll).

4. 124 S. Ct. 2451 (2004).

5. *Id.* at 2458-59.

6. *Id.* at 2461 (quoting *Hoffman v. United States*, 341 U.S. 479, 486 (1951)).

7. *Id.* at 2457.

8. This assumption elides important issues that are examined in the NRC Report, *supra* note 1.

9. This is far from easy. *See generally* Bruce Schneier, *Secrets and Lies* (2003).

10. *See* NRC Report, *supra* note 1.

11. Biometrics can be used for identification or authentication. *See generally* Dutch Data Protection Authority (Registratiekamer), R. Hes, T.F.M. Hooghiemstra, & J. J. Borking, *At Face Value: On Biometrical Identification and Privacy* 2 (1999), available at http://www.registratieka-mer.nl/bis/top_1_5_35_1.html (discussing the various applications of biometrics).

12. *See* Ann Cavoukian, Biometrics and Policing: Comments from a Privacy Perspective 4, in *Polizei und Datenschutz (Neupositionierung im Zeichen der Informationsgesellschaft* (Data Protection Authority ed., 1999) available at http://www.ipc.on.ca/web_site.eng/matters/sum_pap/PAPERS/biometric.htm.

13. *See id.*

14. Again, there are always borderline cases, such as a lost limb, which could reasonably be described as a (henceforth) "permanent," "past" or "present" condition.

15. Similarly, for most people, a criminal record is a fixed fact that cannot be changed. Even here, there are pardons and reversals on appeal, so the categories are somewhat fluid.

16. *See* Philip Redfern, Precise Identification Through a Multi-Purpose Personal Number Protects Privacy, 1 *Intl. J.L. & Info. Tech.* 305, 312 (1994).

17. *See* 8 U.S.C. § 1324a(a)(1)(B) (prohibiting hiring workers without verifying identity and authorization to work in the United States). Employers must complete an INS Form I-9, Employment Eligibility Verification Form, documenting this verification and stating the type of ID they examined. *See* Verification of Employment Eligibility, 8 C.F.R. § 274a.2.

18. *See, e.g.,* Sarah M. Kendall, Comment, America's Minorities Are Shown the "Back Door" . . . Again: The Discriminatory Impact of the Immigration Reform and Control Act, 18 *Hous. J. Int'l L.* 899 (1996).

19. *See* Julie E. Cohen, A Right to Read Anonymously: A Closer Look at "Copyright Management" in Cyberspace, 28 *Conn. L. Rev.* 981 (1996), available at http://www.law.georgetown.edu/faculty/jec/read_anonymously.pdf; Julie E. Cohen, Lochner in Cyberspace: The New Economic Orthodoxy of "Rights Management," 97 *Mich. L. Rev.* 462 (1998), available at http://www.law.georgetown.edu/faculty/jec/Lochner.pdf.

20. *See* Chad Woodford, Trusted Computing or Big Brother? Putting the Rights Back in Digital Rights Management, 75 *U. Colo. L. Rev.* 253 (2004).

21. For a discussion of related concerns, *see* Daniel J. Solove, Access and Aggregation: Public Records, Privacy and the Constitution, 86 *Minn. L. Rev.* 1137 (2002).

22. Personal Responsibility and Work Opportunity Reconciliation Act of 1996, Pub. L. No. 104-193, 110 Stat. 2105 (1996). Samuel V. Schoonmaker, Consequences and Validity of Family Law Provisions in the Welfare Reform Act, 14 *Journal American Academy of Matrimonial Lawyers* 1, 10 (Summer 1997); Valerie Collins, Identity Cards and Numbers: The Debate Continued, 10 *Int'l Rev. L., Computers & Tech.* 142 (1996).

23. Smaller-scale versions of this have happened abroad. For example, during the Cold War,

the West German government kept a secret list of persons who it deemed unfit for government employment due to their political activities. *See* Wikipedia, Radikalenrlass, http://de.wikipedia .org/wiki/Radikalenerlass.

24. The classic survey of the potential dangers of a national ID system remains Roger Clarke's list of the dangers of "Dataveillance." Roger Clarke, Information Technology and Data-veillance, 31 *Commun. ACM* 498-551 (Nov. 1987), available at http://www.anu.edu.au/people/ Roger.Clarke/DV/CACM88.html.

25. *See* Michael A. Sprow, The High Price of Safety: May Public Schools Institute a Policy of Frisking Students as They Enter the Building?, 54 *Baylor L. Rev.* 133 (2002).

26. For example, data matching to combat fraudulent applications for benefits.

27. For example, building up lists of frequent protestors against government policies.

28. An agency shall "maintain no record describing how any individual exercises rights guaranteed by the First Amendment unless expressly authorized by statute or by the individual about whom the record is maintained or unless pertinent to and within the scope of an autho-rized law enforcement activity." 5 U.S.C. § 552a(e)(7).

29. 5 U.S.C. § 552a(e)(1).

30. *Id.* at (e)(6).

31. Erik Baard, Buying Trouble, *Village Voice* (June 24, 2002), available at http://www.vil-lagevoice.com/issues/0230/baard.php.

32. Data provided in a driver's license application is currently protected against release to the private sector-but not to many government agencies-by the Driver's Privacy Protection Act of 1994 (DPPA), 18 U.S.C. §§ 2721-25. *Cf. Reno v. Condon*, 528 U.S. 141 (2000) (upholding con-stitutionality of DPPA).

33. Another, less persuasive, analogy would treat the data as having been left in the govern-ment's plain view. And it is settled that the police may examine anything left in plain view. *See Florida v. Riley*, 488 U.S. 445, 450-51 (1989) (search of home from helicopter does not violate Fourth Amendment).

34. Codified at 5 U.S.C. § 552A(b). The restrictions on law enforcement agencies as regards investigatory records-a potentially broad category-are somewhat less strict.

35. *See* Michael Adler, Note, Cyberspace, General Searches, and Digital Contraband: The Fourth Amendment and the Net-Wide Search, 105 *Yale L.J.* 1093 (1996).

36. *Id.* at 1097.

37. On TIPS, *see* William Matthews, *Ashcroft Offers TIPS Assurances* (July 26, 2002), avail-able at http://www.fcw.com/fcw/articles/2002/0722/web-tips-07-26-02.asp.

38. *See* Timothy Garton Ash, *The File: A Personal History* (1997).

39. For a surprisingly pessimistic assessment by a former privacy commissioner, *see* David H. Flaherty, *Protecting Privacy in Surveillance Societies* 406-07 (1989).

40. On profiling, *see generally* EPIC, Profiling and Privacy Page, http://www.epic.org/pri-vacy/profiling/. Examples of predictive profiles in use today include W.A.V.E. and Mosaic 2000. *See* Jon Katz, *After Columbine: Geek Profiling*, (January 23, 2001), available at http://features. slashdot.org/article.pl?sid=01/01/23/2341238.

41. The case of Richard Jewel is instructive as to the costs to the victim of a false positive. *See generally* http://www.hfac.uh.edu/comm/media_libel/cases-conflicts/tv/jewell.html.

42. Megans Law-type statutes stigmatize sex offenders by notifying neighbors of their presence. *See generally* Dan Markel, Are Shaming Punishments Beautifully Retributive? Retributivism and the Implications for the Alternative Sanctions Debate, 54 *Vand. L. Rev.* 2157 (2001).

43. According to T. Markus Funk, A Mere Youthful Indiscretion? Reexaming the Policy of Expunging Juvenile Delinquency Records, 29 *U. Mich J. L. Ref.* 885, 903 n. 85 (1996), the term originates with Richard S. Harnsberger, Does the Federal Youth Corrections Act Remove the "Leper's Bell" from Rehabilitated Offenders?, 7 *Fla. St. U. L. Rev.* 395 (1979).

44. For some thought-provoking if rather cold-hearted arguments as to why some common forms of social forgiveness might be harmful, see Funk, *supra* note 43.

45. *See* NRC Study, *supra* note 1, at ch. 2.

46. *Cf.* Sinclair Lewis, *It Can't Happen Here* (1935).

47. *See, e.g.,* Roger Clarke, *Information Technology: Weapon of Authoritarianism or Tool of Democracy?* (June 1994), available at http://www.anu.edu.au/people/Roger.Clarke/ DV/Paper-Authism.html.

48. *Cf. Rumsfeld v. Padilla*, 542 U.S. 426 (2004).

49. *See* U.S. Bureau of the Census, *Housing Issues Motivate More Than Half of Movers, Census Bureau Reports* (May 24, 2001) (giving 16 percent figure for year 2000), available at http://www.census.gov/Press-Release/www/2001/cb01-90.html.

50. Employers and insurers are already relying on credit scoring. *See* Insurance Credit Scoring, available at http://www.indianafarmers.com/docs/Credit%20Score%20 Brochure%20 Final%20Version.pdf; Insure.com, How Your Credit History Affects Your Auto and Home Insurance Premiums, available at http://info.insure.com/auto/creditscores.html.

51. *See* A. Michael Froomkin, Flood Control on the Information Ocean: Living With Anonymity, Digital Cash, and Distributed Databases, 15 U. *Pitt. J. L. & Com.* 395 (1996), available at http://www.law.miami.edu/~froomkin/articles/ocean.htm.

52. The problem is equally real with a national ID system without a card, but is easier to visualize with a tangible example.

53. So named after *Terry v. Ohio*, 392 U.S. 1 (1968).

54. Robert C. Johnston, 15 States Link School Status, Student Driving, *Education Week*, (Nov. 6, 1996), available at http://www.edweek.org/ew/ewstory.cfm?slug=10drive.h16.

55. *See* A. Michael Froomkin, The Death of Privacy?, 52 *Stan. L. Rev.* 1461 (2000), available at http://www.law.miami.edu/~froomkin/articles/privacy-deathof.pdf.

56. *See, e.g.,* Simson Garfinkel, Will a Mandatory ID Keep Us Safe?, *Privacy J.*, (Apr. 2002) (discussing the recent attempts by the states and DOT to create a standard driver's license and link the databases, making a de facto national id).

57. *E.g.*, Family Educational Rights and Privacy Act of 1974, 20 U.S.C. § 1232g (2002); Video Privacy Protection Act of 1988, 18 U.S.C. § 2701 (2002); Driver's Privacy Protection Act of 1994, 18 U.S.C. §§ 2721-25 (2002); Children's Online Privacy Protection Act of 1998, 15 U.S.C. §§ 6501-03 (2002); Privacy Act of 1974, 18 U.S.C. §§ 2510-22, 2701-09 (2002); Electronic Communications Privacy Act of 1986, 5 U.S.C. § 552a (2002).

58. 5 U.S.C. § 552A.

59. *Cf. Lamont v. Commissioner of Motor Vehicles*, 269 F. Supp. 880 (1967) (denying injunction to block sale of DMV registry data).

60. Some state legislatures tried to sell driver's license data to private companies, but the public rebelled. Florida, for example, planned to charge one cent per image. Citizens complained, and the Florida legislation died. *See* Robert Lemos, The Dark Side of the Digital Home, ZDNet News (Feb. 7, 1999), available at http://zdnet.com.com/2100-11-513639.html?legacy=zdnn.

61. A fuller account of these developments can be found in Froomkin, *supra* note 55.

62. The obligation to comply with data protection rules would thus run with the data, just as do the obligations under the European Data Protection Directive. On the Directive *see generally,* Joel Reidenberg & Paul Schwartz, *Data Privacy Law* (1996).

63. It may also make whistleblowing more difficult and dangerous.

64. Roger Clarke suggests additional protections are needed if the system relies on ID cards. *See* Roger L. Clarke, *Chip-Based ID: Promise and Peril* (1997), available at http://www.anu.edu.au/people/Roger.Clarke/DV/IDCards97.html.

65. OECD, *Guidelines on the Protection of Privacy and Transborder Flows of Personal Data* (Sept. 23, 1980), available at http://www.oecd.org/document/0,2340,en_2649_34255_1815186_1_1_1_1,00.html [herinafter OECD Guidelines].

66. *See, e.g.,* Marc Rotenberg, Fair Information Practices and the Architecture of Privacy (What Larry Doesn't Get), 2001 *Stan. Tech. L. Rev.* 1, 45 (2001) ("It is generally understood that the challenge of privacy protection in the information age is the application and enforcement of Fair Information Practices and the OECD Guidelines."). *See also* Paul M. Schwartz, Privacy & Democracy in Cyberspace, 52 *Vanderbilt L. Rev.* 1609 (1999).

67. *See, e.g.,* Gary T. Marx, *Ethics for the New Surveillance in Visions of Privacy* 39 (Colin J. Bennett & Rebecca Grant, eds. 1999).

68. *See* Froomkin, *supra* note 55.

69. Privacy Act of 1974, Pub. L. No. 93-579, 88 Stat. 1896 (codified as amended at 5 U.S.C.A. § 552a.

70. *Cf.* Fred H. Cate, The EU Data Protection Directive, Information Privacy, and the Public Interest, 80 *Iowa L. Rev.* 431, 438 (1995).

71. *See* Jessica Litman, Information Privacy/Information Property, 52 *Stan. L. Rev.* 1283 (2000) (summarizing and critiquing these arguments).

72. *Id.*

73. There are things we do not allow to be sold in any circumstances, such as babies and limbs and (in most states) sex, but information is unlikely to be added to that select group.

74. Consumers suffer from rational privacy myopia, valuing each bit of data at marginal value, whereas the buyer-aggregator understands that a profile is worth more than the sum of the parts. The buyer is thus willing to pay average value of the bit (modulo transactions costs), which will usually be higher than marginal value for all but the most sensitive data. Hence the observed behavior that Americans will sell their privacy for a frequent flyer mile. *See* Froomkin, *supra* note 55, at 1501.

75. The U.S. government sometimes suggests that current privacy rules such as the Privacy Act may not apply to data held by its contractors subject to government directives. *See, e.g.,* U.S. Department of Homeland Security, *Report to the Public on Events Surrounding JetBlue Data Transfer* (2004), available at http://www.dhs.gov/interweb/assetlibrary/PrivacyOffice_jetBlueFINAL.pdf. I believe this argument misreads the Privacy Act. But whether or not it

does, the loophole should not be available for data indexed via a national ID card or it would erase any meaningful privacy protections.

76. Obviously, creating such a right for data collected in the context of law enforcement investigations would be even more protective of personal privacy, but most would probably find the cost unacceptable.

77. There will undoubtedly be a few exceptions to this principle, *e.g.*, government employees in sensitive positions such as the CIA.

78. *See Lynn v. Rusk*, 389 F. 2d 940, 948 (D.C. Cir. 1967) (stating "the passport, [is] an official document that has consistently been regarded as the property of the Government.").

Currently, the Passport Act, 22 U.S.C.A. § 211a, defines the government's authority to grant and issue passports. Executive Order No. 11295, 31 F.R. 10603 (Aug. 5, 1966).

79. The modern passport cases begin with *Kent v. Dulles*, 357 U.S. 116 (1958) (overturning the secretary of state's decision to deny passports because Congress had not given him that power). The decision avoided the core constitutional issues of a right to a passport as an aid to the right to travel, but the narrowing construction suggested the Court was concerned about it. In a 1965 decision, *Aptheker v. Secretary of State*, 378 U.S. 500 (1964), the Court held that a statute making it a criminal offense for a member of the Communist Party to apply for, renew, or use a passport was unconstitutional on its face. Nevertheless, in 1981 the Court held that even in the absence of explicit statutory authorization, the government could revoke the passport of a U.S. citizen if there was a substantial likelihood of "serious damage" to national security or foreign policy as a result of a passport holder's activities in foreign countries. According to Chief Justice Burger, the Constitution's due process guarantees called for no more than statement of reasons and opportunity for prompt hearing *following* the revocation of the passport. *See Haig v. Agee*, 453 U.S. 280 (1981).

80. *See* 22 C.F.R. § 51.70.

81. *Id.*

82. Although there is no fundamental legal reason why this transaction could not be prohibited, such action seems far less secure politically than a regime in which the government owned the number and set the rules, thus making it impossible for individuals to waive a restriction they do not control.

83. As the OECD Guidelines contemplate exceptions for law enforcement, this is less protection than it might be.

84. First Amendment limits on preventing persons from sharing what they know are one constraining factor. *See* Eugene Volokh, Freedom of Speech and Information Privacy: The Troubling Implications of a Right to Stop Others from Speaking About You, 52 *Stan. L. Rev.* 1049 (2000).

85. *See* Eric Poggemiller, Note, The Consumer Response to Privacy Provisions in Gramm-Leach-Bliley: Much Ado About Nothing?, 6 *NC Banking Inst.* 617 (Apr. 2002).

86. For a particularly evocative vision of what that might be like, *see* David Brin, *The Transparent Society* (1998).

PROMOTING PRIVACY AND SECURITY THROUGH THE MARKET

Part 4

15 CONTRACTS, MARKETS, AND DATA CONTROL
Raymond T. Nimmer

Raymond T. Nimmer is dean and Leonard H. Childs Professor of Law, University of Houston.

This chapter uses the prism of contract law to deal with issues about who should control use of data created or exchanged in a voluntary transaction (transactional data) that can be linked with an identifiable person.

.   .   .

Data control activists argue that increased controls in individuals are needed *and* that protecting individuals' rights requires regulation. I disagree and instead argue for allowing voluntarily undertaken contractual obligations and market forces to define the scope of data control. That voluntary regime should be displaced only when broad consensus exists that particular uses of the particular data should be restricted.

I. THE LANGUAGE OF DATA CONTROL

A. Difference Between Privacy and Data Control
Both privacy and data control policy focus on the relationship of governments, businesses, and individuals to data about individuals. But "privacy" and "data control" address vastly different public policy questions.

In 1888, Judge Thomas Cooley described privacy as the "right to be left alone."[1] That phrase captures the essence of the concept of privacy in this country. "Privacy" centers on a right to be free from unwarranted intrusions and from undesired disclosure of otherwise confidential and sensitive facts about an individual. It posits a right to keep places and information away from the government and from the public. Two themes define most privacy law: (1) whether the person has a reasonable expectation of privacy with respect to the information or place and (2) whether wrongful disclosure would be highly embarrassing to a reasonable person.[2]

But "privacy" in this sense is not what modern activists think about when they use that word to assert the need to protect or control transactional data. Arguments for data control propose that one party (data subject) should control the other's (controlled party) use of data that both know, whether or not those data are confidential or sensitive, accurate or inaccurate. Alan Westin, for example, described "privacy" as involving the "claim of individuals . . . to determine for themselves when, how, and to what extent information about them is communicated to others."[3] He meant "data control." A later author described privacy as "an individual's claim to control the terms under which . . . information identifiable to the individual . . . is acquired, disclosed, and used."[4] These descriptions center on control, rather than privacy.[5]

A shift from privacy to data control is a shift away from protecting against wrongful acquisition or disclosure of private information of a sensitive nature and toward a broader claim to control all information personally identifiable to the individual. The focus becomes "personal" or "personally identifiable" information, rather than "private" information. "Personal information" is *any* information relating to a natural person "[who] can be identified, directly or indirectly [by the data]."[6]

B. Language and Assumptions of Data Control

Traditional United States law assumes that each party is free to use or disclose information created or obtained in a transaction unless a confidential relationship exists or the party agreed to confidentiality restrictions. Data control activists would replace that with an assumption that transactional data are restricted in use. The obvious question is "why"?

To understand the answer, we need to understand the language of data control. Advocates of control tend to use the language of property rights and governmental regulation. The rhetoric of rights and regulation, however, deflects attention from the transactional character of the context defined by agreements, relationships, market choices, and voluntary interactions. In that context, it is neither awkward nor improper to rely on the voluntary choices to allocate data control. Law should intervene only when needed where the risks of harm and the failure of the market are so significant that the need for control clearly outweighs the cost of regulation.

C. "Rights Talk" and Property Issues

Property "rights talk" is often used by control activists.[7] This language emphasizes terms such as *ownership, rights, infringement, waiver,* and the *right to exclude.* The assumption is that one person owns data unless he or she waives those rights. The controlled party is not required to agree—the rights exist as a matter of law. Property rights language implies that if the owner waives rights in *its* information, the waiver is a transfer *from* the owner *to* the other party.[8] Once law identifies the owner, the argument goes, law should prevent the rights from being taken away without consent.

For data control advocates, ownership always vests in the individual. The rights are enforceable against the controlled party, which is often assumed to be a business. One underpinning for data control policy is the need to protect the "rights" of individuals.[9]

For nonprivate data, however, rights talk is not a useful model. The basic flaw lies in the assumption about ownership. Ownership is grounded in the fact that the individual can be associated with what the data describe. But the assumption that the individual owns the data is not based on meaningful analysis. If Party A and Party B enter into a transaction to sell a car for a stated price, the transactional data might be the following:

> On July 1, at four in the evening in New York, Party A of 11 Post Street purchased Party B's Mercedes for $38,000 cash. Party A received the car and the title certificate at that time.[10]

What is the basis of the claim that Party A owns these data and B does not? Both parties have equal claims. Indeed, traditional United States law assumes that both are free to use them.[11] That premise is targeted for reversal by the data control movement.

D. "Regulation Talk" and Government Control

"Regulation talk" speaks of rules, mandates, compliance, and agency oversight. The assumption is that markets and voluntary interactions will not produce the *right* results and that government intervention is required. As with "rights talk," the themes of regulation talk are widely used in the data control movement.[12] Data control policy posits that markets will not protect what the control advocate believes should be protected because corporations dominate and individuals are powerless without regulatory help. As we shall see, however, markets indeed respond to data control concerns.

Regulation has a narrow role in a market economy, but control activists describe the need for regulation in broad terms covering the entire economy. Because it cannot be that there is a market failure or high risk of injury for all nonprivate data throughout all of the economy, this premise entails less of an argument about selective failure and more of a rejection of the idea of markets and voluntary interactions.

I reject that view, but even if it were accepted, constitutional and other values limit it as applied to information. Data control by *agreement* does not offend First Amendment values, but controls imposed by law should face strict limitations.[13] Permitted governmental restraints on First Amendment speech require narrowly tailored rules and strong governmental interests.[14] The likelihood of the restraints being invalid increases as the strength of the government interest diminishes. That occurs as regulation moves away from protecting truly private, sensitive, or harmful information. "Rights talk" and "regulation talk" here are at odds with First Amendment values in reference to use of transactional data. And even beyond First Amendment values, broadly intrusive regulation of the use of information would have severe social and economic consequences.

E. "Contract Talk" and Agreed Allocations
Transactional data result from voluntary interactions in contractual or pre-contractual relationships. Yet few discussions of data control approach the issue using "contract talk" and contract themes.[15] "Contract talk" speaks of agreements, exchanges, performance, expectations, and markets. Individual agreements and aggregated decisions in a market yield the most efficient exchange of value and sustain individual choice and autonomy.

From this perspective, transactional data are simply one part of an exchange. The issue is how the parties' agreement handles the right to control those data.

F. Data Control as Business Regulation
In the United States, traditional privacy litigation focused on the relationship between the individual and the state. In contrast, data control also centers on the right of one *private* party to control another *private* party.

Within this focus, data control themes discriminate among types of private uses. The Data Protection Directive, for example, *excludes* coverage of "the processing of personal data . . . by a natural person in the course of a purely personal or household activity."[16]

Given the exclusion of "consumer" uses, what is the policy of data control?

The policy concentrates on regulating the relationship between individuals and businesses as much as it does on ideas of privacy. Data control law is often business regulation. The goal is to rearrange the relationship between an individual and a business by giving the individual a right to control uses of information created or transferred in an interaction between the two.

II. THE COSTS AND BENEFITS

A. Data Control Policy Supports

What interests are served or harmed by data control? We can address this only briefly in the space available. We begin with pro-control interests.

Controls protect human dignity of the subject. The traditional idea of privacy is closely associated with protecting human dignity, autonomy, intimacy, and sense of self. Control supporters often link data control to similar principles.[17] But as one moves from traditional privacy and toward control of nonsensitive, often public data, the affinity between the claimed right and these core values lessens, especially for data created by interaction of both parties.

Controls protect accuracy. Some justify data control as preventing dissemination and use of false information.[18] Because most data control issues do not involve intentional misrepresentation by the controlled party, the true issue involves a right to cure and prevent errors. In ordinary cases, however, the person possessing transactional data also has an interest in ensuring that the information is accurate. Incorrect information exists. But the legal policy should protect *both* parties' interest in accuracy. Not surprisingly, data control laws address accuracy by placing obligations and potential liability on the controlled party (a business) with rights given to the data subject (the individual).

Controls prevent harm from third parties. Some argue that data control is needed to protect an individual from harmful third-party use of *accurate* data such as in identity theft or stalking.[19] In most cases, this type of misuse is separately punishable against the wrongdoer. The costs and liability risk here, however, are imposed on an entity that, in most cases, is not the person that engages in identity theft or stalking. In addition, whereas identity theft and stalking are often mentioned, control advocates routinely include other, far less threatening uses of data within their view of misuse to be prevented, but on these other issues there is likely to be greater variation in public response. For example, some regard mailing lists as a serious intrusion. Others do not.

Controls encourage autonomy in conduct. Arguments for control sometimes claim justification in the idea that control will enable the individual to engage in conduct the disclosure of which would be embarrassing.[20] Control reduces the fear of disclosure. Of course. But the behavior may or may not be socially beneficial. Also, the strength of the effect varies across different individuals, data, and uses. Variability argues against a broad, undiscriminating data control regime.

Controls encourage disclosure to the controlled party. Data control in the individual might encourage disclosures in the relationship to which it applies. This is one reason for the presumptive confidentiality in relationships between doctors and patients, and lawyers and clients. These relationships serve significant social functions and depend on the free exchange of information. The same rationale, however, is not present for all other relationships. Once again, the variation argues for selective control, rather than a broad data control regime.

Controls allow controlling a public reputation. Being able to control what others can reveal gives a person the ability to shape the person's public image. This, of course, involves misdirection or deception, and many believe promoting it is inappropriate social policy.[21]

B. Data Control Costs

However one evaluates the strength of reasons for creating control rights, two things are clear.

First, the strength of the supporting rationales varies across different transactions, different subject matter, and different individuals.

Second, although it is politically incorrect to oppose privacy protection, the idea of *data control* is not one in which only good things flow from expanding control.[22] Here are some negative impacts.

Controls reduce autonomy and speech. Each step expanding control restricts the autonomy and choice of the controlled party. Some may believe that, if the control target is a business, this is not a problem. But that ignores benefits that come from allowing individuals and firms flexibility to act in the most efficient and effective manner. Further, even if the target is nonconsumer use of data, that does not mean that individual users are not affected. We will see that shortly in the case of Ms. Lindqvist's Website.

Controls impose large compliance costs. Data control regimes impose compliance costs (such as for staff, systems, and monitoring required to comply) and opportunities lost because information is no longer available to be effectively used.[23] These costs arise because the controlled party must act in a manner that allows it to respond to the control demands of the other party regardless of whether a particular data subject cares about data control.

Controls impede other transactions. Data control also imposes costs on transactions *other than* the one in which the data were created or transferred.[24] Control makes it more difficult and costly to obtain information for a subsequent transaction and, in some cases, impossible. Sometimes that information may be only marginally relevant, but in other cases it may be vital to assess risk and whether or not to engage in that other transaction. Data control increases the costs of that subsequent transaction, makes it more risky, or simply results in the transaction not occurring.

Controls support deceptive behavior. Data control is conducive to fraudulent or otherwise deceptive conduct.[25] The ability to prevent another from revealing information may serve positive purposes, or may be used improperly. The controlling person has an ability to conceal.

Controls inhibit free interaction. Data control reduces the flow of information in commerce and society. This can be discussed through the lens of increased costs, but it has independent significance in a society that values personal autonomy and free speech. These values are threatened *as to the controlled party.* Control encumbers the free choice of the person in possession of the data. Consider a husband whose wife is admitted to a hospital. The husband calls to learn her status—asking for personal data. The hospital, however, was unable to obtain consent from the wife before emergency admission. Quite obviously, the hospital should give the husband proper information. But how does that fit with a data control regime that states that a person cannot disclose transactional data to another without consent of the subject? And if the answer is that any control regime will make exceptions, who will make those decisions and what is the effect of such detailed regulation on the overall ability to interact in society? Which regulators are perfect?

Controls inject regulation into ordinary transactions. Data control laws admit regulators into too many parts of our ordinary behavior, and they cannot always get it right. Even if they do, many would prefer the right to go our own way. Indeed, this is precisely the type of privacy protection that may be most appropriate.

C. The Early Record—Ms. Lindqvist

Data control advocates assume that the regulatory impact will concentrate on abusive cases. The early record confirms that this will not be true. Consider Ms. Lindqvist's Website.[26]

Lindqvist was convicted of a violation of the Swedish data protection law; on appeal, the Swedish court referred questions to the European court about the data protection directive. The facts were that, in addition to working as a maintenance worker, Lindqvist was a catechist in the local parish. She set up Internet pages on her personal computer to allow parishioners preparing for confirmation to obtain information. The Church's Website linked to that site. The pages also contained information about Ms. Lindqvist and her colleagues, sometimes including their names, telephone numbers, and the like. Ms. Lindqvist also described, in a mildly humorous manner, her colleagues' jobs and hobbies. At one time, she reported that a colleague had injured her foot and was working halftime on medical grounds. "Mrs. Lindqvist had not informed . . . the [data supervisory authority]" of her Website. She was convicted of violating Swedish data protection law and appealed.

The European court provided the following observations:

1. The act of referring . . . by name or by other means, for instance by giving their telephone number or information regarding their working conditions and hobbies, *constitutes the processing of personal data.* . . .

2. Such processing of personal data is *not covered by any of the exceptions* in [the] Directive. . . .

3. Reference to the fact that an individual has injured her foot and is on halftime on medical grounds constitutes *personal data concerning health* within the meaning . . . [of the] Directive. . . .

This prosecution reflects the data control mind-set. None of the Website data were private. Yet posting yielded liability. The chilling effect is clear. A rule that places Ms. Lindqvist in the judicial process is ludicrous. But if her conduct should not be regulated, what distinguishes it from the behavior of a small business that uses data about the sale of a television to contact the buyer with product information?

Lindqvist's problem was not simply an overzealous regulator. Given a mandate to regulate data, regulatory action such as this can be expected.

III. DATA CONTROL THROUGH THE PRISM OF TRANSACTIONS

A. Transactions and Voluntary Ordering

Because transactional data arise in a contractual relationship, any rule on data control will pass through the filter of contractual choices and market adjustments. Any law will produce adaptations in transactions, and these will not necessarily be confined to the regulatory result sought.

The costs imposed by a data control regime may be manifested in increased price, reduced net income, or other transactional adaptations. The effects will vary depending on the data preferences of the parties, the type of data involved, the nature of the transaction, the nature of the controlled use, and other factors. But the costs should be imposed only if they are justified by overriding benefits. However, these "benefits" also vary. We should not impose high costs for low, intermittent gains and should not impose any costs unless the gains clearly outweigh the adverse impact.

In transactional relationships, the impact of law filters through adjustment by markets, contracts, and relationships.[27] But why not accept those as the primary shaping instruments, rather than making them a target for suppression by regulation? That is the perspective I suggest. Transactions involve exchanges made because each party decides that the transaction gives value to it that exceeds what it has in the absence of the transaction. These exchanges should be controlled by the parties, not by regulators. That is best achieved by the presumption that, if the parties have not otherwise agreed, either party can use information. This is the traditional presumption in U.S. law, and it should be overridden only if data control interests clearly and decisively outweigh interests in speech, disclosure, and autonomy with respect to both participants, and clearly justify the costs and dislocations that a data control regime imposes.

B. Transaction and Allocation of Data Control

Allocation of a right to control transactional data is best left to voluntary choices in an open market that allows the market and the parties to adjust for differing preferences and different sensitivities. Rather than regulated control, the market is more likely to efficiently differentiate as parties see fit in light of their own interests.

There are two ways of describing transactions to which data control issues apply. One treats data control as part of a mix establishing the overall value of a transaction for each party. Consider the following:

> Party A will sell a car for between $10,000 and $12,000 cash. A values data rights in the transaction at $1,500, which it builds into the sales price. Party

B is willing to purchase for between $9,000 and $11,000, without considering data rights.

If B is indifferent to data control, a transaction should occur between $10,000 and $11,000, giving A the right to use the data.[28] In effect, the data rights allow B to acquire a car for less in cash because the data have value. In contrast, a data control regime will either deny A the ability to obtain data rights or impose procedural or other steps (costs) to obtain and exercise that control. If A is prevented from obtaining data rights by law, there will be no sale because B will offer less than A's lowest price (that is, $10,000 + $1,500 cash).[29]

Data control rights may be a non-cash asset that either augments an individual's ability to purchase or hinders it. Control affects the price if a party attaches value to it or if it imposes unavoidable costs. But the impact will vary. In general, if an individual is indifferent to it (that is, places zero value on controlling the data), but a business values it, there is a shift toward lower prices. In contrast, if individuals highly value the right to control data, and the seller's value for it is low, we would expect a shift to allow individuals to control because this enables sales at a higher price. The calculus changes when we consider compliance and other costs of data control.

An alternative analysis is that product price and data control are separate. No transaction occurs unless there is "separate" agreement on both issues. This model assumes that data control is a potentially controlling factor in all transactions.

If agreement is clear on the goods, and the parties are indifferent to data control, agreement on that issue should occur in order to enable the purchase. A default rule allowing use of data leaves costs steady, whereas a rule giving control to one party imposes compliance costs.

If both parties value control highly, but in opposite directions, disagreement blocks the transaction. In effect, the buyer might say, "I never let anyone use my name and address," while the seller might say: "I offer this service only because I want to use those data."

For some, data control has overriding significance. But there will be variations in individual preferences and on the type of data and use. More people would refuse a transaction in order to prevent disclosure of intimate details of their sex lives than would reject a transaction because they do not wish to be on a mailing list.

C. The Market for Data Control Rights

The foregoing assumes that there is a market in which data control interests are relevant. Is there a market? The answer is "yes."

When we talk about a market, we can be referring to a case in which each individual deal is arranged under unique terms by the parties to the specific deal, or we can be referring to a situation in which businesses who are repeat participants arrange offers and standard deals to meet the demands of the customers with whom they deal.

Modern information systems allow tailored choices within a mass-market environment ("mass customization"), and these may manifest in the form of a platter of privacy options.[30] There are clear indications of a market sensitive to data control. For example, although few companies had privacy policies in the early 1990s, by the late 1990s, such policies were virtually ubiquitous.[31] A report in 2003 commented,

> We in the United States have generally allowed free market concepts to dictate the development of best practices in the commercial acquisition and use of non-sensitive personal information. As evidenced by the almost universal existence of Internet privacy policies . . . this approach has worked.[32]

Not all of the policies would satisfy a control advocate's goals. Indeed, a control advocate would respond to this study by asking whether the privacy policies were "adequate," but would answer based on the advocate's standard of adequacy.

Most privacy policies make commitments beyond what law requires even though few create the elaborate restrictions sought by data control theories. But the point is that the market defines adequacy from the perspective of the participants. The development of these policies means that businesses in an open market have made commitments not mandated by law. That occurred because of business judgments that the policies were desired by customers and benefited the companies. That is how markets work.

Today it is often true that neither party in a transaction greatly values control of the data.[33] The value of control is less important than obtaining (or selling) the goods, services, or software at an acceptable price. This is one reason why online providers make "privacy" commitments. Many customers ignore privacy options because they simply do not care.

One contested issue in control debates is whether the individual should have (1) the right to opt out of use by the controlled party or (2) the right to opt in to allowing use. From a transactional context, these options state alternative "default" rules. The track record is that, presented with an option, most individuals ignore it: they neither opt in, nor opt out.

One can debate the cause of this pattern. But one cause is that many individuals are indifferent to the issue. Most purchasers are concerned with whether the goods or services work, cost less, and are supported, than with whether the vendor will list the buyer among those who made a purchase from it. Indeed, most purchasers are willing to freely give that information to their friends. What then is the rationale for imposing huge compliance costs and shifts in transactional dynamics to achieve a result for which most persons are indifferent? The answer, from the data control perspective, is that the policy advocates believe that the individuals *should* care and, in the absence of that, will impose what they believe individuals *should* want.

D. Contract Law and General Themes

Contract law is the primary source of law with respect to transactional obligations. The premise of contract law is to enforce voluntarily assumed obligations. Contract law enforces agreements, and an "agreement" is

> the bargain of the parties in fact as found in their language or by implication from other circumstances, including course of performance, course of dealing, and usage of trade as provided in this [Act].[34]

The reference to usage of trade reflects that contract law relies on contextual information to fill in terms of an agreement, or to interpret them. The theory is that parties contract with reference to context and that the legal implications of the agreement should be understood with it in mind.[35] This makes contract law a living, evolving entity, rather than a fixed body of rules; that evolution may ultimately incorporate evolving, general, and actual expectations about data control.

Contract law exists because it is socially important to support voluntary relationships as an integral part of an open market. In limited cases, agreed terms might be overridden by policy. The support for enforcing contractual choices, however, means that this is uncommon. The dominant premise lies in the idea of enforcing voluntarily assumed obligations.

E. Contracts: Default Rules and Trade Practices

Other than rules about creating a contract, most contract law rules set out what are described as "default rules." A "default rule" governs only if the agreement does not establish contrary terms. Other rules are default standards—they do not prescribe an outcome but set a standard such as "reasonable" or "good faith" conduct. For transactional data, the default rule has been that both parties can freely use the information, except for transactions with indicia of confidentiality.[36]

Extensive contract law literature addresses from what source the content of default rules should be derived. Clearly, however, a default rule should be adopted only if it promotes efficiency or another overriding goal in widespread, *heterogeneous* cases.[37] Default rules that work only in narrow, definable instances should be confined to those types of instances.

Beyond this, there are two principles about the derivation of default rules:

- Default rules should reflect what parties of this type would ordinarily agree to if they considered the topic.[38]
- Default rules should force disclosure by a party of special circumstances in order to avoid the default rule ("penalty defaults").[39]

Of these, the most influential is the first: default rules support contracts by providing predictable, commonsense outcomes reflecting what similar parties would have expected the rule to be. The goal is to facilitate agreements in light of the premise that the business of law is to enforce the parties' expectations.

In contrast, some argue that in limited cases contract law should adopt a "penalty default rule" approach. But the relationship of a penalty default concept to actual contracting practice is suspect. The theory is that a party with special circumstances will know of the default rule and will seek a contractual change, thereby signaling that a special case is present. In fact, that assumes away the significant complexity in actual contracting. Once that complexity is considered, it is often not possible to predict the impact of a "penalty default" rule.[40]

One author has argued for a data control rule that permits only functionally necessary processing of personal data.[41] This proposes a "penalty default" based largely on the assumption that the business is in a better position to know that it has *special uses* for the information and should be forced to indicate that by seeking agreements to allow the use. But what are special uses? Clearly, they are not the ordinary commercial uses of ordinary, nonsensitive data. Indeed, for most purposes, the reverse premise is more accurate. That is, a right to use nonsensitive data is most often presumed, whereas a desire to prevent use would be the exception or special case. The default rule should be that each party is free to use the data, and that imposing controls requires an agreement to that effect.

F. Default Position: Party Autonomy

The traditional default rule is that a person is free to use and disclose information that is not cloaked in indicia of confidentiality, except in relationships such as doctor-patient or lawyer-client.[42] In those latter settings, one can identify specific and strong social benefits that support presumptive confidentiality (control). More recently, various sector-specific and data-specific statutes have identified particular types of information (for example, financial data) that should not be used without permission.

Strong reasons support retaining the traditional premise. These include the simple question of costs, which are imposed on all transactions by a different default rule or by a regulatory data control regime, even when the individual or both parties are indifferent to data control. The track record is that, when faced with a choice, most individuals accept the status quo.

The reasons also relate to core assumptions about how our economy is organized. It emphasizes the right to use and disseminate information, even if the result is uncomfortable to others. That is a consequence of the First Amendment. But even beyond the First Amendment, this theme carries weight. Furthermore, for most transactional data both parties often have equal claims to having created the information itself. The image that data held by a party to a transaction are "personal" to the other misstates the context.

Even in strong data control laws, the approach has not been to cloak all information with presumptive control rights in one party.[43] Different types of data for different types of uses present very different balances. Privacy preferences differ. Markets are better able to adapt to diversity than are statutes or regulations.

For the control advocate, the traditional rule is unsatisfying—it does not respond to "the problem," does not "protect" *rights*, and does not *regulate* "fair practices."[44] Ultimately, the control advocate suspects that the result will be that no limits on use will emerge through market transactions. But that is not supported by the facts. As seen above, there has been a sea change in the extent to which companies offer privacy policies. These policies make commitments that go beyond current law, even though they stop short of what rules data control advocates desire.

This is a market response. But what about the greater sensitivity of some people about some uses of some data? Mass markets react more to aggregate desires than to individual interests. If one person in a million desires a result, that person is unlikely to achieve it through market reactions or bargaining in a mass market. Yet the same problem exists in the reverse in a regulated response, in which the question would be, Why set an intrusive rule for all parties in all transactions based on demands of a small number? There are situations in which a minority should be protected, but data control is not one, except for narrow issues. In many cases for most data, neither party is concerned about the other's use of transactional data. The traditional rule of no data control is efficient because it does not impose compliance costs or require dealing with an issue about which neither party is concerned; it is also the least intrusive because it allows information to be freely available.

To be clear about one point: the argument is not that control advocates should not worry because companies will act in the individual's best interest. They will not always do so. The argument is that markets ordinarily work and that freedom of choice works.

G. Exception: Harmful Information Not Generally Used

There are situations in which the default rule should shift and give control to the individual. But the best approach is to be highly selective. Neither all personal data nor all uses of personal data are equal. In contract law, a selective approach can be implemented by a default rule giving presumptive control to the individual for *some types* of information and, in even more narrow cases, requiring contrary agreement under disclosure standards that protect the individual.

The question is, When should that occur? The answer: it should occur only when (1) the risk of harm or misuse clearly and conclusively outweighs costs of control and the general interests in enforcing contracts and enabling free dissemination and use of information and (2) markets will not predictably account for such risk.

Outside traditionally confidential relationships, this will typically involve a combination of four conditions:

1. The data are delivered by one party to another (rather than created in a transaction).
2. The data are of a type that, as viewed by a reasonable person, the disclosure or use would proximately threaten physical, monetary, or significant emotional harm.
3. The disclosure or use is of a type that is not normally expected.
4. The disclosure or use does not further other socially desirable purposes, such as prevention of fraud, free speech, or the like.

The first condition identifies the only context in which one can argue that the one party (data subject) has a claim to ownership of the data because the information is not jointly created but conveyed from one person to the other. The receiving party's interest is defined solely by the voluntary conveyance to it. Information brought to the transaction by one party presents a context in which to ask what reasonable expectations a person had in delivering the data. Even here, however, not all information or uses of information are the same, and in most cases no reasonable expectation of confidentiality exists.

The second condition sets risk of significant harm as a criterion. If parties are dealing with innocuous information, reasons for restrictive rules are weak, and it is most likely that neither party reasonably expects nondisclosure or nonuse. Indeed, when no proximate risk of harm exists, there is no basis to impose restraints. The formulation here recognizes that the harm might involve substantial emotional harm, as in traditional privacy law, as well as significant risk of financial or physical harm. On the latter issues, the question is not whether the use or disclosure actually causes the harm, but whether the disclosure will proximately contribute to the risk of such harm. In many cases, information will be known or easily findable without a disclosure by the transaction recipient. In such cases, merely being one potential source should not change the basic presumption about a right to use information.[45]

The third recognizes a trade practice or expectation element. A decade ago, social security numbers were used in numerous ways that today would be regarded as high risk. At some level, practices associated with a particular type of information place its disclosure or use in a particular way outside the ordinary. When that occurs, contract law properly should assume a treatment consistent with ordinary practice unless the parties agree otherwise.

The fourth recognizes that data control engages a balancing of general social interests and that this balance will often weigh in favor of preserving contractual choice and free-flowing information. The contrary result favoring imposed or presumptive controls should be undertaken only in clear cases in the absence of contract terms providing otherwise.

Let's take the case of a person's social security number as an illustration. For many years, social security numbers were widely used identifiers. More recently, fear of identity theft, stalking, and misuse has begun to lend an aura of sensitivity and risk to disclosure of these numbers.[46] How should law treat the obligations of a person who receives the social security number of the other person as part of a transaction? Under the approach outlined earlier, use in a manner that is consistent with ordinary usage of such numbers would not be regulated or subject to a default rule of data control. On the other hand, public disclosure might be a breach because it entails nonordinary use that exposes the data subject to a risk of harm through identity theft. If the recipient of the number desires to use it in this manner, it must obtain assent.

Results such as these can be achieved under contract law over time without a legislative or regulatory mandate.

IV. CONCLUSION

The view presented here cuts against a control activist's approach to using law to force results that the activist desires, but it is a view that recognizes the traditions and current character of the law in this country as to transactions voluntarily undertaken. Although imposed data control may work some benefits, it inevitably incurs palpable costs and significant detriments if imposed across commerce. The costs are not justified.

In any event, markets and businesses are responding to concerns about data control. The best approach is to allow markets to continue to redefine and adjust relationships, reserving intervention of law to those narrow cases in which serious risks exist.

NOTES

1. Thomas M. Cooley, *The Law of Torts* 29 (2d ed. 1888).
2. *See* Raymond T. Nimmer, *The Law of Computer Technology* ch. 16 (1997, 2006).
3. Alan Westin, *Privacy and Freedom* 7 (1967).
4. Jerry Kang, Information Privacy in Cyberspace Transactions, 50 *Stan. L. Rev.* 1193, 1202 (1998).
5. Privacy tort claims based on data control theories typically fail. *See Dwyer v. American Express*, 273 Ill. App. 3d 742, 652 N.E. 2d 1351 (1995).
6. European Union Directive on the Protection of Individuals with Respect to the Processing of Personal Data and on the Free Movement of Such Data, 12004/4/94 COR 3 (en) art. 2(b) (July 20, 1995) (Brussels) (hereinafter Data Protection Directive).
7. *See* Richard S. Murphy, Property Rights in Personal Information: An Economic Defense of Privacy, 84 *Geo. L. J.* 2381 (1996) ("Such information, like all information, is property. The question the law must answer is: Who owns the property rights to such information—the individual involved, the person who obtains the information, or some combination?"); Kang, *supra* note 4 at 1246: "[P]rivacy enthusiasts insist that the individual self-evidently owns her personal information."
8. Murphy, *supra* note 7, at 2381.

9. *See* Data Protection Directive, art. 1 ("Member States shall protect the fundamental rights and freedoms of natural persons, and in particular their right to privacy, with respect to the processing of personal data.").

10. All of this data would be "personal data" if both parties are individuals. In addition, there might be incidental data, *e.g.*, what color shirt A was wearing, whether B arrived with any other party. The Data Protection Directive covers all of this: "'personal data' shall mean any information relating to an identified or identifiable natural person." Data Protection Directive art. 2(a).

11. *See Dwyer v. American Express*, 273 Ill. App. 3d 742, 652 N.E. 2d 1351 (1995).

12. *See* Joel Reidenberg, Setting Standards for Fair Information Practice in the U.S. Private Sector, 80 *Iowa L. Rev.* 497 (1994).

13. *See Cohen v. Cowles Media Co.*, 501 U.S. 663, 111 S. Ct. 2513, 115 L. Ed. 2d 586 (1991) (claims based on estoppel not precluded by First Amendment).

14. *See Universal City Studios, Inc. v. Corley*, 273 F. 3d 429 (2d Cir. 2001) (intermediate scrutiny permits enforcement of strong state interest that does not affect substantially more speech than necessary for the governmental objective).

15. *Compare* Kang, *supra* note 4 with Lee Kovarsky, Tolls on the Information Superhighway: Entitlement Defaults for Clickstream Data, 89 *Va. L. Rev.* 1037 (2003).

16. Data Protection Directive art. 3.

17. *See* Kang, *supra* note 4 at 1193, n. 64; Charles Fried, Privacy, 77 *Yale L. J.* 475, 482 (1968).

18. *See* Data Protection Directive art. 6(d).

19. *See Remsburg v. Docusearch, Inc.*, 816 A. 2d 1001 (N.H. 2003) (stalking); *In re Crawford*, 194 F. 3d 954, 958 (9th Cir.1999) ("In an era of rampant identity theft, concern regarding the dissemination of SSNs [social security numbers] is no longer reserved for libertarians inveighing against the specter of national identity cards.").

20. *See* Murphy, *supra* note 7 at 2381: "An activity that may generate embarrassment or reprobation from some sectors of society will not occur if the activity carries with it a significant risk of being disclosed."

21. *See* Murphy, *supra* note 7 at 2381:"When the only interest is in reputation, it is usually inefficient to limit disclosure of true information."

22. *See, e.g.*, Richard A. Posner, The Right of Privacy, 12 *Ga. L. Rev.* 393 (1978).

23. *See* IBM & Ponemon Institute, *The Costs of Privacy Study* (2004) ("[For] 44 large U.S.-based organizations . . . spending ranges from less than $500k to over $22 million dollars [annually]."). *Compare* AEI/Brookings, *The Value of Online Information Privacy: An Empirical Investigation* (Oct. 2003) (average value individuals place on privacy as between $30.49 and $44.62).

24. *See* Murphy, *supra* note 7.

25. Posner, *supra* note 22.

26. *See Bodil Lindqvist v. Åklagarkammaren i Jönköping*, No. C-101/01, Judgment of the Court dated Nov. 6, 2003, at Numbers 13 and 14, Court of Justice of the European Communities, available at http://curia.eu.int/jurisp/cgi-bin/form.pl?lang=en.

27. *See* Raymond T. Nimmer, Breaking Barriers: The Relationship Between Contract and Intellectual Property Law, 13 *Berkeley Tech. L. J.* 827 (1998); Charles J. Goetz & Robert E. Scott,

The Limits of Expanded Choice: An Analysis of the Interaction Between Express and Implied Contract Terms, 73 *Cal. L. Rev.* 261, 266 (1985).

28. *See* R. H. Coase, The Problem of Social Cost, 3 *J. L. & Econ.* 1, 6-8 (1960) (in the absence of transaction costs, rational players transact in a manner that produces a long-run equilibrium that maximizes value).

29. The actual value of data control to *individuals* may be far less. *See* AEI / Brookings, *supra* note 23 (average value as between $30.49 and $44.62).

30. *See* Stan Davis, *Future Perfect* (1996). *See also* Online Privacy Alliance, *Privacy and the Top One Hundred Websites: Report to the Federal Trade Commission* (June 1999) ("[83 percent] of the Top 100 Websites . . . offered at least one form of choice [on data privacy].").

31. *See* Online Privacy Alliance, *supra* note 30: "93% (93 sites) of the Top 100 Websites have posted at least one type of privacy disclosure (a privacy policy notice or an information practice statement). 59% of the Websites posted both types of disclosures."

32. *See* Gary R. Gordon & Norman A. Willox, *Identity Fraud: A Critical National and Global Threat* 38 (Economic Crime Institute of Utica College & LexisNexis Co., 2003).

33. *See* Alan Westin, Testimony before U.S. House of Representatives, Committee on Energy and Commerce, Subcommittee on Commerce, Trade, and Consumer Protection, Hearing on "Opinion Surveys: What Consumers Have to Say About Information Privacy" (May 8, 2001); AEI / Brookings, *supra* note 23.

34. UCITA § 102(a)(4) (2000 Official Text); UCC § 1-201(a) (1998 Official text) (same).

35. UCITA § 102(a)(4) (2002 Official Text); UCC § 1-201(a)(1) (1998 Official Text).

36. *See Dwyer v. American Express*, 273 Ill. App. 3d 742, 652 N.E. 2d 1351 (1995).

37. *See* Alan Schwartz & Robert E. Scott, Contract Theory and the Limits of Contract Law, 113 *Yale L. J.* 541 (2003).

38. *See* Charles J. Goetz & Robert E. Scott, Enforcing Promises: An Examination of the Basis of Contract, 89 *Yale L. J.* 1261 (1980).

39. *See* Ian Ayres & Robert Gertner, Filling Gaps in Incomplete Contracts: An Economic Theory of Default Rules, 99 *Yale L. J.* 87 (1989).

40. *See* Raymond T. Nimmer, Images and Contract Law-What Law Applies to Transactions in Information, 36 *Houston L. Rev.* 1 (1999); Ian Ayres & Robert Gertner, Strategic Contractual Inefficiency and the Optimal Choice of Legal Rules, 101 *Yale L. J.* 729 (1992).

41. *See* Kang, *supra* note 4 at 1193.

42. *See* Raymond T. Nimmer, *The Law of Computer Technology* § 16:10 (1997); Richard S. Murphy, *supra* note 7 at 2381, 2408.

43. *See, e.g.*, Data Protection Directive art. Art. 7(a) ("data subject has given his consent unambiguously").

44. *See* Reidenberg, *supra* note 12.

45. *Commonwealth v. Duncan*, 817 A. 2d 455 (Pa. 2003) ("[It] is all but impossible to live in our current society without repeated disclosure of one's name and address. . . . There is nothing nefarious in such disclosures.").

46. *See Remsburg v. Docusearch, Inc.*, 816 A. 2d 1001 (N.H. 2003) (issue of whether disclosure is embarrassing); *Bodah v. Lakeville Motors Express, Inc.*, 663 N.W. 2d 550 (Minn. 2003) (yet no privacy tort).

16 THREE ECONOMIC ARGUMENTS FOR CYBERINSURANCE

Jay P. Kesan, Ruperto P. Majuca, and William J. Yurcik

Jay P. Kesan and William J. Yurcik are faculty at the University of Illinois at Urbana-Champaign in the College of Law and the National Center for Super-computing Applications, respectively. Ruperto P. Majuca is faculty at the Weber State University Department of Economics. They can be emailed at kesan@uiuc. edu, rupertomajuca@weber.edu, and byurcik@ncsa.uiuc.edu, respectively. The authors thank Lauren Gelman, Anupam Chander, and Peggy Radin for organizing a terrific symposium that featured many insightful presentations. They also thank Lauren Gelman and Anupam Chander for insightful comments, and Carl Nelson for helpful discussions on the measurement of cyberinsurance welfare gains. Last, they thank the other participants in the symposium for their helpful comments and suggestions.

The Internet has radically changed the way business is carried out and it increasingly dominates our professional and personal lives.[1] Yet software vulnerabilities are extraordinarily pervasive. They expose Internet businesses to both risks[2] and liability[3] for property damage, business interruption, defamation, invasion of privacy, theft of credit card numbers, malpractice, and consumer fraud. The increase in the availability of hacker tools has made it easier for criminals to exploit these vulnerabilities.[4] Already, high-profile firms such as Microsoft, Amazon.com, eBay, Yahoo, and CNN.com have suffered denial-of-service (DOS) attacks, rendering these firms unreachable for significant periods of time.[5] Also, hackers have interfered with the Websites of several government agencies.[6] And not only intrusions but even internal attacks can be a problem, as employees can illegally obtain credit card data or the firm's proprietary design.[7] *InformationWeek* estimated overall that computer viruses and hacking caused damages of $266 billion in the United States and $1.6 trillion worldwide in 1999.[8]

Privacy issues also account for many of the disputes occurring as a result of the Internet.[9] This is because even though organizations and businesses that manage personal information on the Internet have a duty of confidentiality,[10] few of these organizations and businesses have security sufficient to protect personal information such as credit card and social security numbers.[11] Nevertheless, privacy law suggests that courts will hold firms liable for harm to individuals.[12] Specific claims of liability may arise from (1) a tort based on privacy violations, (2) a breach of an implied contractual duty, (3) a violation of regulations intended to safeguard privacy, or (4) federal legislation intended to safeguard personal data online.[13] As a result, an increased regulation of Internet privacy will almost certainly arise out of the growing concern over the security of online data.[14]

We examined several possible solutions to Internet security and privacy problems that ranged from technological solutions to a wide array of legal-based approaches (regulation,[15] penal legislation,[16] tort liability,[17] contract law,[18] quasi-contracts,[19] and fiduciary trust law). Each of these solutions relied primarily on nonmarket remedies.

In this work, we generated a market-based solution for improving Internet security. We specifically examined cyberinsurance. In Section I, we examine how cyberinsurance can result in better IT safety. In Section II, we discuss how cyberinsurance can facilitate standards for liability to be set at socially optimal levels. In Section III, we show that cyberinsurance increases social welfare. Finally, in Section IV, we conclude our discussion.

I. ECONOMIC ARGUMENT 1:
CYBERINSURANCE INCREASES IT SAFETY

In a separate paper,[20] we argued that traditional insurance policies, which are designed to cover traditional perils of fires, floods, and other forces of nature, are inadequate to cover damages to cyberproperties, which do not have physical form. The inability of traditional insurance to deal with the new cyberthreats underscores the need for new insurance products specifically designed to cover the Internet. In the next three sections, we present three primary economic arguments for creating cyberinsurance, because it will result in greater IT security, facilitate the adoption of settings that will optimize security, and solve the current market failure.

Suppose that a firm has an income in good state (I_1^e), and there is a probability p that it will lose $L^e = I_1^e - I_0^e$ (where I_0^e is the income in bad state) in the event of a cyberattack. E-commerce losses may be (1) direct losses from the attack or intrusion, (2) business interruption (loss of productive time) and reputation losses, or (3) third-party liability (suits for damages associated with privacy, defamation, and so on). All of these potential losses are risks for which the firm would like coverage.[21] In the good state (occurring with probability 1 – p), the firm has utility, $U(I_1^e - \gamma s)$, associated with its income in the good state minus the expenditure on insurance. In the bad state (which occurs with probability p), the firm has utility associated with its income in the good state minus the loss and the expenditure for insurance plus the amount the insurer will pay the insured in the event of a loss: $U(I_1^e - L^e - \gamma s + s)$.[22]

As illustrated in Figure 16.1, by purchasing insurance coverage of amount s, a firm moves from E to F. A firm spends γs on insurance premiums so that in the event a loss occurs, the insurer will pay out s. The firm gains from purchasing cyberinsurance because the firm moves from point E to point F, thereby moving to a higher indifference curve. The firm moves from point E (no insurance) to either point F (full insurance), if $\gamma = p$ (premiums are actuarially fair),[23] or point P (partial insurance), if $\gamma > p$ (insurance prices are higher).

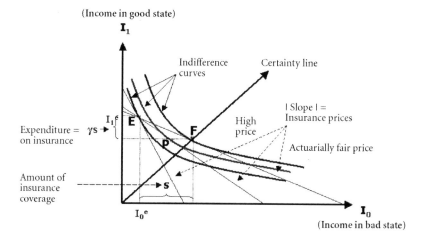

Figure 16.1. Expenditure on cyberinsurance and amount of coverage

Firms use different methods to protect themselves against damages. These methods include outsourced insurance (cyberinsurance), self-insurance, and self-protection. Both self-insurance and cyberinsurance protect firms against loss or redistribution of income from "good state" to "bad state," that is, they are both designed to reduce the *size* of the loss.

Cyberinsurance differs from self-insurance in that a firm purchases cyberinsurance from a third party while self-insurance is an internal investment reserved for use only in the event of a loss.

In contrast to both cyberinsurance and self-insurance, self-protection attempts to reduce the probability of losses occurring in the first place. Self-protection, also called loss prevention, is analogous to a burglar alarm that reduces the probability of someone breaking into a house. In cybersecurity, self-protection may manifest in any of the following forms: authentication processes, antivirus software, firewalls, virtual private networks, intrusion detection systems, vulnerability scans, and official security policies explicitly stating unacceptable behaviors.

Self-insurance, also called loss protection, is analogous to a sprinkler system that minimizes damage to a burning house. In cybersecurity, self-insurance may manifest in any of the following forms: IT staffs who restore data and normal functions, software backup strategies, disaster recovery planning, and any investment or purchase of equipment or services that reduce the potential loss.

Our intention is to show that (1) cyberinsurance and self-protection are "complements" (cyberinsurance increases self-protection),[24] (2) cyberinsurance and self-insurance are "substitutes" (an increase in expenditures on one would decrease the amount spent on the other); and (3) self-insurance decreases self-protection (the "moral hazard problem").[25] An implication of our analysis is that cyberinsurance does not lead to less self-protection, that is, that it does not create a moral hazard.

Cyberinsurance results in higher investment in security, increasing the level of safety for IT infrastructure. Accordingly, new insurance products may make the Internet a safer business environment because cyberinsurers can require businesses to minimize losses using economic incentives.[26] Cyberinsurers are able to base a firm's insurance premium on the insured firm's investment in security processes, thereby creating market-based incentives for e-businesses to increase information security.[27]

In contrast to the moral hazard argument that insurance will result in a reduction of self-protection, investment in IT security occurs at a higher rate in firms that have cyberinsurance than in those firms that don't have cyberinsurance.[28] Because cyberinsurance and loss prevention activities are complements,[29] insurers can insist that software companies deliver safe products and exert pressure on software engineering firms to improve IT security in order to decrease exposure to various claims. In addition, insurance companies have an incentive to monitor hackers in order to minimize the amount of damage the companies would have to pay out to its insured firms. In summary, private enforcement by insurance companies would supplement enforcement efforts of both firms and law enforcement.

As shown in Figure 16.2, a firm has a choice between self-insurance (associated with the bowed-out transformation curve) and cyberinsurance (associated with the straight lines representing the insurance prices). The transformation curve is bowed-out because the "law of diminishing marginal returns" applies to investment in self-insurance products; each additional dollar of good-state income invested on self-insurance is less productive than the previous dollar invested.

Starting at point E, a firm facing an actuarially fair price would move from E toward S_1 (via self-insurance) or from S_1 to point F (via cyberinsurance).

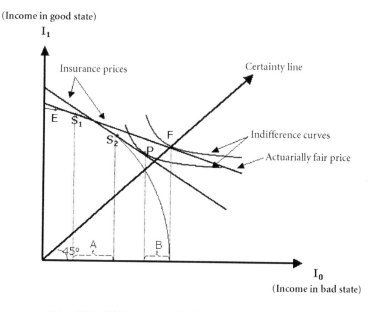

Figure 16.2. Self-insurance and cyberinsurance as substitutes
SOURCE: Adapted from Ehrlich & Becker, *supra* note 24, at 635.

If, however, insurance prices increase, as represented by a steeper price line, the firm would instead have self-insurance up to point S_2 and cyberinsurance up to point P. Thus, as a result of the increase in the insurance prices, the amount of self-insurance increases by the horizontal distance between S_1 and S_2 (represented by A), and the amount of cyberinsurance would decrease by the horizontal distance between points F and P (represented by B).[30] This demonstrates that self-insurance and cyberinsurance are substitutes.

Self-insurance, unlike cyberinsurance, is likely to result in a moral hazard in that self-insurance and self-protection act as substitutes. Generally, if the price of insurance is independent of self-protection expenditures, the reduction in the probability of the hazard would be exactly offset by the increase in the "loading factor" (which measures the deviation from the fair price). The loading factor, in turn, reduces the demand for self-insurance.[31] Because the price of self-insurance is independent of the probability of loss, there would likely be either a large demand for self-insurance and a small demand for self-protection, or the converse.[32]

Cyberinsurers can actually promote self-protection by basing cyberinsurance premiums on the insured's level of self-protection. Figure 16.3 graphically represents these relationships. We conclude that cyberinsurance is better than self-insurance for promoting an increase in Internet security.

Cyberinsurance does not merely benefit firms. In addition, consumers realize increased privacy and safety. Customers of firms who purchase third-party liability cyberinsurance also receive coverage against fraudulent trans-

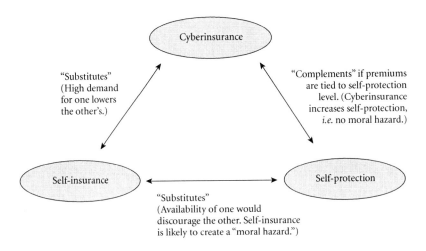

Figure 16.3. Cyberinsurance, self-insurance, and self-protection

actions in cyberspace.[33] By using cyberinsurance, firms benefit consumers in several distinct ways. First, insurers that offer third-party cyberinsurance will pressure firms to fix security problems[34] such as data leaks.[35] Second, even in the absence of legislation expressly holding firms liable for data leaks,[36] competition pressures will cause firms to develop more secure Websites to protect their reputations vis-à-vis other firms.[37] Third, cyberprotections positively affect third-party Websites by not allowing compromised systems to serve as a platform for attacking other systems. In addition to reducing the risks of intrusion into other firms' IT infrastructure, customers' personal information residing in those other firms' databases is safer.[38] In short, not just the insured firm but also other networks and customers derive safety benefits from cyberinsurance.

II. ECONOMIC ARGUMENT 2:
CYBERINSURANCE FACILITATES OPTIMAL LIABILITY

Standard liability laws provide efficient incentives for product safety[39] by functioning as a Pigouvian tax[40] that deters harm or internalizes damages caused by the injurer to the victim.[41] Conversely, a liability tax imposed on suppliers of risky goods may discourage the suppliers from developing new, safer products out of a fear of exposing themselves to liability.[42] Lawmakers, therefore, must correctly answer the question of when liability has become too expansive.[43]

As is true for other goods, there is an optimal amount of security. Figure 16.4[44] shows the socially optimal level of precaution. Thus, if p is the probability of a cyberattack, x the amount of precaution, L the monetary value of the loss from a cyberattack, and w the cost of precaution (per dollar of

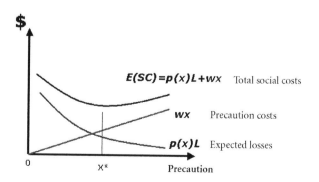

Figure 16.4. Socially optimal precaution level

unit), the expected social cost equals the costs of precaution plus the expected cyberloss:[45] $SC = wx + p(x)L$. The line $p(x)L$ is downward-sloping because increased precaution decreases expected losses. Extra precaution, however, also increases costs (that is why the line wx is upward-sloping). The socially optimal level, x^* in Figure 16.4 (where the total social cost costs are at minimum), is achieved by striking a balance between the gain from the additional investment in security and the cost associated with extra security:[46]

$$w = -p'(x^*)L$$

(marginal social cost) = (marginal social benefit)

The government can encourage firms to implement a socially optimal level of precaution using three distinct liability regimes (1) no liability,[47] (2) strict liability, and (3) negligence rule.[48] In general, if the potential victim, but not the injurer, can take precaution, then the no liability regime is optimal.[49]

If, on the other hand, the injurer, but not the victim, can take precaution, strict liability with perfect compensation results in efficient precaution when the injurer internalizes the marginal gains and costs of precaution.[50] However, when both the injurer and the victim can take precaution, neither the no liability nor the strict liability standard can cure the problem of inefficient incentives. In this case, a negligence rule in which the legal standard is equal to the efficient level of care results in efficient precaution.

In the case of a simple negligence rule (illustrated in Figure 16.5), the optimal level of precaution is x^*. Society can set the rule that the injurer is at fault whenever x_i falls below x^*. This is the forbidden zone in Figure 16.5 in which precaution by the potential injurer is deficient. Hence, whenever $x_i < x^*$, the injurer is liable. Otherwise, if x_i is equal to or greater than x^*, the injurer is not at fault, and therefore not liable.[51]

Because both the potential injurer and the victim can take precautions to strengthen cybersecurity, a negligence rule with a legal standard equal to the efficient level of care results in efficient precaution.[52] In theory, the liability system results in efficient precaution if x^* is set at just the right amount. Also, because the cost of bringing a liability suit is high,[53] liability rules do not work for many injuries in which losses are smaller than the costs of bringing an action.[54] Litigation costs may be especially high for cybersecurity because the question of whether a victim of a computer intrusion can be held liable for subsequent damage initiated from his or her system is an unsettled issue.[55] Another danger is that the expansion of liability can coincide with increased regulatory standards, particularly when liability and regulatory rules are not

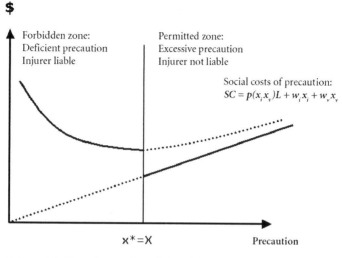

Figure 16.5. Simple negligence liability rule
SOURCE: Adapted from Cooter & Ulen, *supra* note 44, at 327.

coordinated.[56] There are also problems associated with a regulatory regime, not the least of which is the information requirement necessary to quantify the risks in order to set the regulatory standard at the proper level.

Lawmakers do not feel market pressures for precise risk categorization and therefore are not always exact in their appraisal of long-term latent risks.[57] This causes a problem in that if regulation overshoots the estimate, that is, sets a standard higher than the socially optimal level, innovation can suffer. If, on the other hand, lawmakers set the standard too low, injurers responsible for accidents and product defects will not recognize a sufficient deterrence. Furthermore, regulatory agencies may be susceptible to lobbying by powerful interest groups opposed to stricter standards.[58]

The administrative costs of updating regulations are far higher than the costs of adjusting premium rates.[59] This is where market-based deterrence can offer definite advantages. Because insurers pool information and are experts at assigning proper prices to risk and developing safety standards, they are thus better than regulators at determining an optimal level of insurance.[60] Also, because precise risk categorization requires a predictable relationship between safety practices and liability, it is best for insurers to use their superior information to create a level of reasonable care that causes firms to set loss prevention measures to efficient levels.[61] One way of accomplishing this is by cyberinsurers requiring insured firms to set their loss prevention activities equal to the level that will bring about the socially optimal level of care.[62] In sum, because of the high transaction costs associated with the liability system, as well as the problems associated with a regulatory regime,[63] market-based incentives such as cyberinsurance are a better alternative than either a liability regime or regulatory system at deterring harm and setting IT security at the socially efficient level.

III. ECONOMIC ARGUMENT 3:
CYBERINSURANCE INCREASES SOCIAL WELFARE

The current level of uncertainty associated with traditional insurance policies results in an underinvestment in insurance, thereby causing an insufficient amount of profit-smoothing by firms and an inefficient level of risk-sharing throughout society. Similarly, the absence of markets for bearing of new Internet risks lowers the welfare of those who find it advantageous to transfer those risks, as well as those who, because of pooling and superior expertise, are willing to assume such risks.[64] In short, a market failure exists because of the absence of markets.[65] By creating markets for the trading of Internet risks, this shortcoming is overcome and the market solution is allowed to work, resulting in greater societal welfare.

The amount of welfare society gains from cyberinsurance is a measurable amount. This value can be calculated in dollars for varying levels of risk aversion and the probability of a cyberattack occurring. The market value of income, which, in Figure 16.6 (Section III[A]), is the y-intercept of the "budget line" tangent to the indifference curve, can be used as a measure of welfare. Thus, by comparing the market value of income in the first-best case with full cyberinsurance to the situation when there is no cyberinsurance, we are able to provide dollar estimates of society's welfare gains from cyberinsurance.[66]

In the next section, we develop a general methodology for calculating welfare gains from cyberinsurance and perform calculations for specific examples.

A. General Methodology for Measuring Welfare Gains from Cyberinsurance

Figure 16.6 illustrates that the firm starts at point E (without cyberinsurance), which is associated with the lower indifference curve. If there is a cyberinsurance market, the firm can go to point F by buying insurance at the price γ per

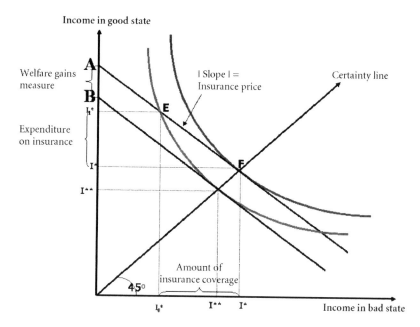

Figure 16.6. Measuring welfare gains

dollar of coverage. In Figure 16.6, the firms pay the insurer $I^e_1 - I^*$, and if the attack occurs, the cyberinsurer pays the insured firms $I^* - I^e_0$. By entering into this trade, the firm is able to attain a higher indifference curve by fully insuring. The measurement of the change in welfare is the line $\overline{AB}$ (the difference between the y-axis intercepts of the "budget lines" tangent to those level curves).[67]

The following steps indicate how to measure welfare gains $\overline{AB}$:

Step 1: Get data on income in good (I^e_0) and bad (I^e_1) states.

Step 2: Get data on p (the probability of an attack) and γ (premium per dollar of cover), and calculate A. Here, we assume actuarially fair premiums.

Step 3: Assume a particular parametric form of the utility function, and then calculate $\overline{U}$ (the expected utility of the lower indifference curve). Assume a constant relative risk aversion among firms. (We will calculate the gains for varying levels of risk-aversion coefficient.)

Step 4: Calculate I^{**}.

Step 5: Calculate B and subtract from A. This is our measure of welfare gains (the distance of line $\overline{AB}$).

B. An Example: Calculating Welfare Gains for Year 2000 DOS Attacks

Step 1:   Gross Profit (2000) From Yahoo!Finance

Yahoo	$951,759,000
eBay	$335,971,000
Amazon	$655,777,000
Total	$1,943,507,000 <= we use this figure as I_0^e.

From The Yankee Group: The companies' lost revenues, the lost market capitalization due to plunging stock prices, and the cost of systems security upgrades due to the DOS attack resulted in more than $1.2 billion.[68] This means that I_1^e = $3.143 billion ($I_0^e$ + the $1.2 billion damages).

Step 2: Because industry reports indicate that cyberinsurers charge premiums that range from $5,000 to $60,000 per $1 million of coverage (depending on the extent of the risk and the assets and protection extended),[69] we calculated for p = γ = 0.005, 0.01, 0.02, 0.03, 0.04, 0.05, and 0.06. As an example, in the case where p = γ = .06, I_1^e = A − 0.06 I_0^e => $3.1435 billion = A − 0.06*$1.9435 billion => A = $3.26012 billion.

Step 3: As mentioned, it is common in the asset-pricing and macroeconomics literatures to assume a constant relative risk aversion (CRRA) utility function:[70]

$$u(I) = \begin{cases} \dfrac{I^{1-\sigma}}{1-\sigma} & for\ (\sigma > 0, \sigma \neq 1) \\ \log(I) & for\ (\sigma = 1) \end{cases}$$

This suggests that the firm's willingness to take risks (in *percentage* terms) is constant for all income levels. In other words, the firm doesn't become relatively more or less risk-averse across different levels of income.

The firm's willingness to assume risk is determined by the curvature of the utility function, $\sigma = -\dfrac{u''(I)}{u'(I)} I$, the Arrow-Pratt[71] coefficient of (relative) risk-aversion. Higher σ's correspond to a higher aversion to risk.[72] Literature suggests that reasonable levels of risk-aversion are such that σ is between 1 and 3. We therefore calculate the welfare gains (and the premiums) for varying levels of risk aversion within the range such that σ = 1, 1.5, 2, 2.5, 3.

As an example, for σ = 2 and p = γ = .06, we calculate

$$\overline{U} = .06\frac{1.9435^{(1-2)}}{1-2} + (1-.06)\frac{3.1435^{(1-2)}}{1-2} = -0.33 .$$

Step 4: For our example ($\sigma = 2$ and $p = \gamma = 0.06$), we have

$$\overline{U} = .06 \frac{I^{**\,(1-2)}}{1-2} + (1-.06)\frac{I^{**\,(1-2)}}{1-2} = -0.33 \quad \Rightarrow \quad I^{**\,-1} = -\overline{U}$$

$$\Rightarrow \quad I^{**} = -\frac{1}{\overline{U}} = \$3.0312 \; billion.$$

Step 5: For the same example ($\sigma = 2$ and $p = \gamma = .06$), we have $I^{**} = B - 0.06 * I^{**}$

B = 1.06 (I**) = 1.06 * \$3.0312 *billion* = \$3.2131 *billion*
Welfare gains = A − B = \$47,040,870.76.

We performed the same calculations for $\sigma = 1$, 1.5, 2, 2.5, 3, and $p = \gamma = 0.005, 0.01, 0.02, 0.03, 0.04, 0.05, 0.06$ with the results presented in Tables 16.1 and 16.2 (Section III[C]). We calculated the welfare gains for both (1) DOS attacks against Yahoo, eBay, and Amazon.com, and (2) worldwide virus and hacking attacks. As Tables 16.1 and 16.2 show, the welfare gains from the presence of a cyberinsurance market can be quite substantial. For instance, assuming constant relative risk-aversion and actuarially fair prices, we calculated that in the case of the DOS attacks against Yahoo, eBay, and Amazon, the availability of cyberinsurance would have resulted in welfare gains to the insured firms of as much as \$78.7 million for a firm with a high degree of risk aversion ($\sigma = 3$) facing a high probability of an attack ($p = \gamma = 0.06$). Overall, we calculate that if cyberinsurance were available, the welfare gains associated with insuring worldwide security breaches and virus attacks in 2000 could have approached \$13.16 billion.[73]

C. Calculating Cyberinsurance Premiums

We also calculated the total premium that the insured would be willing to pay for varying levels of risk-aversion and attack probabilities. Following Cochrane (1997),[74] the premiums may be calculated as follows:

$$(I_m - \Pi)^{(1-\sigma)} = p \cdot I_0^{e\,(1-\sigma)} + (1-p)\cdot I_1^{e\,(1-\sigma)}$$

where Π is the total amount of premium paid and $I_m = p \cdot I_0^e + (1-p)\cdot I_1^e$. Solving for Π, we have:

$$\Pi = I_m - \left[p \cdot I_0^{e\,(1-\sigma)} + (1-p)\cdot (I_1^{e\,(1-\sigma)}) \right]^{\frac{1}{1-\sigma}}.$$

As with the welfare gains calculations, we calculated the premiums for $\sigma = 1$, 1.5, 2, 2.5, 3 and $p = \gamma = 0.005, 0.01, 0.02, 0.03, 0.04, 0.05, 0.06$. Tables 16.1 and 16.2 present our results.

Table 16.1.   Premiums and welfare gains: Year 2000 DOS attacks (in $Mn)

Risk-Aversion Parameter σ =	1	1.5	2	2.5	3
Premiums					
p = γ = 0.005	$1.55	$2.54	$3.67	$5.03	$6.62
0.01	$3.08	$5.02	$7.29	$9.96	$13.10
0.02	$6.09	$9.90	$14.34	$19.54	$25.60
0.03	$9.03	$14.64	$21.17	$28.75	$37.54
0.04	$11.90	$19.25	$27.76	$37.60	$48.93
0.05	$14.69	$23.72	$34.14	$46.10	$59.79
0.06	$17.42	$28.07	$40.30	$54.26	$70.15
Welfare Gains					
p = γ = 0.005	$1.59	$2.57	$3.73	$5.09	$6.69
0.01	$3.23	$5.19	$7.49	$10.18	$13.35
0.02	$6.69	$10.58	$15.12	$20.41	$26.60
0.03	$10.37	$16.17	$22.89	$30.70	$39.75
0.04	$14.28	$21.95	$30.80	$41.03	$52.81
0.05	$18.41	$27.92	$38.85	$51.41	$65.79
0.06	$22.76	$34.08	$47.04	$61.84	$78.69

Table 16.2.   Worldwide cyberinsurance premiums and welfare gains (in $Bn)

Risk-Aversion Parameter σ =	1	1.5	2	2.5	3
Premiums					
p = γ = 0.005	$0.20	$0.30	$0.41	$0.51	$0.62
0.01	$0.40	$0.60	$0.81	$1.02	$1.23
0.02	$0.79	$1.19	$1.60	$2.01	$2.43
0.03	$1.17	$1.76	$2.37	$2.98	$3.61
0.04	$1.54	$2.33	$3.12	$3.94	$4.76
0.05	$1.90	$2.88	$3.86	$4.86	$5.88
0.06	$2.26	$3.41	$4.58	$5.77	$6.98
Welfare Gains					
p = γ = 0.005	$0.24	$0.34	$0.45	$0.55	$0.66
0.01	$0.56	$0.77	$0.97	$1.19	$1.40
0.02	$1.44	$1.85	$2.27	$2.69	$3.12
0.03	$2.64	$3.26	$3.88	$4.51	$5.16
0.04	$4.16	$4.98	$5.81	$6.65	$7.51
0.05	$6.00	$7.02	$8.06	$9.11	$10.18
0.06	$8.16	$9.38	$10.62	$11.88	$13.16

IV. SUMMARY AND CONCLUSIONS

A case study of the new cyberinsurance market confirms that our predictions are consistent with the emerging cyberinsurance practice.[75] Cyberinsurers developing coverage policies have required applicants to provide top-to-bottom physical and technical analysis of security, networks, and procedures,[76] or to fill in a detailed online questionnaire, consisting of about 250 queries, to assess the applicants' security risks and cyberprotections.[77] A typical cyberinsurer such as American International Group (AIG), Inc., Marsh, or Insuretrust would categorize an applicant firm into one of several risk classifications and tie the premiums to the level of the firm's security, giving discounts to firms that have installed a professional security system.[78] Insurers also utilize monitoring of the firm's security processes,[79] third-party security technology partners, rewards for information leading to the apprehension of hackers,[80] and expense reimbursement for post-intrusion crisis-management activities.[81]

Thus, we conclude that there are theoretical foundations, as well as market-based evidence, to support the view that the creation of new insurance products results in (1) better IT safety infrastructure and increased Internet security; (2) standards based on the optimal amount of care; and (3) overcoming the market's failure, thereby increasing overall societal welfare. These results are consistent with the results we found in our survey of the nascent and immature cyberinsurance market.

NOTES

1. Brian D. Brown, Emerging Insurance Products in the Electronic Age, 31 *Fall Brief* 28 (2001).

2. Ernst & Young reported that 34 percent of the 1,400 organizations surveyed admit of less-than-adequate ability to identify if there are intrusions in their systems, and 33 percent admit of lack of ability to respond. Insurance Information Institute, *Computer Security-Related Insurance Issues* (Sept. 2003), available at http://www.iii.org/media/hottopics/insurance/computer (last visited Apr. 14, 2004).

3. Potential e-litigation may relate to product liability claims (*e.g.*, incorrect configuration or negligent design of hardware and software); computer malpractice suits associated with negligent provision of services; denial-of-service flooding attacks and other security breaches; intellectual property violation; and domain name and meta-tagging controversies. Robert Paul Norman, Virtual Insurance Risks, 31 *Fall Brief* 14, 15 (2001).

4. Nicholas A. Pasciullo, *Insurance and High Technology: CyberInsurance: Consistency in Claims and Coverage Resolution*, available at http://www.whitewms.com/CM/Publications/publications141.asp (last visited Apr. 23, 2004).

5. Nancy Gohring, Cyberinsurance May Cover Damage of Computer Woes, *Seattle Times* (July 29, 2002), available at http://www.landfield.com/isn/mail-archive/2002/Jul/0133.html (last visited Apr. 23, 2004); Timothy A. Vogel, Dealing with Cyber Attacks on Network Security, 48 *Prac. L.* 35, 36 (Apr. 2002).

6. *Id.*

7. Daintry Duffy, Prepare for the Worst, *Darwin Mag.* (Dec. 2000), available at http://www.darwinmag.com/read/120100/worst.html (last visited Apr. 24, 2004). Employee-related security losses represent 41 percent of total loses.

8. Tim McDonald, Report: Year's Hack Attacks to Cost $1.6 Trillion, *ECommerce Times* (July 11, 2000), available at http://www.ecommercetimes.com/perl/story/3741.html (last visited Apr. 24, 2004); Will Knight, Hacking Will Cost World $1.6 Trillion This Year (July 11, 2000), available at http://news.zdnet.co.uk/internet/security/0,39020375,2080075,00.htm (last visited Apr. 24, 2004). Estimating the damages caused by security breaches is inherently hard; hence, these figures may be subject to debate. The costs associated with security incidents involve not only transitory costs such as lost business, decreased productivity, repair, hacker prosecution, and media-related costs, but also long-term effects such as loss of potential new customers, reduced trust of present customers and business partners, higher insurance costs, and other intangible costs (Huseyin Cavusoglu *et al.*, The Effect of Internet Security Breach Announcements on Market Value: Capital Market Reactions for Breached Firms and Internet Security Developers, 9 *Int'l J. Electronic Com.* 69, 72 (2004), available at http://info.freeman.tulane.edu/huseyin/paper/market.pdf (last visited July 25, 2005). In estimating these figures, InformationWeek and Reality Research and Consulting used company downtime figures of about 50,000 firms they surveyed. They calculated that the 6,822 person-years productivity loss in North American businesses and the 3.3 percent unanticipated downtime in worldwide businesses translated to $1.6 trillion in lost revenue. Aside from surveys, another method used to estimate the cost of security incidents is the event study method (*see infra* note 72 for a description of this method), which is used to measure the impact of security breaches on the firm's market capitalization (for a survey of studies conducting estimates of the cost of security incidents, *see generally* Ashish Garg *et al.*, The Financial Impact of IT Security Breaches: What Do Investors Think, *Info. Sys. Security* (2003), available at http://www.auerbach-publications.com/dynamic_data/2466_1358_cost.pdf [last visited July 25, 2005]). Cavusoglu *et al.*, *supra* this note, used this technique to estimate that attacked firms lost, on average, $1.65 billion (or 2.1 percent) of their market capitalization within two days of the security breach occurrence.

9. Courts recognize four types of privacy invasion (1) intrusion upon a person's solitude or private affairs, (2) revelation of embarrassing private facts, (3) publicity that puts him or her in a false light, and (4) appropriation of his or her name or likeness. Wendy S. Meyer, Notes, Insurance Coverage for Potential Liability Arising from Internet Privacy Issues, 28 *J. Corp. L.* 335, 337-38 (2003) (citing Martic C. Loesch & David M. Brenner, Coverage on the Technology Frontier, Corp. Officers & Directors Liability *Litig. Rep.*, Feb. 17, 1998, at 9; Joel E. Smith, Invasion of Privacy by Sale or Rental of List of Customers, Subscribers, or the Like, to One Who Will Use It for Advertising Purposes, 82 *A.L.R.* 3d 772, 773 (1978)).

10. *Id.* at 335.

11. *See, e.g., Hawking Cyberinsurance* (Mar. 12, 2001), available at http://www.zdnet.com.au/news/business/0,39023166,20208314,00.htm (last visited Apr. 25, 2004) (reporting that during the 2001 World Economic Forum, hackers who espouse the globalization cause had breached databases acquiring the participants' confidential data, including those of Microsoft chairman Bill Gates and former U.S. secretary of state Madeleine Albright, and accessed credit card numbers for 1,400 people.). *See also* Insurance Information Institute, *supra* note 2 (citing a 2002 survey by St. Paul Companies of 501 IT and risk managers at 460 U.S. companies which found that only 55 percent of the respondents said that they have reviewed existing coverages for e-risk coverage).

12. Meyer, *supra* note 9, at 341.

13. *Id.* at 338-41.

14. *Id.*

15. *See* Daniel J. Solove, The New Vulnerability: Data Security and Personal Information, Chapter 6 in this volume.

16. *See* Susan W. Brenner, Should Criminal Liability Be Used to Secure Data Privacy? Chapter 13 in this volume (examining the option of enacting "public welfare"-type legislation to impose criminal sanctions for data privacy violation).

17. *See* Jennifer A. Chandler, Improving Software Security: A Discussion of Liability for Unreasonably Insecure Software, Chapter 8 in this volume.

18. *See* Raymond T. Nimmer, Contracts, Markets, and Data Control, Chapter 15 in this volume.

19. *See* Marcy E. Peek, Beyond Contract: Utilizing Restitution to Reach Shadow Offenders and Safeguard Information Privacy, Chapter 7 in this volume.

20. *See* Ruperto P. Majuca *et al.*, *The Evolution of Cyberinsurance*, ACM Computing Research Repository (CoRR), Technical Report cs.CR/0601020 (2006), available at http://arxiv.org/pdf/cs.CR/0601020.pdf.

21. The insurer will pay the firm s in the event that a cyberloss occurs and the price of insurance is γ per dollar of cover.

22. The firm chooses the insurance coverage, s, such that its expected utility from both the good and bad states is maximized. That is, the firm chooses s to

$$Max\ EU = pU\,(I_1^c - L^c - \gamma s + s) = (1 - p)\ U\,(I_1^c - \gamma s).$$

23. The first-order (optimality) condition equates the slope of the indifference curves and the "budget lines":

$$\frac{p}{1-p}\,\frac{U'(I_1^c - L^c + [1-\gamma]s)}{U'(I_1^c - \gamma s)} = \frac{\gamma}{1-\gamma}\ \cdot\ \gamma = p \Rightarrow\ U'(I_1^c - L^c + [1-\gamma]s) = U'(I_1^c - \gamma s) \Rightarrow L^c = s.$$

That is, the firm will fully insure if the insurance company charges an actuarially fair premium.

24. Self-protection is encouraged if the price of insurance is negatively related to the amount of self-protection. Overall, the optimal amount of self-protection is likely to be larger with cyberinsurance than without cyberinsurance if p is not very small. Isaac Ehrlich & Gary Becker, Market Insurance, Self-Insurance, and Self-Protection, 80 *J. Pol. Econ.* 623 (1972).

25. The term *moral hazard*, also known as the *hidden action* or *principal-agent* problem in economics, concerns actions of a party that may be unobserved by the other parties that could result in negligence by the former. *See* Meyer, *supra* note 9, at 348.

26. Hazel Glenn Beh, Physical Losses in Cyberspace, 8 *Conn. Ins. L. J.* 55, 80-81 (2002). Insurers, too, can pool knowledge about risks, identify systemwide vulnerabilities, demand that the insured undergo prequalification audits, and adopt proactive loss prevention strategies.

27. *See* Jeffrey Kehne, Note, Encouraging Safety Through Insurance-Based Incentives: Financial Responsibility for Hazardous Waste, 96 *Yale L. J.* 43, at nn. 12-14 (1986) (insurance caused increased safety in fire prevention, aviation, boiler, and elevators).

28. *See* Ehrlich & Becker, *supra* note 24.

29. The presence of cyberinsurance increases the amount spent on self-protection as an

economically rational response to the reduction of insurance premium, and thus results in higher levels of IT security in society.

30. Ehrlich & Becker, *supra* note 24, at 636.

31. *Id.* at 642-43.

32. *Id.*

33. This is analogous to the third-party coverage for motor-vehicle accidents, in which the third-party liability coverage of the injurer contributes directly to the security of the potential victim.

34. Right now, there exist specific security regulations requiring firms in the financial and health care sectors to ensure the security and confidentiality of customer data; for other industries not covered by specific regulations or consent decrees, the National Strategy to Secure Cyberspace (www.whitehouse.gov/pcipb) as well as several commentators suggest that there is a general duty to protect the information under their control. *See* Thomas J. Smedinghoff, Defining the Legal Standard for Information Security: What Does "Reasonable" Security Really Mean? Chapter 1 in this volume.

35. Note that consumers' prices will increase because part of the insurance costs will be passed on to them by the insured companies. Exactly how much will be passed on to the consumers and how much will be borne by the firm depend on the elasticities of the supply and the demand curve. Security, in this case, is "internalized," *i.e.*, it is incorporated as part of the product's or service's price.

36. In reality, absent any express legal provision exempting the firm from liability, cyberinsurers have incentives to be cautious and require firms to adopt safety measures because injured customers may resort to privacy common law tort principles. It is in the interest of the insurer to have clearly defined liability obligations and to resolve any ambiguity in favor of precaution.

37. An analogous idea is when local governments compete for consumers who "vote with their feet" in the choice of local community to live in. *See* C. M. Tiebout, A Pure Theory of Local Expenditures, 64 *J. Pol. Econ.* 416 (1956).

38. *See* Jay P. Kesan and Ruperto P. Majuca, Cybercrimes and Cyber-Attacks: Technological, Economic, and Law-Based Solutions, in *Cybercrime and Security* (Pauline C. Reich, ed., 2008). (Compromised computers can be used to launch attacks against other systems, as in the case of distributed DOS attacks.)

39. Another objective of liability laws is to compensate the victim. Carl Shapiro, Symposium on the Economics of Liability, 5 *J. Econ. Perspectives* 3, 5 (1991).

40. Arthur C. Pigou (1877-1959), a British economist who pioneered welfare economics, wrote in his influential work *The Economics of Welfare* (first published in 1920) about the divergence of social and private costs and benefits. To correct for this, he proposed the imposition of a tax on externalities. Thus a Pigouvian tax is one enacted to correct the effects of negative externalities. Ronald Coase in The Problem of Social Cost, *J. L. & Econ.* 1 (1960), proposed instead the definition of proprietary rights to correct the externalities problem when transaction costs are low.

41. When a party is held responsible for injury to another, the externality is internalized. Shapiro, *supra* note 39, at 4.

42. *See* Kip Viscusi, Product and Occupational Liability, 5 *J. Econ. Perspectives* 71 (1991).

43. Shapiro, *supra* note 39, at 5.

44. This graph and subsequent discussions are drawn from Robert Cooter & Thomas Ulen, *Law and Economics*, 320-37 (4th ed., 2004). *See also* Steven Shavell, *Economic Analysis of Accident Law* (1987).

45. The expected cyberloss includes all types of cyberlosses to society including spillover (external) losses, loss of faith in e-commerce, loss of privacy for individuals, and so on.

46. One cost of IT security is its trade-off with convenience. The rule in IT is that security is inversely proportional to convenience. Colleen Brush, *Surcharge for Insecurity*, available at http://www.esmartcorp.com/Hacker%20Articles/ar_surcharge_for_insecurity.htm (last visited Apr. 23, 2004).

47. Section 230 of the Communication Decency Act (CDA) (47 U.S.C. § 230) protects Internet Service Providers (ISPs) from libel claims resulting from defamatory materials posted by subscribers, and the Digital Millenium Copyright Act (DMCA) (17 U.S.C. §512(c) (2003)) shields ISPs from liability associated with hosting any form of material that infringes some copyright. Thus, in *Zeran v. America Online (AOL), Inc.*, 129 F. 3d 327 (4th Cir. 1997), the court held that AOL is not liable for defamatory messages posted by an unidentified third party. But *see Stratton Oakmont, Inc. v. Prodigy Serv. Co.*, N.Y. Sup. Ct. (May 24, 1995).

48. In some sense, both no liability and strict liability are just special cases of the negligence rule: in the latter the due care is set so high that no injurers can meet it, while in the former the due care is set so low that all injurers meet it. *See* Shapiro, *supra* note 39, at 6.

49. Cooter & Ulen, *supra* note 44, at 323-25. The victim chooses the level of precaution that minimizes his or her total costs, which occurs when his or her marginal costs is equal to his or her marginal benefit. If only the victim can take precaution, a strict liability rule with perfect compensation results in zero precaution.

50. *Id.* If the injurer (but not the victim) can take precaution, a *no liability* rule yields zero precaution. *Id.* at 324. A rule of *strict liability* with deficient compensation results in the injurer externalizing part of the harm and does not provide incentives for optimal precaution. *Id.* at 326, n. 9.

For an example of strict liability regime, *see* Comprehensive Environmental Response, Compensation, and Liability Act (CERCLA), 42 U.S.C. §§ 9601-27, 9651-75, 6911a (1988 & Supp. IV 1992); 26 U.S.C. §§ 4611-12, 4661-62 (1988 & Supp. IV 1992) (enacting a retroactive strict liability regime to address concerns pertaining to the formation and disposal of hazardous wastes). Meyer, *supra* note 9, at 344-45.

51. This corresponds to the permitted zone in the figure.

52. *See* Chandler, *supra* note 17 (suggesting the imposition of negligence-based liability against the manufacturer of a software that falls below the standard of security).

53. Shapiro, *supra* note 39, at 5. There is some empirical evidence-for example in the health-care industry-suggesting substantial costs related to enforcement of liability rules: less than 50 percent of money paid for liability insurance actually reached the victims, whereas 80 percent of the premiums are returned to the insured in the form of benefits. *Id.* at 7.

54. Kehne, *supra* note 27, at 410.

55. For instance, in the case in which e-commerce sites are being targeted by hacktortionists, some believe that the real party at fault is the firms that don't patch their systems. *See* Lawrence M. Walsh, *On the Cutting Edge* (Apr. 2001), available at http://infosecuritymag.techtarget.com/articles/april01/departments_news.shtml (last visited Apr. 23, 2004). Some others believe

that the real culprit is Microsoft's software holes that needed patching because the hacktortionist targeted U.S. e-commerce sites using unpatched NT and IIS Web servers. Brush, *supra* note 46.

56. Viscusi, *supra* note 42, at 72.

57. Kehne, *supra* note 27, at 410-11.

58. Id. at 411 and n. 29, citing Noll, The Economics and Politics of Regulation, 57 *Va. L. Rev.* 1016, 1028-32 (1971); P. Quirk, *Industry Influence in Federal Regulatory Agencies* (1981) ("Well organized opponents of controls may 'capture' the agencies that regulate them and exert direct pressure on the content of regulations.").

59. *Id.* at 412.

60. *Id.* at 410.

61. Thus market-based pricing of risk and precaution can at least augment regulatory standards and can internalize the costs and benefits associated with IT security better than a case-by-case application of the "Learned Hand" formula. *See U.S. v. Carroll Towing Co.*, 159 F. 2d 169 (2d Cir. 1947). Judge Learned Hand's rule can be reformulated as: the injurer is negligent if the marginal cost of his or her precaution is less than the resulting marginal benefit. Cooter & Ulen, *supra* note 44, at 333-35.

62. Thus, for instance, insurers have lobbied considerably for mandatory air bags in automobiles and pressured the government to force industries to change. Beh, *supra* note 26, at n. 130 (citing Robert Kneuper & Bruce Yandle, Auto Insurers and the Air Bag, 61 *J. Risk & Ins.* 107 (1994), available at 1994 WL 13386236).

63. Insufficient expertise in characterizing risk, political lobbying, and high administrative costs.

64. Kenneth Arrow, Uncertainty and the Welfare Economics of Medical Care, 53 *Am. Econ. Rev.* 941, 946 (1963).

65. In general, a market failure exists if any of the three conditions for the equivalence of competitive equilibria and social optimality fail to hold. These conditions are (1) existence of markets (*i.e.*, "marketability" of all goods and services relevant to costs and utilities), (2) existence of some set of prices that will clear all markets (*i.e.*, existence of competitive equilibrium), and (3) nonincreasing returns. Id. at 942-44. In this case, the absence of markets for the bearing of Internet risks results in a violation of condition 1 and results in a reduction in welfare below that fully obtainable by society.

66. This is similar to the international macroeconomic approach of measuring welfare gains from trade. *See* Earl L. Grinols & Kar-Yiu Wong, An Exact Measure of Welfare Change, 24 No. 2 *Can. J. Econ.* 428 (1991); Earl L. Grinols, A Thorn in the Lion's Paw: Has Britain Paid Too Much for Common Market Membership?, 16 *J. Int'l Econ.* 271 (1984); Douglas A. Irwin, The Welfare Costs of Autarky: Evidence from the Jeffersonian Trade Embargo, 1807-1809, 13 *Rev. Int'l Econ.* 631 (2005); Daniel M. Bernhofen & John C. Brown, An Empirical Assessment of the Comparative Advantage Gains from Trade: Evidence from Japan, 95 *Am. Econ. Rev.* 208 (2005); Robert C. Feenstra, *Advanced International Trade: Theory and Evidence* (2003).

67. Note that the level surfaces are maximized exactly at the intersection of the "budget lines" with the 45° line, as a particular characteristic of expected utility optimization:

$$\frac{\partial U / \partial I_0}{\partial U / \partial I_1} = \frac{p}{(1-p)} \frac{du/dI_0(I_0)}{du/dI_1(I_1)} \Rightarrow \frac{\partial U / \partial I_0}{\partial U / \partial I_1} = \frac{p}{(1-p)} \text{ at } (I_1 = I_0).$$

Also, if we assume constant relative risk-aversion, the utility functions are homogenous, which means that the lines tangent to the utility curves are parallel. *See* Carl P. Simon & Lawrence Blume, *Mathematics for Economists* (1994), for a general discussion of homogenous functions in economics.

68. Russ Banham, Hacking It (Cyberinsurance)(Statistical Data Included), *CFO, Mag. for Senior Fin. Exec.* (Aug. 2000), available at http://www.findarticles.com/cf_dls/m3870/9_16 /63916347/p1/article.jhtml (last visited Apr. 24, 2004). Gohring, *supra* note 5. A security incident's impact on the stock prices is usually estimated using event study analysis, a method used extensively in finance, accounting, and management science to measure an event's (*e.g.*, mergers, regulatory changes, and so on) impact on the stock price of firms (*see generally*, Cavusoglu *et al.*, *supra* note 8, for an application of this technique to computer security events). In general, the market value of the firm's equity following the attacks is subtracted from its market value immediately prior to the attack, and the calculated return is adjusted by substracting the market's return. This technique relies on the assumption that markets are efficient, in which case the new public information (*e.g.*, the security breach) is immediately incorporated into the stock price (*see* Eugene F. Fama *et al.*, The Adjustment of Stock Prices to New Information, 10 *Int'l Econ. Rev.* 1 (1969)). The DOS attack lends itself to this type of analysis because the attacks are a landmark in the catalog of Internet attacks and the relevant time period for capturing the new information flow can be shrunk arbitrarily to capture a specific security event (unless of course if the researcher did not carefully eliminate all other factors that may affect the firm's market valuation). Other studies corroborate the huge and significant impact on the DOS attacks to the stock market price of firms, particularly for substantially Internet-only firms such as Yahoo, eBay, and Amazon, whose market returns are much more affected by security breach announcements than are those of conventional firms (*see* Michael Ettredge & Vernon Richardson, *Assessing the Risk in E-Commerce*, Proceedings of the Thirty-Fifth Hawaii International Conference on System Sciences (2002), available at http://papers.ssrn.com/sol3/papers.cfm?abstract_id=268737; *see also* Garg *et al.*, *supra* note 8, which estimates an even higher market capitalization loss associated with the Yahoo, eBay, and Amazon DOS attacks).

69. *See* Becca Mader, Demand Developing for Cyberinsurance, *Bus. J. Milwaukee* (Oct. 11, 2002), available at http://www.milwaukee.bizjournals.com/milwaukee/stories/2002/10/14/focus2.html (last visited Apr. 24, 2004).

70. Note that for $\sigma = 1$, the CRRA utility function is simply the log-utility function, which means the level curves are Cobb-Douglas utility function. Also, in a two-"good" case, the level surfaces of CRRA utility function are constant elasticity of substitution (CES) utility, where the elasticity of substitution $1/(1-p)$ is equal to the reciprocal of the risk-aversion coefficient, and the log-utility case ($\sigma = 1$) corresponds to the Cobb-Douglas level sets:

$$CRRA: \quad U = p\frac{I_0^{1-\sigma}}{1-\sigma} + (1-p)\frac{I_1^{1-\sigma}}{1-\sigma} = \overline{K}.$$

$$CES: \quad [a_1 I_0^p + a_2 I_1^p]^{\frac{1}{p}} = K => a_1 I_0^p + a_2 I_1^p = \overline{K}.$$

71. John W. Pratt, Risk Aversion in the Small and in the Large, 32 *Econometrica* 122 (1964).

72. For a general introduction on the economics of uncertainty, *see* Hal R. Varian, *Micro-economic Analysis* (3d ed. 1992), at 173-92.

73. Our calculations of the welfare gains are broken down for various levels of risk-aversion and probabilities of cyberattack occurring. For our calculations of worldwide welfare gains, we used worldwide gross domestic product (GDP) data (*see* The World Bank Group, *Data and Statistics: World Development Indicators 2004*, available at http://www.worldbank.org/data/wdi2004/index.htm) as the income in bad state and $1.6 trillion as the worldwide loss from hacking and viruses (*see supra* text accompanying note 8).

74. John H. Cochrane, Where Is the Market Going? Uncertain Facts and Novel Theories, 21 *Econ. Perspectives* 3 (1997).

75. For a case study of the cyberinsurance industry, *see* Majuca *et al.*, *supra* note 20.

76. How a typical step-by-step formal assessment may be done is shown in this PDF document: http://common.ziffdavisinternet.com/download/0/2274/Baseline-NetDiligenceMap.pdf (last visited Apr. 24, 2004), in Eileen Mullin, Project Map: Hedging Your Security Bets with Cyberinsurance, *Baseline Mag.* (Aug. 9, 2002), available at http://www.baselinemag.com/article2/0,3959,656097,00.asp (last visited Apr. 24, 2004).

77. This has allowed firms to assess their risks and become better aware of their security needs and has also allowed insurers to engage in an ongoing dialog with the firms about their security risks. Insurance coverage to firms with fewer cyberprotections; with a greater percentage of their business online; or in a highly regulated business subject to high penalties, such as financial firms, are considered to be higher risk. Mullin, *supra* note 76.

78. Banham, *supra* note 68.

79. Engaging in dialog between insurer and insured about their risks is important to developing coverage.

80. Duffy, *supra* note 7.

81. Security software vendor Tripwire, Inc. offers a 10 percent premium discount on Lloyd's of London's e-Comprehensive cyberinsurance policy to customers who use their product. Wurzler Underwriting Managers also offered clients a 5 percent to 30 percent premium break if they use Linux or Unix servers rather than Windows NT because these systems are less susceptible to attack. Marcia Savage, *Tripwire, Lloyd's Partner for Cyberinsurance* (Sept. 11, 2000), available at http://www.techweb.com/wire/story/TWB20000911S0008 (last visited Apr. 22, 2004). Preston Gralla, Electronic Safety Net: Cyberinsurance Policies Can Offer Protection When Technology Fails, *CIO Mag.* (Dec. 1, 2001), available at http://www.cio.com/archive/120101/et_article.html (last visited Apr. 22, 2004); Anna Lee, Notes, Why Traditional Insurance Policies Are Not Enough: The Nature of Potential E-Commerce Losses and Liabilities, 3 *Vand. J. Ent. L. & Prac.* 84 (2001).

INDEX

Abercrombie, 248

Access to information, legislation based on, 57–58

Accountability, in social assurance model, 190–91

Ackerman, Bruce, 241*n*4

Action threats, 255–56, 259

Acxiom, 137–39, 142, 145

Administrative security measures, 26, 28

Affiliate information sharing, 148*n*11

Agreement, defined, 336

Alexa Internet, 60, 68*n*4, 70*n*52

Amazon.com, 60, 68*n*4, 69*n*38, 70*n*48, 345

American Bankers Association, 214

American Electronics Association, 254

American Financial Services Association, 214

American International Group (AIG), 359

Andrews, Adelaide, 211

Anti-benchmarking clauses, 158, 177*n*21

Antitrust law, 94, 285

Aptheker v. Secretary of State, 321*n*79

Arbitration, 8, 49

Architecture, information: control-oriented, 75, 82–83, 120; growth-oriented, 82–83, 88*n*54; security and, 118–20; vulnerability and, 120–21

Article 29 Data Protection Working Party, 98

Ashcroft, John, 119, 304

AT&T, 68*n*4

Attributes captured by ID cards, 298–99

Audit controls, 28

Audits, external, 30

Authorizations, 300

Auto-ID Center, Massachusetts Institute of Technology, 246

Automated Clearinghouse (ACH), 233

Autonomy, 330, 338–39

Avenue A, 52*n*20, 63

Ayres, Ian, 241*n*4

Ballon, Ian, 8, 9–10

Bank of America, 112

Bankruptcy, 218

Bill of Rights, 272

Biographical data, 275–76, 290*n*39

Biometric information, 298–99

Boards of directors, security responsibilities of, 30–31

Bots, 78, 87*n*37, 91, 163

Boyer, Amy Lynn, 121–22

Brandeis, Louis, 128–29, 138, 271

Breach of confidentiality, 122

Breach of trust, 97–100

Brenner, Susan, 8, 14

Browsewrap agreements, 78–81, 88*n*42, 88*n*43, 88*n*51

Buffer overflows, 170

Burger, Warren, 321*n*79

Business: anti-privacy stance of, 5; and consent requirement, 6; and FTC enforcement, 64; information security responsibilities of, 30–31, 49; information security standards for, 23–30; obligations of, 9, 20–23, 121–24; privacy burdens on, 8; public welfare offenses and, 284–88

Business Roundtable, 31

California: credit practices in, 211, 217; privacy security law in, 4, 7, 43, 49–50,

Market failure: cyberinsurance and, 354; defined, 364*n*65; disclosure of security breaches and, 13

Marks & Spencer, 248

Marsh, 359

Mary Poppins (film), 232

Massachusetts Institute of Technology, 246

MasterCard, 2, 3, 214

Matwyshyn, Andrea M., 10

McGraw, Gary, 170, 178*n*38

Media, disposal of, 28

Medical malpractice, 126–28

Mens rea, 284

Michelin, 249

Microsoft, 10, 11, 48, 51*n*15, 65, 98–100, 102, 131, 264, 345

Model Penal Code, 284

Monopoly, obligations resulting from, 167–68

Moral hazard, 348, 361*n*24

Most restrictive rule, 93, 95–97, 99–100

MSBlaster worm, 174

National Association of Insurance Commissioners, 24

National Cyber Security Partnership (NCSP), 40*n*59, 156–57

National ID cards, 295–316; anonymity/pseudonymy and, 311; benefits of, 298–301; components of, 296, 298–300; constitutionality of, 295–96; current privacy situation and, 297; dangers to liberty from, 301–8; and data ownership, 312–14; de facto system of, 14, 296, 308–9; *de jure* system of, 14; psychological effect of, 309; public opinion on, 316*n*3; suggestions for, 310–12; symbolic effect of, 308

National Security Agency, 68*n*4

Nation-states: contests between, 97; extraterritorial regulatory capability of, 94; influence of, in international system, 102–4; and international privacy regime, 93; privacy regulation in, 95

Negligence: credit practices and, 213–14; design defects and, 198–200; economic loss and, 162, 164–65, 167; privacy security and, 193; services and, 192–95; socially optimal level of precaution and, 352; software security and, 161–75

.NET Passport, Microsoft, 51*n*15, 65, 94, 98–100, 131

New Hampshire, 253

New York state, 66

Nimmer, Raymond, 6, 7, 14–15, 55

Nissenbaum, Helen, 112

Nonconsensual transactions, regulation of, 96

Notice: conspicuousness of, 77–78; European requirements on, 98; legislation based on, 57–58

Notification laws, 33–34, 46–47

Object Name Service (ONS), 246, 256

Office of the Comptroller of the Currency (OCC), 24, 226, 227

Office of Thrift Supervision, 24, 227

Open source software, liability regarding, 197

Opt-in consent systems, 6, 335–36

Opt-out consent systems, 6, 58, 335–36

Organizational code, 73, 75, 82, 84*n*1, 89*n*56, 89*n*60

Organizational security measures, 26

Organization for Economic Co-operation and Development, *Guidelines on the Protection of Privacy and Transborder Flows of Personal Data*, 311–12

Outsourcing, 9, 29

Palmer, Charles C., 178*n*36

Park, John, 285

PASS cards, 251–52, 255–56

Passports, 9, 250–51, 262, 313, 321*n*79

Past attributes, 299

Patches, software, 158–59, 162–63, 169, 176*n*8, 177*n*24, 201

PATRIOT Act, 67*n*4

Payment system, 232–33

Peek, Marcy, 8, 11

Penalty default rule, 337

Permanent personal attributes, 298–99

Persistent facts, 299

Personal Identity Verification card, 252, 260

Personal information: biographical data, 275–76; collection and use of, 111, 113; commodification of, 280, 293*n*69; control of, 138–39, 279–80, 291*n*49; cost of, 94; data control and, 326; defined, 47, 326; dossiers of, 111–12, 118–21, 139, 149*n*20; inaccurate, 58, 116–17, 119, 305–6, 329; individuals' sale of, 320*n*74; leaks of, 117–18, 122–23; legal regime concerning, 226–30; misuse of, 114–17; monetary value of, 320*n*74; principles concerning, 124; as property, 146, 280, 282–84, 292*n*57, 312–14; on RFIDs, 255, 258–59; right to privacy of, 129–30, 136*n*106; sensitive, 224, 227, 231–32; sources of, 149*n*21; tool data, 274–75; vulnerability of, 111–13, 118–21, 139. *See also* Data abuse; Data privacy; Data protection; Data security; Databases